The OFFICER'S GUIDE TO
POLICE PISTOLCRAFT

The Complete Guide to the Reality-Based Tactics, Techniques, and Philosophy of The New Paradigm of Police Firearms Training

Michael E. Conti

SABER PRESS

North Reading, MA

A Subsidiary of Saber Group, Inc.

www.sabergroup.com

The Officer's Guide to Police Pistolcraft
by Michael E. Conti

First Edition

ISBN: 978-0-9772659-0-9
Printed in the United States of America

Published by Saber Press, a wholly-owned subsidiary of
Saber Group, Inc.
268 Main Street, PMB 138
North Reading, Massachusetts 01864, USA
Tel./Fax: (978) 749-3731

Direct inquiries and/or orders to the above address
or contact us online at **www.sabergroup.com**

Copies of this book are available at special discounts for
bulk purchase. Special editions or book excerpts can also
be created to specifications. For details, contact the
Special Sales Manager at Saber Press.

All text, photographs, and illustrations by the author
unless otherwise noted.

On the cover: Background image is an example of a .31 caliber, Colt Model 1849 Pocket Revolver, believed to be the first pistol officially issued to the members of any U.S. police department. In the foreground is a modern, .40 S&W caliber, SIG Sauer P226 DAK semiautomatic pistol equipped with a Safariland RLS LED light.

This Book

presented to

by

Date

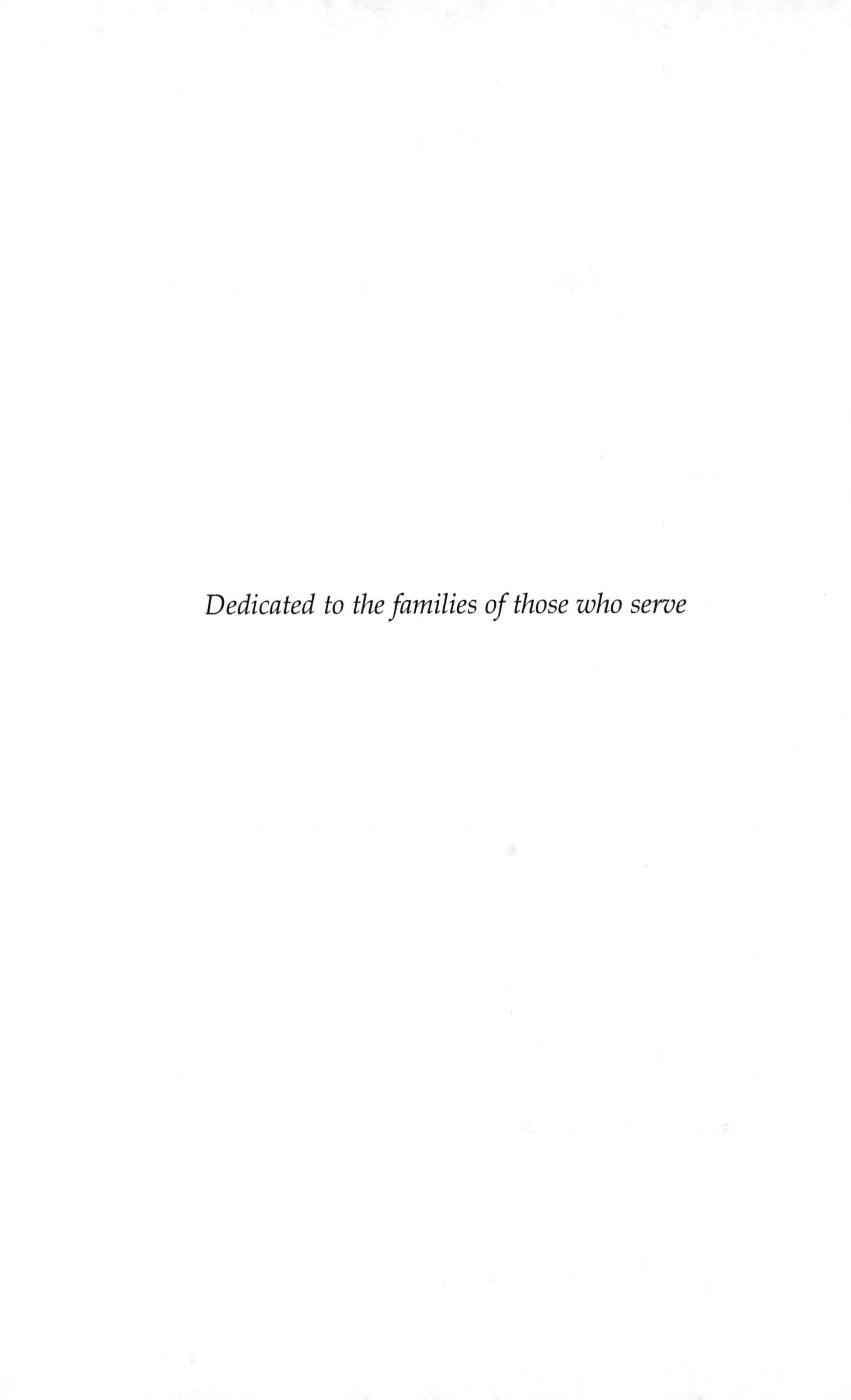

Dedicated to the families of those who serve

Table of Contents

WARNING

A Note on the Use of Lethal Force

The express purpose of this book is to present an overview of the New Paradigm Police Firearms Training Program to the trained police officer, military, or security professional. It is in no way meant to replace or contradict any department's or agency's current policies or procedures.

The justified use and employment of any type of weapon, regardless of its intended level of force, is a subject that must be addressed by each individual department or agency. Federal law, state law, departmental rules, regulations, policies, and procedures must all be satisfied.

Today, in the United States, the use of deadly force by a law enforcement officer is generally only permissible as a last resort, when in the reasonable and considered opinion of the individual police officer there exists an imminent threat of death or serious bodily injury to himself or someone else.

It is imperative that each officer operating in the field knows and understands both the meaning and the intent of all applicable standards regarding the use of any level of force option available to him. It is also imperative that he be able to clearly and reasonably articulate his actions, especially when those actions involve the employment of any level of force.

As civilian, military, and security professionals, we must also be familiar with various federal statutes and court rulings that have a direct impact on what actions we may take and how they may affect our liability exposure while performing our duties.

Your department, unit, or agency is responsible for your training in this area. Once properly trained, the onus of responsibility for adhering to this training is then placed squarely on the individual officer.

Neither the author nor the publisher is responsible for the use or misuse of any information contained in this book. It is presented for information purposes only.

Attention! Firearms training is a dangerous activity that can lead to serious injury or death if not properly and safely performed. All training must be conducted at approved ranges and under competent supervision.

Acknowledgements

I wish to extend my deepest thanks and gratitude to all who have assisted me in the production of this *Officer's Guide to Police Pistolcraft.*

I have been blessed and honored to have had the support and encouragement of a small circle of family, friends, and close associates for many years and through many interesting and often trying times. I will forever be indebted to you all for reasons too numerous to fully list here, though I would like to cite a few.

To my wife, Kathy, our children, Katie and Nick, and my parents, Margie and Jim, thank you for providing not only love and support, but also for your patience, understanding, and many sacrifices made on my and the work's behalf.

An additional word of thanks is also due Kathy and Katie Conti for all their assistance in proofreading and editing. You have made it a much stronger book through your efforts and I truly appreciate all the time you gave me.

To my friends and staunch allies, in addition to loyalty, honesty, and dedication to the mission we have all embraced, I would like to thank you for the trust you each have given me. It is one of the things I truly value. Your trust has also inspired me to try my best to live up to the expectations we have all placed on one another. I believe I have become a better person as a result, and owe that to you as well. This is especially directed to Paul Wosny, Donna Losardo, Paul "Yoda" Damery, Richard Lane, Pat McAdam, and Bill Burroughs, six of the most hard working, dedicated, and professional individuals I have ever known. I am privileged in your friendship.

To those very special members of our circle who have gone on ahead, thank you for all you taught us. You are greatly missed, but your presence is felt always.

To all the police officers, service members, and security personnel who have participated in training programs, operations, or otherwise contributed time, energy, and experience to assisting us with moving our efforts forward, thank you.

Know that our thoughts are with you wherever you may be.

Introduction

The "New Paradigm" of police firearms training is a reality-based approach to firearms training first developed in the early part of the New Millennium. It was created because the long-entrenched, sight-oriented, marksmanship-based approach employed by the police industry for decades hadn't been working.

This opinion was based upon data regarding actual police-involved deadly force encounters that had been collected and analyzed for more than thirty years. The result of this analysis indicated that the average officer missed with more than 80% of the rounds he fired at real-world threat subjects.

This poor performance record was compounded by the fact that the vast majority of police-involved shootings have always been, and continue to be, close-range affairs, with more than 80% occurring with the officer and offender twenty feet and closer, and more than half taking place within a distance of *five feet.*

How "New" is the New Paradigm?

The New Paradigm program is—in many ways—the latest rebirth of a system of combat pistol shooting and training that reached its apex more than sixty years ago! How can this be, you may ask?

In Chapter 1 we will take a brief look at the history and development of police pistol training. When looked at in this context, it becomes apparent that two distinct approaches to this subject—one marksmanship-oriented, the other combat-oriented—have been struggling for dominance since the beginning of the twentieth century.

One of the main reasons the struggle has gone on for so long is because, like the two entwined snakes in the illustration on the following page, both approaches appear similar at first glance. Closer examination, however, reveals that one is better suited for mortal combat than the other.

Since the occupation of the law enforcement officer inevitably brings him or her into contact with dangerous situations and people, the need for a system of weapons training that allowed officers to develop reliable, life-saving skills with their most commonly available firearm—*the handgun*—was imperative.

And, as these skills overwhelmingly need to be employed against other human beings during terrifying instances of close quarter violence, logic demanded that the combat-oriented training approach be embraced as the only sane choice.

Untangling the Snakes

Incredibly, the argument between marksmanship-oriented and combat-oriented training approaches has been fought and won in a repetitive cycle throughout the past century and into the new.

One of the primary reasons for this constant struggle has been because prior to the development of the New Paradigm program, there had never truly been a system of pistol training designed exclusively for the members of the civilian police profession. Police officers' training programs had always been derived from, or at least heavily influenced by, outside sources.

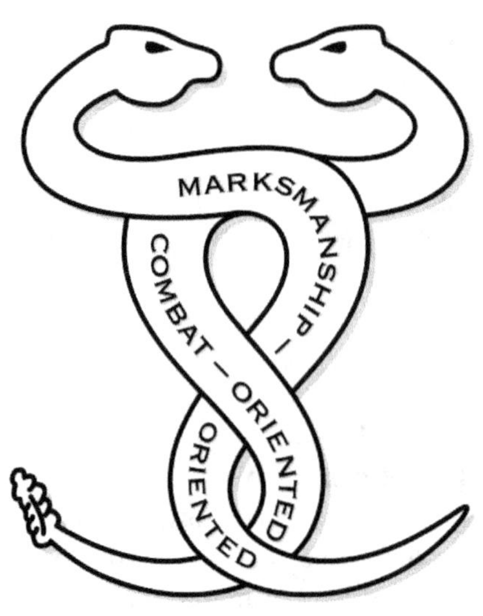

Untangling the Snakes

Both military and non-police civilian influences, while well-meaning, have generated a great deal of confusion in this regard.

This confusion has also undoubtedly been compounded by the tremendous volumes of work produced by numerous authors, trainers, pundits, and gurus, all extolling the universal virtues of their own particular brand of pistolcraft.

As a result of all these influences, and in the absence of a needs-driven, police-specific training approach, what had generally occurred over the years had been the adoption of a variety of training methodologies based upon individual police trainer's *beliefs*.

If the trainer's beliefs were influenced by a champion IPSC pistol competition shooter, then that trainer would most likely be a staunch proponent of highly stylized positional shooting stances and demand that the shooter's focus always be on the pistol's sights while firing the weapon.

Should the trainer's beliefs have been formed based upon the teachings of a proponent of the combat-oriented, point shooting school, then that trainer would just as avidly demand that the training emphasis be on the development of close combat pistol fighting skills that disregard the sights.

For many, many years, the divide between these two camps had been unmistakably clear, and the basis of never ending arguments and controversies.

Over the last few years, however, a third camp has been established. The folks in this camp share beliefs from both the sighted and point shooting schools.

"Can't we all get along?" seems to be the mantra, and to a great degree I concur with the sentiments expressed by the members of this group.

However... the specific matter of *police* firearms training demands that we don't simply agree that the symbolic, entangled snakes are similar enough to justify our ignoring their differences. It demands that we untangle them, recognizing and appreciating both for what they are, and then, after careful determination of our mission-specific needs, *that we choose one or the other.*

Then and only then will our training philosophy be based upon actual, objective need, not simply a subjective belief system rooted in limited exposure, incestuous training practices, or the guru-based cult of personality.

As noted previously, after careful analysis, the combat-oriented approach was selected for use in the development of the New Paradigm police firearms training system.

Defining the Combat-Oriented Approach

When defining the combat-oriented approach to police pistol training, most people naturally and understandably focus on the physical techniques that are used to aim and fire the pistol at the threat.

While this is a critical and intrinsic component of the combat-oriented approach, it is far from the most important!

Of even greater importance than the techniques used to aim and fire the pistol are the techniques used to prepare the officer to operate effectively in the "element of danger," and to assist in the *development of sound judgment and decision-making skills.*

These aspects of police firearms training—while often acknowledged as the most critical components—often receive the least amount of actual training attention!

The hallmark of the reality-based, New Paradigm combat-oriented training approach is that the training emphasis is focused on preparing our officers as thoroughly as possible to know *when* to use the pistol as well as *how* to use it effectively when needed. This focus on mental preparation as opposed to pistol aiming technique is absolutely critical, for being trained to respond and act appropriately when operating with a pistol in your hand is the hard part of the equation. The development of the actual physical skills required to aim and fire the pistol accurately and effectively is much easier to achieve.

In regard to the specific aiming and firing techniques best suited for combat-oriented police firearms training, I wish to make something clear: while many have interpreted the adoption of the combat-oriented approach to be a condemnation of sighted shooting techniques, this is *not* the case.

Both sighted shooting and point shooting techniques are intrinsic components of the New Paradigm training system.

In fact, in a perfect world, both techniques would receive equal time and emphasis during training iterations.

The reality, however, is that the world is far from perfect.

Most of us rarely get to participate in training programs as often as we should. When we do get to the range, the actual amount of training time is often less than ideal, and very often the emphasis is placed on training activities that don't actually prepare us to do with the pistol what our duties will require us to do.

That is why the New Paradigm program, being based on the realities of our world and our profession, places the physical skills training emphasis on the development of the close quarter point shooting skills that statistics indicate we will most likely need while performing our duties.

Though statistically less-likely, since we may also be required to employ the pistol to display precision-aimed and fired rounds at threat targets under certain circumstances, we also need to understand how to employ the pistol using sighted aiming and shooting techniques.

Unlike the traditional markmanship-oriented approach to this aspect of police pistolcraft, however, our focus is on developing both of these skills to prevail over human threats in actual situations, not simply to pass a competition-inspired target shooting course.

Police Pistolcraft and The Officer's Guide

The textbook, *Police Pistolcraft: The Reality-Based New Paradigm of Police Firearms Training* was first published by Saber Press in September 2006.

The intent of *Police Pistolcraft* was to provide the professional law enforcement firearms instructor with a comprehensive textbook detailing the concepts, approaches, tactics, and techniques of the New Paradigm training system.

In the short time since its release, *Police Pistolcraft* has been widely hailed by many in the professional police training community. Numerous positive reviews have been published in commercial magazines and professional journals.

The New Paradigm program is also in use, in whole or in part, by training entities in the United States, Europe, and Canada. As of this writing, the book is being used as an instructor manual for programs being conducted at the Massachusetts State Police Academy, Hocking College, and Penn State University, among others.

Calibre Press and the Law Enforcement Training Network (LETN) also produced and released a three-part video training series based on *Police Pistolcraft* in the Fall of 2007.

Please understand that I am stating this bluntly here neither as a boast nor in an attempt to stroke my ego. I try not to take myself too seriously, for I have seen just how slippery a slope that can be. However, for me and those with whom I associate, the *work* is *everything* and we take *it* very seriously.

I cite the reception the book has received only to emphasize that the research, materials, philosophy, and approach imbued in the New Paradigm program have been vetted by a diverse array of professionals in the training and educational fields. (A complete listing of peer reviews and readers' comments can be found on our website, **www.sabergroup.com**.[1])

As for this book, *The Officer's Guide to Police Pistolcraft* has been produced in response to numerous requests from police firearms trainers, supervisors, and line officers.

Many trainers and supervisors have expressed a desire to have a manual that can be issued to those they train, a manual that does not include all the instructor-level information found in the original *Police Pistolcraft* textbook.

Many individual officers have written or called requesting a distilled (and physically smaller) version of the book that illustrates the tactics and techniques used in the system, while allowing for easier transport, storage, and use at the range.

It is in response to these requests that I have formatted and produced this "Officer's Guide." I hope it is of use to you.

Mike Conti
Andover, Massachusetts
July 2009

---

[1] Additional information and training materials are also available on the website.

Police Pistolcraft. Published by Saber Press, 2006.

"Too many people will see this book in the context of the 'sighted shooting versus point shooting' controversy. That view misses the point. Though there is a point shooting component to the approach of the author, there is also an equal emphasis on sighted shooting.

The real message of this book is that police firearms training must be based on the requirements of the job, rather than the various forms of competition upon which nearly all police firearms training is based."

- **Gilbert DuVernay**
Police Pistolcraft Book Review
ILEETA Review, October/November 2006 [2]

2 International Law Enforcement Educators and Trainers Association. (www.ileeta.org)

CHAPTER 1

The New Paradigm

FIRST U.S. LAW ENFORCEMENT OFFICERS

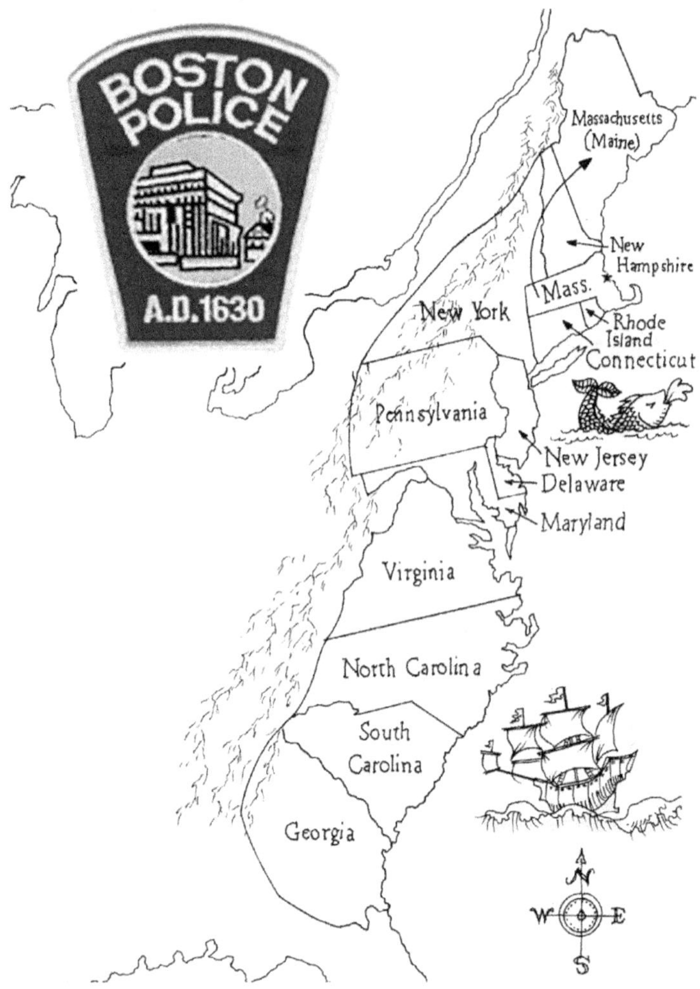

The first organized law enforcement presence in the 13 colonies was established in Boston, MA in 1631. The "Night Watch" initially consisted of 1 officer and 6 men. Members of the Night Watch were subsequently equipped with a badge, a rattle to call for assistance, and a six-foot long, blue and white painted pole. The pole had a rounded "bill" on one end and a hook on the other. The bill was used as a weapon. The hook was used to grab fleeing criminals whose names would later be recorded in a book. *"Hook 'em and book 'em!"*

SECTION 1

The Development of Police Firearms Training

October 11, 1928. Everett, Massachusetts Police Department's first outdoor pistol practice. An auspicious and formal affair! Most U.S. municipal police officers never received any firearms training whatsoever prior to the mid 1920s. Note the "bullseye" target shooting stances being used and the lack of visible gunbelts and holsters. (Photo courtesy Everett PD.)

To fully understand the importance of the New Paradigm of Police Firearms Training it is necessary to have a basic knowledge of how police firearms training has developed and changed over the past century and into the new.

This is especially true in light of the fact that there have been many influences on the development of police firearms training, not all of them beneficial.

The Development of Police Firearms Training

While the development and employment of the first handgun can be traced to the 1300s, and the combat use of this short weapon in its many variations has been documented through the ensuing centuries, the story of modern law enforcement employment of the handgun truly begins in the nineteenth century. Prior to this time period, the vast majority of police officers in this country conducted their duties unarmed—at least officially.

It wasn't until 1857 that the Baltimore City Police Department became the first U.S. police agency to officially authorize and issue a handgun to its officers for daily carry and use.

Even after the issuance of pistols became more commonplace, the vast majority of modern American law enforcement officers didn't carry their handguns in holsters in plain view as is customary today. Whether in uniform or plainclothes, their pistols were generally carried concealed, usually in their pockets, and often beneath several layers of clothing. Presentation of the handgun from such a carry location was neither fast nor easy. This was not of great concern at the time, however.

The handgun was chosen for use specifically because it was so easily concealed and portable, not because it was regarded as a more desirable weapon than a shotgun or rifle.

While long guns such as the shotgun and rifle had always been the preferred type of defensive/offensive firearm, the handgun emerged as a respected deadly offensive weapon in its own right during the American Civil War (1861-1865). Prior to this time handguns were most often employed as a weapon of last resort, just ahead of the edged weapon, and used at fairly close distances.

The occurrence of several interconnected events led to this change in perception and use. These events included the rise of horse-mounted guerrilla irregulars; the development of the lightning-fast, close-quarter form of mounted combat they employed; and most of all, the availability of the short, easily manipulated pistols they used that allowed the guerilla fighters to perform as efficiently and effectively as they did.

After the war ended, these new methods and techniques of close quarter pistol fighting found their way to the western United States, as veterans from both sides sought out the possibilities of wealth and adven-

The .31 caliber Colt Model 1849 Pocket Revolver. The Baltimore City Police Department first issued this pistol to its members in 1857. As its name indicates, this gun was generally carried concealed in a pocket, even by uniformed officers.

ture offered by the quickly disappearing frontier.

One of the most well-known of these efficient horse-mounted pistol fighters would later gain fame as a celebrated Indian fighter and lawman. His given name was James Butler Hickok, but he would be immortalized in American history and pistolero mythology as "Wild Bill."

The Wild, Wild West & Emergence of the American Pistolero Mythology

Hickok and other noted Western gunmen of this period would have a far-reaching effect on the types of pistol selected and developed for close combat use, as well as how the pistol was carried and employed. Just how influential the Western gunmen's choices of weapons, holsters and techniques were can be illustrated by the proliferation of articles and books published at that time and the resultant adoption of similar weapons, holsters and techniques by lawmen across the nation.

The spread of the classic American "pistolero mythology" was ensured by the publication of articles appearing in magazines from *Harper's New Monthly* to a veritable flood of dime novels (example shown above) depicting the exaggerated or more likely fictitious deeds of Western pistoleers, both good and bad. The hero in these stories (as was often the case in real life) was invariably armed with at least one percussion revolver that he carried exposed, usually in a holster hung from a gunbelt worn around the waist. He would also possess the ability to draw that revolver with lightning speed and to hit his target with amazing accuracy.

A review of the numerous books, articles, movies and popular culture of the U.S. reveals that the influence of the American pistolero mythology is unmistakably with us still, both in general society and within the subculture of the law enforcement community.

The Police-Involved Gunfight: Then & Now

Stripping away the mythology so lovingly wrapped around the Western lawman, his weapons and equipment, we can discern that little has actually changed in regard to the typical police-involved gunfight.

Using Hickok as an example, we can state that with only one documented exception (the July 21, 1865 gunfight with Dave Tutt), the vast majority of Hickok's confirmed gunfights occurred at fairly close ranges and in low-light environments. They were overwhelmingly fast and furious events involving only a few rounds fired, and usually involved one or more participants operating under the influence of some type of mind-altering substance.

The above description still accurately describes the vast majority of police-involved shootings as experienced by present-day lawmen.

Organized Police Firearms Training

Early police handgun training ranged from non-existent to strictly target shooting using unrealistic positions and techniques. Policies and guidelines relating to the selection, training, carrying, and use of pistols by the police were practically non-existent during the mid to late 1800s (Morrison, 1996).

It was not until 1895 that any type of formalized police revolver training was instituted in the United States of America.

Roosevelt Leads the Charge

Theodore Roosevelt, the newly-appointed New York City Police Commissioner, looked into the specifics of what his officers were doing with their firearms and how they were performing on

Photo inset above: New York City Police Commissioner Theodore Roosevelt, "The Reformer."

the streets. What he found was that his officers were prone to accidental discharges with their weapons and also that they performed miserably when employing their pistols during actual gunfights.

Based upon these facts, Roosevelt instituted regular firearms training and inspections for the members of the New York City Police Department in 1895. These first formalized training sessions were generally conducted semi-annually and consisted of dry-fire practice followed by an extremely abbreviated target shooting session (Berman, 1987).

After Roosevelt left the position of Commissioner, police firearms training basically ceased for the NYPD, though a basic course of revolver practice did continue in some form (Morrison, 1996).

The New York City Police Department's experiment with police firearms training, though rudimentary in the extreme, proved to be much more than the vast majority of police officers at the time received. Most municipal police officers never received any firearms training whatsoever prior to the mid 1920s.

Early Military Influences

Despite the desire to create non-military oriented, civilian police forces, one of the primary influences on early police firearms training was the U.S. military. This came about for a number of reasons, most significantly because both the military and civilian police establishments shared a number of similarities. They wore uniforms, had defined chains-of-command, were organized along similar lines, and were armed.

When the members of civilian police agencies found themselves in need of firearms training programs, the availability of the U.S. military model proved quite attractive. After all, the military had already established firearms training programs devoted to a number of specific weapon systems including handguns. To put it bluntly, the work in this regard had already been done, and the adoption of the established military training and qualification courses would eliminate the need for the members of the civilian police forces to research and create their own.

Unfortunately, what was either overlooked or intentionally ignored was that these programs had been developed expressly for military training and qualification purposes, not civilian law enforcement training purposes. The adoption of these training courses and approaches was a mistake, for even though it provided a means for training large numbers of police officers in mechanical technique, it did not address the specific mission and environments the officers would be tasked to deal with.

This error in judgment would continue to confuse the issues surrounding civilian police firearms training for decades to come, and is, in fact, still influencing civilian police firearms training to this day.

Luckily, there have always been a few individuals and organizations who thought police handgun training needed to be based on the realities and demands of the profession, and who worked hard to establish and institute viable, worthwhile firearms training to meet these specific needs.

The Wild, Wild East

Shanghai, China during the 1920s and 1930s was not only equal to any of the American Western frontier towns of the late 1800s in regard to providing opportunities to engage in close quarter pistol combat, but was by many accounts vastly superior.

The forces of law and order in what has often been described as the toughest city in the world during that era were represented primarily by the Shanghai Municipal Police (SMP) Department.

Two British police officers assigned to the SMP would exploit the opportunities presented by the rampant lawlessness and numerous criminal elements to develop an unprecedented body of knowledge of effective close quarter combat methods and techniques. Chief among these skills would be the art and science of pistolfighting.

The boss of the operation was SMP Assistant Commissioner William E. "Dan" Fairbairn. While a competent marksman, Fairbairn's primary interest and strengths lay in hand-to-hand combat skills, with a strong emphasis on edged weapon techniques. A former Royal Marine, Fairbairn would also be instrumental in developing the prototypical versions of the modern riot control squad and police tactical operations or SWAT team.

Working with Fairbairn was another Englishman named Eric A. Sykes. Sykes, originally a firearms and ammunition salesman, also served as a special police officer for the SMP and was in charge of the police sniper element. Sykes, having a greater interest and stronger skills with firearms than Fairbairn, complemented Fairbairn and ensured that the training they provided as a team was equally balanced between armed and unarmed fighting techniques.

Together they trained all of the indigenous members of the SMP, as

William E. Fairbairn

Eric A. Sykes

well as numerous American military personnel who were stationed in prewar Shanghai. During the time they served with the SMP, Fairbairn and Sykes were involved in more than two hundred violent incidents, many of them involving the use of handguns and close quarter combat. They developed a no-nonsense attitude toward both the weapons they carried and the techniques they used to employ them. Their systems were based on the experiences they had in the field while performing their jobs, and their jobs were quite simply to enforce the law while operating as police officers—not soldiers—and deal with often armed and dangerous criminals in heavily populated environments.

As a result of their personal experiences and observations, Fairbairn and Sykes developed a system for close quarter pistol fighting that incorporated the natural reactions exhibited by human beings when engaged in close quarter pistol fights. The system was primarily designed to be used while armed with a semiautomatic pistol, but would be effective, according to Fairbairn, with any type of one-hand gun.

The Basic System

The basic system consisted of having the shooter stand square to the target, holding the pistol in the dominant hand. The shooting arm was then locked out to the front, the pistol held in line with the center of the body. By bending the wrist slightly toward the dominant side of the body, the bore of the pistol was directed straight out from the body's centerline.

Keeping both eyes open and the arm locked out, the pistol was then raised along the centerline of the body until it was at or just below eye level and in line with the target. As soon as the pistol was in line with the target, the hand convulsed and the pistol was fired, with the shooter's focus being maintained on the target, not the sights.

Also included in this segment of training were blocks of instruction on other close quarter and various shooting positions; engaging moving targets; and engaging targets while the shooter was on the move. In addition, methods for using the pistol to engage the occasional threat target at distances beyond the normal close ranges encountered in pistol fights were taught. These included the use of a two-handed grip and firing from behind cover while using the sights when time and distance permitted.

The Mystery Shoot

Practical, dynamic courses of fire were also included in the training, as was a course Fairbairn described as a "mystery shoot." The mystery shoot as employed by Fairbairn and Sykes required the student officers to navigate a course of fire on a range that had been modified by screening walls and various props to resemble real-world environments. Human looking dummy targets, both threat and non-threat types, would then be activated by the instructors as the student moved through the simulated environment, and the student would have to react to the target and take appropriate action.

The combination of the basic pistol training program (that instilled safe handling skills and developed confidence in the student officer's ability to use the pistol to hit a man-sized target) and the psychological training benefits generated by programs like the mystery shoot produced extraordinary and well-documented results.

According to Fairbairn and Sykes, the members of the SMP, trained as indicated above, engaged in no less than 666 armed encounters with criminals over a twelve and a half year time period (approximately 53 encounters per year).

In the close quarter encounters where pistols were used by the police officers, more than 260 criminals were killed and 193 wounded, compared to 42 officers killed and 100 wounded.

Statistically, this means that the pistol-equipped members of the SMP suffered an average of 3 officers killed and 8 wounded per year during more than a decade of incredible street violence, compared to an average of 21 criminals killed and 15 wounded per year during this same time period. (It is interesting to note that police firearms training being conducted in the United States during this same time period primarily consisted of target-shooting style qualification courses of fire, utilizing highly-stylized marksmanship oriented positions and techniques as shown in the photograph on page 17.)

Return to England

Shortly after World War II began, both Fairbairn and Sykes were called home to England and immediately commissioned as captains in the British Army. Their original mission was to train the poorly equipped British Home Guard to repel a German land invasion. Eventually they were tasked to train Allied commandos and intelligence personnel in their hard-learned techniques of close quarter combat.

In 1942, Fairbairn was sent to the United States to assist the newly formed Office of Strategic Services (OSS) in setting up a training program for guerrillas and intelligence operatives. It was there he would meet a young U.S. Army lieutenant named Rex Applegate.

Colonel Rex Applegate, the COI, OSS, and MITC

The son of a pioneering Oregon family, Rex Applegate was commissioned a lieutenant in the U.S. Army's Military Police Corps after graduating from the University of Oregon in 1940. In 1942, he was assigned to the Coordinator of Information (COI), forerunner of the Office of Strategic Services (OSS), which would later evolve into the CIA.

One of the missions given him at the time by World War I Medal of Honor winner Colonel William J. "Wild Bill" Donovan was to "learn everything there is to know about close combat."

Applegate took the mission to heart.

While initially researching this broad topic, Applegate ended up in Deadwood, South Dakota, the place where another "Wild Bill"—James Butler Hickok—had met his end in 1876 when he was assassinated by Jack McCall.

Rex Applegate

Applegate stated that he found a letter written by Hickok that had been stored for years in the basement of the Deadwood City Hall. In the letter, the accomplished western gunfighter reportedly explained how he had managed to defeat so many opponents in close quarter pistol combat.

In Hickok's words, "I raised my hand to eye level, like pointing a finger, and fired."

This basic description of Hickok's pistol fighting technique intrigued Applegate, but the method wasn't made completely clear to him until after Fairbairn arrived in the U.S. from Britain in 1942.

It was then that Applegate and Fairbairn met and worked together for more than a year. During this time, Applegate and Fairbairn polished not only what would become known as the *point shooting technique*, but also how the system was taught.

The Point Shooting Technique

The mechanical movements of the technique were simplified and based on people's normal reactions to stress and fear—not highly stylized stances and marksmanship techniques that fell apart when true danger from an armed opponent was introduced into the equation.

The basic technique (illustrated in Chapter 4) worked in training and was proven time and again in the field.

While the techniques themselves were effective, the job of truly preparing the students for real world encounters required another level of training that would address the mental conditioning aspects so often overlooked by conventional police firearms training programs. This level was addressed by ramping up Fairbairn's mystery shoot program.

Formally renamed the "House of Horrors" program, the course, set up in the basement of a building, was designed to simulate experiences the students would most likely be encountering in the field.

The House of Horrors

The House of Horrors program was conducted by an instructor who would direct one student at a time through a lowlight, danger-fraught environment. The student would be armed with the basic tools of the trade: a firearm and a fighting knife. As the student walked through darkened rooms and along hallways littered with debris, uneven surfaces, and in some cases, simulated dead bodies, he would be confronted with dummy and live role players dressed to present both enemy and friendly figures.

The enemy figure would be dressed, equipped, and even speak like the actual known enemy, such as Nazi soldiers. Often, the enemy figures would be equipped with blank-firing weapons to add to the sensory input.

Friendlies would be dressed like Allied soldiers or civilians. If the student reacted appropriately to the figure or scenario, either by shooting, knifing, or holding his fire, then the instructor would praise him with a simple and immediate, "Good work, that's right, good job."

If the wrong choice was made, the student would experience a great deal of the emotional stress and disappointment such a mistake in an actual situation would generate.

Many of the students who were trained by these methods (as well as the OSS instructors themselves) used the point shooting technique successfully in behind-the-lines operations.

The system—to include the House of Horrors program—continued to be taught at the Military Intelligence Training Center (MITC) located at Camp Ritchie, Maryland throughout the remainder of the war.

Among the many government, military, and law enforcement personnel trained in this system during this time were members of the U.S. Federal Bureau of Investigation.

The FBI

One of Rex Applegate's assignments during his time with the OSS was to serve as President Franklin Delano Roosevelt's personal bodyguard. While working this assignment, Applegate reportedly became acquainted with Frank Baughman, a high-ranking official of the FBI.

Baughman, then in charge of the FBI's laboratories and training division, was especially interested in firearms training.

Modern FBI Academy "Hogan's Alley" patch. (Courtesy of Dan Meany.)

After Applegate was transferred to Camp Ritchie in 1943, he invited Baughman to the MITC to observe the training they were administering. According to Applegate, Baughman was particularly impressed with the point shooting technique and the methods used to teach it. After Baughman returned to Washington, he recommended adoption of the point shooting technique and the training system being used to teach it, to include the House of Horrors program.

Shortly thereafter, a young FBI agent named Hank Sloan was sent to Applegate at Camp Ritchie for training. When he returned to Washington, Sloan, at the direction of Frank Baughman, incorporated the point shooting technique into the FBI's firearms training curriculum.

According to Applegate, the point shooting technique was an intrinsic component of the FBI's firearms training program until Baughman changed assignments approximately seven years later. Hank Sloan, who would eventually become the officer in charge of firearms training at the FBI Academy in Quantico where he served for almost 30 years, reportedly eased out the point shooting system as taught by Applegate and replaced it with a firearms training system of his own shortly after Baughman left.

The bastardization of the point shooting technique had begun. It was during the period from 1950-1960 when the "FBI crouch" and its attendant training methodologies appeared.

The FBI crouch involved a variation of the point shooting technique that was more highly-stylized than the Applegate version.

It also required more initial training time to learn, and a greater amount of practice time to maintain proficiency. The result was a firearms training system that was not as easily taught, assimilated, or retained as the Applegate version. Since this version was also referred to as "point shooting," the very name began to be associated with a complicated and inefficient method of handgun deployment.

It was also during this time that the FBI became associated with the now famous "Hogan's Alley" training course. This course, similar to the House of Horrors and other earlier programs, was also modified by the FBI.

They altered this concept as well by taking the fear out of it and turning it primarily into a marksmanship course.

Whereas the House of Horrors incorporated 3-dimensional targets and role players who would actually move and shoot (blanks) at the trainee, Hogan's Alley was populated only with two-dimensional plastic, paper, or cardboard targets.

The games had begun.

Going Hollywood

At the same time this was occurring, a number of other factors came into play to further taint the whole concept of point shooting.

For years Hollywood had popularized the Western with numerous short movies and feature-length films. Then, as television found its way into more and more homes during the late 1940s and early 1950s, Hollywood began recycling these films on the small screen. Soon, Western-themed television series were all the rage, and the public couldn't get enough of programs like Gunsmoke, The Lone Ranger, Wild Bill Hickok, etc.

Unfortunately, many of the people who would later find their way into U.S. law enforcement were raised on images such as the hero gunslinger walking slowly toward the villain on a dusty town road, squinting into the high noon sun, drawing and firing his pistol—only after the bad guy made his move first of course—at hip level and defeating the black-clad desperado with a single dramatic shot.

Across the U.S. the "sport" of fast-draw exploded along with the popularity of the Hollywood "screen slinger." Much time, money, and excitement were devoted to this game that required the participants to draw and fire a western-style single action revolver from a customized cowboy rig as fast as possible. Accuracy, like reality, had nothing to do with this activity; the guns were loaded with blanks.

Soon thereafter, the very term "point shooting" began to be viewed synonymously with others like "hip shooting," "instinct shooting," and "trick shooting."

The Modern Technique

Amid the national fever of fast-draw and shooting games during the 1950s emerged a loosely knit, southern California-based organization of sport shooting enthusiasts that called themselves the "Bear Valley Gunslingers."

Jeff Cooper, a Marine Corps veteran of World War II, headed this organization. Cooper and others in the club shunned the fast-draw games and focused on the development of live fire sporting competition courses that were conducted for fun.

When asked about this period of development, Cooper once said, "We started with nothing. Just a bunch of guys enjoying themselves. We started having contests using the point shooting systems," but the courses were developed and expanded from there.

One of the primary ways the courses were initially "developed and expanded" was by incorporating live fire "combat shooting courses" utilized at that time by various national and international law enforcement agencies. Among these courses was an adaptation of the FBI's Hogan's Alley reaction course—a watered down, marksmanship-oriented version of the House of Horrors training program.

A critical juncture in the development of police firearms training had been reached.

Competition "shoots" began to be held an average of once a month. A large number of police officers were drawn to these competitions in the San Bernardino Mountains. Courses of fire began to be developed that promoted and rewarded speed and accuracy more than tactical sensibility. Techniques and stylizations such as the one now commonly known as the "Weaver Stance," designed to allow the participant to efficiently employ a two-handed hold to better shoot at and hit non-threatening static and moving targets during these competitions, were adopted.

The games and the rules became more complicated. The firearms and carry gear followed suit, becoming more refined, expensive, and less practical. Cooper began to write extensively about the guns and techniques being employed.

The Bear Valley Gunslingers renamed their organization the "Southwest Combat Pistol League." Big money, high-profile shooting contests like the Bianchi Cup, Steel Challenge, and Second Chance competition helped popularize the sport and established champion gamesmen as the new "combat handgun masters."

Cooper and other popular gun magazine writers of the time declared the birth of a "new technique of the combat pistol," consisting of the Weaver Stance, quick draw, quick sight picture, and surprise shot break. Another bedrock component of the new technique was the preference for big bore 1911-type single-action, semiautomatic pistols, most notably in .45ACP caliber.

With the rejection of the fast-draw games and the "gunslinger" image also came an indiscriminate rejection of any technique even remotely related to, or described as, instinct, hip, or point shooting.

Finally, within the course of a relatively few years, assisted by the establishment of popular shooting schools such as Cooper's American Pistol Institute (API) and the development of organizations like the International Practical Shooting Confederation (IPSC) and United States Practical Shooting Association (USPSA), the term "combat handgun shooting" became synonymous with the unrealistic, competition-based shooting games conducted at these types of matches.

The cart had been placed before the horse and the "new technique"—which has now become, for our purposes, the old paradigm—was firmly established.

The National Rifle Association

The NRA has had a tremendous influence on police firearms training, especially during the period from the end of World War I through the beginning of World War II (Morrison, 1995). During these years the NRA Police School provided training for many members of the U.S. civilian police forces. While the majority of this training was similar to that provided by the military, the NRA did recognize that the police mission was different from the military mission, and made attempts to address this in training.

The NRA Police School was disbanded shortly after the start of World War II due to a loss of federal funding.

In 1960, the NRA formally re-established the Police School as the "Police Training Department" under its Education and Training Division. Through this entity the NRA again began offering structured training courses for police officers. Gradually, the emphasis shifted from providing training for individual officers to the training of law enforcement firearms instructors.

In 1979, the Police Training Department was reorganized into a separate division called the Police Activities Division. Gaylord W. "Eliot" Ness, a retired U.S. Army Lieutenant Colonel, was placed in charge. In 1981, under Ness's direction, the Police Activities Division began to offer training for security officers as well as sworn police officers. At this time, police pistol "combat" competitions were also incorporated into the programs, and the division's title was changed to the Law Enforcement Activities Division (LEAD).

Rifle, submachine gun, and "tactical" handgun courses have also been added since that time. Many of these programs are available to members of law enforcement tuition-free, or at reduced-cost.

As of this writing the vast majority of training provided through the NRA LEAD programs are still based on what we consider the old paradigm training model, though signs of positive change are being seen.

Hocking College

For well over thirty years after the establishment of the Modern Technique the vast majority of U.S. law enforcement agencies centered their handgun training programs on the highly-stylized, sight-oriented, marksmanship-based shooting techniques that were developed to assist gamesmen achieve victory during shooting competitions.

In essence, various types of stationary or moving targets were fired at from different distances to record the success or failure of the officer's ability to achieve hits on these targets.

In order to best achieve hits on these paper, plastic, or metal training targets, the emphasis was placed on using highly-stylized stances and the pistol's sights—especially the front sight—at all distances and under all conditions.

During these same thirty or so years, however, U.S. law enforcement officers consistently averaged hit rates of less than 15% when engaged in actual real-world, predominantly close-quarter gunfights during which the targets not only shot back, but usually shot first.

Unbelievably, this situation was allowed to continue virtually unabated until the 1990s.

The first documented organizational challenge to the Modern Technique took root in early 1992, when two police firearms instructors at Hocking College in Nelsonville, Ohio, noticed a disturbing trend after they introduced Simunition training ammunition and dynamic simulation training into their firearms program.

Steve Barron and Clyde Beasley, both steadfast proponents of the Modern Technique, were at a loss to explain why their students' demonstrated abilities to hit their target during standardized qualification courses all but evaporated when they were faced with targets that shot back.

They were further dismayed as they observed their students' carefully taught and ingrained stances and techniques consistently disintegrate time and again while they participated in any type of dynamic interactive simulation training.

Like many other police firearms instructors across the U.S., however, Barron and Beasley were faced with an unyielding philosophy. The Modern Technique was the only acceptable way to train police officers, even though it only seemed to be effective when used on the training range firing line.

Barron and Beasley struggled privately with these issues for several more years. The first solution they tried was the one most often provided by the same people who had ushered in and reinforced the Modern Technique, namely, "If your students aren't hitting in dynamic encounters, real or simulated, then you're either not training them properly in the Modern Technique, or you're not training them enough in the Modern Technique!"

So they provided more training to their people, who became even more proficient on the static firing line—only to see these reinforced skills "crash and burn" as well during dynamic encounters.

After more than three years of trying to figure out a viable solution, their search led them to Rex Applegate.

The Reemergence of Applegate

Both Barron and Beasley established a solid working relationship with Rex Applegate. In addition to providing them with written and video-taped information, Applegate personally trained them both in the point shooting technique in 1995. This collaboration eventually resulted in Hocking College officially adopting the point shooting technique after approximately two years of study and experimentation by Barron and Beasley.

According to Barron, the results have been both dramatic and outstanding. He succinctly summed up his opinion regarding this matter in the book *Bullseyes Don't Shoot Back* (Paladin Press) with the following quote:

"Point shooting was developed to win gunfights, not competitive games. It was developed for average people, not gun enthusiasts. Most importantly, it is combat proven. Simply put, it works!"

East Meets West

Around this same time, several other U.S. police firearms instructors also found their way back to Applegate and the point shooting technique, including Lou Chiodo of the California Highway Patrol. Chiodo instituted the technique into his agency's firearms training program and noted a dramatic improvement of his students' abilities on the firearms training range.

Lou Chiodo

In addition, numerous real-world police-involved gunfights have indicated an enormous turn-around in the abilities of CHP officers to hit suspects presenting an immediate threat during spontaneous, dynamic encounters.

This turn-around, Chiodo believes, can be directly attributed to the training.

The New Paradigm

On the East Coast, my own personal journey (described in Chapter 2 of the book *Police Pistolcraft*) also led me to Applegate and the point shooting technique.

Both were inspirational in the formation of the Massachusetts State Police Firearms Training Unit and the designing of the New Paradigm Police Firearms Training Program that was officially adopted in May 2000.

While the basic point shooting technique was incorporated in the New Paradigm program much as it had been in the Hocking College and CHP programs, we also took the emulation of the original MITC approach a step further by recreating and implementing a House of Horrors program based upon the original.

The combination of both the point shooting technique and the House of Horrors course is a powerful one, producing beneficial training and operational results the likes of which haven't been seen (to my knowledge) in the United States since 1945.

Of course, unlike the MITC Program, the New Paradigm program was formatted and designed to train the modern U.S. law enforcement officer, *not* the soldier or commando. This factor is significant, and must obviously be considered by the members of civilian law enforcement agencies prior to implementing any type of firearms training program based on the MITC model.

After years of research and work, drawing from many of the resources described above, we were able to create an easily-reproduced, cost-efficient, customized training program that better serves the needs of our department and the citizens of Massachusetts.

It was christened the "New Paradigm" in order to differentiate it from the many others that had been produced since that critical juncture took us in the wrong direction in the late 1950s.

The rest of this chapter will provide a brief overview of the philosophy, design and implementation of the New Paradigm police firearms training program as it has evolved to date.

Founding members of the Massachusetts State Police Firearms Training Unit. From Left; Trooper Dana Pullman, Sergeant Bob Sheehan, Trooper Mike Conti, Trooper Kevin Ford, Trooper Johanna Lawlor, and Trooper Donna Losardo. (Photograph courtesy Massachusetts State Police archives.)

SECTION 2
Training for the Real World

Police firearms training must prepare our officers to perform as well as possible while they employ the handgun in the real world.

While this may seem to be a given, all too often the focus of police firearms training is actually to assist the officers to perform safely and effectively on the range during training iterations, and to pass marksmanship courses so they may be deemed "qualified" with their pistols by their department or agency.

Unfortunately, these types of training "activities" actually do little more than assist the officer to be safer while handling his weapon under controlled conditions on and off the range.

For when using the pistol for real in actual situations, the concept of "control" is often both fluid and tenuous.

It's All About Control

Police officers use their pistols to assist them in controlling out of control behavior. That, after all, is the purpose of any level of force we employ. From our mere presence, through the use of verbal commands, empty hand techniques, chemical agent weapons, impact weapons, and finally, up to and including the employment of deadly force by means of our firearms or otherwise, it is all about *control.*

The level of force employed by the police officer is directly dependent upon the level of force perceived being employed against him or others. Therefore, when we feel the need to draw, point, and/or fire our pistols, it is because we believe we are facing a serious immediate threat to ourselves or others that must be stopped. Bottom line: *lives are at stake.*

Real World Conditions

We know from the data that has been developed over decades that in the vast majority of cases, we will be dealing with a close proximity threat, most often (85%) from about seven yards and closer. We also know that more than half the time (53%) the threat suspect will be five feet and closer to us when the lead starts to fly. As far as distance goes, that is only a step-and-a-grab away!

We also know that in the vast majority of cases we will be dealing with a spontaneous threat. That means that the suspect will more than likely make the first violent move, putting us behind the eight ball and the reactionary lag.

Common sense tells us that we may face a deadly threat at any time of day or night, from anyone or any direction. Statistics tell us that we're most likely to face an armed violent assault during the hours of darkness, or in low-light environments.

The typical police-involved deadly force encounter is usually over in a matter of seconds, with only a few critical rounds fired.

Most officers will face their moment of truth and terror alone or with a partner, while performing their regular day-to-day patrol functions.

Aside from using our pistols to save our own life or someone else's life through the immediate employment of deadly force when faced with an immediate threat of deadly force, we may also draw our weapons in the real world for a number of other reasons such as:

- when searching areas or locations where a deadly threat could be present;
- to assist us to control individuals who are displaying any type of behavior that would cause a reasonable officer to believe the suspect could immediately present a threat of death or serious bodily injury to the officer or others;
- to stop the suffering of a seriously injured animal when other options are not feasible.

While any of these situations could be expected to generate a great deal of stress on the average, normal human being, the first two listed above would likely generate more stress than the last as they require (or could potentially require) the officer to recognize, deal with, and ultimately control at least one threatening human being during a potentially life threatening event.

Additional stress may also be generated because officers do not operate in a vacuum. Besides having to deal with a threatening suspect or suspects, they may also be required to make life and death decisions while simultaneously trying to process information regarding other people present on the scene or in the area.

Add to this mix that, as a result of the stress, the officer's own body will be pumping powerful, naturally occurring chemicals into his blood stream that will elevate his heart and respiration rates, induce perceptual narrowing, and limit to varying degrees his control over his own thought processes and actions, and you begin to get a picture of what must be dealt with while operating with gun in hand as a law enforcement officer.

And we're not through yet! The "icing" on this multi-layered "stress-cake" is found in an officer's innate fear of injuring or killing an innocent person, or the sometimes overwhelming (and often erroneous) fear of being sued for using his firearm for any reason whatsoever and losing his home, career, and very possibly even his family as a result.

These are the everyday deadly force realities faced by the modern police officer while operating in the real world.

To assist him to cope with them, our society provides him with the basics in the form of a badge of **authority**, a **firearm** that may be used only under specific circumstances in support of that authority, and **training** to prepare and enable him to employ both in ways that our society deems appropriate.

While the badge and gun are the most visible components of this deadly force triangle, it is the training component that provides the critical foundation for their proper, confident, and efficient employment.

In order to best achieve this goal, a viable training program must prepare the officer to deal with these realities by exposing him to them *before* he actually experiences them in the real world, allowing him to develop the physical and decisional skills he will need to succeed.

The New Paradigm program facilitates this through mechanisms described in the rest of this chapter.

The Deadly Force Triangle

SECTION 3

Psychological Manifestations of Stress

There are a number of ways that stress affects the human being's ability to take in and process information. If you are not aware of these potential effects, they can add to your stress levels when you experience them while participating in an already stressful encounter.

In order to be better prepared to deal with them, you will need to understand what they are and how they are commonly manifested. Then, when you experience them yourself (preferably in training the first time), they will be both less distracting and disturbing to you.

We will start with an overview of the common perceptual distortions you will be most likely to experience while participating in high-stress activities. For more in-depth information on this subject, I recommend you read *Deadly Force Encounters* by Dr. Alexis Artwohl and Loren W. Christensen.

Common Perceptual Distortions

1) ***Auditory Exclusion:*** When this occurs you may not hear or remember what was heard during an event. You may also hear sounds but be unable to interpret them clearly.

2) ***Auditory Magnification:*** Sounds are intensified, sometimes excluding other sounds. Very often the sound that is intensified is one that is perceived to be critical for survival. For example, you may hear an officer giving commands to a threat suspect while the sound of a nearby cruiser's siren is completely excluded.

3) ***Tunnel Vision:*** You may only see or remember seeing specific components of the total visual tableau. This is commonly illustrated when someone facing a suspect armed with a pistol can describe the suspect's pistol and hand quite clearly while being unable to describe the suspect's face or much else.

4) ***Heightened Visual Clarity:*** You may see specific components of the total visual tableau in high resolution / great detail. Using the example of a suspect armed with a pistol, you may recall seeing the hairs on the suspect's hand quite vividly even at a distance. During a critical incident I was involved in, I experienced a variation of this effect when the suspect began

firing his rifle out the window. At that moment, I lost my color perception, and could see the entire scene only in high definition black and white. This effect lasted for several minutes but was not disturbing to me because I was aware these types of distortions were not only possible but normal.

5) ***Dissociation:*** You may feel detached from the events as they occur. You may even have the feeling of watching yourself during the event, and wondering why you are taking certain actions as you perform them.

6) ***Intrusive Thoughts:*** Some people report having thoughts that were distracting, such as seeing an image of their family or even the written report they were going to have to submit as a result of their actions during the event. Many others, however, have reported thoughts that related to similar past experiences and were in fact helpful in determining their actions in the current event.

7) ***Automatic Behavior:*** Sometimes described as going on "auto pilot," this distortion may be linked with dissociation and memory distortions. The auto pilot distortion is often a positive one, as the subconscious takes over and you perform as you have been trained. It becomes problematic, however, should you have been trained improperly, or worse, if you have received no training for this specific type of circumstance. In the former case, you may find yourself doing something completely illogical such as stopping during a shooting encounter to recover an empty magazine because that is how you trained at the range. In the latter case, you may respond in a completely improper manner, such as by throwing your loaded pistol at a threat suspect and then running away. (Both of these examples actually occurred during police-involved shootings.)

8) ***Temporary Paralysis:*** You may feel as if you are "freezing up" during an event. This may be linked to the slow motion time distortion (see below), for if you begin to perceive things "slowing down" and are not aware that it is a common effect, it may raise your stress levels significantly enough to induce the temporary paralysis (i.e. "Oh my God, I'm freezing up!..." and then you do).

9) ***Time Distortions:*** Time distortions, during which people and events seem to be moving faster or slower than they actually are, are a well known by-product of the type of stress induced during critical situations. Many

officers have described this distortion, most commonly relating how they and subjects they were dealing with suddenly appeared to be moving "in slow motion" during the height of the action. A generally smaller percentage of officers report the opposite type of time distortion, during which people and events seemed to speed up.

The **slow motion distortion** is believed to be simply the result of the brain's functioning being accelerated in response to the stress and the natural chemical cocktail being dumped into the system. Both alter the way the brain takes in and processes available information. The faster the brain processes the information, the slower everything appears to be happening.

While potentially disturbing, this distortion can also be used to the officer's advantage if he is aware of it and prepared to exploit it. (Officers have reported that when experienced and recognized, this effect can produce the feeling of "having all the time in the world" to take proper, careful action in order to stop the threat.)

There are other aspects of time distortions that need to be explored in order to better understand this potentially disturbing effect.

First, regarding the **fast motion perception**: This perception may possibly be linked to memory distortions (see below). Our studies and experiences also indicate that the vast majority of people facing what they perceive to be an immediate deadly threat *to them personally* will experience a feeling not so much of events speeding up, but rather of their own reaction time being too slow, making them feel as though they need to hurry or rush. For example, when facing an immediate threat, an officer may have an overwhelming feeling that there isn't enough time to access and focus upon the sights of his pistol even though there actually is. This feeling is often described as "intense" and will typically override the sight-oriented marksmanship skills and techniques commonly taught and emphasized during old paradigm range training programs. (It is also the primary reason for the incorporation of the point shooting technique into the New Paradigm training program and the emphasis placed upon it.)

As for the **slow motion perception**, it is not uncommon for officers to describe events occurring in extreme slow motion—even though they *also* may have the feeling of "not having enough time."

10) ***Memory Distortions:*** Memory distortions include memory gaps or loss, faulty memory, and false memory. **Memory gaps**, sometimes referred to as "critical incident amnesia," are extremely common. It must be under-

stood that I am not describing a state of confusion; I am describing people experiencing *lost time*—that is, not being able to recall parts or even entire sequences of a dramatic incident they had participated in just moments before.

Although many studies have been conducted on this phenomenon and its existence is widely accepted, the intense reality of a memory gap must be experienced firsthand to truly be understood. For even though someone can describe the effects to you, and you can grasp the concept intellectually, it doesn't become a concrete part of your reality until it happens to you. While interviews with people who have been involved in critical situations can shed some light on the intensity and commonality of memory gaps, I believe that many people do not report that they experienced memory gaps in the field because they quite simply *don't remember what they don't remember.*

Memory gaps may also be linked to fast motion distortions, as parts of the incident are lost resulting in a "missed frames" effect, if you will, similar to watching a film and having it skip ahead, altering (in this case shortening and speeding up) the time line.

Faulty memories and false memories can result for a number of reasons to include the power of suggestion. It is possible that faulty and false memories are also connected to memory gaps. Should someone experience a memory gap, a suggested piece of information may be incorporated into the memory by the brain and used to "fill in" the gap. It is also possible that in the absence of suggestions from an outside source, the brain may tend to fill-in the memory gap with a memory fragment from a similar or even an unrelated experience.

Perceptual Sets

Perceptual Sets can be described as perceptions or expectations that are established *prior* to an encounter that influence perceptions *during* that encounter. If, say, you go into a situation strongly believing that someone has a gun, you may indeed see a gun during that encounter, *even if there actually is no gun present.* It is even possible that, under the right conditions, you may see and/or hear the gun being fired at you, rounds whistling by your head.

Often, all that is needed is something to *suggest* what it is you are expecting to see, and your brain fills in the rest of the image. This image then becomes a mental "Kodak moment," filed away as true memory.

SECTION 4
Physical Manifestations of Stress

Along with perceptual distortions as described in the preceding section, when involved in a critical incident you may also experience one (or many) of the common physical manifestations induced by stress and the powerful chemical cocktail dumped into the system as a result.

Common Physical Manifestations

During a critical incident you may experience dry mouth, shaking hands, pounding heart, trembling, sweating, hyperventilation, upper body quiver, and hyperactivity. These are the most common effects. You may also experience feelings of dizziness, exhaustion, and even nausea during or after the event.

Most of the physical reactions cited above are usually most apparent *immediately after* the event, for it is *then* that the full effects of the chemical dump are felt.

The common misperception regarding the effects noted here is that they are simply a result of "the fear catching up with you." In actuality, of course, once the event is over, the fear has been dealt with one way or another. What you are left to deal with are the effects of the chemicals coursing through your bloodstream.

Doubtful?

Read the description of the effects again. Then compare them to the side-effect warnings found on many prescription medication bottles.

When coming down from the effects of the stress-induced chemicals, you are best advised to drink water and to avoid stimulants like caffeine. You may also find it beneficial to perform mild calisthenics afterward to help burn off the excess adrenaline. Additional information regarding dealing with post-shooting events is included in Chapter 7.

Additional Physical Manifestations

While the physical manifestations of stress described above are those most often thought of when discussing this subject, there are additional aspects relating to this subject that need to be explored. Based upon our training and experiences, I believe these aspects are linked to the stress-induced psychological effects noted in Chapter 1 §3. They are provided here for consideration.

Hollywood Stylizations

Holding the pistol up next to the head is a well-known Hollywood-inspired practice that is commonly derided in the police industry. Often referred to as the **"High Sabrina"** (named for one of the characters on the old "Charlie's Angels" television show), the technique as illustrated in the photo places the officer and those around him in a great deal of danger. For should the officer experience an unintentional discharge while holding the pistol in this manner, there is a very good chance that he may inadvertently shoot himself or someone else in the head. At the least, the officer could easily inflict serious injury to himself or others close to him by exposing their unprotected ears, eyes, and faces to the loud report and hot, high-pressure gasses that follow the bullet out of the muzzle.

While this technique is most strongly discouraged, officers can be observed employing it in the real world all too frequently. I believe this to be a result of repeated exposure to this technique while watching television shows and movies, causing this stylization to be imprinted on the subconscious, and being expressed unconsciously during real world events.

If you find yourself employing this stylization, or observe one of your fellow officers doing so, you should take immediate corrective action in order to avoid serious injury or death.

The **"Peter Gunn"** is another movie-inspired Hollywood stylization that occasionally surfaces. Named for a television detective series popular in the late 1950s and early 1960s, this stylization is characterized by the officer holding the pistol pointed in one direction, while moving toward danger in the opposite direction, usually while moving close to a wall or other vertical surface.

In addition to hindering your ability to deal effectively and efficiently with an immediate threat, this practice also often results in your pointing your pistol at any officer unlucky enough to be following behind you.

You must remember that when operating with a pistol in your hand in the real world, you should always keep the "muzzle first to danger!"

The "Peter Gunn" Hollywood Stylization

Trigger Affirmation

When involved in high-stress situations, it is possible that you may place your finger on the trigger with no conscious awareness on your part, despite being extensively trained to keep the finger off the trigger until ready to fire. You must strive to ensure you are aware of where your finger is at all times in relation to the trigger when operating with gun in hand. And again, in the interest of safety, if you observe a fellow officer to have his finger on the trigger at an inappropriate time you should make him aware of it. Bruised egos and hurt feelings heal much faster than gunshot wounds.

The Reassurance Grip

The "reassurance grip" is the term I've come up with to describe an unorthodox two-handed grip we've seen demonstrated enough times by different officers to rate its own moniker.

Never taught by any firearms instructor that I am aware of, this grip has been observed primarily during dynamic simulation training iterations, though I would expect it also occurs in the field. This dangerous grip consists of placing the non-dominant hand around the slide as shown in the photograph below. It is performed without conscious awareness just as are the Hollywood stylizations described previously. When questioned about the grip, officers could provide no rational explanation for it, except to mention that it made them "feel better" holding the pistol in that manner. Hence the moniker, "reassurance grip."

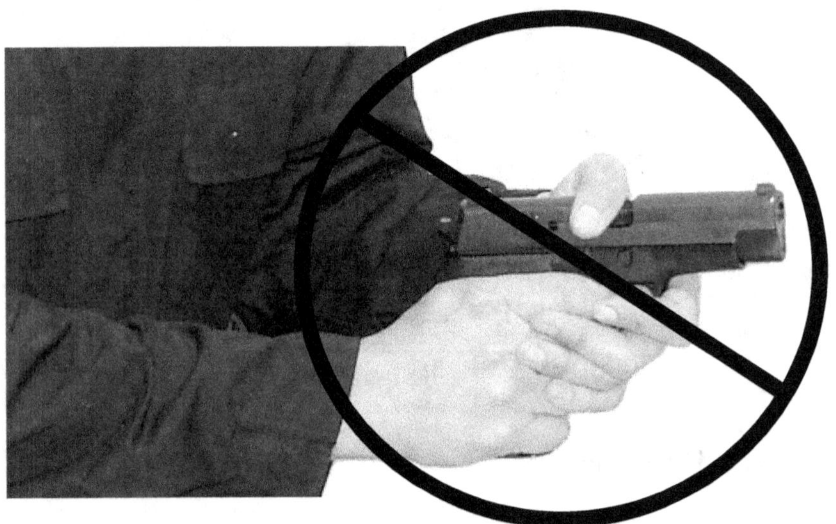

The Reassurance Grip

One interesting theory regarding this grip was offered by Professor Greg Morrison after I described it to him during a telephone conversation.

He felt that it could suggest a subconscious desire to hold and employ the pistol as if it was a stick or club.

"After all," he observed, "we have had more historical experience using blunt impact weapons than firearms, which are still relatively new tools, evolutionary-wise."

Regardless of its cause, this is yet another potentially dangerous physical manifestation of stress that you must be aware of in order to avoid it. You should also bring it to the attention of others should they exhibit this behavior during training or in the field.

SECTION 5

Countering the Effects of Stress by Breathing

There are a number of ways to counter the effects of stress through proper training and personal preparation. Several approaches are outlined in Chapter 7.

In this section, I offer an overview of the most basic and effective technique, one with which we are all familiar—breathing.

Combat Breathing

Controlling the breathing cycle to calm and strengthen the mind and body has long been practiced by martial artists.

A common "Zen breathing technique" requires the practitioner to slowly breathe in through the nose, allowing the air to fill the lower part of the lungs as well as the upper. Once the lungs are full, the practitioner then consciously holds the breath deep within the chest cavity for a few moments, usually four seconds or more. Finally, the breath is *slowly* released through the mouth, using the lips to regulate the flow.

The amount of power that can be developed through this process is incredible. Certain breathing exercises I have been taught over the years, for instance, produce the same physiological results as physical exercise, increasing both strength and stamina.

In regard to the statistically-likely police-involved gunfight, while some proponents of the old paradigm style of training still insist on incorporating breath control into the marksmanship-based shooting cycle (usually characterized by an acronym such as *BRASS*, for *Breathe*, *Relax*, *Aim*, *Squeeze*, *Surprise*), most instructors today will concur that the most important thing an officer should be concerned about in regards to breathing, is that he or she is *still able to do so* after those few terrifying moments are over.

Though I agree with the basic logic of this position, I also know from personal experience that police officers are often involved in stressful activities of longer duration than the typical, spontaneous police-involved gunfight. While these activities may eventually lead up to the gunfight (such as when an officer is searching for a suspect in a building or through a wooded area), they are, in and of themselves, inherently stressful.

If this stress is allowed to increase unabated, it can reach levels high enough to drastically impair the officer's judgment, reaction time, and performance. This is why it is important to understand how to properly regulate your breathing cycles before, during, and after dangerous and stressful encounters. In addition, you should practice this technique both when involved in static training on the range and especially during dynamic training iterations.

The technique outlined below, while sometimes described as something fairly new under the title of "Autogenic" or "Combat" breathing, has literally been known and practiced for thousands of years. This in itself would seem to serve as a testament to its effectiveness.

To truly appreciate the stress-harnessing power of controlled breathing, however, you need to try it yourself.

The Combat Breathing Cycle:

1) Breathe in deeply through the nose for a slow 4-count

2) Hold the breath, pushing it down into the lower abdomen for a 4-count

3) Blow the air slowly out of the lungs through the mouth for a 4-count

4) Wait for a 4-count before beginning the next inhalation

5) Repeat.

By the second or third cycle, you should feel your body relaxing as your respiration and heart rates slow. I have also found that I can easily cause my blood pressure to drop significantly (both systolic and diastolic levels) by using this technique combined with mental imagery (described in Chapter 7 §3).

SECTION 6

The Integrated Duty Pistol Training Course (DPTC) Concept

Individual, traditional police firearms training programs are usually designed to accomplish a number of goals simultaneously. Often, the actual stated purpose of the course is not achieved, in many cases because there is no clarity of purpose.

This is crucial. For without clarity of purpose, true goals cannot be defined. In the absence of defined goals, confusion, misunderstanding, personal preferences, prejudices, and ego enter. This often results in training programs that not only fail to serve their stated purpose, but which may also produce negative results in those being trained.

In order to fully eliminate the possibility of confusion on the part of the course designer or trainee, each level of training must first be identified, then isolated, then addressed.

Individual, mission-specific courses of fire can then be created to assist the student officer to achieve the specific identified goals of each. Once these goals have been achieved, the student officer "graduates" to the next level of training.

Each course of fire is linked to the next, allowing for consistency in the training approach and techniques employed.

Ultimately, each course of fire is revealed to be a single component of an overall training matrix, the purpose of which is not to assist the officer to merely demonstrate technical competence with the weapon under controlled conditions in training, but to prepare the student officer to employ his firearm, when necessary, in the real world, under real world conditions.

In order to best accomplish this goal, all of the training courses must be realistically designed around the three main elements involved: 1) the people being trained; 2) the equipment they are employing; and 3) the environment in which they will be working.

Included in the "environment" considerations are the actual physical characteristics of the environment as well as the social and political realities that must be addressed. The latter considerations are best addressed through the identification and integration of pertinent federal, state, and local laws (as well as departmental policies and procedures) into all of the training segments. An overview of each level of training included in the New Paradigm program is provided in this section.

DPTC 1: Skill Builder Training Courses (The Foundation)

Purpose

Level One courses of fire are designed to assist the student officer in the development of individual, mission-specific pistol handling and manipulation skills.

These skill building programs help the individual officer to develop and polish critical skills that he will most likely need while operating in the field in real situations, under extreme circumstances. The drills are carefully chosen, kept simple and consistent, and allow the students enough repetitions to develop a solid mental and physical grasp of the techniques.

Targets

The targets used for this level of training serve only as a diagnostic tool that will allow the instructor to gauge the ability of the participating officer to successfully deliver rounds to a specified target area. For this reason, only neutral-stimulus, or no-threat types of targets should be employed for DPTC 1 level courses.

The **NPT-1 Target** shown at right has been specially produced by Law Enforcement Targets, Inc. for use in DPTC 1 level courses of fire.

(www.letargets.com)

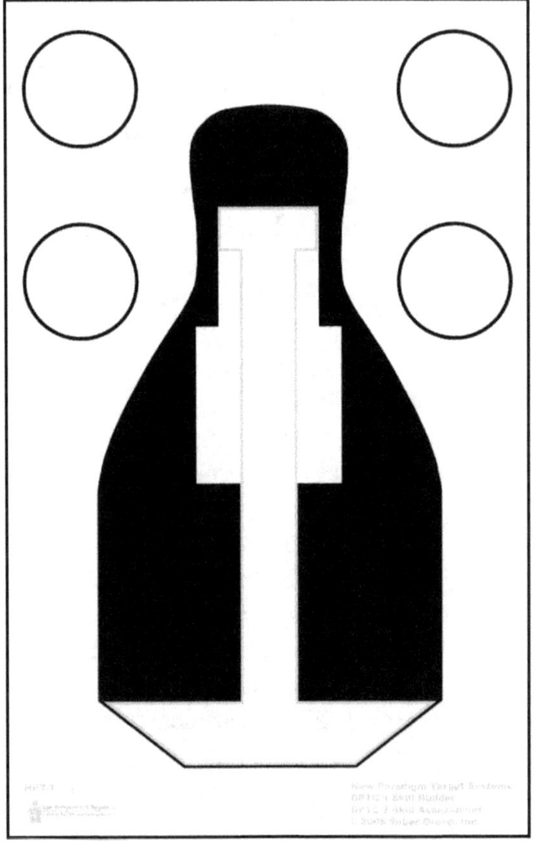

Conduct

DPTC 1: Skill Builder Training Course, Example

Level One courses of fire consist of a number of separate drills, performed one after another. Examples of these types of drills are listed below.

Each of these specific drills will be explained and illustrated in later chapters.

1) The Reset or "One Hole" Drill........................Chapter 12

2) The Point Shooting Exercise..........................Chapter 5

3) Stoppage Clearing Drill.................................Chapter 4

4) Close Proximity Drill....................................Chapter 5

5) Transition Drill..Chapter 7

In addition to assisting the individual officer to analyze/develop and improve his own tactical pistol skills, these types of exercises also allow the instructor to gauge the ability of the participating student officer to successfully deliver rounds to a specified target area, employ verbalization, and manipulate the weapon while performing multiple separate and linked actions.

The incorporation of the various positions, tactics, and techniques that are employed during these courses of fire are intended to provide the participating officer with an opportunity to employ them safely under controlled conditions so they may best be learned and assimilated.

Trained and experienced instructors must also be able to evaluate the participant's ability to properly and safely perform these techniques under controlled conditions, and assist the participants in the improvement of marksmanship, safe handling skills, and additional techniques as needed.

DPTC 2: Marksmanship & Safe Handling Skills Assessment Tests

Purpose

Level Two courses of fire require the student officer to demonstrate that he has achieved the necessary skills to accurately deliver rounds to a specified target area in a safe and proficient manner using the duty pistol. Rounds are fired from the prone, kneeling, and standing positions. Rounds are also delivered while the student officer manipulates, controls, and employs a flashlight in combination with the pistol.

This course of fire most closely resembles a traditional old paradigm, marksmanship-based "qualification" type course.

Keeping to our clarity of purpose, the express focus of this program has been placed on 1) safe and efficient manipulation of the pistol and flashlight; 2) safe and efficient positioning of the body and pistol in relation to the environment and cover; and 3) the effective employment of the pistol from these various positions to deliver aimed rounds to a specific target area, while the officer is operating in a controlled environment and under the effects of minimum induced stress.

Both **point shooting** and **precision shooting** skills are evaluated during Level 2 courses of fire. In contrast to old paradigm courses of fire, the majority of rounds are fired from closer distances and utilize point shooting skills. The ratio of rounds fired employing point shooting as compared to precision shooting techniques has been calculated to more accurately reflect the percentages indicated by actual police-involved shooting situations.

Targets

Targets for this level of training also serve only as a diagnostic tool that will allow the instructor to gauge the ability of the participating officer to successfully deliver rounds to a specified target area.

For this reason, only neutral-stimulus (no-threat) types of targets such as the **NPT-1** should be employed.

Conduct

DPTC 2: Marksmanship & Safe Handling Skills Assessment Tests Training Course, Example

Level Two courses of fire consist of a number of separate drills, performed one after another. Examples of these types of drills will be explained and illustrated in later chapters.

Drills in Level Two courses may include having the student:

1) Deliver precision-aimed (sighted) rounds from the prone position, behind cover, from 25 yards distance, using a two-hand hold.

2) Deliver precision-aimed (sighted) rounds from the kneeling position, behind cover, from 17 yards distance, using a two-hand hold.

3) Deliver a series of 2 aimed (Point Shooting/Full Extension) rounds from the standing position, from 7 yards distance, using a two-hand hold.

4) Deliver a series of 2 aimed (Point Shooting/Full Extension) rounds from the kneeling position, from 7 yards distance, using the non-dominant hand, and a two-hand hold.

5) Deliver a series of 2 aimed (Point Shooting/Full Extension) rounds from the standing position, from 4 yards distance, using a one-hand hold.

6) Deliver a series of 2 aimed (Point Shooting/Full Extension) rounds from the standing position, from 2 yards distance, using a one-hand hold while employing a flashlight in combination with the pistol.

7) Deliver a series of 2 aimed (Point Shooting/Body Point) rounds from the standing position, from 1.5 yards distance, using a one-hand hold.

8) Deliver a series of 3 aimed (Point Shooting/Body Point and Full Extension) rounds from the standing position, from 1 yard and 2 yards, respectively, using a one-hand hold.

DPTC 3: Combination Drill (Movement, Cover, Judgment, Verbalization, & Safe Handling Skills Assessment Tests)

Purpose

Level 3 courses of fire require the student officer to demonstrate that he has achieved the ability to perform a number of interrelated skills, i.e., adeptly exit the cruiser, properly move to a position of cover, use cover in an efficient manner, recognize an immediate threat, employ verbal commands, use good judgment while employing deadly force, engage a moving target, or fire effectively while on the move. All of these objectives can be accomplished in an efficiently designed and safely run course of fire. A sample DPTC 3 level training course is described and explained in this section.

Targets

Targets for this level of training will serve as diagnostic tools that allow the instructor to gauge the ability of the participating officer to successfully deliver rounds to a specified target area. More important, these targets will also serve as threat or no threat stimuli, requiring the officer to employ judgment before, during, and after firing his weapon.

There are many target options, 2D and 3D, available to use for this type of course. A few examples are shown here.

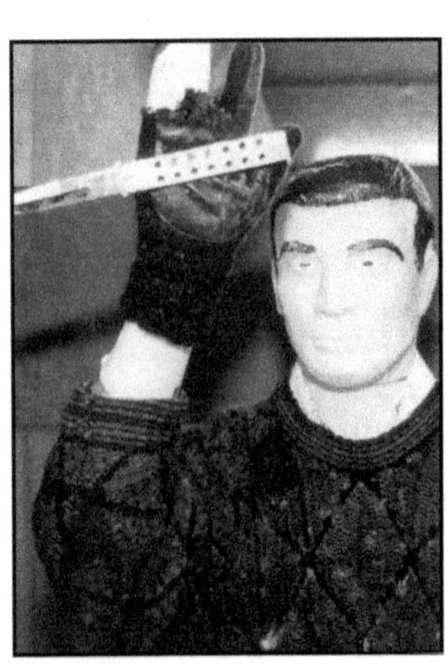

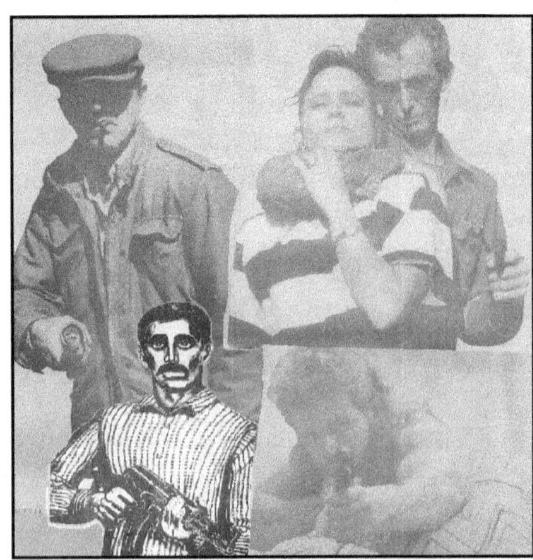

Conduct

DPTC 3: Combination Drill Training Course, Example

The Level 3 series of courses are truly the "transitional courses" of the program, taking the foundational pistolcraft skills that have been developed and introducing them into more police-specific, reality-based activities while still maintaining the controlled atmosphere of the training range.

Level 3 courses are designed to be extremely time efficient and yet have a high training value. One such course (shown being conducted in photo) addresses all of the below listed critical training needs and can be completed, on average, in about three minutes time per student. This includes an individual critique and debriefing.

1) efficient vehicle (cruiser) escape technique
2) tactical movement while controlling a pistol
3) use of cover
4) use of verbalization while controlling representations of both threats and no-threats
5) scanning / observation of environment while controlling representations of both threats and no-threats
6) engaging a threat from behind cover while the threat is moving through a less than sterile environment
7) decision making skills regarding the if, when, and how of employing deadly force during a spontaneous, high-risk situation while trying to control representations of both threats and no-threats

DPTC 4: Scenario-based, Dynamic Interactive, Experiential Learning / Diminished Light Training

Purpose

The Level 4 "House of Horrors" course is the most intense and critically productive segment of the entire New Paradigm program. In essence, it is the defining component of the program.

The primary purpose of the House of Horrors training course is to assist each officer in attaining, developing, and reinforcing his individual tactical thinking and operational skills and abilities, thereby producing a more competent, confident, and safer police officer.

In addition, the course also provides the following benefits:

- inoculates officers against the effects of stress and body alarm reaction
- allows assessment of officer's behavior in realistic situations
- allows remediation of behavior as necessary
- illuminates areas of training deficiency, both individual officers' and departmental, and allows for correction
- facilitates the reinforcement of good tactics and techniques
- facilitates the reduction of poor tactics and techniques
- enables the development of judgmental / decisional skills and allows for instructor assessment of same
- allows for the testing of new tactics and techniques
- increases morale and confidence
- enhances liability insulation for all department personnel

Not only does the Level 4 course allow the participants to experience extreme situations under controlled conditions in a training environment, where trained instructors are available to provide information, guidance and assistance to them as needed or requested, but it also provides instructors and students with an excellent means of verifying the officer's individual skill retention levels, while allowing for the identification and reinforcement of strengths, the identification and improvement of weaknesses, and for the immediate identification and correction of any observed operating errors.

In addition, when formatted and administered correctly, these courses will allow the student to see, through his own eyes, exactly what the effects of stress are and how they may affect the individual. The degree of success attainable in this regard will be directly dependent upon the training, knowledge, and observation skills of the instructor, as well as upon the instructor's ability to properly debrief the students immediately upon completion of the course.

Finally, by allowing students to experience the effects of stress as they employ the actual equipment, tactics, and techniques they will use while operating under conditions similar to those they are preparing for, we are able to educate them as never before and simultaneously inoculate them against these same, often debilitating effects.

The specific desired result of this type of training is to produce officers who can and will operate at a higher level of efficiency in the real world. This becomes possible as officers develop improved cognitive and judgmental abilities, which in turn will serve to improve their physical performance levels.

The end result is a more confident, efficient, effective, and above all, *safer* police officer.

Targets

In addition to serving as diagnostic tools that allow the instructor to gauge the ability of the participating officer to successfully deliver rounds to a specified target area, Level 4 House of Horrors training program targets also serve to present specific visual, auditory, and pain stimuli to the participant, requiring the officer to employ judgment before, during, and after firing his weapon. For this reason, realistic 3D interactive threat-type and no-threat type targets are employed.

Instructor (left) and student in the House of Horrors.

Conduct

In essence, the instructor, following closely behind the student officer, directs the student officer from station to station through the training area. Subdued guidance and support in the form of directions and advice is provided by the instructor throughout the course.

At various stages, the student officer will be presented with a threat and/or no threat stimulus which he will be expected to deal with appropriately.

Upon successful completion of this course of fire, the student will have been exposed to a number of reality-based, interactive and dynamic training scenarios, similar to those that may most likely be encountered while operating in actual working environments.

Contrary to common beliefs, training courses of this type do not require expensive facilities or complicated equipment in order to produce beneficial results. There are a number of options that may be employed to conduct this type of high-value training safely, and with a minimum dedication of assets.

Similar to the Level Three courses, each officer participating in the Level Four course receives individualized instruction while participating in high-yield critical skills training that satisfies practically all of the current requirements and meets all of the standards mandated by statute and case law such as:

- Moving targets
- Reduced light training
- Judgmental/decisional training
- Use of cover
- Realistic environments
- Policy reinforcement
- Force level integration and transition
- Relevance to assignment (patrol, investigations, undercover, etc.)

Additional Information

Additional information regarding the design, construction, and administration of each DPTC level of training is available in the text, *POLICE PISTOLCRAFT: The Reality-Based New Paradigm of Police Firearms Training.* (Available from www.sabergroup.com)

CHAPTER 2

Weapons & Equipment

SECTION 1

The Pistol: Basic Tool of the Trade

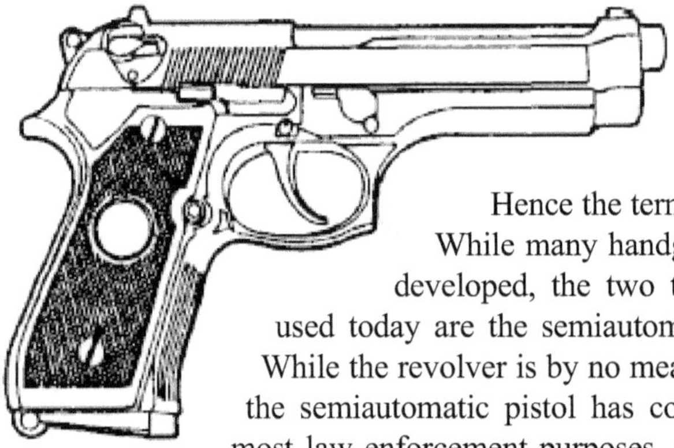

A pistol is defined as a firearm designed to be held and fired with only one hand. Hence the term, "handgun."

While many handgun designs have been developed, the two types most commonly used today are the semiautomatic and the revolver. While the revolver is by no means an obsolete design, the semiautomatic pistol has come to be favored for most law enforcement purposes, and will, therefore, be focused upon in this book.

The majority of handguns currently in use by the police industry share many common traits. In the interest of keeping this section to a manageable size, specific design characteristics unique to each make and model will not be addressed except when using one model pistol or another to illustrate individual techniques. The techniques themselves are, for the most part, adaptable to the various pistols most likely to be encountered.

As for the detail work (since that is where the devil reportedly resides), each individual officer will (or should) be thoroughly trained by his department, agency, or unit with the specific weapon he will carry.

How Semiautomatic Pistols Function

The basic functioning or "cycle of operation" for the vast majority of semiautomatic pistols is the same.

- First, you insert a magazine containing ammunition into the receiver or grip of the pistol.
- Then you pull the slide fully to the rear and release. As the slide moves forward, it strips the top round from the magazine and pushes it into the chamber. For pistols with exposed hammers, depending upon the trigger action, the hammer may remain in the cocked position or automatically lower. Either way, unless a mechanical safety is engaged, the pistol is ready to be fired.
- The weapon will fire one round each time the trigger is pressed.
- Each time a cartridge is fired, the slide and/or barrel recoils

(moves rearward) a short distance while locked together. This permits the bullet and expanding powder gases to escape from the muzzle before the unlocking is completed. The barrel then unlocks from the slide which continues to the rear, extracting the empty cartridge case from the chamber and ejecting it from the weapon. As the slide travels rearward the recoil spring is compressed and the next round in the magazine is raised into position by the magazine spring pressing on the follower.

- At the end of the slide's rearward movement, the recoil spring expands, forcing the slide forward. The round is then pushed into the chamber as the barrel and slide lock together. The pistol is ready to fire again.
- This same cycle of operation continues until the ammunition is expended. With most (but not all) semiautomatic pistols, as the last round is fired, the magazine follower presses up on the slide stop, forcing it into the recess on the bottom of the slide and locking the slide to the rear. This action indicates that the magazine is empty.

Trigger Actions

To avoid confusion, a few terms relating to the trigger mechanisms, or actions, incorporated into modem handguns need to be addressed. The first term is **double action.**

It is often argued that this term refers to a pistol's ability to be fired in two ways—either by manually cocking the hammer to the rear and then pressing the trigger, or, with the hammer down, pressing the trigger fully rearward, causing the hammer to cock and then release. It can also be argued, however, that the name double action is derived from the term *double acting* trigger, originally used to describe the two actions that take place when the trigger is pressed on a handgun designed to be fired from the hammer-down configuration. (Pressing the trigger both cocks and releases the hammer.) Adhering to this variation of the terminology would allow a weapon so designed to be referred to as double action, regardless of its ability to be fired from the manually achieved full-cock position.

The second term is **single action.** Firing a weapon single action means that a press of the trigger will cause the hammer to be released from the fully cocked position, firing the weapon. The hammer may be brought to the fully cocked position either manually, by thumbing it back, or, in the

---

Illustrations on pages 60, 62, and some material on pages 60-61 have been adapted from FM 23-35, Headquarters, Department of the Army, Washington, DC, 3 October 1988.

case of a semiautomatic pistol, by the slide's rearward travel. Confusion is sometimes generated by the fact that when some double action semiautomatic pistols are fired, the cycling of the slide cocks the hammer. Once in this condition, the weapon is then commonly referred to as being in *single action mode*.

If you are employing a **double action only** semiautomatic pistol, the hammer will follow the slide forward each time the action is cycled, requiring the shooter to press the trigger fully rearward, raising and releasing the hammer for each shot. (For the purposes of this book, the Glock pistol's unique **Safe-Action** may be considered as double action only.)

Because my goal here is to present the information in a straightforward, uncluttered fashion, I am simply going to employ the terms double and single action in the following manner throughout this book:

Double action — a single press of the trigger raises the hammer fully rearward and then releases the hammer to fire the weapon.

Single action — the handgun is fired by pressing the trigger with the hammer at the full-cock position. The hammer may be brought to the full-cock position either manually by thumb-cocking or by being slide-cocked.

Basic Characteristics of the Semiautomatic Pistol

The semiautomatic pistol has been in use since the late 1800s. While many developments in materials and design have occurred since then, the basic characteristics remain the same.

Magazine fed — The semiautomatic pistol is invariably magazine-fed. While a few models have been configured differently, the vast majority use a self-contained, removable magazine that is loaded while removed from the pistol and then inserted into the handle or grip of the weapon.

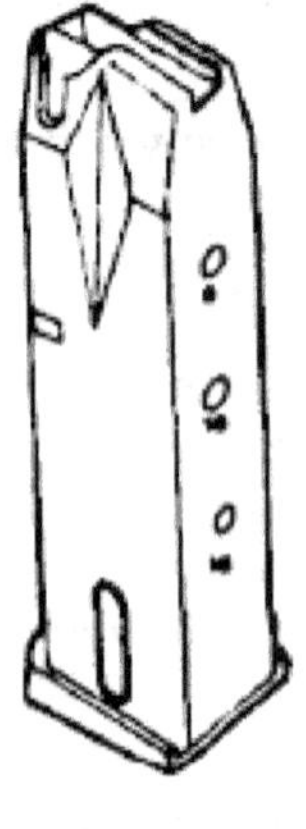

M9 Magazine

Slide action loaded — While there are variations, most semiautomatic pistols require the slide to be fully retracted and released to load the first round from the magazine into the chamber.

Recoil-operated — Most semiautomatic pistols utilize the rearward movement of parts of the weapon in recoil to operate the action. In other words, upon firing, an equal amount of energy drives the bullet forward while

Common Characteristics of the Semiautomatic Pistol

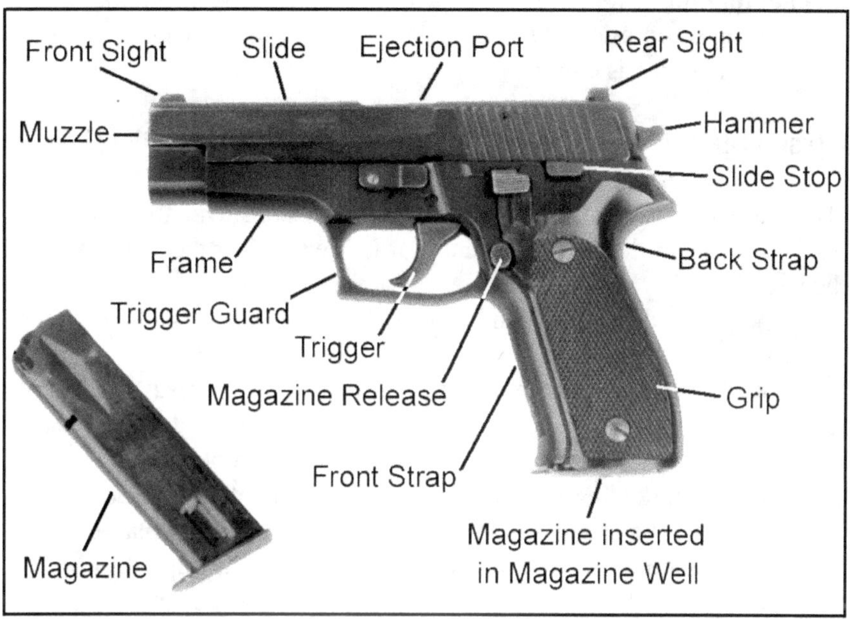

Exploded Views of Semiautomatic Pistol and Magazine

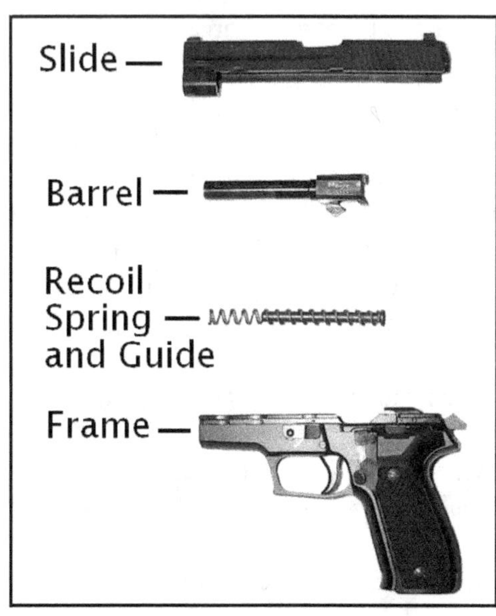

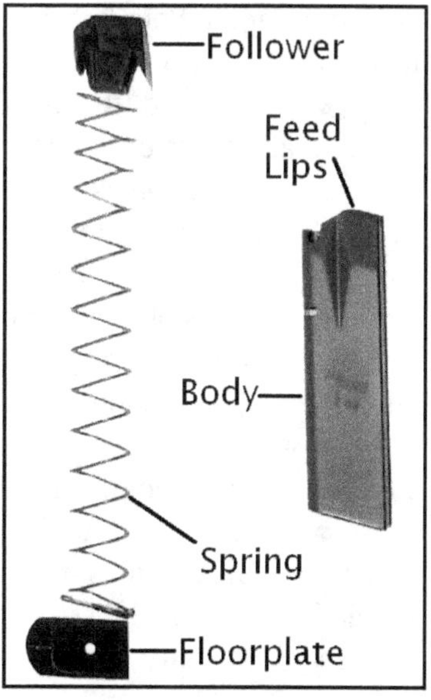

simultaneously driving the barrel and slide to the rear. (See "**How Semiautomatic Pistols Function**" above for a fuller description).

Semiautomatic — One round is fired each time the trigger is pressed until the magazine is empty.

Desirable Characteristics of the Semiautomatic Pistol

There are a number of quality semiautomatic pistols available for use. In most cases, your department, agency, or unit will select the pistol you will be issued.

A quality duty pistol can be judged in part based upon the following criteria:

- The duty pistol should be configured for combat use, not for competition shooting applications. The more complicated the pistol and its components, the more likely you are to experience problems with it.
- When holding it, you should be able to comfortably and securely grip the pistol while the first pad of your index finger is placed on the trigger. You should not have to constantly readjust your grip when firing.
- For double-action weapons, dry-firing the weapon 50 to 100 times as quickly as you can will give you an accurate gauge of the required trigger pull as well as your current hand strength. If you experience difficulty doing this, you will have to improve your hand strength or request another weapon. Your best bet would be to prepare for firearms training by increasing your hand strength. (See Chapter 4 §6.)
- When held, the pistol should fit comfortably into your hand and feel like an extension of your arm. Some people express this quality by referring to a weapon as being a "natural pointer," meaning that when held in a solid grip and extended toward the target, the weapon points to a specific spot on the target as naturally as your index finger would.
- The pistol should not be so large or unwieldy that it is uncomfortable to carry on your person, whether in the uniform duty holster or while wearing plainclothes.
- The pistol should be equipped with a set of rugged sights that your eyes can quickly acquire and align.
- The pistol should provide you with the highest ammunition capacity available for similar models of its size and quality. Reloading should be simple and fast.
- The duty pistol should not be equipped with any type of

manually-operated, mechanical safety that renders the weapon inoperable. This includes magazine disconnectors that don't allow a chambered round to be fired if the magazine has been removed from the pistol.

"Firepower" Reality Check

Whichever type of pistol you carry, you must always understand that it is a *handgun*, a tool that is limited by its size and the operator's skill. Too often, I have seen the gleam in an officer's eyes when issued a new high-capacity semiauto and heard the word *firepower* attributed to it. The armament aboard the *USS New Jersey* qualifies as firepower. No handgun does.

Caring For the Semiautomatic Pistol

Taking care of your pistol is the best defense against the always-present Murphy and his confounding "laws." When cleaning firearms, you don't need to go overboard, but you do need to be thorough. After safely disassembling your weapon, make sure you clean off any carbon, lead residue, rust, dirt, or fouling. Carbon generally looks dull compared to shiny clean metal surfaces and can be easily spotted once you learn what to look for.

To avoid excess wear when cleaning metal parts, be sure to use brushes made of a softer material than that of your weapon's components. Stainless steel bristles on bore brushes or cleaning brushes are **not** recommended.

A rag lightly dampened with a quality firearm's cleaning solvent should be used to thoroughly wipe down all metallic components of the pistol. A nylon brush and a dry rag can then be used to clean these and all other parts of the weapon. Pay special attention to any moving parts or areas where metal-to-metal contact occurs.

Slide: Slides require extra attention at the face of the bolt where the extractor and firing pin hole are located. Make sure to clean the area under the extractor claw with a nylon brush, and use both the brush and the rag to clean the slide rail cuts (the grooves the frame rails are inserted into). The area at the rear of the slide, any channels, grooves or cuts, and both the front and rear sights will also tend to collect dust, dirt, rust, and fouling.

Barrel: The outer and inner surfaces of the barrel must be cleaned so all carbon buildup, dirt, and rust are removed. Pay particular attention to the lands and grooves of the bore of the barrel, as well as the feed ramps and

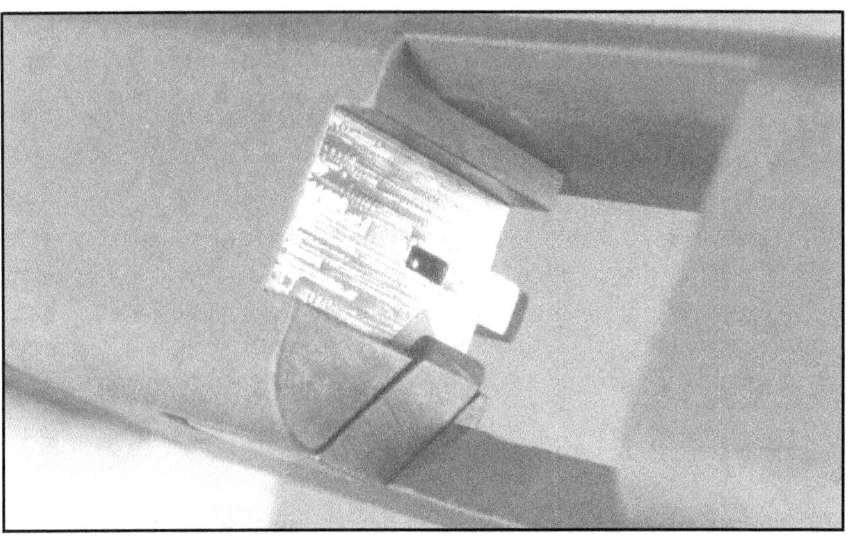

The face of the bolt. Note the extractor (lever protruding over the face of the bolt from the side) and the firing pin hole. This area should be kept clean and dry. Over lubrication in this area will cause excessive fouling when firing, as well as possibly contaminating the primer of the chambered round if the weapon is left loaded for a long period of time. Though not highly likely, the explosive compound within would be inactivated should the slightest bit of oil leach into the primer. This could be deadly should you need that round to stop an immediate threat.

chamber. A Hoppe's BoreSnake can be used to clean the feed ramps, chamber and bore with only a few passes, or you can use a cloth patch dampened with solvent and run through the bore with a rod, followed by a bore brush. When using the second method, make sure to run dry patches through the bore after brushing and repeat the process until the patches come out clean.

Frame (or Receiver): All areas of the frame should be brushed out with the nylon brush and wiped down with your rag. The rails of the frame along which the slide moves also need to be thoroughly cleaned. Don't remove grip panels unless you have been trained to do so. Grip screws should be cleaned and checked to ensure they are not loose. When checking grip screws on semiautomatics, be careful not to over-tighten them. With some models, it is possible to turn the screws in far enough to either "lock" the magazine in or prevent insertion.

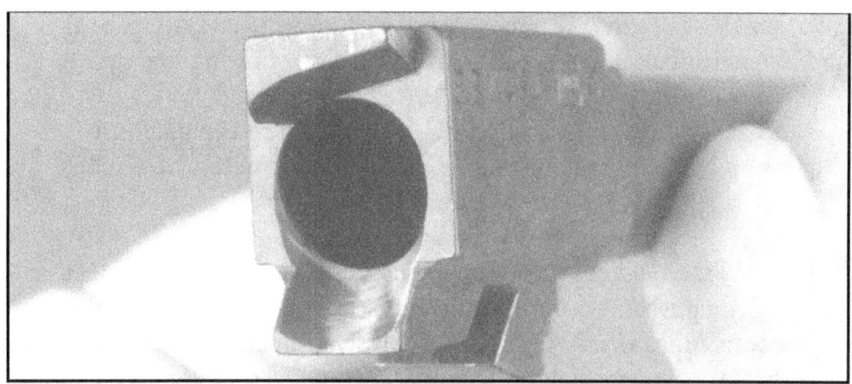

(Above) A close-up of the feed ramp and chamber of a Glock barrel. Pay particular attention to both these areas when cleaning any semiauto pistol barrel, as carbon buildup here will cause feeding and extraction problems.

Magazine: The magazines must also be disassembled (if possible) and all components brushed off and wiped out, preferably with a clean, dry cloth. The magazine feed lips and follower should be checked for damage.

Lubrication: Lubricating the weapon after it's cleaned is critical. A clean, dry gun can be as prone to stoppages as a dirty one because of excessive heat and friction caused by metal-to-metal contact. This is especially true with some aerosol cleaners, as they tend to remove all of the oils and grease from the pores of the metal, including internal parts the average user may not be able to access in order to relubricate.

If you do use aerosols, make sure you consult with an armorer regarding these concerns, because metal fatigue is a real possibility, *especially* if you are using a strong degreasing solvent.

When lubricating, keep it light but, again, be thorough. The weapon should not be dripping with oil or grease when you are finished, but should have a subtle sheen and should function smoothly when the action is worked. Pay particular attention to any areas that show wear from friction.

Basic Pistol Cleaning Kit

There is a vast array of handgun cleaning equipment available on the market. You should use that which works best for you. After more than 25 years and having used practically every tool, solvent, and device available, my basic pistol cleaning kit now consists of the following four items:

- a lint-free rag
- a military-style, double-end, nylon-bristle cleaning brush
- a bottle of combination cleaner-lubricant-preservative (CLP)
- a Hoppe's BoreSnake Bore Cleaner

Using only these 4 items, a thorough, inspection-grade cleaning can usually be accomplished on most semiautomatic pistols in about 15 minutes. Fast doesn't mean rushed, however. Always remember that should you need to go to your pistol while working, it will be because your life or someone else's life is in jeopardy.

Devote your time and energy to servicing your pistol accordingly.

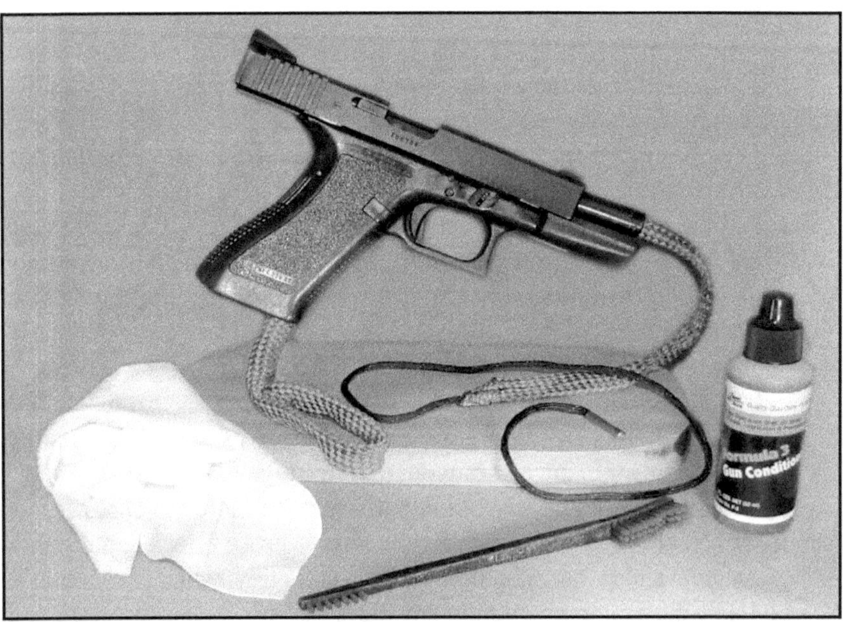

One of the best tools available to thoroughly and quickly clean the feed ramp, chamber, and bore of your pistol is the Hoppe's BoreSnake. It can be used with the barrel removed or while the pistol is assembled as shown for a quick touch-up cleaning. Add a lint-free rag, nylon brush, and combination cleaner-lubricant-preservative and you have everything you need to clean your pistol.

SECTION 2
Ammunition

How Pistol Ammunition Functions

"Round" is the term used to describe a single unit of ammunition. For a modern small arms cartridge the round is made up of a combination of cartridge case, primer, propellant, and bullet.

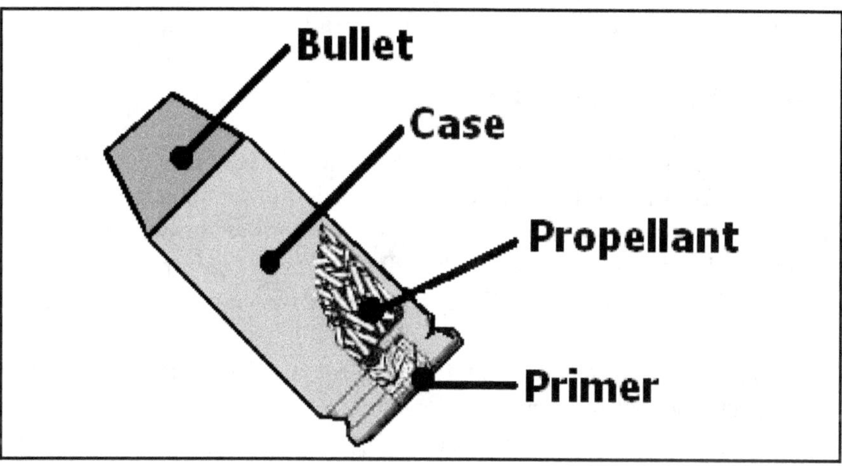

The chambered round is fired in the following manner:

- The trigger is pressed causing the hammer and/or firing pin to be driven forward, striking the primer located at the base of the cartridge case. The impact partially crushes the primer igniting the explosive compound within it.
- The flash from the primer then ignites the propellant in the case. The propellant burns at an extremely fast rate. As it burns, it produces a great deal of hot gas.
- The gas quickly expands within the case and produces pressure. As the case body is surrounded by the steel of the chamber and the base of the case is pressed up against the steel of the locked bolt, the bullet, merely crimped into place in the case, provides the path of least resistance for the pressure to escape.
- The pressure produced by the expanding gas forces the bullet out of the case and into the barrel. Once in the barrel, the bullet makes contact with the spiral-cut lands and grooves in the bore. This forms a seal behind the bullet (keeping the gas from escaping around it) and causes the

bullet to rotate (spin) as it travels through the bore.

● As the bullet exits the end of the barrel, it continues to spin much like a properly thrown football does in flight. The spinning provides for a stable trajectory, or flight path. Drag is also influenced by bullet spin. The faster the spin, the less likely a bullet will "yaw" (turn sideways) or tumble in flight. The bullet continues to travel until it either strikes something in its path or the energy that propelled it forward is depleted, in which case it will simply fall to Earth as a result of gravity.

Ammunition Trajectories

After exiting the bore, the spinning bullet generally travels in a straight line on the **horizontal axis**. Extremely high winds may influence the bullet's horizontal trajectory (the reason sighting adjustments on the horizontal plane are referred to as "windage"), but the effects of even very strong winds will be negligible at the normally close ranges handguns are typically used (50 yards and much, much closer).

The bullet's trajectory on the **vertical axis** is a slightly different matter, and one that is often misunderstood.

To understand vertical axis bullet flight, a few basic concepts must be understood.

First, when the shooter uses the sights to verify that the muzzle is pointed at a specific target, he looks through the sights and aligns them so they are pointing at the specific spot he wishes the bullet to impact. This imaginary line is called the **Line of Sight**.

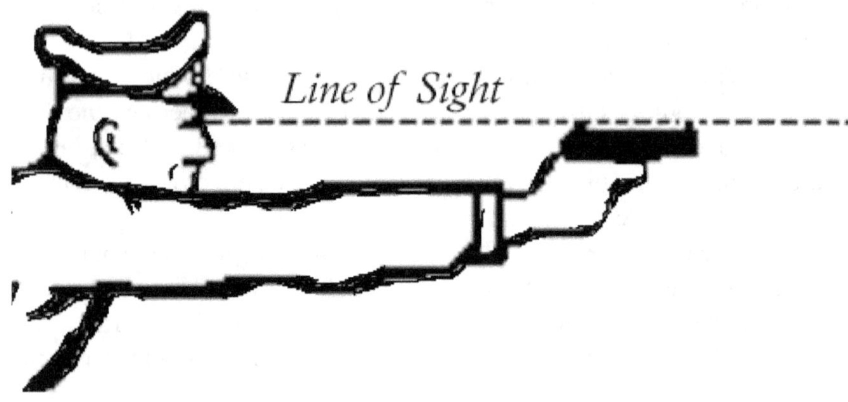

The second concept concerns the actual **Bullet Flight Trajectory**. Simply stated, as a result of the typical handgun's design, the bullet enters the atmosphere at a point slightly lower than the sights of the pistol and, therefore, slightly lower than the shooter's line of sight.

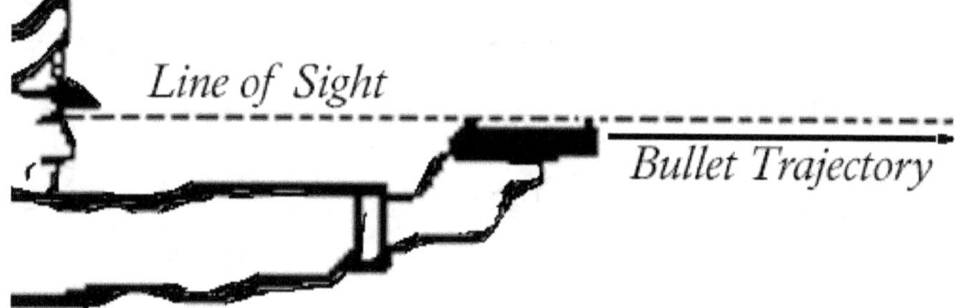

The third concept is referred to as **Zero**.

By design, the barrels of handguns are either angled **slightly** upward, or the sights are set to cause the shooter to hold the front end of the weapon at a slightly upward angle. This causes the bullet to travel on a **slight upward trajectory** for part of its flight, until the forces of gravity exert their downward pull on the bullet and cause it to drop to the ground.

"Zero" simply describes the point at which the shooter's line of sight and the bullet's actual flight trajectory intersect. Sights can be altered or adjusted to change this intersecting point to varying degrees.

What is often misunderstood is how little the pistol bullet actually deviates on the vertical axis at closer distances.

Generally speaking, a pistol that has its sights zeroed for 25 yards will launch the bullet on a flight trajectory just slightly below the line of sight, usually about .8". This distance becomes incrementally smaller out to 25 yards, at which point the bullet's path and the shooter's line of sight intersect.

After that point, the bullet continues on its slight upward trajectory for a very short distance until it reaches the apex of its flight. It then begins an immediate and dramatic descent.

As most pistol rounds are not loaded with tremendous amounts of propellant, the energy that propels the bullet forward is quickly depleted as the bullet continues on its flight. Air resistance compounds this effect, slowing the bullet during its entire flight, but significantly shortening the arc downrange. That's why the apex of the trajectory is not at the midpoint of the flight, but closer to the launching point.

A diagram illustrating the flight path of a .45 caliber, 250 grain jacketed hollow point bullet fired at a velocity of 1,000 feet per second is provided here to illustrate typical pistol bullet trajectory.

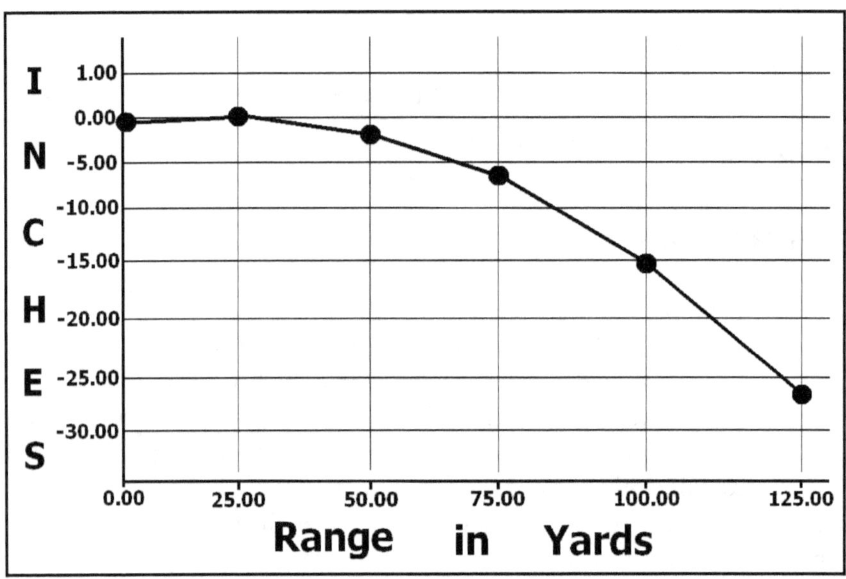

Police Applications for Long Range Pistol Shooting

At the risk of offending marksmanship-oriented purists, for most police purposes, the considerations regarding pistol bullet long range flight trajectories detailed above are largely irrelevant.

Statistically, most police shootings will occur at close ranges and will not involve the use of the sights. Should the use of the sights be possible at these close ranges—we'll say 25 yards and in—most police officers will have neither the knowledge nor the need to know that the bullet will likely impact less than an inch or so below their point of aim. I base this statement on the realities that 1) most police officers (and shooters in general) do not have the ability to shoot up to the inherent accuracy of their handguns under the best of conditions, and 2) that the "best of conditions" will very, very rarely exist during an actual shooting situation.

It must be understood that the focus of *police* pistol training is to ensure that our officers know 1) *when* to shoot, and 2) are trained well enough with their handguns so they have the best chance of hitting the intended target under real world conditions.

A final word regarding long-distance pistol shooting: the techniques needed to deliver accurate aimed fire at varying distances while using the sights are provided in Chapter 5. With a little practice, it is entirely possible to employ these techniques to hit human-sized (and much smaller) targets out to ranges greater than 100 yards with the handgun.

Don't be afraid to try it during training. It is not difficult to do once you know how high to hold your point of aim so the bullet's line of flight will impact on the desired target area.

As an example (and generally speaking), to deliver a pistol bullet to the mid-torso area of a man-sized target 100 yards away, simply line up the sights using the center of the target's head for an aiming point. If the round is fired straight and true, the bullet will impact approximately 15 to 20 inches below the aiming point.

How Bullets Work

A bullet works by **lacerating and crushing tissue** as it passes through it.

Again, generally speaking, the larger the bullet, the more tissue gets cut and/or crushed. The more tissue that gets crushed or cut, the greater the likelihood that a critical organ will be damaged or destroyed, resulting in an incapacitated attacker.

When a bullet enters the human body, it creates two types of wound cavitation: **temporary** and **permanent**. While much has been made of the effects of temporary wound cavitation, the permanent wound cavity is the most significant. (Additional factors such as deformation and/or fragmentation of the bullet will also influence wound cavitation.)

The **temporary wound cavity** is created as a result of the continued forward acceleration of air or tissue in the wake of the bullet. This causes the wound cavity to be temporarily stretched outward. This occurs in combination with the "**pressure wave**" that may be generated by the transfer of kinetic energy from the bullet to the body. The human body, however, being extremely elastic and flexible, may not be affected to the point of incapacitation as a result of either the temporary wound cavity or pressure wave.

The **permanent wound cavity**, on the other hand, is created as the bullet passes through the tissue and organs and destroys that in its path or "track." While there are never any guarantees when it comes to the effect a bullet or bullets may have when fired into a human being, the permanent wound cavity is more likely to produce the desired incapacitating result.

Stopping Power

One of the more controversial issues relating to handguns concerns the matter of "stopping power."

Stopping power can generally be defined as the ability of a bullet to immediately stop (incapacitate) a human aggressor once it enters the body. A great deal has been written about this subject, and proponents of the various theories sometimes tend to get emotional when discussing it.

Very often, theories are based upon physics and science (e.g., the performance of a faster and lighter bullet vs. the performance of a heavier and slower bullet, the effect of pressure waves, etc.), bullet design, and various performance testing methods. There are also a great many theories based largely upon subjective information, anecdotal evidence, and personal opinion.

While there is still much that is not known regarding this subject, after extensive study of a great deal of the voluminous data produced by the research into this question and seeing firsthand the effectiveness of various types of weapons and ammunition on humans, the unscientific opinion I have come to share is this; there are no magic bullets, and no guarantees as to how any type of bullet will perform when fired into a human body. There are just too many variables to allow definitive conclusions to be drawn.

As for general guidelines, ammunition intended for law enforcement purposes must be capable of penetrating the body deeply enough to damage critical organs and/or disrupt the central nervous system (the brain and spinal cord). It should also be designed to expand reliably (though, again, there are no guarantees when it comes to bullet performance in the real world) so as to create the largest permanent wound cavity.

Penetration: Reliable penetration into soft body tissue for a minimum depth of 12 inches is generally recommended, though depths up to approximately 18 inches are preferred. That human beings often wear clothing that bullets may need to be fired through is another consideration that enhances the need for effective penetration capabilities.

Expansion: Many bullets are designed to expand upon contact with tissue. In order to aid in incapacitation of a human being, expansion of the bullet should occur later rather than sooner, for early expansion increases drag and will result in less penetration. Some bullets have metal jackets that are designed to peel back from the lead core and form jagged "talons" during expansion. The razor sharp talons dramatically enhance the lacerating effect of these bullets when they perform as designed. As noted previously, however, expansion cannot be guaranteed as many things may impede or prevent it.

Placement: The most important consideration in regard to effecting incapacitation of a human being with a bullet is placement. This is especially true when it comes to a limited weapon such as a handgun. I have seen people that had been shot with similar pistol bullets exhibit effects ranging from immediate death to strong annoyance. The determining factors were simply the bullet's specific location and angle of entry into the body, and the resultant damage caused by the bullet as it passed through the body on its unique track, or path. If this seems logical to you, it's because it is.

Achieving Incapacitation

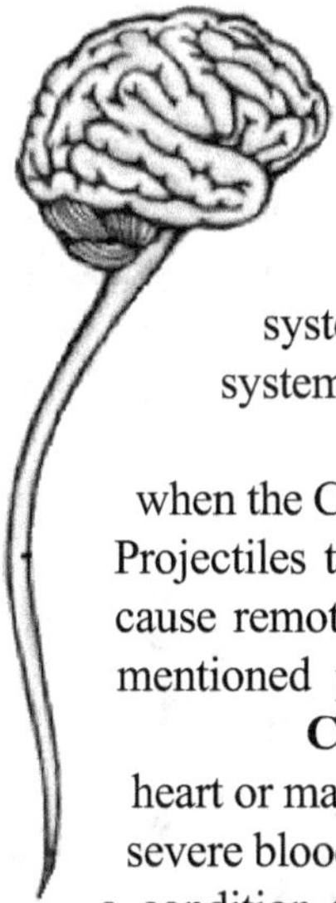

Our goal when shooting a subject who presents an immediate threat of death or serious bodily injury to us or others is to achieve incapacitation of that subject as quickly and efficiently as possible. The best way to do this is to damage or destroy the central nervous system (CNS). Inflicting severe damage to the cardiovascular system is the next most effective method.

Rapid neurological incapacitation is achieved when the CNS (brain or upper spinal cord) is disrupted or destroyed. Projectiles that do not make direct contact with the CNS may still cause remote neurological damage as a result of the pressure wave mentioned previously.

Cardiovascular collapse is achieved when damage to the heart or major blood vessels of the torso cause massive bleeding and severe blood and fluid loss. This often results in **hypovolemic shock**, a condition that disrupts the heart's ability to pump enough blood through the body to sustain life.

The primary advantage of rapid neurological incapacitation over cardiovascular collapse is the time factor. Disrupting or destroying the CNS is like shutting off the switch of an electrical system. Inducing cardiovascular collapse, on the other hand, is similar to draining a hydraulic system. It takes time. Also of note: If a human being's heart were instantaneously destroyed, there would still be sufficient oxygen within the brain to support full, voluntary action for 10-15 seconds. That is a long time to be dealing with a dead man still walking, fighting, shooting, or stabbing!

Reliability

It is critical that the duty ammunition you carry functions reliably in your weapon. To ensure this, it is extremely important that you fire a minimum of several hundred rounds of the exact same ammunition you intend to carry through your weapon *before* you carry it into the field.

When training with your pistol for certification purposes, you should be required to participate in at least one documented course of fire while using the same brand and type of ammunition you will be carrying on duty.

It is also very important that you periodically inspect not just your weapon and magazines, but the ammunition you carry as well. It is not uncommon for rounds to become damaged during day to day use. Check for dented casings, damaged primers and deformed bullets. Any questionable rounds should be immediately replaced.

Bullet compression is another potentially hazardous condition that occurs when pistols are loaded and unloaded on a daily basis. Due to repeated impacts of the bullet against the feed ramp and chamber when being loaded time and again, the bullet may become compressed deeper than it should be into the case. (Two similar .40 S&W rounds are shown below. Bullet at far right is compressed.) This can result in a failure to feed.

Should such a round be fired, the compressed bullet will cause an increase in chamber pressure. While most high quality pistols firing factory ammunition should be able to handle the increased pressure, the use of lower quality weapons or "hot" ammunition (loaded out with more propellant than normally recommended) could prove dangerous to the operator or others.

SECTION 3
Carry Gear

There is an enormous amount of gear on the market that caters to every imaginable weapons system and user preference. The choice of which gear you use may be decided for you by your department or agency, or you may have a great deal of leeway in your selection. Some officers may even have to completely outfit themselves. Whatever the case, try to keep it simple, clean and professional.

Today's police officer often has to carry so much equipment on the duty belt that there is hardly any room left for the sidearm. If possible, you must avoid this overcrowding, especially around your weapon and your spare magazines. Shun the extraneous bangles, beads, whistles, and bells that police officers are so often fond of, and practice accessing the different gear you do carry before you need to get to it under stress. A brief review of the most common carry gear follows.

Duty Belt

The duty belt may be made of leather or nylon. Regardless of which type you use it should be wide enough and strong enough to keep its shape and not deform because of the weight of the items carried on it. A good, secure buckle or closing device is mandatory, and you should wear it while running or exercising to find out how secure it really is.

Duty Holster

A good holster that keeps the pistol secure yet allows you to get it out in a hurry is paramount. A thumb-break-type securing device, considered the minimum in some circles and more than adequate in others, is preferable to a retaining strap both for securing the weapon and presenting it cleanly and efficiently.

While **security-type holsters** continue to become increasingly popular with many police agencies, it seems to me that to a great degree the emphasis for weapon retention has been taken off the operator and put on the holster. This is not good, especially when you consider the false sense of confidence an officer may develop about his weapon's security, as well as the fact that many of these holsters incorporate various safety catches and internal design components that make it difficult for anyone to get the weapon out, including the officer.

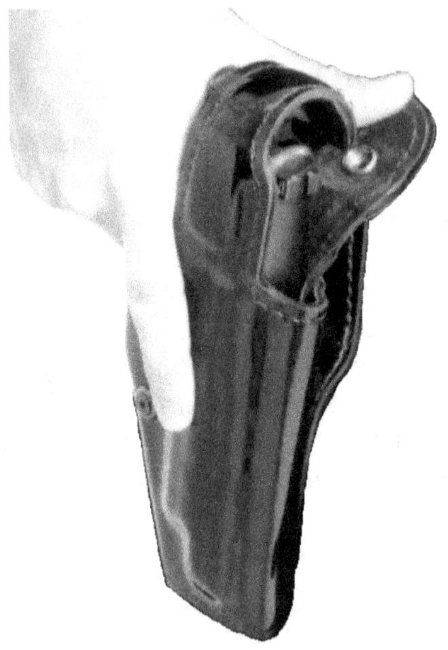

You must practice drawing your pistol so the movements needed to get it out of the holster and into your hand become automatic. This is especially critical when using security-type holsters.

If you have been issued or prefer to use one of these holsters, then you must devote whatever time is necessary to developing a fast, consistent draw. Regardless of the configuration, the duty holster should not allow the trigger finger access to the trigger prior to presentation of the piece.

It must, however, allow the middle finger to snug up comfortably against the bottom of the trigger guard. The holster must also allow access to the magazine release button while the weapon is secured.

Another holster option is found in the popular **Kydex® holsters** currently flooding the market. Kydex is a hard, thermoplastic alloy with a hardness of 90 on the Rockwell R scale. Originally used in aircraft interior component production, Kydex has been adapted to produce holsters molded specifically for individual models of handguns. The finished product is strong, extremely rigid, abrasion and chemical resistant. Kydex holsters are also fairly inexpensive compared to their leather counterparts.

Many Kydex holsters are produced in open top designs, using small hooks or other internal components to keep the pistol secured. Retention screws are usually provided with these types of holsters to allow you to adjust the fit to best suit your needs. For police purposes, I would recommend a model that provides both a retention screw and an adjustable thumb break strap. Such models are readily available.

The smooth interior finishes found on most Kydex holsters also provide for a smooth presentation of the pistol.

Kydex holsters are produced with both paddle and belt loop accessories. The connection between the holster and the belt attachment component tends to be the weak link of the design in some models. As with any equipment, a Kydex holster should be thoroughly tested for quality and performance prior to using it in the field.

Kydex holster

Paddle Holster

Paddle holsters provide a more convenient method for attaching both pistol and holster to your belt than do holsters that require you to weave your belt through the holster's loops or slots.

The price for that convenience is security, for with a paddle holster not only do you need to be concerned about the holster keeping the pistol secured within it, but you need to be concerned about the holster and pistol staying secured to your belt as well.

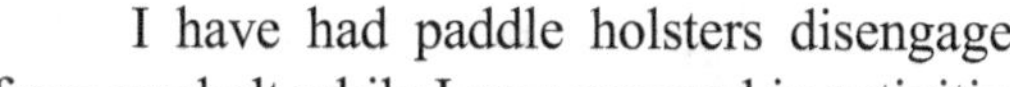

I have had paddle holsters disengage from my belt while I was engaged in activities such as running and negotiating obstacles. Several officers I know have also had the disturbing experience of drawing their pistol during a real world situation only to find their hand filled with both pistol *and* holster.

So if you do choose to use a paddle holster, select one that provides for secure attachment to your belt, practice your presentation and recovery frequently, and be aware of the potential problems it may present.

Pancake Holster

Pancake holsters are designed to provide a low profile to aid in concealment of the pistol. These types of holsters are made to be worn on the outside of the waistband (**OWB**) or the inside of the waistband (**IWB**).

OWB models are normally provided with a clip and/or belt loops/slots to attach to the belt or waistband.

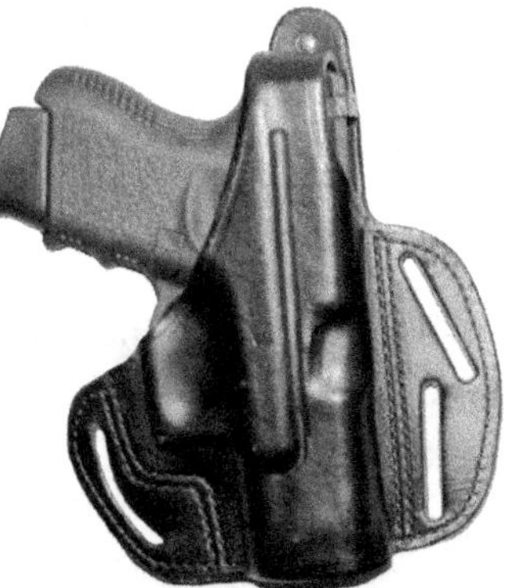

OWB Pancake holster

IWB models are normally provided

only with some type of clip or tab to attach the holster to the belt or waistband.

IWB holsters should be constructed so there is material above the waistline between the user's body and the pistol. Otherwise, sweat becomes a problem. One method for using IWB holsters is shown in Chapter 9.

Shoulder Holster

Some officers working plainclothes assignments prefer to wear a shoulder holster. Some find it more comfortable; others simply like the way it looks.

Whatever your reason for wearing a shoulder holster, you must keep the tactical priorities ahead of any other consideration. Above all, a sound shoulder holster rig must provide security as well as safe, easy accessibility to the weapon.

The shoulder holster you wear should not require you to unintentionally cover anyone with your weapon while it is being drawn. Holsters that configure the weapon to be carried while pointing straight to the rear require additional safety measures to be employed while drawing the weapon—especially under stress. As always, the trigger finger must remain well off the trigger and outside the trigger guard while drawing the weapon.

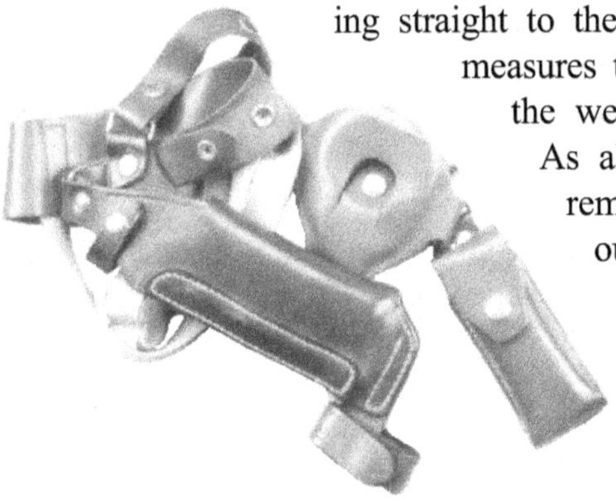

Shoulder holster rig with handcuff and magazine cases attached

Reholstering the pistol is another issue that must be addressed, because the use of both hands is often required to reholster when using a shoulder rig. Very often, an officer's attention and focus will be shifted away from a suspect or threat area while he tries to reholster, leaving him vulnerable to a devastating surprise attack. This tactical weakness must be prepared for and countered by proper training methods and practice. (See Chapter 4 §11.)

During my career, I have occasionally worn a shoulder holster for various assignments where it proved to be advantageous, but I prefer to try and carry the same way all the time to avoid confusion under stress. If you carry your weapon on your hip most of the time and then occasionally carry it somewhere else, you run the very real risk of trying to present your pistol from a place where it ain't. And those few moments while your conscious mind adjusts may prove deadly.

Ankle Holster

I have never warmed up to the concept of an officer carrying his primary defensive/offensive tool strapped to his ankle, at least in all but the most delicate of situations. If you carry a backup weapon there, that's one thing, but not a primary weapon.

While assigned to work in an undercover capacity, I was told by a few of my fellow narcotics officers that the detection of a pistol could possibly identify us as police officers and jeopardize an operation. Some of these officers preferred the ankle holster, while a few others felt they were best served by going into an undercover situation unarmed.

Although I understood the obvious need for flexibility when working in an undercover capacity, and believed that the ultimate decision of how or even whether to carry should be left to the officer involved, the way I saw it, it was better to possibly jeopardize an operation than risk being caught unarmed, or, in the case of an ankle holster carry, beaten to the draw by one of the players who kept his pistol neatly tucked in his belt.

As far as the risk of being "made," well, when you're working undercover, you're usually playing the role of a bad guy, and, as we all know, bad guys carry guns too. There are better ways to conceal a weapon that still leave it accessible when you need it than strapping it to the body part that is physically farthest from your hand. So unless you've got an overwhelmingly good reason to carry on your ankle, you're probably better off leaving ankle holsters to Popeye Doyle of The French Connection fame.

Of course, if you are determined to use an ankle holster, you must devote the time required to develop at least two methods (one high, one low) of drawing the weapon from it quickly and efficiently, as well as a sound tactical method of reholstering. Two techniques for presenting the weapon from an ankle holster are illustrated in Chapter 7 §2.

Magazine Carrier

Magazine carriers (also called cases or pouches) should be of good quality

Nylon magazine carrier in vertical-carry position

and reliably retain the magazine until it is intentionally drawn.

Leather or nylon duty models are usually produced with a protective flap that covers and secures the magazines. Any carriers so equipped should have a dependable closure device. A metal snap is preferable to Velcro. Kydex® magazine carriers are also available.

Your carrier should hold the magazine securely, yet allow you to access it quickly when needed.

Most carriers designed for uniformed duty belts allow you to attach them to the belt in either the vertical or horizontal position.

I have found the **vertical-carry position** considerably easier to access than when the pouches are carried horizontally. Besides ease of access, especially when kneeling or prone, the vertical-carry position also conserves precious space on the usually crowded duty belt. Magazine carriers worn vertically should be located on the belt on the shooter's support side, as close to the (centered) belt buckle as possible, rounds pointing inboard toward the buckle.

Magazine carriers worn in the **horizontal-carry position** should be located on the belt in front of the holster, with rounds pointing up and magazines being removed from the carrier toward the centerline of the body.

Leather magazine carrier in horizontal-carry position

It's a good idea to routinely remove your magazines from the carrier and wipe them down between training periods. This should also be done any time you clean your pistol.

More than once I have observed officers at the range trying to work with gear that was hopelessly rusted, fouled, or inoperative because of lack of maintenance. In addition to showing a lack of care and respect for your equipment and yourself, allowing vital equipment to fall into such a state of neglect demontrates a lack of concern for the safety of your fellow officers as well.

This is something we cannot allow. *Ever!*

Properly Configuring the Duty Belt & Equipment

There are a number of ways to arrange the equipment on the duty belt. A few suggestions are provided here for consideration.

The Duty Belt

The duty belt should fit snugly around your waist, but should not be so tight it causes discomfort. **Keepers** (small straps designed to be wrapped vertically around the inner and duty belts and secured) should be used to keep the duty belt from slipping or hanging below the waistline.

Many officers prefer to use a **buckleless inner trouser belt** with the duty belt. The inner belt is laced through the trouser's belt loops and secured with Velcro®. The outer belt is then put on over the inner belt and secured with keepers. Some inner belts and duty belts are lined with Velcro so that no keepers are needed as the belts stick together.

The Duty Holster

The duty holster should be kept clear of other equipment so the presentation of the pistol is not impeded. The holster should be situated on the belt so the hand, raised from a natural hanging position by your side, falls easily upon the grip of the pistol. (See Chapter 12 §2.)

Magazine Carriers

Magazine carriers worn either vertically or horizontally on the belt should be placed so there is nothing between them and the belt buckle. This includes cell phones and pagers!

Handcuff Case

Handcuff cases should be worn off to the side, though some officers prefer to wear them toward the front. Many officers place the handcuff case directly on the small of their back, centered over the spine. The most common reason given for this is that it allows access to the handcuffs with either hand. Please note that this practice is extremely dangerous!

No equipment, including a handcuff case, should ever be worn near or directly up against the spine!

Severe injury can result should you fall or suffer an impact there. Injury may also be incurred simply by the day-to-day pressure exerted on the spine as you walk, run, or sit up against the back of a chair or car seat.

Some officers have adopted the practice of carrying a rolled up pair of **medical gloves** at the bottom of the handcuff case. If you do not normally carry protective gloves while working, you may want to consider this. Having to deal with blood or other bodily fluids while effecting an arrest is not unheard of. Non-latex materials such as vinyl or nitrile rubber are recommended due to the increasing rate of latex allergy in the general population.

Additional Equipment

In addition to the basic equipment listed above (flashlights will be discussed in detail in Chapter 8), officers are often required to find room on the duty belt for a portable radio, baton, and aerosol subject restraint spray (ASR).

Any number of additional pieces of gear can also be seen worn on police officer's belts, to include a cell phone, pager, Taser, medical kit, flash and gas grenades, rebreather device, explosives and detonator, lockpicks, electronic surveillance equipment (including night vision video camera and monitor), a forensic kit for gathering crime scene evidence, grappling hook... you get the picture. As I stated earlier, when it comes to your duty belt, do your best to keep it simple, clean, and professional.

CHAPTER 3

Safety

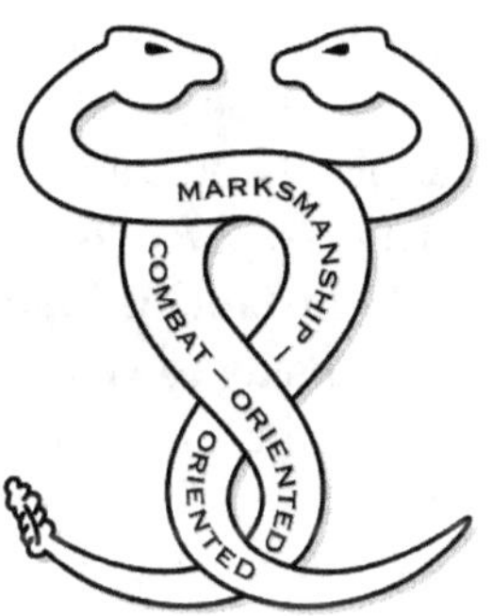

SECTION 1

Safety: Everyone's Responsibility

In this chapter, we'll be taking a look at safe weapon handling both on the range and at home. The following chapters will address various pistol skills, development methods, and techniques, as well as some of the responsibilities we must deal with in regard to their use while on or off duty.

We will also explore methods for ensuring that our weapons do not fall into the wrong hands or cause any unnecessary safety problems while in our possession or while being kept in our homes.

Safety As a Compulsion

When handling or working with firearms, you must ensure safety at all times. Forget about developing good safety *habits*; when it comes to deadly weapons such as the pistols we carry, you need to take it a step further and develop good safety *compulsions*.

All it takes is a single instant, a lone moment when you are distracted or inattentive for tragedy to result.

So forget about the savoir faire and appearing debonair—keep it real and keep it safe instead.

You MUST check and recheck to ensure that the weapon you or anyone around you is holding is safe, clear, and empty when doing anything other than firing it or preparing to fire it.

You must also develop the compulsion to **always be conscious of the muzzle's direction.** This is the #1 critical safety compulsion, followed closely by **keeping your fingers off the trigger until ready to fire.**

The "One Round" Reality Check

Whenever handling or working with any firearms, keep this in mind: As police officers, we carry our guns day in and day out, both at work and when bringing them into our homes. It is not unusual that after a while we may sometimes start to think of them as just another piece of gear. But each of us *must* remember, all it takes is *one round.*

If just *one round* comes out of the end of that barrel, and goes into your body or someone else's, no matter how much we may want to, ***we can never call it back***.

And that one round can change or end your life or someone else's life *forever.*

We must never forget exactly what it is we are dealing with when handling a firearm—it is *a deadly, deadly weapon.*

Safe Direction

The term "safe direction" is frequently used when working with firearms, as in, *"Always keep the muzzle pointed in a safe direction..."*

When asked to define the term, most officers will offer another term, "downrange," in response.

Usually the conversation stops there. However, if we ask the next question, "Where is downrange on the street or in your home?" we open a whole new can of worms, for **there is no downrange in the real world**. There are only safe, less safe, and unsafe directions in which to point the weapon.

Stray bullets might not be stopped by a floor or wall, but may pass through into another room or even outside. Ricochets off of walls, floors, or other surfaces (including water) are another possibility.

One common solution for providing a safe direction at home includes designating a specific corner of a room in the house or apartment for this purpose. Any corner chosen should be constructed of surfaces that will not cause ricochets, yet will also not allow a round to penetrate and exit into either another room or outside of the building.

Rooms located in basements are preferable. Other options include placing a drum or barrel filled with sand in a designated location at which the muzzle may be pointed while loading and unloading the weapon.

The simplest solution, as usual, is right in front of us (as well as in back of us, in this case).

Body armor—after you have taken it off and placed it on a floor, chair, couch, or bed—provides a portable bullet-trap in any secure room in your home. This option is demonstrated in Chapter 4.

***SAFE DIRECTION*: Any direction in which a discharge would result in no loss of life, no injury, and limited property damage.**

SECTION 2
Safety On the Range

Lead Safety

While some firearms training facilities are beginning to require the use of clean or lead-free ammunition (a trend I believe will become the norm eventually), most still do not.

Lead, whether contained in the projectile, propellant, or primer, is a hazardous material.

Airborne lead particles are produced with every round fired when the ammunition contains lead-based components. If precautions are not taken, these hazardous particles can enter the human body through several methods: inhalation, absorption, and ingestion.

Inhalation: Particles enter through the respiratory system and are absorbed into the bronchial aveoli.

Absorption: Particles are absorbed through the skin and hair follicles.

Ingestion: Particles are ingested through the mouth.

Once lead is introduced into the body through one of these routes, it works its way through the blood stream and soft body tissue and eventually is stored in the bones. The reason this occurs is because the human body cannot differentiate between lead and calcium.

Having been present while countless rounds had been fired on all types of ranges for many years, I was a bit surprised when I first learned how lead actually entered and was stored in the body. In addition to standing in lead-contaminated clouds generated by a line of shooters on windless days, the first thing I thought of were the police calls conducted afterward, and how we would gather the expended shell casings in our hats, dump the casings into buckets, and then place the hats back on our heads—depositing all those lead particles right onto our hair follicles!

Make no mistake, lead is a poison, and if too much is stored in your body, it will kill you.

Some guidelines that should be used to protect you and your family from lead poisoning are provided here:

1. **Don't smoke on the range.** Smoking cigarettes, cigars, or pipes on the range may increase the quantity, and will accelerate the speed of absorption, of inhaled lead into the blood stream.

2. **Don't eat on the range.** Lead particles on your hands and face can be ingested through contact with food.

3. **Don't collect fired brass in hats.** Whenever you collect expended shell casings in your hat, you're simultaneously collecting lead particles as well. If you then dump the casings into a bucket and put your hat back on your head, you've dumped those lead particles on your hair. They can then work their way through the follicles and into the skin.[1] A better idea is simply to collect the casings by hand, place them into containers, and then wash your hands thoroughly afterward.

4. **Decontaminate yourself and your clothing.** Lead particles may attach to all exposed surfaces, including your face, arms, clothing, etc. Wash thoroughly with cold water after training. Use plenty of soap. Pay attention to areas where exposed hair is present, especially facial hair. You may want to change your clothing after you complete training and before returning home. At the least, remove your shoes before you enter your home, especially if there are children or even pets inside, to prevent tracking in lead particles that may be picked up or ingested. Wash range clothing separately from your family's clothing, and let them air dry as opposed to placing them in the dryer. This will further help prevent contamination.

5. **Avoid contaminating others.** Lead particles can be transferred by casual contact. Family and friends should not be hugged or kissed until you've had a chance to shower and change your clothes.

6. **Minimize risks to pregnant officers.** While studies indicate that the amount and levels of noise experienced during normal firearms training iterations seem to pose little danger to the health of the fetus, the possibility of lead contamination being passed from the mother's body to the fetus is very real.[2] For this reason, it is recommend that only 100% lead-free ammunition be used when training pregnant officers if they are required to participate, and there is no medical necessity that precludes their participating in firearms training. (Many agencies require written consent from

---

[1] There is some dispute as to whether the type of lead particulates produced during the firing process are able to enter the body through the hair folicles. Until conclusive evidence is offered, it is best to err on the side of caution.

[2] The Hospital for Women Medical Center's Reproductive Toxicology Center (RTC) has provided clinical information on both subjects. The RTC advises that "some direct effects of environmental sound on the human fetus...include fetal movements and fetal cardioacceleration." "The diversity of sounds reaching the fetus is relatively large, with sounds with frequencies below 2 khz being attenuated very little. The investigation of possible adverse effects resulting from ambient, aversive sound has not yielded any clear associations." Additional research suggests that amniotic fluid reduces the noise levels by 30db (which is greater than most of the ear protection worn by shooters).

the officer's physician prior to allowing them to participate in training.) Other safeguards such as having the officer wear some type of respirator may be employed when training with leaded ammunition.

7. **Participate in lead safety training programs.** Attend all training programs provided by your department or agency to ensure awareness of the hazards of lead.

Hot Brass

Occasionally, when training with semiautomatic firearms on the range, a hot shell casing ejected from one of the weapons will fly through the air and come down on you.

It may unexpectedly fall right into your shirt collar and down your shirt, and once in there start to immediately burn your skin. Usually what happens is it burns hotter and hotter, and then just as abruptly it stops burning as the heat dissipates.

Some casings are so hot that they may even hit your neck and just stick there, and start to *sizzle*.

If that happens to you on the firing line, you must stay focused and maintain your discipline!

Breaking your focus and losing control of yourself and/or your pistol is not acceptable. At the least, a loss of control may result in your being removed from training. At worst, you may experience an unintentional discharge, possibly injuring or killing yourself or others.

You must be prepared to deal with this fairly minor hazard when training with semiautomatic pistols. The best response you can exhibit when the hot brass lands on your skin is to keep your focus locked on the mission at hand, keep your weapon controlled and pointed in the right direction, and finish the drill to the best of your ability.

Flying hot brass is also the reason we always wear baseball-type caps with the brim to the front and wrap-around eye protection when training!

Safety Rules

A review of commonly-accepted **Firearms Range Safety Rules** is provided in this section as a refresher for the veteran and for the benefit of those new to law enforcement or firearms training.

FIREARMS SAFETY RULES

A. CARDINAL RULES OF FIREARMS SAFETY:

1. Treat all firearms as though they were loaded.
2. Keep the muzzle pointed in a safe direction at ALL TIMES!
3. Keep your finger outside the trigger guard until you are on target and have decided to fire.
4. Be sure of your target and what is around *and* beyond it.

REMEMBER THE "LASER RULE": TREAT YOUR FIREARM AS IF IT IS A LASER GUN WITH THE BEAM ALWAYS ON; WHATEVER THE BEAM TOUCHES, IT CUTS THROUGH!

B. SPECIFIC RANGE SAFETY RULES:

1. **Ear and eye protection** are required at all times when firing is being conducted on the range. This includes observers.
2. **Baseball-style hats** with brim (worn to front) are recommended when on the firing line. This is done to minimize the chance of hot shell casings becoming lodged behind the protective eyewear and against the eye.
3. Eye protection is required in the cleaning room to minimize the chance of brush-flicked particles, sprayed solvents, or other contaminants causing injury to the eyes.
4. Immediately upon picking up a firearm, visually and physically check to see it is unloaded.
5. **Check a second time**.
6. Never give a firearm to, or take a firearm from anyone, unless the action is opened and the weapon is confirmed to be safe and clear.
7. Load/reload/unload only after position is taken at the firing point and on command unless directed otherwise.
8. Keep the firearm pointed in a SAFE DIRECTION at all times.
9. Never draw a handgun from the holster on the range unless instructed to.

10. Never draw or reholster with your finger in the trigger guard or on the trigger.
11. NEVER holster a cocked weapon. (**NOTE:** This rule is applicable when using double-action configured, decocking lever-equipped semiautomatic pistols. This rule may be modified depending upon the weapon system used.)
12. Always wash hands before eating, and shower and change clothing (including footgear) at the end of a shooting day. This is in regard to lead as discussed earlier.
13. Never go forward of the firing line unless instructed.
14. Never bend over to retrieve dropped articles on the firing line until instructed to do so by an instructor.
15. No talking on the firing line except by, or with, an instructor.
16. Pay strict attention to the instructor.
17. Never anticipate a command.
18. Never permit the muzzle of a firearm to touch the ground.
19. Conduct a proper safety check of the weapon before and after a training session.
20. Never dry fire on the range unless instructed to do so.

****

Everyone Shares the Responsibility for Range Safety!

****

THE SAFE CONDITION CHECK

Whenever you pick up or hand someone a weapon, first, open the action and render the weapon safe, keeping your trigger finger off the trigger and out of the trigger guard.

Then, have the other person check to verify that the weapon is indeed, <u>absolutely</u> safe, clear, and empty.

These actions will help ensure safety and identify you as a competent professional!

SECTION 3
Safety Off the Range

For many police officers, the only firearm they will ever own or have in their possession will be the one issued to them by their department.

Police officers' feelings toward firearms are as diverse as those found in the society we live in, and it is not uncommon for a police officer to feel a little ill at ease when bringing a weapon into the home, especially when there may be little hands and curious minds roaming about the household.

The specter of a thief breaking into our homes and then leaving with a deadly weapon is also a real consideration.

Take nothing for granted! Secure your firearms! It is up to each of us to protect those around us from the dangers of a firearm improperly used or in untrained or irresponsible hands.

Storage of Firearms

Storing weapons safely in the home is more than simply a good idea. It is a moral, ethical, and in many cases, legal duty.

A few options that can be used to store handguns in the home are provided here.

Safes

Safes are available in a variety of shapes, sizes, and costs. Large floor safes weighing many hundreds of pounds can easily store dozens of pistols and long guns, while small metal wall safes like the one shown below can be used to store only one or two handguns. Many decent safes are available within these two extremes, and should be chosen according to each officer's specific needs.

At the least, some sort of lockable case or compartment should be utilized to store the duty weapon when it's not in use. It is also recommended that the ammunition be kept in a separate locked container.

Metal safes such as the one pictured here can be secured to a wall by installing screws into the wall studs or by using cement wall anchors.

Other Recommended Options

Another option to secure the cleared weapon is a **trigger guard lock**, a device which is secured around the trigger guard and completely covers and prevents any manipulation of the trigger. Shown below at left and installed on a pistol at right. While this type of lock doesn't prevent the pistol from being taken, it does impede its operation. **Note:** The pistol must be unloaded and the chamber must be empty when using this device, as it may be possible to cause a loaded weapon to fire by striking the lock itself.

Cable-type locks can also be used to effectively disable the action of most handguns. To disable the semiautomatic pistol, first remove the magazine and lock the slide to the rear. Then insert the cable into the magazine well and out through the ejection port, and secure as shown below.

Many manufactures now include or have available plastic **lockable gun cases** specifically designed to house their particular weapons. Cases such as the one produced by SIG Sauer shown below are highly recommended, for they provide an easy method for both safely securing and storing your pistol.

Lockable gun cases such as this are highly recommended for use.

Less Desirable Options

One option some instructors used to recommend for use with both revolvers and semiautomatics was to employ **handcuffs** as a firearms disabling device. This was done with the revolver by securing one of the cuffs around the top strap with the cylinder open. With the semiautomatic, the slide would be removed and one of the cuffs secured through the trigger guard, the other through the ejection port of the slide.

Even though this practice is effective at rendering the weapon inoperable, I strongly recommend against it because the metal on metal contact can easily damage the weapon's frame or slide, possibly causing problems in operation.

Yet another option for disabling firearms is being made more readily available by many gun manufacturers in response to political pressure from various quarters. This option is designed into the firearm itself, and usually takes the form of an **internal trigger lock** that is activated by some type of key. While some might choose to go this route when selecting duty weapons, in my opinion any firearm intended for self-defense use should not be so equipped. This is especially true in regard to law enforcement weapons, as they are taken out and re-secured on a daily basis in most cases.

Should the weapon's internal safety device be used regularly, I believe it would only be a matter of time before an officer was found killed or wounded because he drew his pistol in a critical situation and tried to fire, only to find that the trigger had been inadvertently left disabled.

As always, with any type of weapon designed for combat use, the simplest approach is best.

Some handguns such as the Steyr M40 Pistol are being manufactured with an increasing number of internal safety devices. The model shown here includes an internal trigger lock that requires a key to manipulate. The author believes pistols that include safety devices such as these are unsuitable for law enforcement/ combat use for the reasons cited in the text.

Home Firearms Safety & The Junior Detective

When you bring a firearm into your home, it affects everyone who lives there. That is why I highly recommend that any officer who keeps a weapon in the home **discuss firearms safety** with all family members, including children.

We have all heard the stories of police officers' firearms being picked up by small children in the home, and the resulting tragedies that occur. Too often, when you hear about these incidents, the child has turned the weapon on himself, perhaps looking down the barrel when the weapon was inadvertently discharged. Other times, the weapon is discharged by the child and the round strikes someone else. In a recent case, a police officer was shot and killed by his three-year old son while the officer stood in his kitchen talking with his pregnant wife.

Very often tragedies such as these are thought of by police officers (as is common with most people, regardless of profession) as things that *only happen to other people.* We may also dismiss the incident as an aberration, caused by negligence on the part of the officer responsible for the weapon's safe handling and storage.

And many times this is true—the officer did fail to properly secure the weapon, and he or his family members will have to live with the result for the rest of their lives. Having talked with people directly involved in situations like these, I can tell you that I would not wish that burden and heartache on anyone.

Having grown up the child of a police officer in a home where weapons were kept, however, I am also aware of a greater reality, one that has influenced me to not only discuss firearms and their safe handling with my young children, but also to make myself available to them as their own personal firearms instructor, should they desire to learn to shoot.

The reality I am referring to is this: most kids, by the time they are old enough to want to snoop and poop throughout the house, pretty much know where all the hidden stuff in the home is kept.

This includes mom's or dad's firearms.

And if these firearms are deemed to be absolutely off limits, and if the children—especially male children, in my experience—are forbidden to see, handle, or get acquainted with these firearms under adult supervision, then these firearms may become a secret, unimaginably fascinating obsession for that child or children.

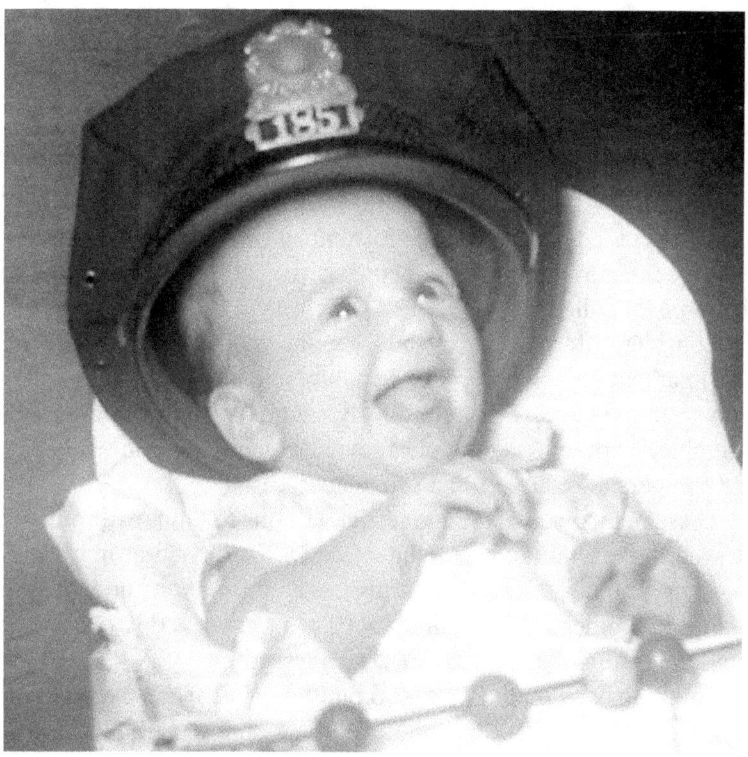

The author at 4 months of age wearing his father's police uniform cover. Just 3 years later, he would get hold of the revolver that went with it.

How do I know this? Well, besides the fact that common sense and numerous recorded experiences indicate this occurs, I was one of them. In fact, the first time I held a real pistol was on a fine summer morning when I was three years old. According to my parents, I climbed up on a chair, crawled across a large table, and opened a metal box where my father kept his .38 S&W Model 10 police-issued revolver. (My father, who was new on the force and working midnights at the time, had apparently placed the unloaded pistol into the green lockable box and shut it without locking it before going to bed.) I then playfully terrified my mother with the weapon (so I am told, I do not recall the event), holding her at gunpoint until my father was woken by my mother's incessant calls; calls she tried to make while conveying urgency to him, and calm control to me.

According to the story, my father got up, unceremoniously relieved me of the pistol, got yelled at by my mother (even after he explained that it was unloaded), locked the pistol in the box, and then took it with him back to bed.

By the time I was around ten, my parents had divorced, I had graduated to the rank of junior detective, and I now had two houses to snoop and poop through. By the time I was twelve, not only did I know where my father then kept his pistol and the green metal box, but I also knew how to get through the intricate series of locks, alarms, and safes to get to my older brother's pistol collection.

Considered too young by my gun-shy mother (who was probably still traumatized by my first pistol-handling exhibition) to be taught about real guns at the time, I surreptitiously taught myself, learning how to disassemble, load, unload, and clean every type of pistol in his collection, from derringers to revolvers and semiautos.

These regular self-training sessions continued until my brother began impromptu lessons about a year later. He was surprised at how quickly I picked it up, and never knew about my covert infiltrations until years later, when the big brother statute of limitations had run out and I was old enough to avoid the beating he surely would have issued me.

Thinking back on those days I count my lucky stars that nothing bad ever happened while handling those guns. I cringe to think of my own kids—or anyone else's—doing the same.

For years I was embarrassed to admit my early proclivity for B&E'ing into areas in my house where I had no business being in order to get to those objects that so fascinated me. Then one day I offhandedly mentioned it to a fellow officer I was working closely with, and he laughed and told me his story.

His father had also been a police officer who worked midnights. Every morning, his dad would come home from work, lock his pistol in a small metal box similar to my father's, place the box high up on a shelf in a cabinet in the kitchen and then go to bed. Starting when he was around nine years old, every afternoon my friend and his younger brother would arrive home from school, and immediately perform the same ritual, day after day. My friend would grab a kitchen chair, place it against the counter, step up on the chair and onto the counter, and then reach way up high and check the metal box.

Each day, my friend told me, the box was locked, and he and his brother would close the cabinet, put the chair back, and go on their way.

Then one day, after a few years of performing their routine, my friend reached up and found the box to be unlocked. Excitedly, he reached into the box, grabbed the revolver inside, turned toward his brother, muzzle pointed at the young man's chest and exclaimed, "We got it!" while pressing the trigger: CLICK, CLICK, CLICK.

As he related this story to me his face went a little pale. Then he said, "I pointed it right at my brother and pulled the trigger three times. Every day I thank God that my father was wise enough to always unload that gun before he put it in that box. When I think of what might have happened…"

Years after he told me this, I started to include both our stories when training to illustrate just how curious and determined children can be when it comes to firearms, especially when they see one of their parents wearing that gun day to day. That exposure and parental identification, combined with the media's often irresponsible portrayal of firearms use, can prove to be an irresistible combination for young minds.

It was after I started including these stories that I began to learn that this attraction, and these types of close calls, are much more common than anyone is even aware of, simply because we tend to cover them up when they occur or are discovered. I have now heard more stories along these lines from other officers than I could have imagined.

It is part of the reality we live with. We should not, *we must not*, choose to ignore it. Rather, we need to deal with it. The way I have decided to do it with my own children is through education, controlled exposure to the weapons, and straight talk.

Far from a new or unique model, this type of education was once an inherent part of many American children's upbringing, when firearms were still generally thought of as the dangerous, though useful and necessary tools they actually are, rather than simply mechanical incarnations of evil or intrinsic components of violent videogames.

So far, it seems to be working. You will have to decide if this approach is right for your family.

Safety In The World

When operating as a police officer in uniform, just our presence alone will often have a calming, civilizing affect on members of the public, as people generally tend to modify their behavior when the police are around.

This is both common and normal. A prime example of this is the way most people will alter their driving habits when they spot the cruiser's markings and light bar, uniformed officer at the wheel. Regardless of how they were driving previously, people tend to slow down and often become models of civility and proper road etiquette.

After enough time on patrol, police officers tend to get accustomed to this, and eventually come to take their affect on the driving habits of others for granted. I first became aware of this as a young trooper one afternoon while off-duty, negotiating my personal car around a notoriously treacherous traffic circle in Revere, MA.

As I smoothly entered the rotary, seamlessly merging with traffic, I was suddenly confronted with several angry motorists blasting their horns and signaling their displeasure with a one-finger salute as they aggressively cut me off and jockeyed for position on the congested roadway.

Frankly, I couldn't believe it! Were they crazy? I was a cop for crying out loud! As I reached down to activate my overhead lights and siren, it dawned on me—pulling them over was going to be tougher than I thought, because I wasn't in my cruiser. *That's why* these too-typical screwball drivers had reverted to true form in my presence, because they had *no way of knowing I was a police officer*.

After this, I began to refer to this condition as "cruiser shock" and would constantly remind myself while driving off duty that I wasn't in a marked sled, and couldn't count on the normal, civilizing effects generated by the uniform and cruiser.

Another version of cruiser shock is also fairly common in the police industry, though this type often proves more dangerous, even lethal.

This type occurs when a police officer, either off duty or operating in plainclothes, becomes involved in a situation and takes action as a police officer. The problem here is that should the officer be afflicted with a case of cruiser shock, *he may know he is a cop* and he may be *acting like a cop*, but no one else may know who he is or what his intentions are—including *other cops*.

Too often when this happens, tragedy results. In December 2000, for example, I believe that the effects of cruiser shock played a part when an off duty Providence Rhode Island Police Officer, Cornel Young, Jr., died after being shot by two of his brother officers while attempting to assist them during the apprehension of an armed suspect.

According to reports, Officer Young came out of a restaurant and moved toward the officers and a suspect who was armed with a handgun.

Officer Young, holding his duty pistol in his hand, was not displaying his badge at the time. The uniformed officers, responding to a report of a fight at the scene, repeatedly ordered both subjects to drop their weapons. From reports based on witness testimony, the armed suspect then threw down his gun. Officer Young, however, apparently either did not hear the uniformed officers ordering him to drop his weapon (perhaps as a result of stress-induced auditory exclusion), or *did not think they were addressing him.* Whatever the reason, he did not drop his weapon and continued to move toward the suspect and officers.

The officers then fired, hitting Officer Young in the chest and head. It wasn't until moments later when other officers arrived at the scene that someone discovered Officer Young's identification in his pocket and announced to the stunned officers, "He's one of *ours*."

Putting all of the media-driven controversy that surrounded this case aside, this was not the first time that an officer dressed in plainclothes had been mistaken for an armed suspect.[1] In fact, anyone who has ever worked undercover or in a plainclothes capacity can probably relate an instance or two during their career when they have been perceived as suspect rather than police officer.

The reason for this is simple. If our weapons are visible when we are not in uniform or otherwise immediately identifiable as a police officer, *we are perceived only as a man or woman with a gun.*

For again, while *we may know* we are police officers, the uniformed officers we encounter will generally have no way of knowing this unless we make it completely clear to them. (In fact, even if we know the uniformed officers personally, the effects of stress on them may preclude them from taking their eyes off our weapons and looking at our faces.)

The uniformed officers, on the other hand, are operating on the assumption that since they are clearly identifiable as police officers, then they must take control of any dangerous or potentially dangerous situation using whatever means are appropriate.

And that is the way it *must* be.

Having worked both in uniform and in plainclothes, I can attest to the

---

[1] Officer Young was black; the officers that shot him were not. Many so-called "community leaders" and members of the media contended that Officer Young was shot down simply because of the color of skin. Some published articles describing the incident completely omitted the fact that he was holding a pistol in his hands when he was shot.

truth of this, as I'm sure can many of my colleagues.

So in the name of off-duty and plainclothes survival, the following ***Off-Range Firearms Safety Guidelines*** are provided for consideration.

OFF-RANGE FIREARMS SAFETY GUIDELINES

1. Unless absolutely required by the circumstances at hand, do not get directly involved when off-duty in plainclothes. This is especially true if you are with family members or other non-law enforcement personnel. If your direct intervention is not required, you may still assist by observing and collecting information that can be given to responding officers after they have arrived and gained control of the scene.

2. If you must intervene, make sure you clearly identify yourself to ALL parties present. If your weapon is out, you must have your badge out as well. The badge can be held next to the weapon, or even better, while holding the weapon in one hand, hold the badge/ID in the other hand high up and over your head. The badge/ID can then be rotated back and forth for 360-degree visibility. This method was strongly advocated by the late Jim Cirillo. He is shown demonstrating both techniques at right.

3. If someone present has access to a telephone, order him or her to call the police. Make sure that the person tells the police officer or dispatcher that you are present at the scene, that you are a police officer, that you are armed, and that you are wearing plainclothes. You should also have the caller describe you and your clothing, and insist that responding officers be advised of this information. *Be adamant about this*, and ensure that the caller confirms that the information has been relayed.

4. When uniformed officers arrive at the scene, or should you be challenged by a uniformed officer, remain calm, do not make any sudden moves, *do not turn toward them or point your weapon toward them or directly at anyone else*. Reholster if you can do so without putting yourself or others in jeopardy.

The late, great Jim Cirillo demonstrating two good plainclothes techniques to help ensure that you are identified as a police officer when pistol is in hand.

Continue to rotate the badge above your head and loudly repeat, "POLICE! I AM A POLICE OFFICER! DON'T SHOOT!"

5. **Once uniformed officers arrive on the scene, THEY are in control of the scene.** Regardless of your rank, position, or department affiliation, you must follow ALL of their commands instantly and without question. Only after they have gained control of the scene or asked you directly should you attempt to explain the situation to them.

6. **Use Common Sense.** Remember that criminals will sometime identify themselves as police officers in order to create confusion or doubt when confronted by the police. Remember that most police officers are aware of this, and that *anyone* armed with a weapon must be treated as a potential deadly threat until they have been positively identified otherwise.

7. **Assume *Nothing*.** It is too easy for mistakes to happen, especially when we are operating under the effects of stress that will be present during any lethal force encounter. And until we have been positively identified, a lethal threat is exactly the profile we present when armed and not readily identifiable as one of the good guys.

SECTION 4

Negligent & Unintentional Discharges

A **negligent discharge** occurs when an officer causes a weapon to discharge because of carelessness, negligence, or improper handling of the firearm.

The onus of responsibility in these cases is squarely on the operator, though the people responsible for training and/or employing that operator may also be held accountable depending upon the circumstances.

In contrast, an **unintentional discharge** normally occurs while working in the field as the result of an involuntary physiological phenomenon commonly referred to as "sympathetic involuntary muscular contraction."

Sympathetic Involuntary Muscular Contraction

A typical, working police officer is likely to encounter many situations throughout his career where he will have cause to draw his weapon. The decision to fire in each case must be made individually and will be based in part on the presence of various factors. Among these are the specifics of the situation itself, the involved officer's training and experience, and (perhaps most important) the officer's perceptions of the events that may be unfolding around him in a matter of moments.

Most of the rest of this book is directed toward helping us physically train and mentally prepare for these crucial moments, our goal being to attain the greatest tactical advantage in any situation and, if necessary, to direct our fire quickly and accurately to stop the threat.

In this section, however, we are going to take a look at what's involved in the effort to *avoid discharging* our drawn weapons when we do not intend to.

For the purposes of this section, because we will only be looking at the problem of not discharging our weapons until we have made the decision to fire, we will start at the point immediately after a threat has been perceived and the weapon has been drawn.

As many of us are aware, one of the most important things we can do to avoid unintentionally firing our weapons while holding or carrying them in the ready position is to always keep our fingers off the trigger until the decision is made to fire. Whether we are searching for an armed suspect, covering one or more suspects at gunpoint while waiting for backup, or even moving downrange in a live-fire exercise, we must make it more than a habit to keep our trigger fingers not only well off the trigger, but also well outside the trigger guard.

As far as getting off the shot when necessary, the time delay experienced with the finger outside of the trigger guard as opposed to having it directly on the trigger has been estimated to be only from one-tenth to three-tenths of a second. Yet the fact remains that even with our trigger finger outside the trigger guard, there are circumstances where an unintentional discharge may occur.

To recognize and avoid these circumstances, we must first take a look at what it is that can cause us to fire whatever weapon we may have in our hands before we have made any conscious decision to shoot.

As previously noted, it's formally known as **sympathetic involuntary muscular contraction**. It is, as its name implies, basically an involuntary, sympathetic contraction of muscles (in this case the muscles of our arms and hands) that occurs when certain conditions or stimuli are present.

As the brain sends signals to the muscles of our bodies, these signals travel along the nerve fibers of our nervous system and through our spinal cords. Under great pressure or stress, these signals can be sent to either or both of our arms without conscious determination on our part.

In most cases it occurs as a result of the individual either being startled or losing his balance, or by way of the "exertion of maximum force." If a weapon is being held in the hand when any of these stimuli occur and the trigger finger is either on the trigger or finds its way there, it is highly likely that an unintentional discharge may result.

It makes no difference whether the weapon is in double-action mode with the hammer down or single-action mode with the hammer cocked—the contraction experienced as a result of this phenomenon will be intense enough to cause the weapon to fire.

Let's take a moment for a closer look at the three main forms of stimuli that can initiate the phenomenon.

1. **Startle Effect:** The muscle contraction may be initiated by a loud and/or unexpected noise, or the sudden appearance of someone or something that causes you to flinch while holding the weapon.

2. "**Postural Disturbance" or loss of balance:** The contraction may be initiated if you trip or fall while holding a weapon as the hands may involuntarily clench around anything being held.

3. **Exertion of Maximum Force:** The contraction may be initiated when you exert great force with one of your hands while holding a

weapon in the other. The signals traveling through the spinal cord to one of your arms are also involuntarily sent to the other arm in these cases. If you are performing a strenuous clenching action with one hand such as pulling on a door handle, wrestling with a subject, or even holding back a K-9 by its leash while holding a firearm in your other hand, it is possible to experience the involuntary contraction.

The obvious problem here is that when the weapon is discharged unintentionally, only the fates control the bullet's trajectory. Unfortunately, there are numerous examples of situations where officers, suspects, and bystanders have been either startled, wounded, or killed as a direct result of involuntary sympathetic contraction.

I know of many instances where this phenomenon has occurred. In fact, in one of these instances, it was my hand that fired the weapon. The stimuli that was present in my case was *exertion of maximum force*.

My situation began as a pursuit of three subjects in a stolen car. After an extremely interesting pursuit that eventually took us into Boston, the suspects bailed out and fled on foot. I ended up alone and chasing two of them up a flight of cement stairs leading into a multilevel garage.

As the suspects reached the door leading into the garage, they found it locked and began charging back in a highly motivated manner toward their escape route, which was blocked by me. Not knowing whether they were armed, and unable to see their hands clearly (as well as being in fear of being barreled over backwards down the narrow cement staircase), I drew my weapon and ordered them to stop. The weapon achieved part of the desired effect as the suspects veered off from their direct path towards me. However, instead of complying with my command, they proceeded to throw themselves over a railing to the garage level below us.

At that instant, I automatically reacted. I reached out and grabbed the suspect closest to me with my left hand, while simultaneously pointing my weapon in my right hand (with my trigger finger on the trigger guard as I had been trained) down and away from the suspect.

At this point, he turned on me before I could reholster and decided we were going to wrestle. As I don't get paid to wrestle, especially with a weapon in my hand, I grabbed the suspect by the throat at a specific spot with my left hand (employing what we used to call "pain compliance" but now refer to in kinder and gentler terms as "transitory discomfort") and pulled him toward the ground as hard as I could. It was right then that I heard the report and felt the familiar rocking of the SIG Sauer pistol in my hand.

Now, for years I had never been able to understand how people could make the boldface claim that "the gun went off by itself. . ."

And I know as well as anyone out there that in all but the rarest of circumstances a gun does not "go off by itself"—someone or something triggers the weapon. But after this experience I can see how someone might feel that way.

I've been involved with firearms since I was a kid, having fired countless rounds through numerous weapon systems. But I tell you now, I never felt my finger clench, come off the trigger guard, and apply at least 12 pounds of pressure to the trigger. It was an unsettling and disturbing experience. Most disturbing of all was the fact that the round that left my weapon could have struck the suspect, me, a bystander, or one of my fellow officers who were arriving on the scene. As it was, I put a round through the windshield of an empty car parked below us; believe me when I tell you I gave a heartfelt prayer of thanks to the Commander topside that that was the extent of the damage.

Am I proud of this experience? No, I am not. But I'm not afraid to admit it happened either. As police officers, we are involved in a dangerous profession and deal with often dangerous adversaries. If you're out there mixing it up, sometimes things are going to happen. It's part of the risk as well as the responsibility we take, and contrary to what many in our society seem to believe, also a risk the bad guys take.

The point here is that we must be aware of the existence of this phenomenon in order to avoid it if we find ourselves in a stressful situation where our weapons are drawn.

The point is NOT to keep the weapon holstered when we feel we are in a potentially life-threatening situation or have cause to be in fear for our safety!

Prevention

Remember, when moving with any firearm in your hands, you must always be conscious of where the muzzle is pointing. You should also keep your finger off the trigger until the decision has been made to fire.

Keeping the trigger finger held well outside and above the trigger guard, extended and placed against the frame of the weapon as shown on the following page, is widely considered the best option.

When holding the pistol, unless you are firing the weapon, you should keep your trigger finger well outside and above the trigger guard, extended and placed against the frame of the weapon as shown above.

Your training will have the greatest influence on your surviving and controlling all aspects of any life-threatening situation you may encounter.

This practice will most assuredly help us keep the phenomenon at bay, but we must always be aware that there are no guarantees when going into a highly stressful or critical situation.

That is why our training is so important: it will have the greatest influence on our surviving and controlling all aspects of any life-threatening situations we may encounter.

CHAPTER 4

Pistol Handling & Operation Skills

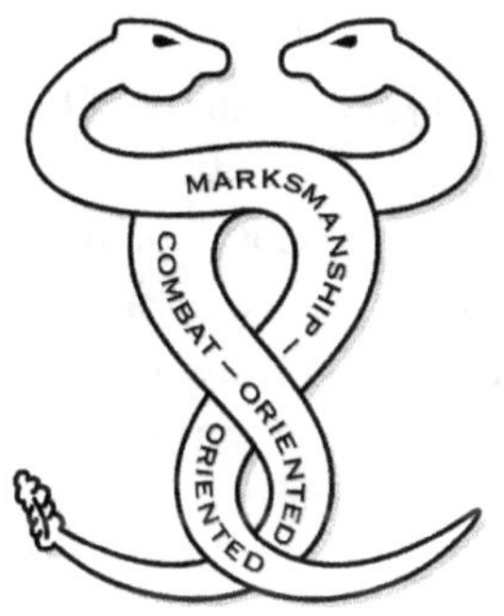

SECTION 1
On Becoming a Pistoleer

Some police officers regard their pistols as a necessary evil, while others regard them as simply another piece of issued equipment.

While both attitudes may be correct to a certain degree depending upon your frame of reference, the ultimate truth of the matter is that the pistol is a lethal weapon that each officer is entrusted with by the society that employs him or her.

In return for this trust, our society expects us to properly and responsibly maintain these deadly weapons, and to train with them so that when we are required to use them, our actions will be reasonable and proper.

No other piece of gear we are issued carries with it the weight and gravity of the firearm. Though the cruiser, impact weapons, or other issued equipment may cause injury or death when used, only the firearm is specifically chosen and employed to administer deadly force when needed.

Statistics still indicate that most police officers may complete a 25 year career never once having to fire their pistols during an actual lethal force encounter. This slim probability induces some police officers to mentally discount the possibility of their having to actually use their pistols to shoot another human being. Some officers go so far as to create what psychologist call a "personal fable," a mindset that allows them to convince themselves that "nothing bad will ever happen to me," or "someone else will take care of me."

This can be a fatal error.

For while none of us *desires* to injure or kill another human being, as police officers, we have accepted the awesome responsibility of having to do just that should the situation require it.

And because we have accepted that responsibility, we have an obligation and a duty to prepare ourselves as best we can to face that moment we hope never comes.

That moment when we may need to use our pistols to take a life in order to save a life.

In order to ensure that we are prepared to use our pistols in as professional and efficient a manner as possible, we each need to accept that our pistols are not simply another piece of equipment that we are issued, and that we are not acting solely on our own behalf while performing in our official capacity.

To this end, it is in our, and in our society's best interest, that we take this responsibility as seriously as it deserves to be taken, and develop our

Legendary Lawman James Butler "Wild Bill" Hickok was also known in his day as the "Prince of Pistoleers."

individual pistolcraft skills to the highest possible degree.

Traditionally, a person who did this was referred to—with great respect, incidentally—as a ***pistoleer***. *(Also: Pistolero (m.), Pistolera (f.))*

Pistoleers on both sides of the law always commanded respect. Outlaws also induced fear in the populace and used their weapons and skills for criminal purposes.

Only a lawman with equal or superior pistolcraft skills was feared and respected by the criminal pistoleer. Since current trends indicate a resurgence in the pursuit of pistolcraft skills by criminal elements in the U.S. and abroad, it only makes sense that we develop our own pistolcraft skills with a renewed sense of purpose and determination. Officers who do this can take pride in their ability to properly, safely, and efficiently handle themselves and their handguns.

The Modern-Day Lawman / Pistoleer is Always Armed

Please note that the use of the terms *pistoleer, pistolero,* and *pistolera* is not meant to be humorous, inflammatory, or frivolous.

These terms are used because they accurately describe a state of mind as well as physical prowess and preparedness.

And in our world today, as many officers seemingly place more emphasis on developing their skills with the computer and other high-tech equipment as opposed to their handguns, the realistic specter of a gunman walking into a mall, school, place of worship, or business and opening fire with a wide array of weapons continues to grow.

That is why the serious, modern-day lawman/pistoleer always carries a pistol, on duty and off, for we never know when our deadly skills will need to be used to save a life.

SECTION 2
Gripping the Pistol

If the Gun Fits

You must be equipped with a pistol you can operate safely and efficiently. One of the most critical steps to ensuring this is the selection of a pistol that fits your hand. Most pistol manufacturers offer various models of their duty pistols to fit different hand sizes. Some also offer adjustable grip and trigger configurations.

You and/or your department will be responsible to ensure this critical aspect of equipment selection and issuance is properly addressed.

Getting a Grip

The importance of a proper, solid, **primary hand grip** on the pistol cannot be overemphasized. Even when using a two-hand hold, only the primary hand is actually wrapped around and making contact with the pistol.

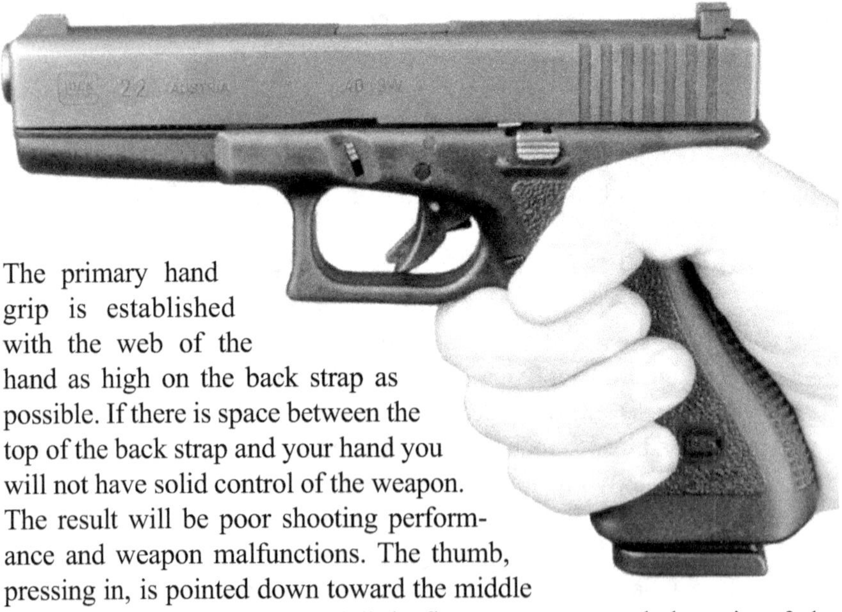

The primary hand grip is established with the web of the hand as high on the back strap as possible. If there is space between the top of the back strap and your hand you will not have solid control of the weapon. The result will be poor shooting performance and weapon malfunctions. The thumb, pressing in, is pointed down toward the middle finger. The middle, ring, and little finger wrap around the grip of the weapon, pressing it straight back against the heel of the hand. The middle and ring fingers provide most of the rearward pressure. There should be no space between the middle finger and the bottom of the trigger guard.

Definitions: Primary & Support Hand

The *Primary Hand* is the hand that is actually gripping and controlling the pistol. It may be your dominant hand or your non-dominant hand.

The *Support Hand* is your other hand. Again, these designations have nothing to do with your being left- or right-hand dominant. It is all about control of the pistol.

Primary Hand Grip, Opposite View

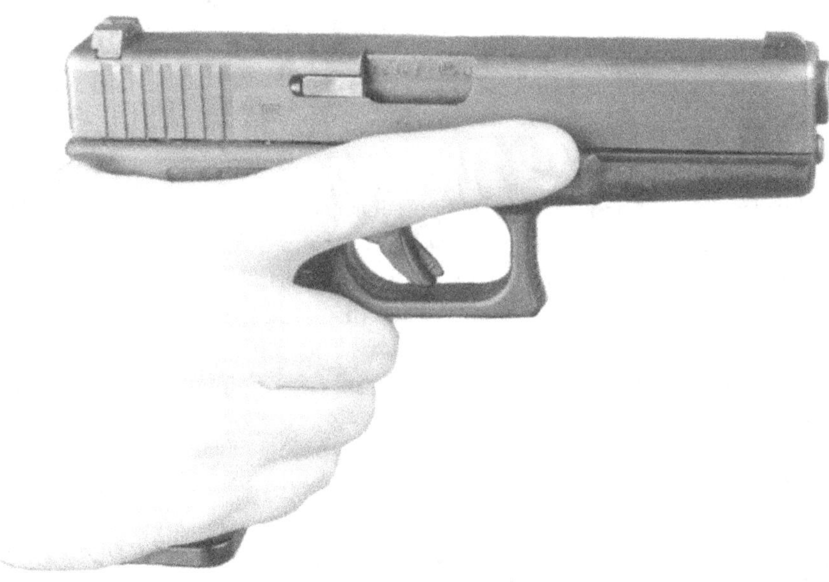

Unless you are firing the pistol, the **trigger finger** should be held off the trigger, outside the trigger guard, and along the frame as shown.

Adding the Support Hand Grip

Thumbs Over Grip #1: The support hand wraps around the front of the primary hand, gripping the primary hand securely. When using the method illustrated above, the support hand thumb presses down on the primary hand thumb, just behind the joint of the distal phalanx (bone at the end of the finger). Note that there is no space or opening where the bases of the thumbs meet. The support-hand index finger is tight up and against the bottom of the trigger guard.

Note trigger finger placement: When firing the pistol, it is best to place the **pad** of the distal phalanx on the trigger.

IMPORTANT: When firing the semiautomatic using a two-hand grip, the support-hand thumb must NOT be placed over the primary hand behind the slide; injury may result as the slide moves rearward! Cuts *bone-deep* are not uncommon! (See Appendix A, page 401, for more information about this hazard.)

Adding the Support Hand Grip (Continued)

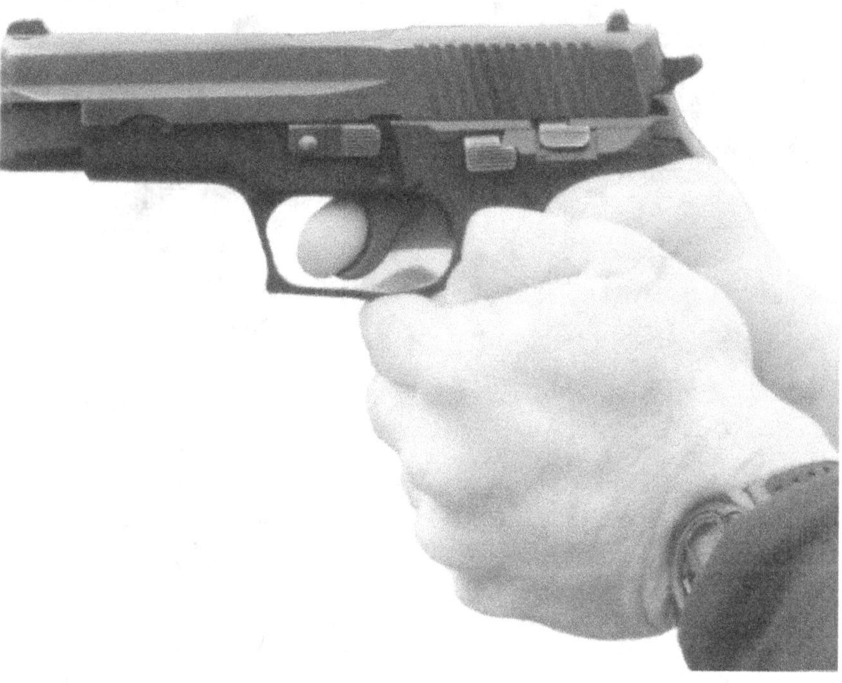

Thumbs Over Grip #2: Similar to Thumbs Over #1, the support hand wraps around the front of the primary hand, again gripping it securely. The support-hand index finger is tight up and against the bottom of the trigger guard.

With this variation, the first pad of the support hand thumb presses down and back on the distal phalanx of the primary hand's thumb. As far as choosing one variation of this grip over the other, you should try both and see which feels better for you. Variables such as weapon design and hand size preclude a simple "one size fits all" solution.

Note: If you can see any part of the pistol grip where the bases of your thumbs meet, then that portion of the pistol is not being fully controlled. Try to position your hands to provide as secure a grip as possible. Your goal is to achieve **stability** and **consistency** with your grip.

Adding the Support Hand Grip (Continued)

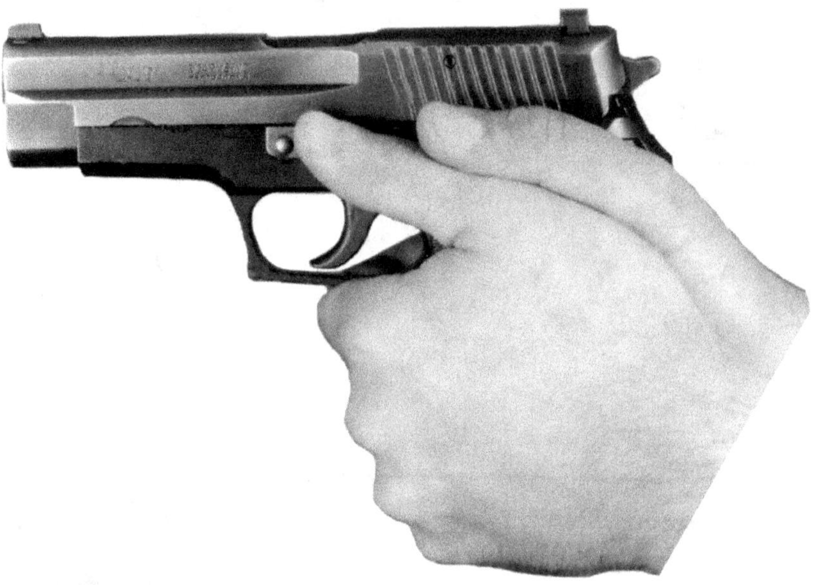

Thumbs Up Grip: Another effective grip configuration. Some refer to this as the S.A.S. Grip, for Britain's Special Air Service. Regardless of what you call it, this grip does provide a superior degree of control when firing using a two hand hold. It may take some time to get used to if you've been using a "thumbs over" grip, but the benefits are worth it. One note of caution: detractors of this grip believe the thumbs up position makes it easier for an adversary to strip the pistol out of your hands.

Note: When using any two hand hold, a **slight isometric tension** between the hands should be maintained. To achieve this, push the primary hand slightly forward into the support hand while pulling back with an equal amount of pressure with the support hand.

You should create enough tension so the hold is firm, but not trembling tight. Approximately 15 pounds of pressure should do it.

SECTION 3
Loading the Pistol

Loading the semiautomatic pistol is as simple as 1, 2, 3.

1 Grip the pistol firmly in your primary hand and point it in a **safe direction**.

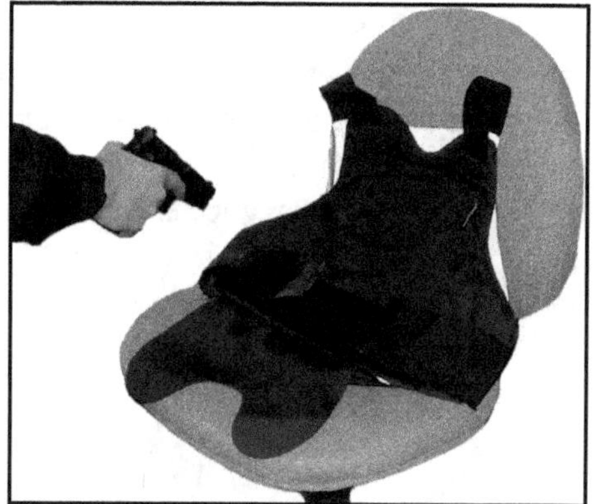

(**NOTE:** Personal body armor that has been placed on a chair provides a safe direction in photo at right.)

2 While keeping the pistol pointed in a safe direction **insert a fully loaded magazine** into the magazine well and push it in until it locks into place. You should hear and feel a "click" when it locks. Then give the floorplate a tug with your support hand to verify it is locked.

3 Grasp the rear portion of the slide with your support hand, pull the slide fully rearward and release, allowing the slide to slam forward, chambering the round. The **overhand method** (left) and the **sling-shot method** (right) are illustrated below. Either is acceptable.

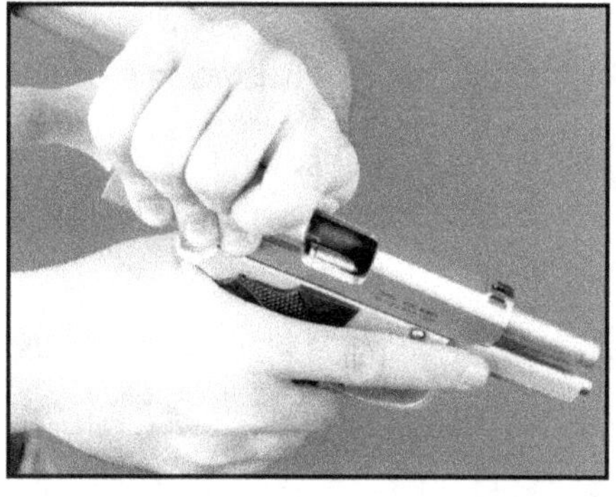

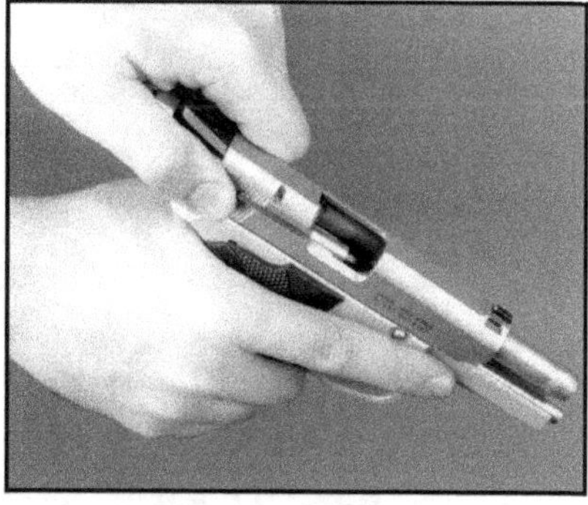

Remember: the slide must be cleanly released and allowed to "slam home." Do not maintain the support hand grip on the rear portion of the slide and "ride the slide" forward as this may induce a stoppage. You must also be sure to keep your fingers off the trigger and muzzle pointed in a safe direction through the entire process.

SECTION 4
Holstering the Pistol

After chambering a round as described in Section 3, you may holster it unless there is an immediate need for you to use your now loaded pistol.

As a general rule, holstering should be performed using only **one hand** whenever possible. Avoid developing the bad habit of reaching across your body and using your support hand to assist by guiding the pistol into the holster or clearing the retaining strap.

The better practice is to place the **index finger** of your primary hand along the slide and use it to locate the opening to the holster, as well as manipulate the retaining/safety strap out of the way if necessary.

Firmly slide the pistol into the holster using a smooth downward stroke. You should place your thumb against the rear of the slide when doing this.

As soon as the pistol is seated, secure the retaining/safety strap, again using only the primary hand to accomplish this. With a little practice it will become second nature.

When holstering the pistol, you should keep your eyes off the holster and on the threat area. You should also avoid using two hands to holster the pistol.

The index finger (as shown in photo at left) can be used to assist you to both locate the opening of the holster as well as manipulate the retaining/safety strap out of the way so the pistol can be placed into the holster.

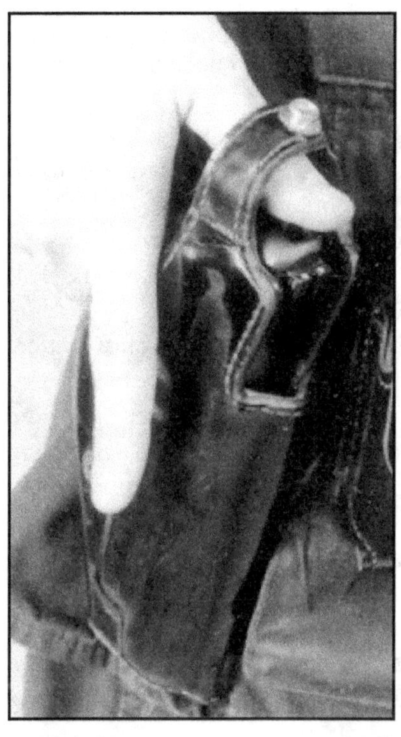

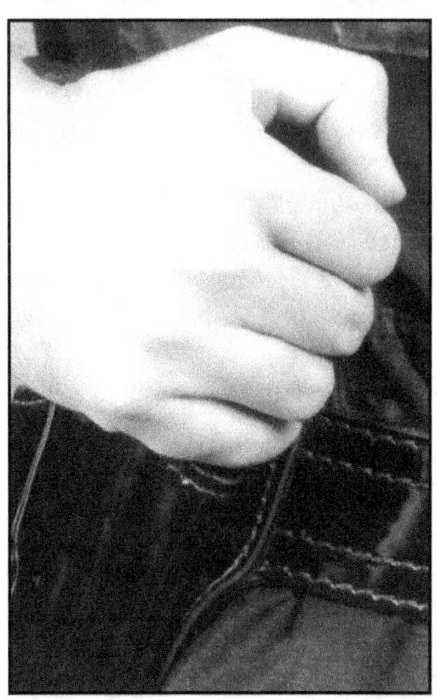

Try to develop the ability to do this without looking at the pistol or holster!

Holstering the pistol is something you may be doing in dim or dark areas when working.

You may also need to holster the pistol while dealing with suspects. You do not want to develop a habit that will cause you to take your eyes off them so you can watch the pistol go into the holster.

Topping Off

Once the loaded pistol is securely holstered, you may remove the magazine from the receiver and "top it off" with an additional round of ammunition. This is done to replace the round that was chambered earlier.

Once fully loaded, the magazine can then be re-inserted into the holstered pistol. Your pistol will then be loaded to full capacity. (Refer to **Appendix B** for additional information on loading the magazine.)

(Top left) Place your thumb on the back of the slide when holstering the pistol. This aids in holstering as well as ensuring the slide stays in battery (forward and locked).

(Left) Securing the retaining/safety strap with one hand as shown becomes easy with a little practice.

SECTION 5
Presenting the Pistol

The "presentation" or drawing of the pistol from the holster is a critical component of your pistolcraft skill set.

In essence, it doesn't matter if you can shoot the sty out of a bird's eye if you can't get the pistol from the holster into your hand when needed. And since most police-involved shootings happen at close range with the adversary making the first move, the time frame will likely be short, meaning you have to be fast. *Fast on the draw*. Like Wild Bill Hickok. It was true then, and it's still true now.

In regard to the development of a smooth, efficient, and fast tactical presentation, I feel it's warranted to clarify that in no way is the idea of any unsafe, boisterous, or foolish activity being promoted here; quite the opposite. As professionals in law enforcement we all realize the destructive capabilities of the weapons we carry and the awesome responsibility that rides in our holsters with them. That is why oftentimes the first reaction to the suggestion of working with our weapons and equipment anytime other than at the range during qualifications, much less the idea of working on and improving our drawing capability, tends to be that we are exhibiting overly aggressive tendencies, or that the individuals who do practice more than they are required to are either dangerous, deluded, or, worse, "itching to kill someone."

In fact, the opposite has proven to be true. A police officer who is truly competent and confident in his pistol and pistolcraft skills is far *less* likely to have to use deadly force in his career. Following are some of the reasons why.

First, an officer who has developed his tactical pistolcraft skills to a high level exudes a **true sense of confidence and bearing** that is detected by the general public and the criminal element. In many instances, this perceived steadiness, or confidence, may dissuade an individual who may be considering taking you on if the opportunity arises.

Second, when we know we are prepared to deal with extreme situations, we will truly be calmer, more observant, and effective. But the confidence must be real and is only achieved through realistic training and practice. In regard to the development of a tactically fast draw, it works something like this:

Entering whatever situation is at hand, we are suddenly faced with what we perceive to be a life-threatening situation. If our training has been followed up by individual practice, what should then happen is that our subconscious mind, reacting faster than our conscious mind, will cause us to draw the weapon. The smoothness and speed of this draw is totally dependent upon the amount of conscious practice we have put into it. If we've done our homework we should suddenly find ourselves looking at the threat over the sights of our weapon.

Since our conscious mind has not had to concern itself with *"Oh my God, THREAT, get my gun out—DAMN SNAP—get the gun OUT—oh God this is it...!"* it is therefore freed up to make the biggest decision of our lives: shoot or not? Again, if we've drawn fast enough, we should have the advantage over an adversary whose conscious mind is (we hope) tied up with the mechanical process of getting to his own weapon. Having the drop on the subject, we can then order, "Police! Don't move!" or, if the threat is perceived by us as immediate or continuing, get off that first round or two on target.

That bears repeating: *on target.* As the legendary Border Patrolman Bill Jordan was fond of saying, "Speed is fine, but accuracy is final."

It's the first hit that counts, not the first shot.

As for practicing your tactical presentation technique, here is a suggestion: to avoid making anyone uncomfortable, practice when you're alone. After unloading your pistol in a safe manner, holster the clear and empty weapon. Secure the pistol in the holster.

Watching yourself in a mirror (if available) helps you to see any obvious mistakes in stance or draw. The use of different starting positions for your hands (e.g., interview position, relaxed by your sides, arms folded) helps build dexterity into your technique.

Then you simply go through the presentation slowly and by the numbers. The key at first is to **ingrain smoothness more than speed**. Speed will increase naturally as you progress.

Remember to draw from a secured holster, incorporating the "un-snap" or whatever movements your holster requires to free the pistol.

The mirror image allows you to see what your adversary would see. A small sticker or piece of tape on the mirror at center-mass height will also give you an aiming point—one that you will begin to draw and point to automatically with a little practice.

The objective is to make the draw as fluid and clean as you can, with as little wasted motion as possible. Only a few minutes per training session are required, perhaps performing the presentation 10 or so times. When counting repetitions, keep in mind that only the correctly executed presen-

Presentation to Body Point Position

1. Start from the commonly taught Interview (or Ready) Position. The stance is wide and balanced; the body is bladed, gun or dominant side away from threat.

2. Move hand directly to holstered pistol and establish the grip high on the backstrap. **Release retaining snap at the same moment.** Begin to simultaneously assume an aggressive forward crouching position. Elbow moves straight back to rear, not out to the side.

tations count.

Important: you must train as you carry. This means practicing the basic movements and techniques while in your working clothes.

For uniformed division personnel, this includes while wearing your patrol jackets, rain coats, sweaters, etc. For plainclothes personnel, this means not only practicing with the different types of clothing worn, but also practicing drawing the weapon from whichever location the individual officer may choose to carry it while in the field.

The time to discover that there is a conflict between the way we carry and the execution of a fast, clean presentation is not at the moment we suddenly realize we need our pistol in our hand.

Presentation to Body Point Position (Continued)

3. Draw the pistol up and out of the holster. Note how the trigger finger position along the side of the slide is already established. Keep the elbow pointed back as opposed to sticking out sideways. A smooth draw is achieved by raising the elbow and allowing the wrist to bend as the pistol is removed from the holster.

"Elbow up" (above), "Elbow down" (right)

More information on the Tactical Presentation is provided in Chapters 5 and 12.

4. Lock the dominant arm elbow against your side as shown. The pistol (gripped securely, wrist locked) is held level and directly in front of the center of your torso. Shooter is in full *forward leaning* combat crouch. Depending upon the distance from, and angle to, the target, you may have to elevate the forearm slightly so the pistol's muzzle points directly where you want it on the vertical plane. This will become automatic with practice. Sometimes referred to as the "third eye" concept, this technique enables you to condition or "calibrate" the muzzle or third eye to "look" where the other two eyes are focused. The support arm may be locked across the upper torso or held up next to the head in a defensive position as shown.

Becoming *One of the Quick*: The Poker Chip Drill

1. Place the poker chip on top of the drawing hand. The drawing hand is placed directly above the holstered pistol. The holster's retaining strap/ device is secured.

The Poker Chip Drill was reportedly used by American gunfighters of the old West to increase their drawing speed. Bill Jordan used to employ a variation of this drill using ping-pong balls during demonstrations.

Jordan was so fast, he could hold his hand (ping-pong ball balanced on top of it), directly above the holstered pistol and draw with such lightning speed that the ball would drop into the emptied holster.

I have found that the Poker Chip drill, when practiced professionally and safely, still provides tremendous benefits to the modern-day pistoleer.

Presentation speed is increased, physical dexterity is improved and more deeply ingrained, and confidence rises as basic skills are strengthened. The fact that it is also a lot of fun to perform, especially when in competition with yourself or others, provides another strong reason for using it, for the more you enjoy working with your pistol, the more positive your attitude toward this potentially life-saving tool.

IMPORTANT! All pistols must be verified to be safe, clear, and empty prior to performing the Poker Chip Drill.

The Poker Chip Drill (Continued)

2. Initiate the presentation. The chip (visible in circle) is allowed to fall naturally off the hand; it is not tossed up or thrown.

Note: Sequence shown in real time. Images enhanced to make chip easier to see in photos.

3. The objective of the exercise is to complete the presentation as cleanly as possible before the poker chip (visible in circle still falling) hits the ground. Most people should be able to achieve this during the first practice session. Once this can be consistently achieved, try to draw and DRY FIRE on target before the chip hits the ground.

SECTION 6
Firing the Pistol

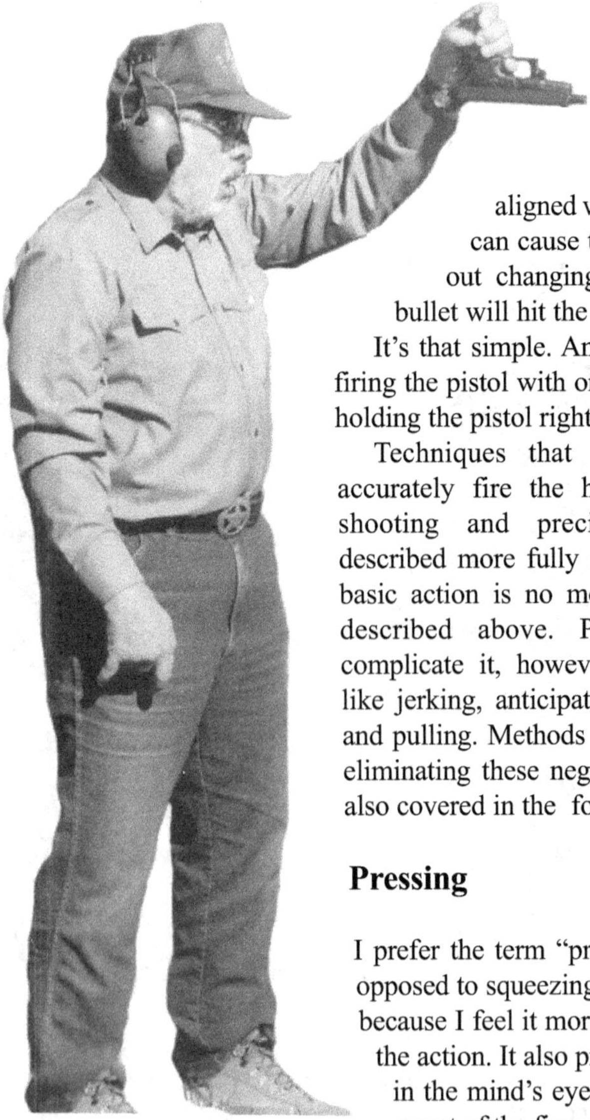

Once the pistol is loaded, point it at the target and **press** the trigger.

If the barrel is aligned with the target and you can cause the pistol to fire without changing that alignment, the bullet will hit the target.

It's that simple. And it works if you are firing the pistol with one hand or two, while holding the pistol right-side up or inverted

Techniques that will assist you to accurately fire the handgun while point shooting and precision shooting are described more fully in Chapter 5, but the basic action is no more complicated than described above. People do tend to complicate it, however, by adding things like jerking, anticipating, heeling, pushing and pulling. Methods for preventing and/or eliminating these negative components are also covered in the following chapter.

Pressing

I prefer the term "pressing" the trigger as opposed to squeezing or pulling the trigger because I feel it more accurately describes the action. It also provides a clear picture in the mind's eye of the desired movement of the finger against the trigger. If you prefer to use another term that is perfectly fine. Regardless of the term you use, you should try to develop the ability to manipulate the trigger in a smooth and consistent manner.

Jim Cirillo shooting his pistol while it is inverted, using his little finger on the trigger. As long as the barrel is aligned properly at the moment of discharge, you will hit your target.

Hand & Finger Strengthening Methods

One of the best ways to develop good control of the handgun is to develop and increase the strength of your hands and fingers.

Wrist and forearm exercises are also recommended. The stronger your forearms, wrists, hands, and fingers, the easier it will be for you to manipulate and control the pistol while firing.

If you are scheduled to begin firearms training in the near future, you should adopt an exercise routine as soon as possible. Begin slowly and increase repetitions and resistance gradually and reasonably. A few exercises are presented below for consideration.

If you already have training or experience with firearms, adopting some or all of these exercises into your training routine is also a good idea, for shooting is both a physical and mental activity. The stronger we are in both departments, the better our advantage.

While all of these exercises will affect the forearms, wrists, hands, and fingers, some provide for more focused development of specific areas.

Forearm & Wrist Exercises

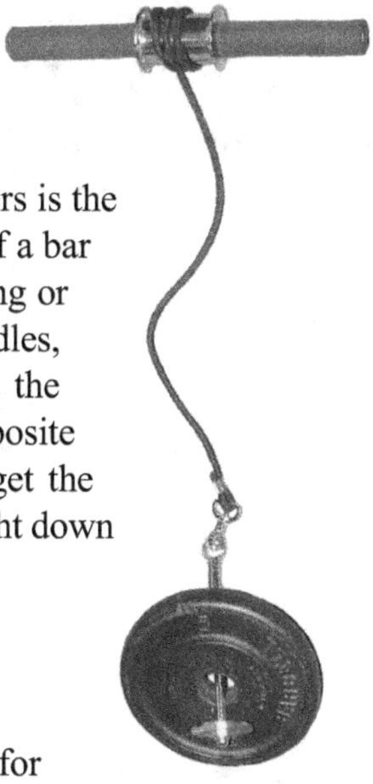

Wrist curls using barbells or dumbbells are excellent exercises to build up forearm and wrist strength. Hands and fingers benefit as well.

One of the best wrist and forearm developers is the **wrist roller** (shown right). This device consists of a bar with a cord or rope attached to it. A weight is hung or fastened to the end of the cord. You grip the handles, palms up or down, and roll the handles raising the weight. Once at the top, roll the handles in the opposite direction and lower the weight back down. To get the most benefit make sure to extend your arms straight down when doing this, not straight out in front of you.

Finger & Hand Exercises

Handgrips provide a tried and true method for improving hand and finger strength. **Rubber balls**, climber's **hand putty**, and other similar devices that can be squeezed and kneaded also work well when used regularly.

The **Grip Master** device is another useful tool, this one specifically designed to develop the individual strength of the fingers. The thumb is held on the side as if gripping a pistol while each finger presses down on its own pad of resistance. The model shown below is equipped with a detachable rubber backstrap and plastic sight radius. This allows you to develop finger coordination as you isolate the trigger finger while maintaining sight alignment.

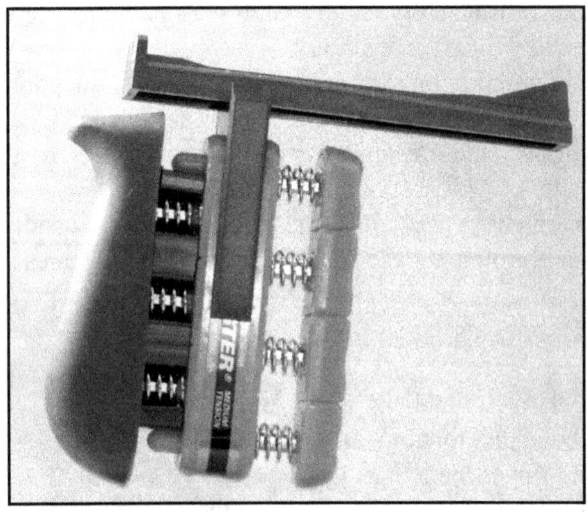

The Grip Master (above) and a standard hand grip exercising device (right). Both are fairly inexpensive, last for years, and provide a convenient method to improve hand and finger strength.

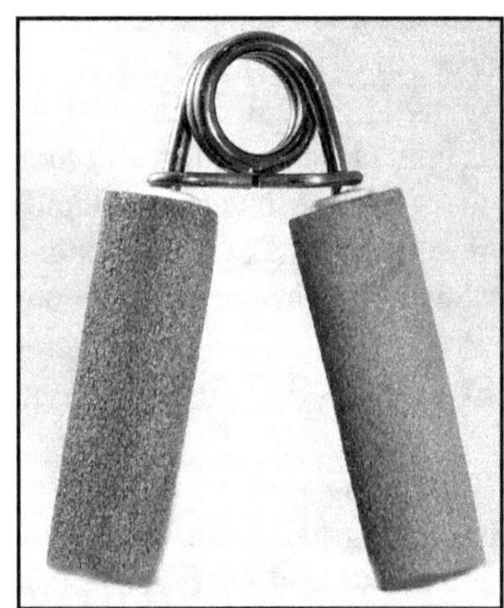

SECTION 7
Reloading the Pistol

Administrative Reload ("Locate, Index, Seat, and Tug")

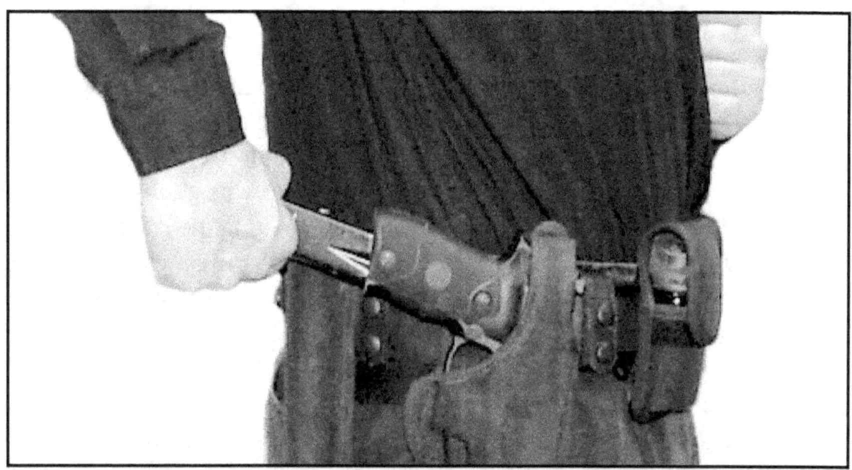

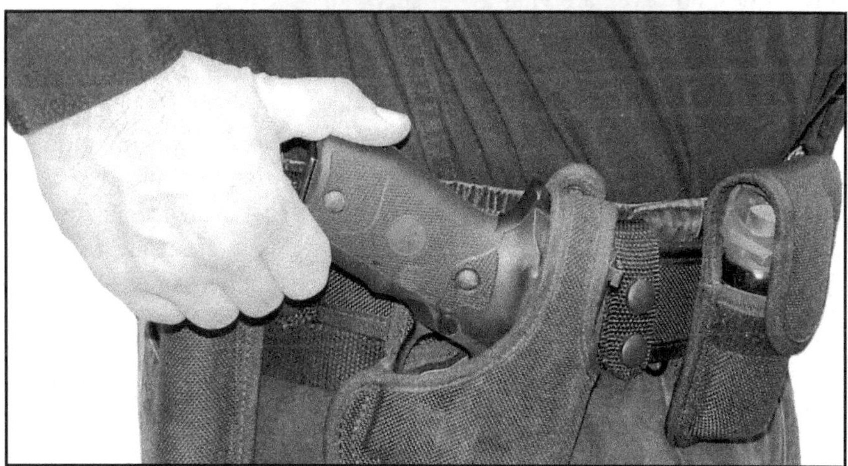

If there is a round in the chamber, remove the empty magazine from the holstered pistol and secure it in a pocket. **Locate** a fully loaded magazine, **index** it, and insert it into the holstered pistol as shown in top photo. Firmly **seat** the magazine in the pistol. Then, **tug** on the magazine's floorplate as shown in the bottom photo to ensure the magazine is locked in. If the pistol has been fired until empty; after inserting the loaded magazine draw the pistol and load as illustrated in Chapter 4 §3 (*Loading the Pistol*). Complete the non-emergency, administrative reload by following the process illustrated in Chapter 4 §4 (*Holstering the Pistol*).

A Few Words About the Combat Reload

The combat or speed reload is used when we have expended so much ammunition during an encounter that the pistol has either run out of ammunition or we feel it is about to.

In training, while performing the combat reload with a semiautomatic pistol, people often have a tendency to want to catch the empty or nearly empty magazine as it falls to the ground. Or they watch the magazine fall to the ground so they can remember where it is. Or worse, they instantly bend down to retrieve it after completing the reload drill.

Why do they do this? Simply to save embarrassment. Once in a while someone picks up the wrong magazine. Then the person next in line is missing one. Usually a ripple effect goes down the firing line with the "extra" magazine found 20 positions to the right or left. Now one of us has to announce that we're short one magazine. This is mildly embarrassing. The reasons we cannot allow ourselves to worry about the expended magazines, however, are vital to our survival.

Training to Win

We know that in a critical or highly stressful situation we will revert to our training. If, in training, we catch, watch, or retrieve our expended magazines, chances are great that we will do just that in an actual situation.

Just as police officers involved in gunfights while using revolvers have been found dead with their hands clutching empty brass shell casings jammed into their pockets (that's how they "saved themselves" from bending over to pick up brass at the range), so could one of us lose precious moments or our focus on the threat in a critical situation as we inexplicably grab for an empty magazine.

Chances are also great that we will never have to reload our weapon during an armed confrontation, even though statistics indicate that approximately 40 percent of the time there will be a potential secondary threat. But if one of us suddenly finds our self alone facing multiple armed assailants, those statistics won't mean nearly as much as proficient shooting skills and a clean, smooth reload.

Please note that the following basic drills are intended for use with semiautomatic pistols that will completely expel a seated magazine with simply a press of the magazine release button. Some pistols require the shooter to press the magazine-release button and then manually remove the magazine with the support hand.

Other pistols may be equipped with the magazine catch located at the rear of the butt of the grip. This configuration, referred to as a heel or "European" magazine release (shown in photo below) also requires two hands to remove the magazine from the weapon before reloading.

If you use a pistol with other than a free-fall magazine, you will need to practice the reload drills accordingly. In some cases, you will still be able to locate and index the fully loaded magazine before removing the empty magazine. In the case of a European release, you are probably best off stripping the empty magazine first, then accessing the loaded magazine.

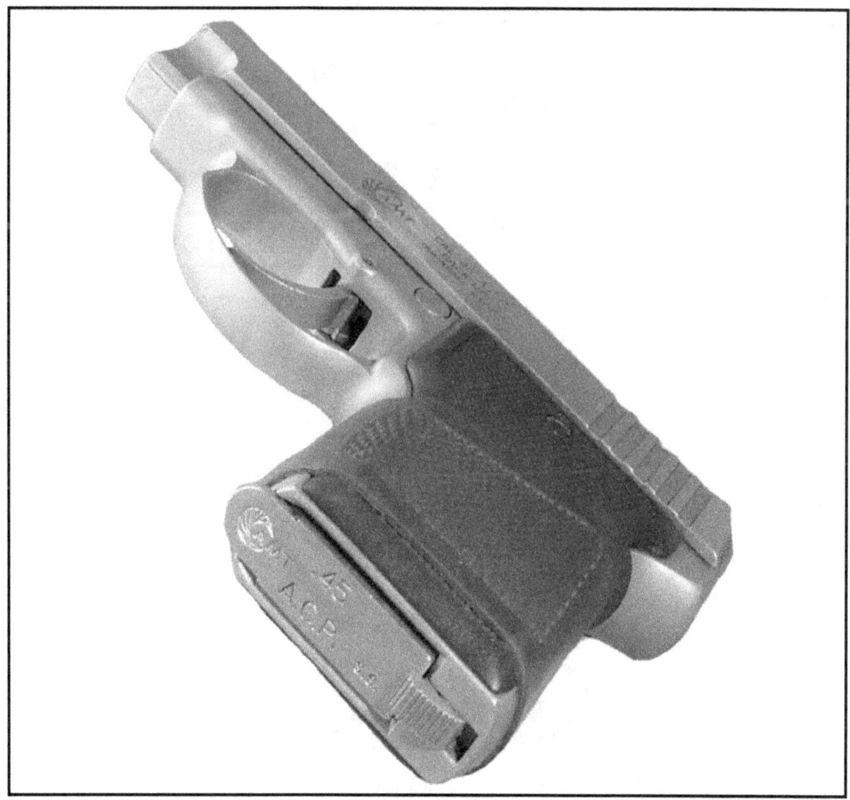

Many smaller-framed pistols such as the .45 ACP caliber AMT BACK UP shown here are equipped with a heel or "European" magazine release.

The Combat Reload ("Locate, Index, Drop, and Pop")

After removing the trigger finger from the trigger, perform the following four steps:

1. **LOCATE** the magazine pouches by placing the support (loading) hand on the center of the duty belt-buckle (as shown at right), and then sweep the hand along the belt toward the support side. The first item encountered should be the magazine pouch.

This movement is incorporated to prevent confusion, for it is not uncommon for an officer to try and load handcuffs, Buck knives, or Mini-Mag lights into the weapon due to failure to properly locate the magazine pouches when performing the reload under stress.

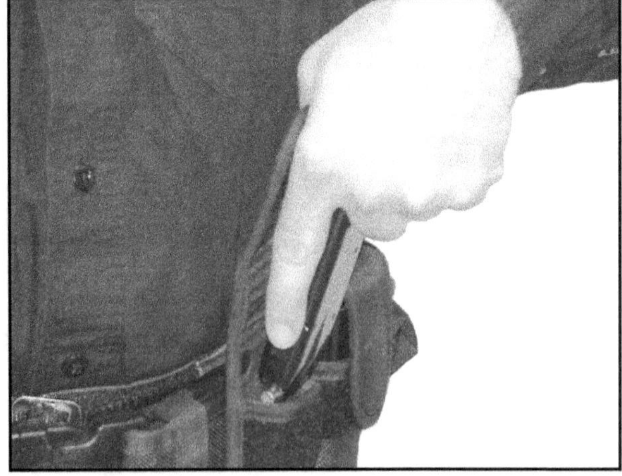

2. Once located, open the *inboard* pouch flap first, then remove and **INDEX** the magazine (index finger placed along front of magazine as shown above). These movements should be practiced until they can be accomplished by feel alone so you don't allow your focus to be turned away from the threat target area.

The Combat Reload (Continued)

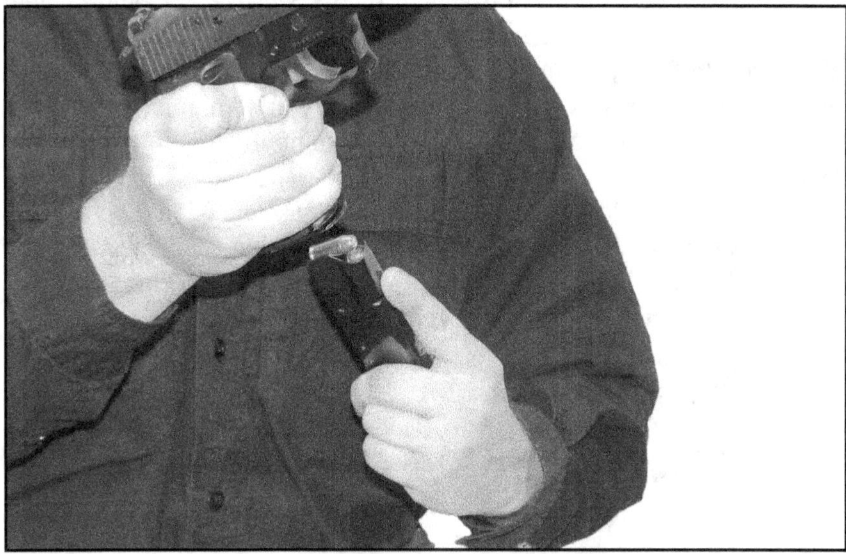

3. (Above) When the loaded and indexed magazine is brought up next to the weapon, the empty magazine is **RELEASED** (**DROP**) and allowed to fall freely from the pistol. **(Note: Pistol in photo has magazine release installed on right side.)**

4. (Right) **INSERT** the fully loaded magazine and seat it firmly, driving it upward (**POP**) by using the heel of the open palm. If the slide has locked open as a result of having fired the pistol until empty, it must be released to chamber a round. Use the overhand or slingshot method to accomplish this rather than depressing the slide release lever, as these methods require less fine motor skills and provide more recoil spring tension to assist the slide in fully closing.

The Tactical Reload ("Locate, Index, Catch, and Seat")

The tactical reload is different from the combat reload, as it requires you to catch and control the released magazine when reloading as opposed to allowing it to fall freely to the ground. It is intended to be used during an extended encounter when you realize you have fired multiple rounds and desire to reload, but want to save any ammunition that is in the partially expended magazine.

It is also employed in situations where the sound of an empty magazine hitting the ground could give away your position, and jeopardize any tactical advantage you may have over an armed adversary. One method of performing this reload is provided here.

1. First, *take cover* where possible. Remove the trigger finger from the trigger. Then **LOCATE** and draw out a fully loaded magazine, **INDEX** it, and bring it up to the pistol.

The Tactical Reload (Continued)

2. Next: Press the magazine release and **CATCH** the expended magazine in the same reloading hand. Maintaining control of both magazines, remove the expended magazine from the weapon.

3. Rotate the fully loaded magazine up and insert it into the magazine well.

The Tactical Reload (Continued)

4. **SEAT** the magazine with an upward press, using the meaty portion of the hand or side of the index finger as shown here. This should be done in a controlled, deliberate manner.
(Note the expended magazine still being held and controlled by the reloading hand.)

5. Finally, place the empty or partially empty magazine *in a pocket.*

! Never place an expended magazine back into your magazine pouch, for it could be the one you grab if you must reload again later in the conflict.

Always try and observe the suspect and his location while performing the reload.

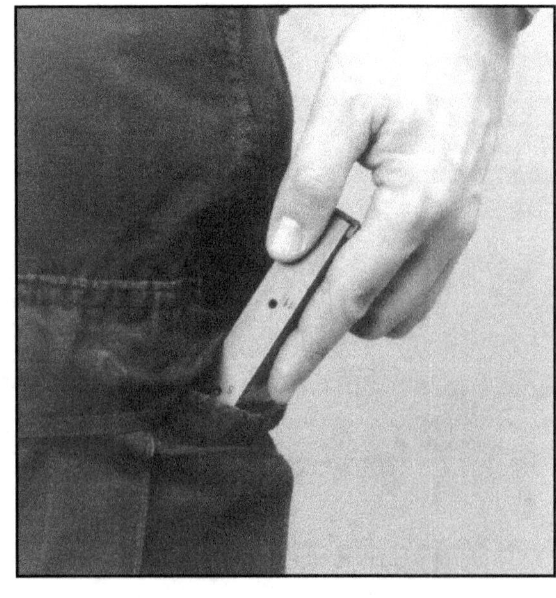

The Tactical Reload (Continued)

Training Note: When performing the tactical reload as shown in this section, **AVOID** using the top of the hand to seat the magazine as shown in this photo as injury may result.

Seat the magazine (as shown in the photo on page 138) with an upward press, using the side of the index finger or meaty portion of the hand.

SECTION 8
Unloading the Pistol

Properly unloading or clearing the pistol to make it safe and empty is a basic activity that can be done practically anywhere at any time if certain precautions are taken. The following method is presented for consideration.

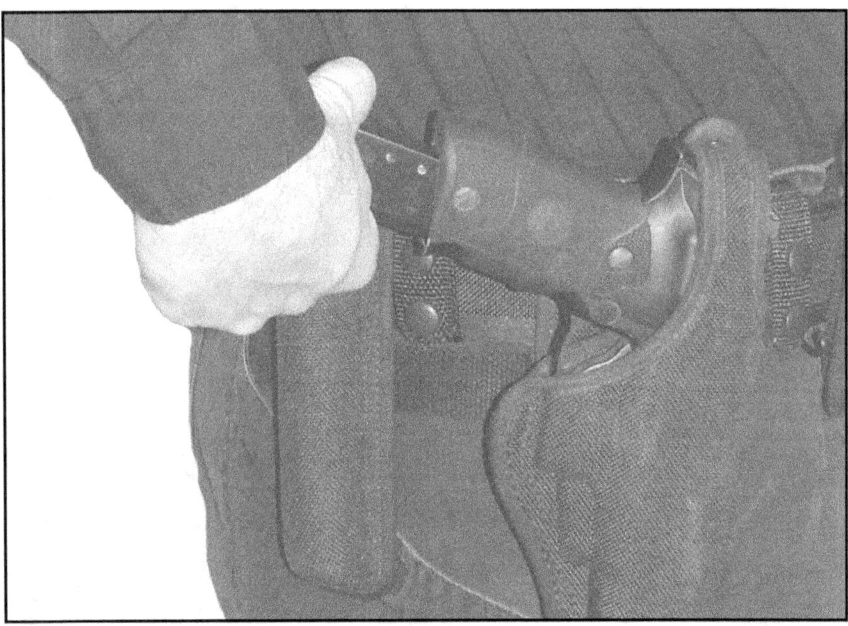

1 Press the magazine release and **remove the magazine** from the holstered pistol as shown above.

Then place the magazine in a pocket or otherwise secure it so both of your hands are free to finish the clearing process.

2 After the magazine has been secured, **draw the pistol** from the holster, keeping your fingers off the trigger and the weapon's muzzle pointed in a **SAFE DIRECTION** as defined in Chapter 3 §1.

Personal body armor may be placed on a chair and used to provide a safe direction in any location as illustrated in Chapter 4 §3.

3 **Cycle the action THREE TIMES** to clear the chamber. Use either an overhand grip or "slingshot grip" as shown in Chapter 4 §3.

If there is a round in the chamber, it should be allowed to eject freely from the pistol. **Never attempt to catch the round or drop it into your hand.**

Then **lock the slide to the rear**. Ensure that the muzzle is kept pointed in the designated safe direction both during cycling and while locking the slide to the rear!

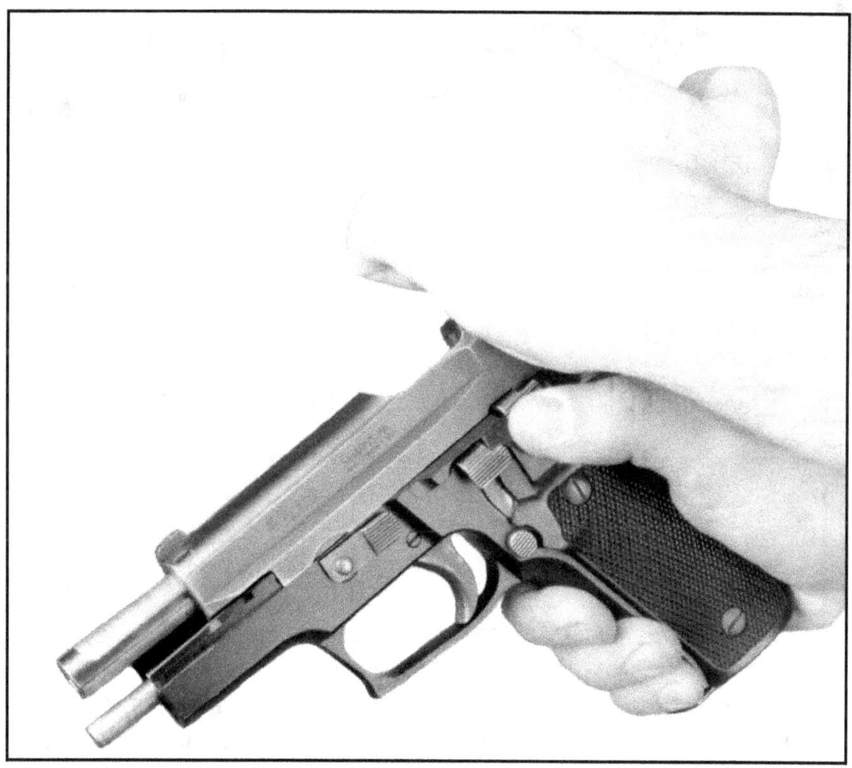

Shown above: Detail of the slide being locked to the rear. The thumb of the primary hand applies upward pressure to the slide release lever as the slide is pulled fully rearward. When you feel the lever move up into the release lever "arresting" notch that is cut into the slide, keep pressing up with the thumb and release the tension on the slide. The slide will then be held to the rear by the lever.

Unloading the Pistol (Continued)

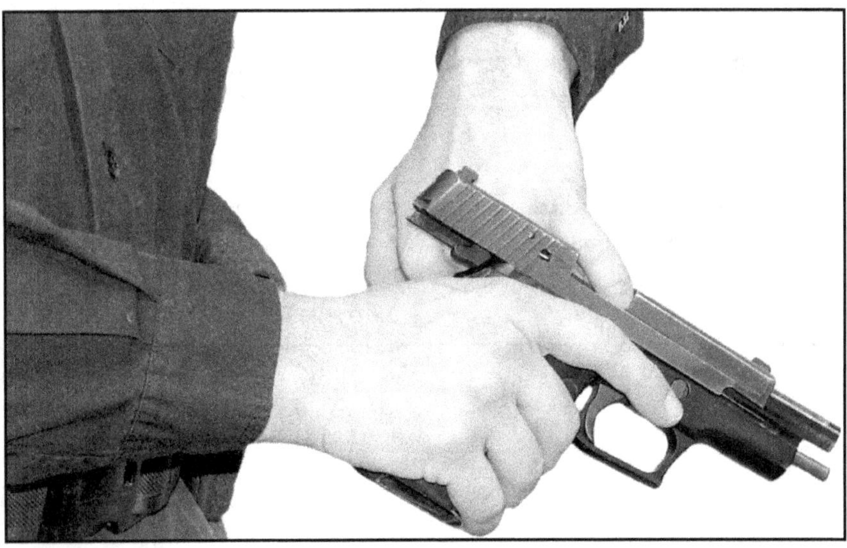

4 While still keeping the muzzle pointed in a SAFE DIRECTION, **visually and then physically inspect** the magazine well and chamber (as shown above) to ensure that the pistol is absolutely safe, clear, and empty of ammunition. Once you are satisfied it is clear, if possible, have *someone else* CHECK and VERIFY it.

? **Why Cycle the Action Three Times?** When cycling the action to clear the chamber (See Step 3 on page 141), the slide should be drawn fully rearward and released three times. The reason I recommend the **Three-Cycle Rule** when clearing the pistol is because it's possible that you might forget to remove the magazine prior to cycling the action. If this happens, you can find yourself ejecting the round in the chamber while unknowingly chambering another round from the magazine. Should this occur, you are now in the doubly-dangerous situation of holding a loaded pistol that you *think* is unloaded. If, however, you do the one-two-three clearing drill habitually, then no matter how tired or distracted you may be, you will get the message that you've overlooked something when those rounds keep ejecting out of the weapon!

SECTION 9

One-Hand Semiauto Pistol Refunction Technique

There are, unfortunately, numerous examples of real-world, police-involved gunfights during which officers were wounded in the hands or arms during the initial stages of an encounter, leaving them vulnerable to further attack.

These types of incidents clearly illustrate why police officers must know how to operate their weapons not only when both hands are available, but also how to make them work when one of the officer's hands is wounded or otherwise unavailable.

Mastering the One-Hand Pistol Refunction Technique shown in this section will enable you to deal with this possibility should it be necessary. *Learn it well.*

Performing the Technique

The technique can be performed with the slide forward or locked to the rear as it may be should the weapon have been fired until empty.

You should practice both with the slide locked to the rear as well as fully forward. Once you master the technique with the slide forward (which is slightly more difficult), then the slide-locked-rearward configuration should be no problem.

Practicing the technique using magazines loaded with dummy rounds is most beneficial. If dummy rounds are not available, simulate retrieving fully loaded magazines and inserting them into the weapon. You should not use empty magazines if they are equipped with followers that cause the slide to lock to the rear during the chambering phase.

Learn the technique by first performing it step by step, as illustrated in the accompanying photographs.

Once you are able to successfully perform the drill using your dominant hand, increase the training value by visualizing yourself being engaged by gunfire and sustaining a wound to your non-dominant arm. You should then seek cover (if possible), keep scanning the area, and execute the technique. Once the refunction technique has been completed, simulate re-engaging the assailant. Repeat this several times.

Then practice the technique as if your dominant hand were injured. This will require you to access the pistol and perform the One-Hand Pistol Refunction Technique using your non-dominant hand. Don't be satisfied until you master the technique with both hands.

Pistol Refunction Technique (Continued)

SAFETY NOTICE: All weapons must be administratively unloaded and verified to be safe, clear and empty prior to practicing this technique!

STEP 1: Eject the Magazine

Take cover (if possible) and **eject the magazine** from the pistol. Some pistols not equipped with "free fall" magazines may require you to hook the magazine floorplate on something to assist in ejection. **Note:** The simulated injured arm/hand should not be placed in the pocket or held behind the back, but simply allowed to hang as if it were disabled.

Pistol Refunction Technique (Continued)

STEP 2: Secure the Pistol

Option 1

After the magazine has been ejected, **secure the pistol**.

The primary recommendation is to keep it simple and just place the pistol in the holster as shown at left. This is probably the best choice, especially for uniformed officers.

Option 2

The second preferred option is to jam the empty pistol between the belt and the body as shown in this photo. This is often the easiest place to secure it when using the non-dominant hand to execute the technique.

Using the belt or the holster also keeps the weapon in a more controllable location than behind the knee or similar positions, and can be employed from a number of positions (e.g. standing, sitting, kneeling, prone, etc.)

Pistol Refunction Technique (Continued)

STEP 3: Retrieve Loaded Magazine

Next, **retrieve** a fully loaded magazine from your carry location.

This must be practiced using both the dominant and non-dominant hands.

Below: Deatil of the magazine being accessed and indexed.

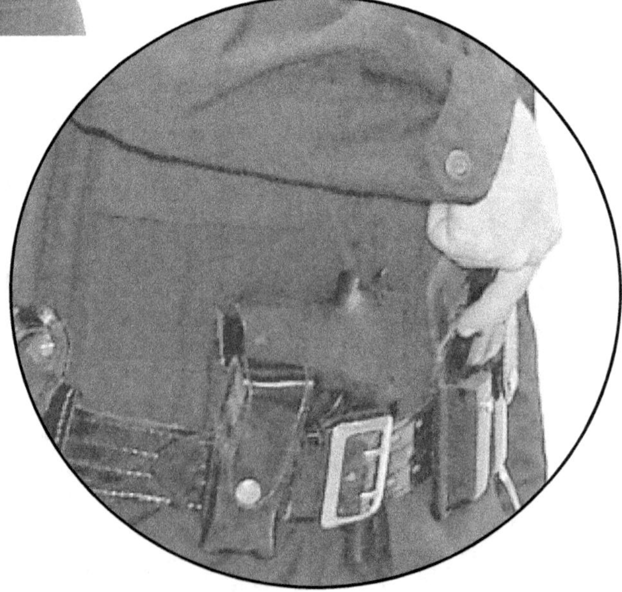

Pistol Refunction Technique (Continued)

STEP 4: Insert Loaded Magazine into Pistol & Seat

Then **insert the magazine** into the weapon and aggressively seat it

Note: This action is simulated if dummy rounds are not available.

Below: Detail of the magazine being seated.

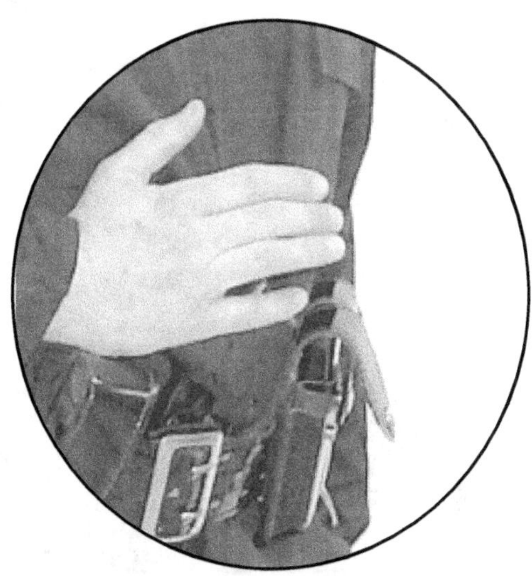

Pistol Refunction Technique (Continued)

STEP 5: Chamber a Round

Chambering, Part 1

Grasp the weapon securely in the "uninjured" hand. **Hook the pistol's rear sight** on the edge of the belt, a pocket, or even the heel of your boot if you are kneeling.

Warning: Do not use the large belt buckle common on many duty belts, because the buckle may be released by the racking action, needlessly complicating the procedure.

Below: Detail of the rear sight being hooked on the holster (left) and on the back of the boot heel while kneeling.

Pistol Refunction Technique (Continued)

Chambering, Part 2

Next, simultaneously push the pistol **IN** (rear sights against the edge of holster, pocket, heel, etc.), **DOWN** (straight down so contact is maintained between the rear sights and the edge), **and MUZZLE AWAY** (from your body).

Care must be taken to do this aggressively, so the slide is fully retracted before release.

Resist the propensity to "ride the slide" slowly, for this can induce stoppages, as well as cause the slide to close around the material of your pants or jacket.

Pistol Refunction Technique (Continued)

STEP 6: Ready!

The pistol is **reloaded and ready** for action as is the injured—but never defeated—officer.

Just *knowing* how to do this can drastically increase your overall confidence levels and chances for survival.

SECTION 10

Semiauto Pistol Stoppages & Clearing Drills

You will occasionally experience a stoppage when firing a semiautomatic pistol. A stoppage is an unintended interruption of the weapon's firing cycle generated by the shooter.

A "malfunction" on the other hand, generally denotes a mechanical failure on the part of the weapon. True malfunctions are fairly rare with modern, high-quality weapons, but they can occur. Firing pins or extractors may fail. Trigger springs may break. Occasionally, even factory-made, high quality ammunition will be defective. It is not unheard of for a round with a damaged casing, no primer cap, or no propellant to slip through the cracks during long production runs, regardless of the level of quality control.

The majority of unintended interruptions we will encounter, however, will be stoppages, and as I've already indicated, these are normally operator-induced.

The most common types of operator-induced stoppages are outlined below, as are the most common reasons for their occurrence. The two primary methods I recommend for clearing stoppages are illustrated as well.

Failure to Feed

A failure to feed occurs when a round is not successfully loaded into the chamber. This is often caused by one or more of the following factors.

Suspect 1: *Improper hold.* When firing a semiautomatic pistol, a firm grip is necessary for the recoil energy to cycle the action of the weapon properly. If some of this energy is bled off through a weak hold, the slide will not travel fully rearward during recoil. When this occurs, a live round is not stripped from the magazine and fed into the chamber. The expended shell casing may be rechambered or fully ejected from the weapon. With anything in between, you will be dealing with another type of stoppage. The possibility of encountering this type of stoppage is greatly increased if the weapon, magazine, or ammunition is dirty.

SEMIAUTOMATIC PISTOL FIRING CYCLE

FEED	(live round into the chamber)
FIRE	(bullet)
EXTRACT	(spent casing from the chamber)
EJECT	(spent casing from the pistol)

Suspect 2: *Improperly seated magazine.* The second most common cause of a failure to feed stoppage is an improperly seated magazine. If the magazine is not firmly locked into place, the top round will be too low for the slide to make contact with it and load into the chamber.

Suspect 3: *Failure to go into battery.* A third variation of a failure to feed is a failure to go into battery. This occurs when a round has been chambered but the slide has not gone fully forward. This is often the result of a dirty weapon, limp-wristed (weak) hold, or combination of both. It may also be caused by a weak recoil spring.

Note: Applying a palm-heel strike (as illustrated here) to the rear of the slide when the slide has not gone completely into battery is a commonly taught technique. Though it is often effective, it is **NOT recommended** for use. If the failure to go into battery was caused by a faulty or deformed round, forcing the slide forward would only exacerbate the problem. Injury to the hand is also a possibility when using pistols with exposed hammers.

The Double Feed

A double feed is a condition that occurs when two rounds are trying to feed into the chamber at the same time. This condition is easily recognized by the way the slide will be held back exposing the breech much further than with a failure to go into battery stoppage. This is generally the most time-intensive type of stoppage to clear.

Suspect 1: A*gain, the most common cause is a weak or loose grip, often combined with a dirty weapon and/or magazine.*

Suspect 2: *May be caused by a weak magazine spring, or other defective magazine component.*

A double-feed. Note that the slide is not locked fully rearward. It is being held open by the misfed round.

Failure to Fire

Your pistol is loaded with a round in the chamber. You press the trigger and nothing happens.

Suspect 1: *Defective ammunition.* When using a modern, high-quality pistol, the ammunition will always be the first suspect when you have a failure to fire. A hard or defective primer that does not detonate when struck by the firing pin is the most common cause.

Suspect 2: *Defective pistol.* The pistol may be the culprit when you experience a failure to fire. Firing pins do occasionally bend, break, or wear down. The springs that drive the hammer or striker forward may become weakened or break. Foreign matter may find its way into the firing pin channel and impede the firing pin's movement.

Failure to Extract

After firing, the slide cycles but the expended casing is not successfully pulled from the chamber.

Suspect 1: *Damaged extractor.* If the extractor is missing, broken, or bent it will not be able to pull the casing from the chamber.

Suspect 2: *Damaged or deformed ammunition.* If the rim of the chambered round's casing is damaged or deformed, or if the case itself has over-expanded, bulged, or split, it may prevent a functional extractor from performing properly.

Suspect 3: *Excessively dirty or fouled pistol.* Extraction may also be impeded by significant fouling (carbon build-up) due to improper cleaning and lubrication of the pistol.

Failure to Eject

After firing, the expended casing is extracted from the chamber but is not successfully ejected from the pistol. This may result in a condition referred to as a "stovepipe" (see opposite page).

Suspect 1: A*gain, the most common cause is a weak or loose grip, often combined with a dirty weapon.*

Suspect 2: *May be caused by interference with the slide during recoil.*

Suspect 3: *May be caused by defective or under-powered ammunition.*

The Stovepipe

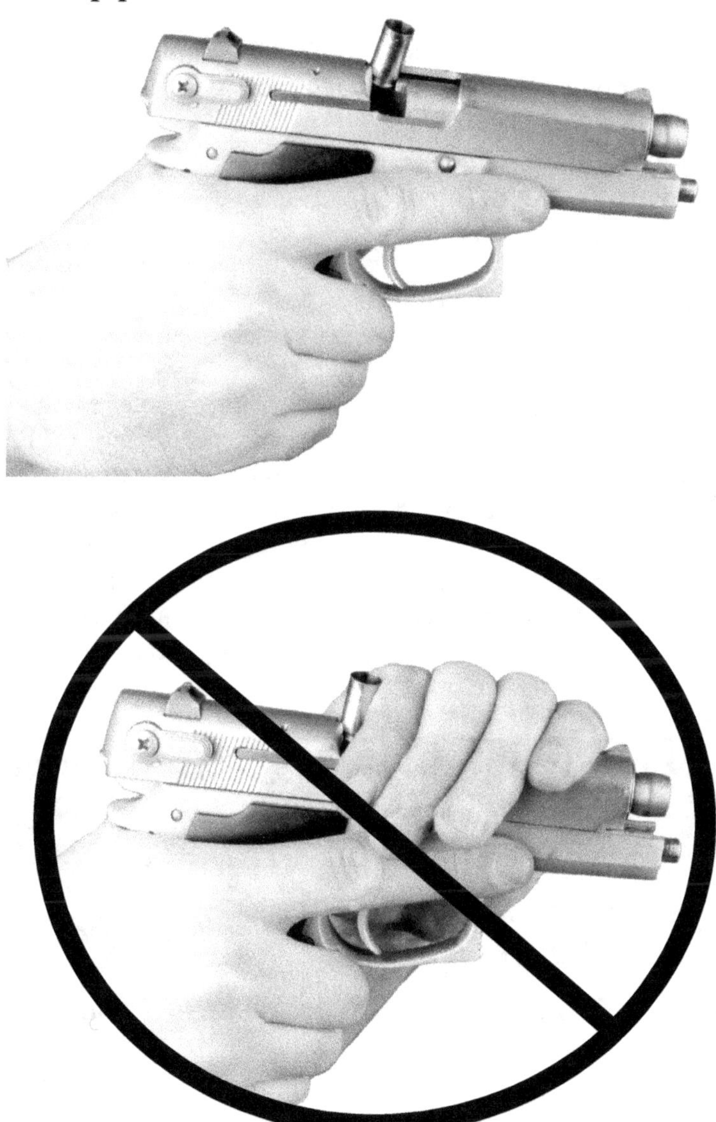

Note: Sweeping the support hand across the top of the slide from behind the front sight back to clear the upended casing is a commonly-taught stovepipe clearing technique. While it's good to be aware of it, the **TIRR Clearing Drill** has made it obsolete it and I no longer recommend it for use.

Stoppage Clearing Drills

The following two stoppage clearing drills will clear the vast majority of stoppages that occur when the semiautomatic pistol's firing cycle—*feed, fire, extract, eject*—is interrupted.

The T.I.R.R. Clearing Drill

The TIRR Clear Drill is a unique variation of the commonly-taught *Tap, Rack, Ready* immediate action drill.

TIRR —pronounced "tear"— is an abbreviation for the drill's sequence; *Tap, Invert, Rack, Ready.*

I have been teaching this drill (sometimes referred to as the "Massachusetts State Police" clearing drill) since developing it in 1994.

The reasons I recommend this drill, however, have nothing to do with its provenance. I recommend it simply because 1) it is more efficient than other clearing drills being taught, and 2) it works better when the operator performing it is engaged in stressful, violent encounters.

In addition to clearing the various stoppages normally cleared by the immediate action drill, this technique also easily clears stovepipe-type stoppages and some double-feed type stoppages.

STOPPAGE TYPE	RECOMMENDED DRILL
Failure to Feed	***TIRR Clearing Drill***
Failure to Fire	***TIRR Clearing Drill***
Failure to Extract	***TIRR Clearing Drill***
Failure to Eject	***TIRR Clearing Drill***
Double-Feed *	***TIRR Clearing Drill***

*** If the TIRR Clearing Drill does not clear the double-feed immediately use the *Double-Feed Clearing Drill***

The success of the technique when used to clear double-feed type stoppages is variable, however, and dependent upon the weapon system used and the severity of the problem encountered. This fact obviously demands that you learn a second, double-feed specific drill as well as the TIRR Clearing Drill.

Both are presented here for your consideration.

How to Perform the TIRR CLEAR DRILL

STEP 1: TAP up on the Magazine

From firing position, first ...

1. **TAP** - Bring the pistol back toward your chest as you tap up sharply on the magazine with the support hand to ensure the magazine is seated and locked.

TIRR Clear Drill (Continued)

STEP 2: INVERT the Pistol

2. **INVERT** - Keep the weapon back toward the chest as you completely invert the pistol. The support hand's forefinger and thumb simultaneously establish a secure "slingshot" type grip on the rear of the slide (see close-up).

Note: You must rotate the pistol *inboard toward the centerline of your body* as shown, not outboard, as some people tend to do.

TIRR Clear Drill (Continued)

STEP 3: RACK the Action

3–4. **RACK** - The primary hand, trigger finger along the frame, is used to *aggressively* punch the weapon forward (as opposed to the support hand racking the slide back) toward the threat, literally pulling the slide from the grasp of the support hand as the slide reaches maximum retraction position. The sharp action of this movement should cause any loose shell casings or misfed rounds to be dislodged. Gravity will then cause them to fall clear of the weapon through the ejection port. As the pistol is driven forward, the primary hand simultaneously corkscrews *outboard* (as shown above right), righting the pistol and bringing it into alignment with the threat as show in the photograph on the following page.

TIRR Clear Drill (Continued)

STEP 4: READY!

5. **READY** - The pistol, once cleared, is immediately ready to be fired if necessary.

More information on the T.I.R.R. Clear Drill (including a video demonstration) is available at our website. www.sabergroup.com

How to Perform the DOUBLE-FEED CLEARING DRILL

If you encounter a double-feed type stoppage while firing (shown right), first, take cover if possible and perform the T.I.R.R. Clear Drill. If this does not immediately clear the stoppage, then ...

STEP 1: LOCK the Slide to the Rear

1. **LOCK** - Lock the slide to the rear (as described on page 141).

Double-Feed Clearing Drill (Continued)

STEP 2: RIP & SHAKE — Remove Magazine from Pistol; Shake Both

2. **RIP** - Remove the magazine and vigorously SHAKE the pistol and magazine. Keep the pistol's **muzzle canted up** to aid in clearing any loose or misfed rounds from the chamber.

Note: Do not discard the magazine that you remove from the pistol unless it is empty, obviously damaged, or you desire to reload a fully loaded magazine. Rather, hang onto it as you clear the pistol and magazine of any misfed rounds, and then re-insert the same magazine into the pistol. This practice (as opposed to the practice of immediately and automatically discarding the magazine during a double-feed clearing drill) is recommended because the magazine in the pistol may be your last or only magazine.

Double-Feed Clearing Drill (Continued)

STEP 3: TAP — Insert Magazine into Pistol and Seat it

3. **TAP** - Reinsert the magazine into the magazine well and drive it forcefully upward using the heel of the palm. **Ensure the magazine seats and locks into place.**

IMPORTANT: Avoid the Hollywood stylization of inserting the magazine partially into the well, releasing contact with the magazine, and then "slapping / slamming" it up into place. In the real world, magazines tend to free-fall from the well and hit the ground when this is done.

Double-Feed Clearing Drill (Continued)

STEP 4: RACK the Action

4. **RACK** - Release the slide by grasping the rear serrations, pull back (top photo) and release, allowing the slide to slam home (inset photo).

IMPORTANT: Do not maintain your support hand grip on the rear of the slide and attempt to assist or "ride the slide" forward; this practice will often induce a stoppage.
Also: Releasing the slide as shown is preferable to depressing the slide release lever, because 1) the extra energy generated by fully compressing the recoil spring will help the slide fully close, and 2) manipulating the slide release lever is a fine motor skill which degrades under stress.

Double-Feed Clearing Drill (Continued)

STEP 5: READY!

5. **READY** - You are then ready to engage, if warranted.

SECTION 11

Tactical Recovery to the Holster

Developing a smooth and efficient presentation of the pistol from the holster is critical for our survival.

Returning the pistol to the holster in a smooth and efficient manner is just as critical a skill—though this skill is often ignored or given short shrift in comparison to the presentation.

More often than not, the police sidearm is drawn and not fired, because the situation is brought under control. Depending on the circumstances, the officer then must either keep the suspect covered until backup arrives, or reholster his weapon in order to secure the suspect.

If it is necessary to fire the weapon to stop a threat during a real-life encounter, then other considerations must also be taken into account. The involved officer may experience tunnel vision, auditory blocking, or any number of other stress-induced reactions as described in Chapter 1 §3 (*Psychological Manifestations of Stress*). This problem becomes magnified if there is more than one assailant present and the officer's focus becomes "locked on" to only one of them.

Statistics indicate that there will be at least a 40 percent chance that the involved officer will be facing more than one potential assailant in any given lethal force encounter; therefore, it becomes obvious that something must be done to counter these effects. One of the best ways to prepare ourselves to deal with these effects is to train ourselves to overcome them.

As noted above, the tactical reholstering, or "recovery," of the weapon is often overlooked or ignored. Watch most any group of police officers training at the range and you will immediately see the magnitude of the problem regarding this simple act.

Many police officers will reholster very quickly after firing. Many more will then reholster with two hands, the support hand crossing over to the firing hand/holster side. Very often this support hand is passed directly in front of the muzzle as the weapon is being brought into alignment with the top of the holster. The support hand may then be used to either hold open the holster strap, clear some clothing, or even guide the barrel of the weapon down and into the holster in a pseudo-military drill movement.

The problem is further aggravated as the majority of these officers will also take their focus off the target/threat area, shifting their heads and gaze onto their own weapon to watch while they reholster. Obviously, when interacting with a suspect on the street, this would be the moment we would be most vulnerable to a renewed or surprise assault—especially if the rounds we fired did not completely stop the threat!

As any competent firearms instructor will only too gladly tell you, you will do for real exactly what you have ingrained in your subconscious mind while training. That is why we must incorporate the tactical recovery into our firearms training, taking into consideration that the dynamics of a situation do not always cease at the same moment we find it either necessary or desirable to reholster.

Bottom line: The recovery of the weapon must be as tactically sound as the presentation.

How to Perform the TACTICAL RECOVERY

STEP 1: Lower the Pistol

Lower the weapon far enough so you can observe the threat area clearly. If the weapon is equipped with a decocking lever that does not disengage the trigger, it should be depressed when the finger is taken off the trigger—regardless of whether the weapon has been fired or not. This ingrained action is performed automatically, providing one more degree of inherent, "built-in" operator weapon-handling safety.

Tactical Recovery (Continued)

STEP 2: SCAN the Area

Scan with your head 180 degrees to the right and left, looking for secondary threats. Statistics indicate that there will be at least a 40% chance that the involved officer will be facing more than one potential assailant in any given lethal force encounter.

Note that **only the head scans**—the weapon remains stationary. If a threat is detected the weapon is then pointed at it. This practice is both faster and safer than waving the entire shooting platform back and forth—faster due to economy of motion, and safer, for no innocent bystanders or other officers will be covered by the muzzle during the high-stress incident.

Tactical Recovery (Continued)

STEP 3: RECOVER to the Holster

(Left) Maintain focus on the immediate surrounding area as you bring the pistol back toward the center-line of your body. If the pistol is equipped with a manual safety, it may be engaged now if required.

(Right) Release the support hand grip. Keep the support hand ready as shown to re-establish the two-hand grip or use for close-quarter physical defense should another threat be presented or the initial threat resumed.

The primary hand continues to return the pistol to the holster. The thumb should be placed against the rear of the slide or the back of the hammer when reholstering as shown in Chapter 4 §4 (*Holstering the Pistol*).

Note that the pistol is returned to the holster as it was removed—using only ONE HAND.

Tactical Recovery (Continued)

STEP 4: SECURE the Holster

(Left) When returning the pistol to the holster, you may place your index finger along the slide and use it to locate the opening to the holster, as well as manipulate the retaining/safety strap out of the way if necessary. The thumb, placed on the rear of the slide (or back of the hammer), assists as the weapon is securely seated back into the holster by a smooth downward stroke. These techniques are also shown in Chapter 4 §4 (*Holstering the Pistol*).

(Right) Once the pistol is seated, the retaining/safety strap is secured, again using only the primary hand.

Remember: Do *not* redirect your focus to the holster; instead, maintain focus on the threat / target area!

Unlike the presentation, the recovery is to be performed *slowly.* If you rush through the recovery in training, you may find yourself inexplicably holstering after firing at a real threat, only to find that you have not successfully stopped it.

CHAPTER 5

Police Combat Pistolcraft Skills

SECTION 1
Combat Stance

Combat is defined by Webster's Dictionary as "armed fighting; battle."

Stance is defined as "the way one stands, especially the placement of the feet."

So it only stands to reason that a good combat pistolcraft stance would be designed to allow us to best fight while armed with a handgun. For too many years, however, that had not been the case, because the emphasis in pistol training had been placed primarily on the "stance" at the expense of the "combat."

Marksmanship Stances

Above: The NRA "Bullseye" Target Shooting Stance.

There are a number of pistol-shooting stances that have been popularized and promoted over the years. Most of these have their roots in stances developed to aid target shooters place bullets accurately into non-threatening, static targets from various distances while the shooter remained not only stationary, but as still as possible.

That is because the target shooter's objective was the development of precision marksmanship-oriented skills as opposed to close quarter combat-oriented skills. As a result, these various marksmanship-oriented skills and stances that were so helpful in achieving high scores while shooting paper targets at the range began to be referred to as "combat stances" when used to train police and military personnel. The NRA Bullseye Stance shown at right is one such stance. While relegated primarily to competition shooters today, this stance was in general use by military and police organizations until fairly late into the last century.

The fact that the shooter stood rigidly upright and placed his support hand on his hip or in his pocket while practicing a "fighting" skill is one indication of just how confused the issue had been. Regardless of whether the stance was intended to have the shooter hold the pistol with one hand or two (as shown below), these marksmanship-oriented stances don't fill the bill for close quarter combat needs.

Weaver Stance... or the *Fitz* Stance?

The well-known Weaver stance is widely credited to California Sheriff Jack Weaver, the man who popularized it for competition use in the 1950s. A remarkably similar two-hand hold and bladed stance, however, can actually be traced back to at least 1930 and a New Englander named John Henry Fitzgerald (shown at left).

"Fitz" as he was known, was an influential force in American pistol shooting for many years.

(This image is excerpted from a photograph in his book, *Shooting,* published by G.F. Book Co., Hartford, CT., in 1930.)

The Combat Stance

Unlike the Marksmanship Stance, the Combat Stance is a **natural fighting stance** that enables the pistol-armed individual to fight a dangerous adversary effectively and efficiently at the close quarter distances where the vast majority of police-involved shootings occur.

That is because the Combat Stance does not rely on unnatural, highly-stylized body postures and configurations to create a stable platform from which to shoot. Rather, you integrate the pistol into a natural fighting posture, and develop (through practice) the ability to effectively shoot the pistol and hit your adversary.

The components of a good combat stance are listed in the box below. They are both basic and natural.

The following sections of this chapter illustrate how we integrate the pistol into the Combat Stance for great effect while fighting.

Components of the Combat Stance

- **Body is squared to the threat, not bladed.**
- **Body is crouched in an aggressive, forward-leaning fighting posture.**
- **Feet are spread comfortably apart, one foot forward of the other. It does not matter which foot Is forward.**
- **Stance is wide enough so you have good balance, but not so wide that you cannot quickly turn or move in any direction.**
- **Knees are flexed.**
- **The heel of your rearward foot is raised slightly.**

SECTION 2
Point Shooting

Body Point Position From the Holster

Interview Position

When performing the presentation it is a good idea to start from a ready position such as the one shown here.

This does two things for us.

First, it allows us to develop a stable, non-threatening "interview" stance that may be used while working.

Note that the stance is wide and balanced, and the body is bladed, gun or dominant side away. The hands are up and open, primary hand placed on top of the support hand. The fingers are not woven or clenched together.

From this stance we may employ a variety of use of force weapons and tactics without telegraphing our intent.

Second, using this stance while training allows us to practice the specific movements needed to draw the pistol and transition smoothly from our non-threatening interview position into a pistol-fighting combat stance.

Body Point Position From the Holster (Continued)

Side View

1. Move the primary hand directly to the holstered pistol and establish the grip high on the backstrap. Release the retaining snap at the same moment. (See detail on next page.)

Begin to simultaneously assume an aggressive forward crouching position as the support arm begins to move to the support side.

2. Draw the pistol up and out of the holster. Note how the trigger finger position along the side of the slide is already established. Keep the elbow pointed back as opposed to sticking out to the side. A smooth draw is achieved by raising the elbow and allowing the wrist to bend as the pistol is removed from the holster.

Body Point Position From the Holster (Continued)

Side View

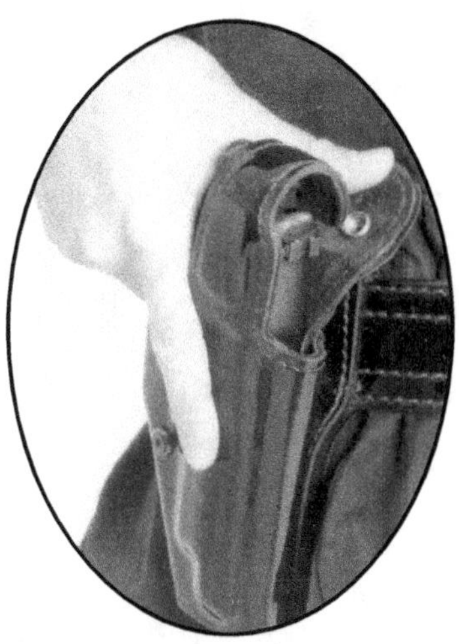

Above: Detail of the retaining snap being released at the same moment the primary grip is established.

Note: This is performed as ONE integrated movement!

3. Lock the primary arm elbow against your side as shown. The pistol (gripped securely, wrist locked) is held level and directly in front of the center of your torso. You are in a full *forward leaning* combat crouch. Depending upon the distance from, and angle to, the target, you may have to elevate the forearm slightly so the pistol's muzzle points directly where you want it on the vertical plane. This will become automatic with practice. Sometimes referred to as the "third eye" concept, this technique enables you to condition or "calibrate" the muzzle or third eye to "look" where your other two eyes are focused. The support arm may be locked across the upper torso or held up next to the head in a defensive position as shown.

Body Point Position From the Holster (Continued)

Opposite Side View

The support hand and arm are held up to protect the head and neck. Hand can be held open or closed. Note that the heel of the rear foot is raised. This assists in promoting an aggressive, balanced, forward-leaning combat stance.

Body Point Position From the Holster (Continued)

Front View

Firing the pistol. The pistol is held on the centerline of the body. The primary arm's wrist may need to be bent slightly outboard to keep the muzzle pointed straight ahead as a result. This is normal.

Full Extension Position From the Holster (**Note:** After completing movements 1-2 as illustrated in the Body Point Position series.)

Side View

1. After the pistol clears the holster, lock your wrist and drive the pistol forward to full extension position. Once fully extended, lock your elbow. To avoid muzzle dipping, the arm may first be locked out holding the pistol pointing at an approximate 45 degree angle to the ground as shown above. The pistol is held centered on the body's vertical midline, yet the muzzle points directly ahead. In order to achieve this, the pistol must be angled slightly to the primary hand side. (This is the same position used when firing from the standing Low Ready Position shown on pages 184-185.)

Full Extension Position From the Holster (Continued)

Side View

2. The primary arm, **wrist and elbow locked**, is then raised like the handle on a pump (pivoting from the shoulder) until it is between your eyes and the intended target point. This is the "vertical lift." As you raise the pistol place your finger on the trigger. At the moment the pistol is locked on target, convulse the primary hand and fire the weapon. EYES ARE ON THE TARGET! When training, hold the pistol at this position for a moment after discharge, and then return it slowly to the low ready prior to performing the Tactical Recovery. (See Chapter 4 §11.)

Full Extension Position From the Holster (Continued)

Two-Hand Hold, Front View

When using a two-hand hold, the support hand grip is established after the pistol is drawn from the holster but prior to driving it forward to full extension.

<u>IMPORTANT</u>: The support hand must not be allowed to pass in front of the weapon's muzzle!

Both arms may be fully extended, elbows locked (as shown), or the support arm elbow may be kept slightly bent and pointed to the ground.

Full Extension Position From the Holster (Continued)

Two-Hand Hold, Side View

The stance illustrated above may be referred to as the Isosceles, the Modern Isosceles, or the Combat Isosceles depending upon minor variations in body position and who you ask.

Regardless of what it is called, when firing the pistol using a two-hand hold keep the wrists locked and the pistol in front of your body along your centerline. The sights may be accessed if possible; however, when point shooting, both eyes are kept open and focused on the threat.

The technique shown above is demonstrated by Bob Taubert, former U.S. Marine and one of the founders of the FBI's elite Hostage Rescue Team (HRT).

Taubert, President of *The Center for Security Studies and Applications, Inc.*, is a well-known and highly sought trainer in the police and military special operations communities.

Point Shooting From the Low Ready Position

Front View

1. The stance is wide and balanced. Place one foot naturally slightly forward of the other. Crouch in an *aggressively forward-leaning posture*.

Raise the heel of the rear foot as shown. The pistol is held in the primary hand at the low ready position, centered on your body. The primary arm is extended; the wrist and elbow are locked. The trigger finger is outside of the trigger guard resting against the frame of the pistol.

The support arm is held out to the side for balance.

Point Shooting From the Low Ready Position (Continued)

Front View

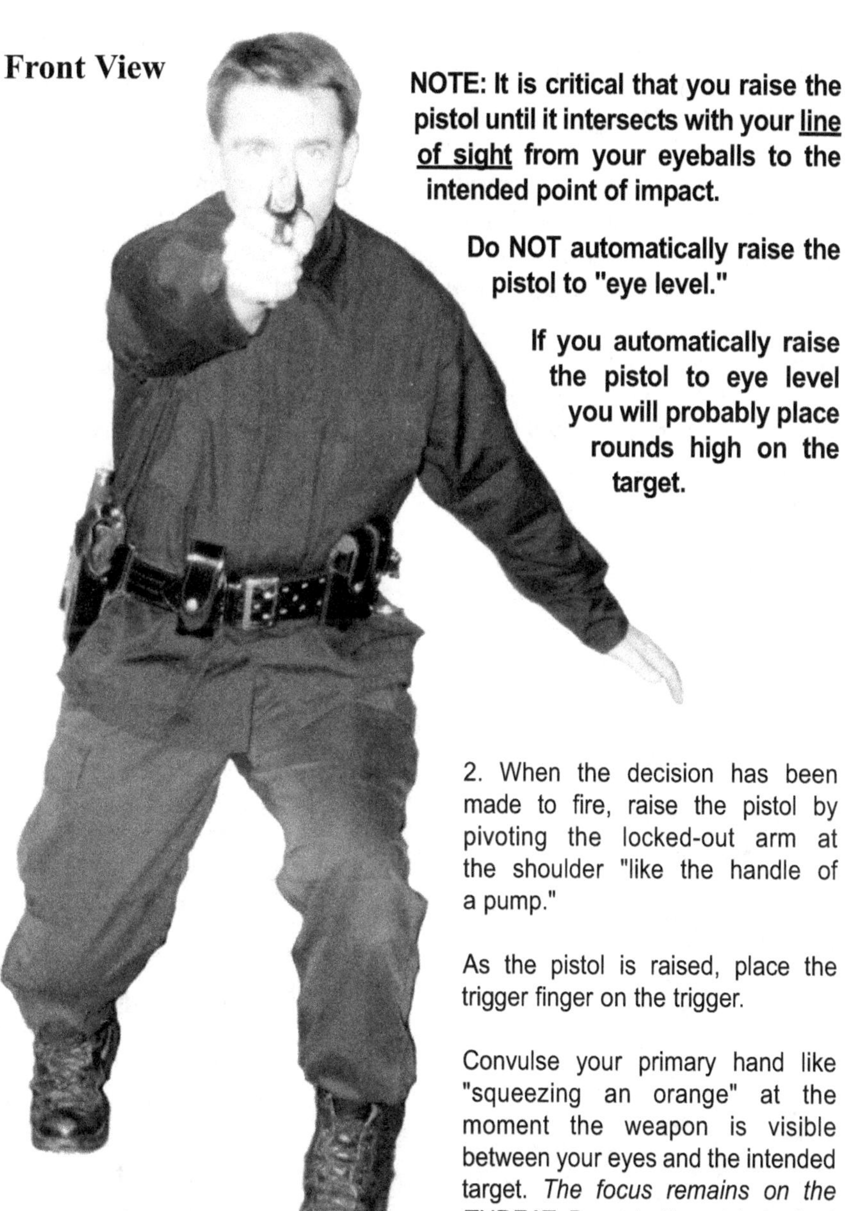

NOTE: It is critical that you raise the pistol until it intersects with your <u>line of sight</u> from your eyeballs to the intended point of impact.

Do NOT automatically raise the pistol to "eye level."

If you automatically raise the pistol to eye level you will probably place rounds high on the target.

2. When the decision has been made to fire, raise the pistol by pivoting the locked-out arm at the shoulder "like the handle of a pump."

As the pistol is raised, place the trigger finger on the trigger.

Convulse your primary hand like "squeezing an orange" at the moment the weapon is visible between your eyes and the intended target. *The focus remains on the THREAT*. Do not attempt to look at or focus on the pistol's sights!

The Close Proximity Drill

This drill is illustrated here to provide an example of a close proximity technique as employed in **DPTC No. 1.** This drill combines both close quarter defensive physical skills and police pistolcraft point shooting skills.

Prior to attempting this drill, you should seek out and receive competent instruction by a trained and certified police firearms instructor.

After instruction and before attempting this drill using live fire, you should perform the drill in three distinct and separate stages as illustrated here using a **safe, clear, and empty weapon**. Only when you can perform the drill safely in a step-by-step manner should you perform it in one uninterrupted sequence.

Once you can consistently perform the drill safely and fluidly, the drill can be performed with live ammunition. The process outlined above should be repeated as you perform the drill slowly, step-by-step, and then in uninterrupted sequence, slowly and fluidly.

Step 1: STRIKE

While standing in front of the target in the *Interview Position* visualize the target attempting to retrieve a deadly weapon from concealment. On the command of **"Make ready...ONE!"** aggressively strike the target in the eyes, throat, or groin.

WARNING! Should your target begin to tip or fall over after you strike it during live fire drills, DO NOT reach out to catch or otherwise prevent it from falling, as death or serious bodily injury may result! LET IT FALL!

Step 2: STEP BACK & INTO BODY POINT POSITION

On the command of **"Ready ...Two!"** take ONE STEP back and present the pistol, assuming the Body Point Position.

NO SHOTS ARE FIRED AT THIS TIME!

Your focus should be on the target's center of mass.

It is imperative that the support arm be held out of the muzzle's line of fire!

Step 3: ENGAGE

On the command, **"Ready... Three!"** fire two rounds into the target.

Then perform a Tactical Recovery to the holster as illustrated in Chapter 4 §11.

The Reactive Movement Drill

This drill is illustrated here to provide an example of a **DPTC No. 2** level exercise. This drill requires you to combine the two point shooting techniques detailed in this section. It also requires you to fire, move, reassess, and fire again, all while maintaining focus on the target and keeping complete control of the weapon using only one hand.

As with the Close Proximity Drill, the Reactive Movement Drill should only be practiced under the supervision of a trained and certified police firearms instructor. Also as with the Close Proximity Drill, this drill should first be performed in three distinct and separate stages as illustrated here using **safe, clear, and empty weapons**. Only when you can perform the drill safely in a step-by-step manner should you perform it in one uninterrupted sequence. Once you can consistently perform the drill safely and fluidly as described here, then you can start the process again using live ammunition. The drill should be performed slowly, step-by-step, then in uninterrupted sequence, slowly and fluidly.

Step 1: MAKE READY

NOTE: When training you must not move or fire faster than you can safely and effectively hit the target.

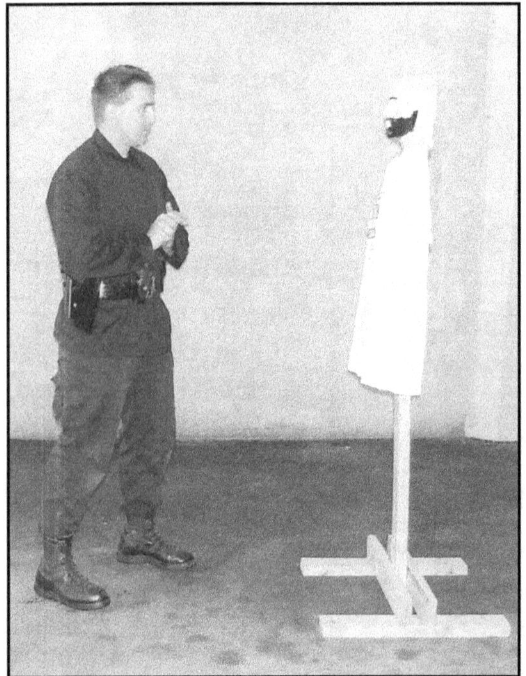

Stand in front of the target in Interview Position.

As with all these drills, your holster must be snapped and pistol secured as worn on patrol.

Step 2: EXECUTE BODY POINT AND FIRE TWO ROUNDS CENTER MASS

On the command of **"Make ready...ONE!"** present the pistol and assume the Body Point Position, firing TWO ROUNDS into the target's center of mass as soon as your position is stabilized.

Step 3: STEP BACK AND INTO FULL EXTENSION POSITION & FIRE ONE ROUND

On the command, **"Ready...Two!"** Take **one step back** (*keeping your body square to the target*) and fully extend your primary hand/arm as shown. Direct your focus and the pistol's muzzle to an alternate target area, preferably the throat or head. Then fire ONE ROUND into this area. **Remember to keep the support arm out of the muzzle's line of fire!**

SECTION 3

Precision Shooting

While point shooting skills can be highly developed, they are primarily intended for close quarter combat use. Precision shooting skills that employ some type of mechanical sight, on the other hand, can be used to great effect at any distance as long as you can physically access the sights and have developed good trigger control.

Because this book is intended as a guide to police pistolcraft as opposed to target marksmanship, we first need to look at the subject of *when* to use the sights rather than just diving into an explanation of *how* to use the sights to aid in precision shooting.

When to Use the Sights

Simply stated, you should use the sights to verify barrel alignment with the target whenever possible.

In regard to the realities of police work, there are certain situations and conditions that may allow you to do just that with the handgun.

Some officers—a very, very small percentage of the overall population in my estimation—are naturally hardwired to be able to access the sights under conditions of close quarter spontaneous combat. These are the Jim Cirillos of the world, a special breed all their own, who in addition to possessing that unique basic ability also devote untold hours to pistol training and practice.

Another small group of officers, most often with extensive military Spec Ops backgrounds (in addition to being what Colonel Dave Grossman refers to as "natural soldiers") and who have received extensive amounts of intensive CQB training, may also be able to overcome and control their natural responses to stress, startle, and fear and switch their focus from that immediate threat to their front sight at the moment of discharge.

For the vast majority of us, however, the likelihood of being able to use the sights of our handguns when facing an immediate deadly threat at close quarters will usually depend on other considerations.

While many would agree that certain factors such as time, distance and availability of cover contribute heavily in the officer's favor in this regard, I have come to believe after years of research, debriefings of numerous officers, and my own personal experiences, that the greatest factor influencing our ability to access the sights is our own perception of where the immediate threat is being directed.

Directed-Threat Perception Theory

If you perceive that the immediate threat is directed *at you personally*, the chances of you being able to take your eyes from the person presenting that threat (or from the weapon in that person's hand) and placing your focus on the front sight of your pistol are slim to none.

If, however, you perceive that the threat is directed *to someone else*, regardless of your distance from the person presenting that threat, then you absolutely may be able to access those sights to verify alignment of the shot.

An example of the type of situation I am referring to was related to me several years ago by an officer in the following way, immediately after we had participated in a meeting during which the relevance of point shooting had been discussed.

This officer and his partner had been dispatched to the scene of what was believed to be a domestic disturbance. As soon as they arrived at the location, the officers heard loud screaming and banging coming from the trailer home. The screaming was so intense that the officers immediately drew their handguns and entered the trailer home, yelling out "Police!" as they rushed into the back bedroom from where the sounds were emanating.

In this room the officers were met with a horrific scene.

"A very large male subject," the officer told me, "was straddled over a small female lying on the floor. As we (he and his partner) entered, the male was in the process of stabbing the woman in the chest with a large kitchen knife. There was blood everywhere. As I watched, the knife was aggressively pulled up and out of the victim, spatters of blood flying off the blade and onto the wall.

I was standing directly behind the assailant, my gun drawn and pointed at him," he continued. "My partner was standing 90 degrees to the side, also facing the assailant, and his gun was also drawn and pointed at the big man."

At this point in the story the officer broke his gaze from the mental image he had been replaying in his mind, looked at me and said, "Now understand what I'm saying here, 'cause I love my partner like he was my own brother, but while we're standing there, guns pointed, blood flying, my partner's yelling at me, saying, 'Shoot him! Shoot him!' Meanwhile, in my own mind, I'm thinking, 'I don't *want* to shoot him, YOU shoot him, YOU shoot him!'

"Finally, as I watched, the knife began to descend again, like in slow motion. I knew I had to shoot to save her, yet I also knew that if I didn't angle the shot correctly, the round could go through him and hit *her*. So what I did was, I lined up my sights as precisely as possible, and stared so hard at them that I could see dust particles on the front sight. The sights, in fact, looked *huge* to me as I fired."

The round entered the back of the assailant's head just as he drove the knife so deep into the victim that it pinned her to the floor. The assailant died at the scene. Unbelievably, the victim survived, owing her life to the officer's actions.

After he finished telling me the story, he said, "So how do you explain that? I was practically right on top of the guy and there's no doubt in my mind as to what I saw."

"... the perception of where the threat is being directed as opposed to the proximity of the officer in relation to the person presenting the threat, is the key ..."

As I considered this, a thought occurred to me. "Let me ask you this..." I started. "At the moment you fired, did you feel that *you personally* were in any direct danger?"

He considered this for a long moment, then replied, "You know, I never really thought about that before. But actually, no, at that moment I didn't. I mean *she* was the one catching the knife, I just wanted to save *her*."

This and many similar stories I've heard have led me to believe that the perception of where the threat is being directed as opposed to the proximity of the officer in relation to the person presenting the threat, is the key to understanding the origins of the conflicting accounts of officers' use of the sights during deadly force encounters.

Indeed, when analyzing reports from the field concerning an officer's ability to access and use the sights, this **directed-threat perception** is perhaps a more important factor than are training memories, involved officers' desires to appear to have conformed to (old paradigm) department training, and the normal stress and confusion experienced during deadly force encounters.

How to use the Sights

First Step: Determining the Master-Eye

Ask most people if they are right or left handed and they will answer instantly. Ask someone if they are right or left *eyed*, however, and they will most likely look at you with an expression similar to that of a hog staring at a wristwatch.

The fact is that one of our eyes *is* usually dominant (preferred for sighting) over the other. Some people—a very small segment of the population—are ***co*-eyed dominant**, which is somewhat analogous to being ambidextrous.

It is important to know which eye is dominant before you begin to learn to shoot using the sights, especially in regard to working with **long guns** (e.g. rifles or shotguns). If you are right handed and left eye dominant—a condition referred to as being **cross eye-hand dominant**—then you will have to make an adjustment either in the way you sight or hold the weapon.

This very common situation can cause problems ranging from mild to severe for the average shooter. If you can catch it early enough, you can eliminate a great many of the complications it causes simply by training yourself to mount and shoot the long gun on the dominant eye side.

Cross eye-hand dominant people who have learned to shoot from their dominant hand side can be easily identified, as they will usually try and maneuver their heads over the weapon's receiver far enough to line up the dominant eye with the sights. This creates undue stress, not to mention discomfort, and usually results in frustration and poor marksmanship.

While it's true that most people can learn to overcome this difficulty simply by getting used to sighting with their non-dominant eye, many people experience a great deal of frustration just trying to get their dominant eyelid to close, especially under stress. In addition, when trying to sight and fire under stressful conditions, many find that their brain will try to restore the natural order and employ the strongest weapons in its physical arsenal—in this case the *dominant* eye—which can induce greater confusion and distress on the shooter.

The good news is that in regard to shooting pistols while employing the sights to verify alignment with the target, the difficulties faced by the cross eye-hand dominant shooter are minimal, and can be pretty much negated simply by ensuring that the shooter is indeed aware of *which of his eyes is dominant.* This is true because of the way the pistol, as opposed to the long gun, is held when firing using the sights.

With the long gun, when you mount the stock on either the left or right shoulder, the sights will naturally be more easily aligned by the eye on that same side. With the pistol, however, the entire weapon system is held well out in front of your face regardless of whether you use one or two hands to grasp it. This allows you to line up the pistol's sights with either eye, simply by slightly angling the weapon on the horizontal plane to the left or right.

By learning sighted fire this way, a lot of confusion is immediately dispensed with.

By way of example, I was taught for years that when firing a pistol with my right hand, I was to sight with my right eye, and when firing with my left hand, I was to sight with my left eye. Now while I agree that it is a great idea to be as flexible and efficient as possible in regard to all forms of pistolcraft skills, including being able to sight and fire with either hand and/or eye, logic indicates that under extreme duress, if you can actually get your eyes to focus on the sights at all, your dominant eye will more than likely be the one called into action as a result of the body's survival mechanisms kicking in.

Logic also indicates that should your dominant eye become damaged or disabled, your brain would automatically shift its resources to the non-dominant eye in order to access the visual information it would find so vital for survival, probably with no conscious awareness on your part.

Requiring people to employ the same hand-same eye technique when training, therefore, might actually do more to add to their confusion should they need to employ sighted fire during an actual event. The only true possible tactical rationale for even teaching people to shoot in this manner, as far as I can see, is to provide them with an advantage they could exploit should they find themselves in a position where they were trying to line up a sighted shot from behind cover, as less of the face will be exposed to incoming fire if the same-side hand and eye are used as you shoot around that cover. While this absolutely has merit, it is a matter I believe is best addressed after the basic skills have been mastered.

Finally, in regard to our co-eye dominant pistol shooters, simply having their condition explained to them (after they've been diagnosed) can instantly clear up years of confusion and help them correct a problem many of them didn't consciously realize they had. For with a co-eyed dominant individual, what often happens is that *both* eyes fight for dominance while the shooter tries to focus on his pistol's front sight. This results in one eye sometimes being used for one shot, and the other for a subsequent shot—all without the shooter's conscious determination or awareness.

After conducting the simple test explained on the following pages, I've had co-eye dominant shooters tell me that for years they had thought that there was something wrong with them, because it seemed like their vision was playing tricks on them as their sight pictures changed from shot to shot.

If You Are Co-Eye Dominant

If you believe you are co-eye dominant, you should try to control the condition as much as possible. Practice half-closing or squinting one of your eyes just enough to blur the image. The neural systems in the brain should then tend to automatically select the unimpeded eye, since both are internally rated as "dominant."

As far as deciding which of your dominant eyes you should use, all things being equal—and in this case, I guess they are—it doesn't really matter except in regard to the tactical considerations described above.

So settle on one of your "Type A" eyeballs, and consciously train yourself to use it consistently.

DOMINANT EYE - the eye which looks directly at an object, while the non-dominant eye views it from the side.

NOTE: The Miles ABC test illustrated on the following pages determines eye dominance based on the limited condition of sighting with your gaze pointed straight ahead. This makes these types of tests appropriate for those involved in activities such as shooting a firearm using sighted fire.

The question of eye dominance, however, is more complicated than hand dominance, and can change under certain circumstances. For instance, ocular dominance has been shown to switch at lateral gaze angles of only 15.5° off center during testing. Eye dominance may also change based upon your age and environmental conditions.

Determining Eye Dominance

1. Donna Losardo demonstrates the Miles ABC test, an effective method for determining eye dominance. First, fully extend the arms and form a small opening about the size of a silver dollar with the hands as shown. Both eyes are open.

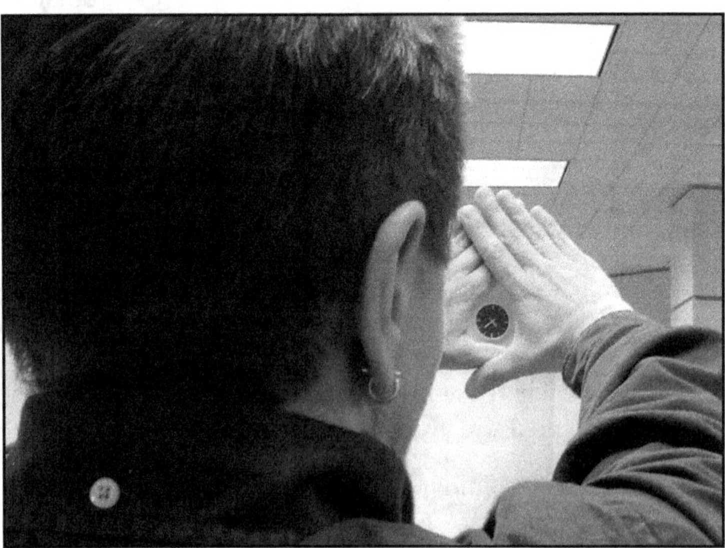

2. **Keeping both eyes wide open** and the arms fully extended, select a distant object (such as the wall clock shown here) and bring the hands up in front of the face. Center the object in the opening formed by the hands.

Determining Eye Dominance (Continued)

3. Then bring the hands back slowly toward the face, while keeping both eyes open and the object centered in the opening formed by the hands.

Whichever eye is looking through the opening once the hands are against the face (as illustrated above) is most likely the dominant eye. This can be verified by performing the test again. If the hands come back to the same eye consistently, you've determined which is the master.

If, however, the opening comes back first to one eye and then the other, you may be co-eye dominant as described in the text.

How to Use the Sights (Continued)

Standard Patridge Front Blade & Rear Notch Configuration

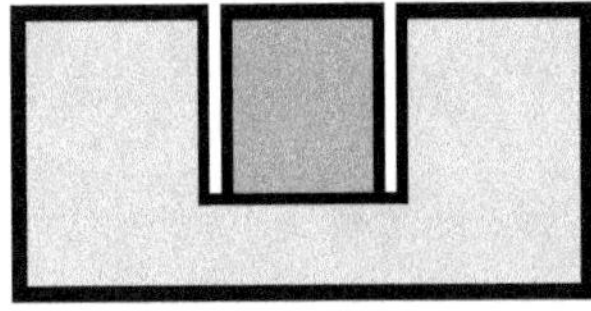

When using typical Patridge-type sights (illustrated at left) to verify that your pistol's barrel is aligned with the object you're going to shoot, place the front sight blade (shown in dark gray) on the object's center of mass, then align the rear notch (shown in light gray) with the front sight so the front sight blade is centered in the middle of the notch.

When aligned properly, you should see the same amount of light on either side of the front blade as you look through the notch (equal light).

The top of the front sight blade should also be even with both tops of the rear sight (equal height).

As you look through the sights at the target, your eyes will only be able to bring one of the three objects—rear sight, front sight, or target—into clear focus.

After **verifying the identification of your target** and ensuring that there is nothing directly around or behind it you are not willing to shoot, focus intently on the front sight, keeping it both aligned with the rear sight and target as described above and in sharp focus.

The sight picture and the front sight focus should be maintained while pressing the trigger to the rear and continued even after the shot is fired. Often referred to as "follow through," this practice helps to increase accuracy and decrease the amount of time it takes to deliver accurate follow-up shots.

The Hexsite™ Sighting System

The Hexsite™

Unlike conventional, Patridge-style iron sights, the patented HexSite™ has been designed to allow the operator to focus on the target, not on the sights, while keeping both eyes open.

Due to the unique design of the HexSite, the operator is able to do just that while still benefiting from the presence of the sights. That is because the HexSite has been designed to be looked *through*, not at, while the operator is engaged in close combat.

This is in direct contrast to the approach E.E. Patridge took over 100 years ago when he first created the sights that would become the standard model for handguns, for Patridge's intent was to create a set of sights that could be easily accessed and *focused upon* while firing. That's because Patridge was trying to produce sights for *target shooting, not combat shooting.*

The Hexsite consists of a rear hexagonal-shaped aperture and a specially-machined front blade sight. The extensively-machined rear aperture offers 16 angular reference points that are subconsciously accessed when the pistol's sights are aligned with the eye and one-another.

What it boils down to is this: while the shooter is seeing the target, the subconscious is "seeing" the sight.

When using the Hexsite for precision shooting, you simply align the sights as described and focus on the front sight as you do with Patridge-type sights.

While the Hexsite is undergoing extensive testing and trials as of this writing, I believe it may one day become the preferred handgun sight for police and military combat applications.

Precision Shooting, Sights, and the "Seasoned" Shooter

Once the eyes reach the age of forty, the lenses normally begin to lose flexibility. This results in the gradual loss of ability to focus on near objects.

As this loss proceeds incrementally, the "point of accommodation" (or the distance away from the eye at which clear focus is able to be achieved) slowly but surely moves further away from the eye.

One way to monitor this cruel wont of nature, if you're of a mind to do so, is to extend your dominant arm as if holding a pistol, and with your other hand hold a piece of paper with some fine print on it just above your dominant arm. Move the paper back and forth until the print appears sharp and clear. This is your current point of accommodation. Then check it every few months or so, and you'll be able to determine just how much flexibility your lenses are losing as that paper has to be held further and further from your eye so you can read it.

Eventually, that piece of paper will be out in front of where the sights on your pistol are located when the weapon is held at full extension. And when that happens, the whole notion of front-sight focused sight picture has become moot, for all three objects—rear sight, front sight, *and* target—will appear blurry as you try and focus on that front sight.

When asked for suggestions by officers who've reached this stage and haven't elected to go with special, multi-lensed shooter's glasses (something I don't recommend for active police officers), I usually advise them 1) don't stress out over it, as it's a natural process, and 2) instead of worrying about it, just *go with it*—for even if both of the sights are a little blurry, you still should be able to line them up properly on the target. Just stay true to form, press the trigger smoothly so you don't disturb the sight alignment and you'll do fine.

Of course, if the shooter's eyesight is such that the *target* cannot be clearly identified, *then* we are dealing with an entirely different matter that must be immediately addressed, either through the acquisition of corrective lenses or other corrective action.

Precision Shooting: It's All About Control

Before we can we use our pistols to control other people's out of control, life threatening behavior, we must first be able to *control our pistols.*

And before we can control our pistols, we must be able to control *ourselves*.

In regard to delivering bullets to such a target with the handgun, our chances of hitting the threat-presenting suspect precisely where it will do the most good are increased substantially if the sights can be accessed and employed properly.

In my first book, *In the Line of Fire*, I noted the two-part "secret" formula for achieving great sighted shooting:

1) properly line up the sights of the weapon on the target, and then
2) cause the weapon to discharge *without disturbing that sight alignment.*

I also offered an acronym that I believed was more accurate than BRASS (Breathe, Relax, Aim, Squeeze, Surprise) and its variants in relating the process best used to deliver precision rounds when more than trophies were at stake.

This acronym, ***CAPS***, stands for *Control, Aim, Press, Surprise.*

C ***ONTROL*** includes keeping your mind as focused as possible and your body functioning as near to normal levels as possible. Simply by employing the "combat breathing" technique described in Chapter 1 §5, you will be able to regain and/or maintain a great deal of control and better achieve both of these objectives. Control also refers to maintaining an effective grip on the handgun itself, something that may be harder than you might imagine especially when operating under stressful environmental and/or psychological conditions.

A ***IM*** is described in the *How to Use the Sights* section above. With Patridge-type sights this can be reduced to "Equal Height, Equal Light—Focus on front sight."

P ***RESS*** the trigger straight back smoothly as possible. Resist the urge to "stage" the trigger while firing double action. This practice of pressing the trigger so slowly that you can see and hear the separate stages of hammer movement is not desirable. Smoothness and speed are the goals.

S ***URPRISE*** doesn't mean we didn't know the pistol was going to fire, because obviously that is the purpose of the exercise. What it means is that we didn't allow our subconscious to alter our grip, stance, or both to *meet, control, or reflexively flinch in anticipation of the shot being fired* and the attendant recoil.

There are several methods that can be used to assist us to avoid and/or overcome problems generated by an inability to achieve this controlled surprise. Five of the best dry-fire and live-fire drills are described below for consideration.

DRY-FIRE DRILLS

DF-1) The Wall Drill: George Harris from the SIG SAUER Academy reportedly developed this effective **dry-fire drill**.

After ensuring your pistol is absolutely **safe, clear, and empty**, face a **blank wall** and get into a good shooting stance.

Keeping the pistol up in firing position, move forward until the muzzle of your pistol just touches the wall. Then back away from the wall about an inch.

DRY-FIRE: Manipulating the action while the pistol is unloaded.

SAFETY ALERT! Always check and recheck your pistol to ensure it is SAFE, CLEAR, and EMPTY prior to dry-firing!

Also: check with your armorer to ensure that your weapon can be dry-fired without damaging it. Some people believe that dry-firing any weapon will cause damage, but there are many that can be dry-fired to your heart's content (while assembled) without worry. Dry-firing any unassembled weapon, however, may result in damage to internal parts.

Snap caps (above) are inert plastic or metal rounds designed primarily to protect the firearm's ignition system. They are constructed with a spring-loaded primer cap that cushions the firing pin when you dry-fire your pistol. Snap caps are available from several manufacturers in a variety of calibers.

Keeping just the sights aligned (there is no target), press the trigger smoothly and steadily until the hammer falls. The goal is to develop smooth trigger manipulation, and this drill assists you in that by eliminating all distractions. Be sure to practice the drill a number of times, working the trigger in single and/or double action depending upon your pistol's action.

DF-2) The Coin Drill: Similar to the Wall Drill, this **dry-fire drill** is conducted by placing a coin (a U.S. dime works well) on the slide just behind the front sight while holding the **safe, clear, and empty** pistol in firing position.

Then manipulate the trigger while keeping the sights aligned and try to do so without disturbing the alignment and dropping the coin. The challenge is to manipulate the trigger repeatedly without having to pick up the coin. (See page 379 for more information.)

LIVE-FIRE DRILLS

LF-1) Ford's Rawhide Technique: An excellent method to help control and then eliminate anticipation problems while live firing is Ford's Rawhide Technique. The name is derived from the person who taught it to me, and the song it brings to mind while you perform it. When trying to help a shooter overcome an anticipation problem, I generally explain it like this:

Part of the brain is always afraid. It is a survival function. The part of the brain that initiates the fight-or-flight response is also with us at the range, when we are firing deadly weapons. It is one of the reasons that some shooters lean way back while firing, for this indicates a subconscious desire to get away from the gun and the firing. It is also this part of the subconscious that speaks to us while we are pressing the trigger. Over and over it says, "Here it comes, it's going to fire, here it comes. . ."

You know this is going on when, as you're pressing the trigger, you feel tense and occasionally see the weapon in your hands dip a bit while you're pressing, but before it fires.

Here is the root of your anticipation problem. One way to rewire your brain, so to speak, is by giving this part of your mind something else to think about. The exercise goes like this:

With the weapon on target, take a deep breath. Align the sights on your target. Focus on the front sight. Then, as you begin a steady trigger press to the rear, you say, out loud, **"Rolling, rolling, rolling, rolling. . ."**

What this does, in effect, is to give the subconscious mind something else to think about, replacing the "Here it COMES, here it COMES . . ."

Therefore, when the weapon discharges, your sights are lined up on target and you are surprised. That translates into a hit.

The key to using this technique is to say the "Rolling, rolling, rolling" in a **monotone** and **out loud**—loud enough for you to hear it. Some people are uncomfortable with this at first, afraid that if anyone hears them talking out loud—seemingly to their pistols—that they will become candidates for the rubber-gun squad.

But the truth of the matter is that most of your fellow officers at the range are so involved with what they are doing that they won't notice. And even if they do, you will be so happy with the results that you won't care.

After using this technique for a while, you will find your anticipation problem clearing up. If it resurfaces occasionally, which it might, simply roll out this training exercise and give yourself a tune-up.

LF-2) The Dummy Round Drill: Another good exercise to help eliminate the all-too-common anticipating or flinching of the weapon is to mix good quality dummy rounds with live ammo when you are practicing at the range. If you are anticipating, it will become extremely obvious when the hammer drops on one of these "duds" and you watch the barrel of your weapon take a nose-dive for the deck in your hands.

Note: Incorporating the TIRR Clear Drill into this drill is also extremely beneficial. (Reference Chapter 4 §10.)

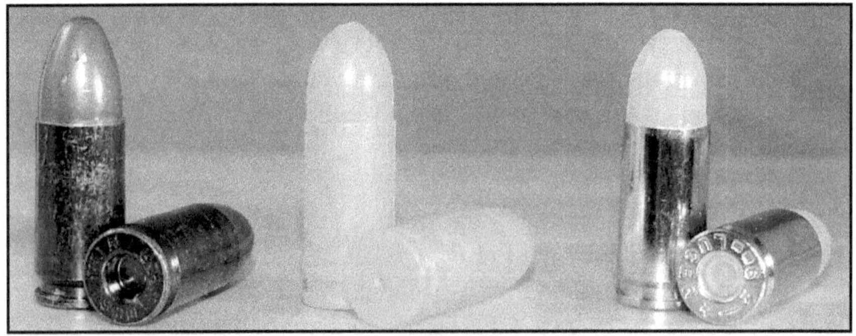

Dummy rounds are made from steel (left), 100% synthetic, orange-colored plastic (center), and brass or nickel cases with bright orange one piece ABS plastic inserts (right). These last rounds, produced by ST Action Pro, Inc. are the best choice. They last a long time, are easy to find on the ground, and don't damage the pistol.

LF-3) The Reset Drill: The Reset Drill is one of the best drills to assist you to improve your precision shooting skills.. Illustrated below with a double/single action pistol, but may be used with any type action.

1. Achieve good stance, grip, and sight *alignment*. Choose and aim at a specific spot on the target. Acquire a good sight *picture*, and focus on FRONT SIGHT. Place finger on trigger.

2. Smoothly press trigger to rear in one stroke, firing weapon. Do not "stage the trigger" by pressing slowly. **CONTINUE to HOLD TRIGGER to REAR** through recoil, **CONTINUE TO MAINTAIN FOCUS ON FRONT SIGHT!**

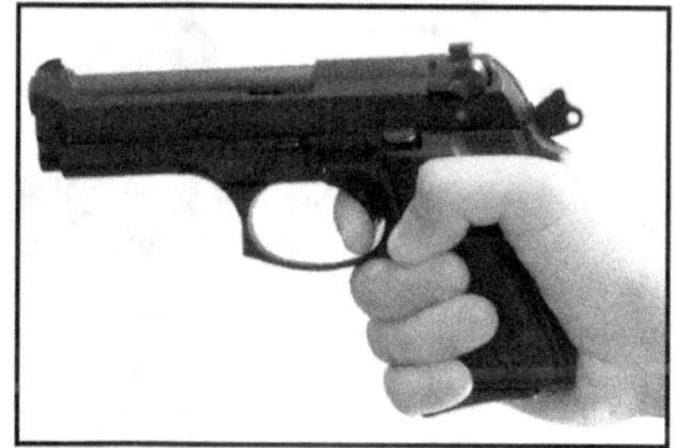

3. Once movement of pistol has stopped, maintain trigger finger contact with trigger and SLOWLY allow trigger to move forward until reset "CLICK" is heard. Then press the trigger *gently* and take up the slack until you feel it re-engage the sear (feels like hitting a "wall") **BUT STOP BEFORE IT DROPS THE HAMMER**... This may take getting used to—*don't give up!*

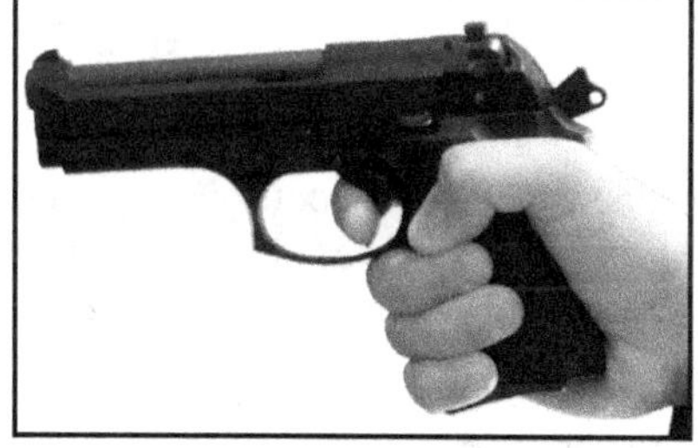

4. Keeping the trigger held against the sear, realign the sights, using the hole generated by first shot as aiming point for next shot. Then **FRONT SIGHT, PRESS and HOLD!** Repeat process for following shots. (Photos by K.P. Conti.)

The Reset Drill (Continued)

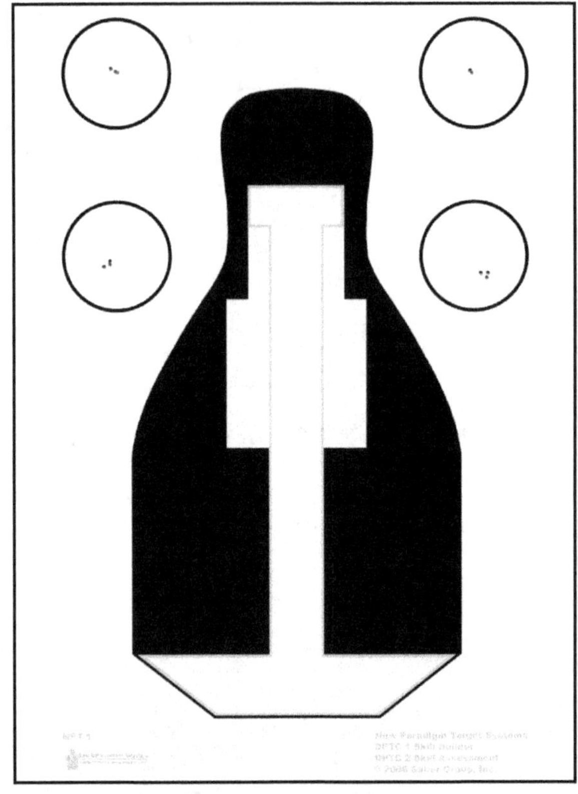

Though you may shoot tighter groups and looser groups than those shown above, these are typical results of the **Reset Drill** after the technique is understood and practiced. Recommended distance from target is 3 yards. (See page 376.)

There are four 3-shot groups visible on the target. Groups are fired in the following sequence during **DPTC No. 1** (Skill Builder Course):

1)Top circle, to right of silhouette: **TWO-HAND HOLD, RIGHT HAND PRIMARY**, then DECOCK (if pistol is so equipped). Next:

2) Bottom circle, to right of silhouette: **ONE-HAND HOLD, RIGHT HAND PRIMARY**, then DECOCK and transfer pistol to left hand. Then:

3) Top circle, to left of silhouette: **TWO-HAND HOLD, LEFT HAND PRIMARY**, DECOCK and finally:

4) Bottom circle, to left of silhouette: **ONE-HAND HOLD, LEFT HAND PRIMARY**, DECOCK, reload, and recover to holster.

SECTION 4
Alternative Shooting Positions

For the purposes of this book, we will only be discussing two alternative shooting positions, the kneeling and the standard prone. Both are employed in the basic New Paradigm Program. Variations of these positions, such as the inverted and downed-officer shooting positions, are used in advanced iterations. These will be included in future editions of this book.

Kneeling

The kneeling position provides us with many tactical advantages. Primarily it makes us a smaller target while still allowing us to deliver rounds from a stable platform and preferably, from behind cover.

Kneeling, One Knee, Unsupported

To assume this position, simply take a step forward with either foot and lower the other knee to the ground. Body positioning from the waist up is consistent with that used in the standing position. Note how the toes of the rearward foot are placed against the ground. This facilitates quick movement from this position. Also note distance from cover. Arm's length plus the length of the weapon is recommended.

Alternative Shooting Positions (Continued)

Kneeling, Two Knees, Unsupported

To assume this position, bring both feet on line and lower your body into a squatting position. When your bent knees are close to the ground, simply transfer your weight forward and allow your knees to make controlled contact with the ground. Then rock your upper body back into a comfortable, balanced shooting position.

This position is ideal for firing from behind cover because you can lean to either side with equal ease and stability.

Again, note the positioning of the toes. By keeping the toes in this position as opposed to straight back, you should be able to get up onto your feet by rocking your weight back over your feet, and then standing up.

Alternative Shooting Positions (Continued)

Kneeling, Self-Supported

The upper body is rocked back, buttocks lowered onto the rearward foot's heel. As pointed out in the previous photographs, the toes of the rearward foot should be pointed forward as illustrated. This will allow for quick movement should it be necessary.

The support arm (above the elbow) is rested on the support knee, avoiding bone to bone contact. The side of the face may be rested against the inside of the primary arm against the biceps, forming a "cheek-weld," and helping to stabilize the shooting platform. (Al Pereira photo.)

Alternative Shooting Positions (Continued)

Prone Position

The prone position can be assumed in a number of ways. When operating in the real world you will probably get there in great haste as a response to shots fired at you, or as a result of tripping, falling, or being thrown to the ground during a struggle.

The method illustrated in this section is provided as a safe, realistic option that may be used during training, as well as having applications for real-world employment.

This method is, in essence, a modified version of the "rollover prone" technique. It is presented in a step-by-step format for consideration.

1 From the Interview Position (left), **KNEEL DOWN AND PLACE BOTH KNEES ON THE DECK** as shown in photo at right.

Note the distance from the cover.

Prone Position (Continued)

2 Once in the kneeling position, **DRAW YOUR PISTOL AND COME TO THE LOW READY POSITION** as shown above.

3 Keeping the pistol pointed in a **SAFE DIRECTION** and **FINGER OFF THE TRIGGER, BEND FORWARD AT THE WAIST** and **PLACE THE PALM OF YOUR SUPPORT HAND FLAT ON THE GROUND IN FRONT OF YOU.**

Prone Position (Continued)

4 **NEXT, PLACE YOUR PRIMARY FOREARM ON THE GROUND,** palm-side facing up, and **ANCHOR YOUR ARM** in position there.

Do not allow the pistol's muzzle to be turned left or right; rather, keep it pointed downrange, in a **SAFE DIRECTION** at all times.

Keep your **FINGERS OFF** the **TRIGGER**, alongside the frame.

5 Finally, **GET DOWN AROUND THE PISTOL.** Once you are prone, adjust your position until you are comfortable and able to achieve a good sight picture from behind cover.

Prone Position (Continued)

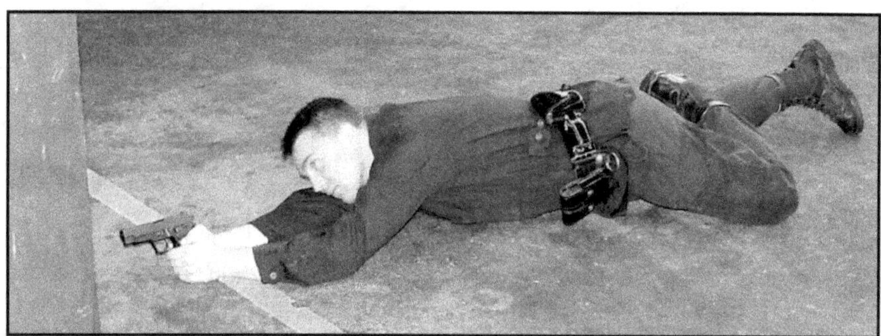

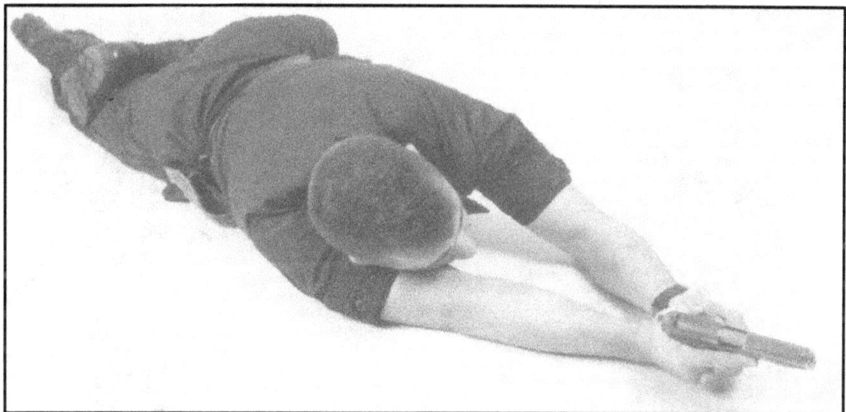

Above: You should try different variations of the prone position to find the one that works best for you. Hooking the support-side foot behind the primary-side knee as shown is one option.

Right: Keeping the arms and hands in contact with the ground while resting the head on the upper arm provides a stable shooting platform while proned out.

SECTION 5
Transition Drill

Transitioning immediately from one level of force option to another must be practiced. Only by practicing can we avoid finding ourselves "freezing up" when faced with a serious imminent threat.

When transitioning from an Aerosol Subject Restraint (ASR) spray or baton to a higher level of force option, the ASR or baton should be immediately released (not thrown—this eats up time!) from the hand and the alternate weapon accessed by the dominant hand.

Don't waste the time required to return the ASR or baton to the carrier prior to accessing the higher level force option when necessary!

Transitioning From the ASR to the Baton

1. While holding the ASR, a threat requiring a higher level use of force option (though not deadly force) is perceived.

2. ASR is released (not thrown or tossed away) as ...

Transitioning From the ASR to the Baton (Continued)

3. ...primary hand begins presentation of baton. There is no hesitation. Baton is accessed and...

4. ...presentation of baton is completed.

Transitioning From the ASR to the Pistol

While holding the ASR, a deadly threat is perceived by the officer.

The ASR is released and allowed to fall freely to the ground as...

... the primary hand begins the presentation of the pistol.

There is no hesitation!

The holstered pistol is accessed and...

Transitioning From the ASR to the Pistol (Continued)

...presentation of pistol is completed.

You should also practice issuing a verbal challenge when performing this drill. A simple command such as "POLICE! Don't move!" is preferable to long or complicated commands.

Cover should also be accessed and utilized whenever possible.

(Transition techniques demonstrated by Paul Damery.)

PLEASE NOTE!

Transitioning from deadly force (pistol) to a lower level of force (ASR, baton, empty hands) should also be practiced.

It must be understood that when transitioning from the pistol to a lower level use of force option, the pistol should be reholstered first, *not released to fall to the ground or into the wrong hands*!

While this may be obvious, we realize that we will act as we have trained. And if we have not practiced transitioning to both higher and lower level force options, then we will not be sure just what we will do in an actual situation.

TRAIN AS YOU FIGHT!

SECTION 6
Moving Target: Engaging One and Becoming One

Engaging Moving Targets: The Basics

In the real world a human being can move in many directions. The following guidelines are intended to assist you in the development of the skills needed to accurately engage a moving subject who presents an immediate deadly threat.

Laterally Moving Target

When engaging a threat that is moving laterally across your field of view, take cover if possible and employ one of the following techniques.

Tracking Technique: Concentrate on the front sight if possible. If not, focus on a specific part of the suspect's anatomy while keeping the pistol pointed and locked on target. Track the moving target while pressing the trigger as smoothly as possible. **Continue to move the weapon with the target before, during and after firing.** Do not stop the movement to take the shot when tracking, as your rounds will more than likely impact behind the target. In regard to "leading" the target:

- If the target is moving laterally or obliquely (on an angle) toward or away from you at a speed of less than 10 miles per hour, at distances inside 15 yards, move the weapon with the target, concentrating on a specific spot on the target through the sights. There is no lead.

- For distances of 15-20 yards, move the weapon with the target, concentrating on the front leading edge of the target through the sights.
- For distances greater than 20 yards (to 30 yards), lead the forward edge of the target by approximately 4 inches.

These guidelines regarding lead are based upon average pistol ammunition velocities. The best way to learn the most effective way to employ your pistol when engaging a moving target is to practice using the ammunition you will be carrying on duty.

Trapping Technique: Trapping is best used from behind cover when the moving subject presents an immediate threat to others, or is currently moving laterally or obliquely away from you. This is because the trapping technique requires you to focus your vision not directly on the threat subject, but at a point slightly ahead of his perceived route of movement. (It is important to note that trapping is also best performed by employing the pistol's sights—something that may be extremely difficult, if not impossible, to do when facing a threat perceived to be coming directly at you.)

To perform the technique, as noted above you **pick a spot directly in front of the moving subject's direction of travel and focus at that point.** Remaining in a stationary position, press the trigger when the subject physically intersects with your aiming point.

Overtaking Technique: This third technique is used to catch up to and "overtake" a threat subject already on the move.

With this technique, you align your pistol on the horizontal axis of the threat subject's direction of travel and swing your pistol using a tracking movement toward the target. Once you catch up to the target, you have two options.

The first is to continue with a smooth tracking action and employ the Tracking Technique as described previously.

The second option is to move your weapon's sights through the target and stop at a point slightly ahead of the target. The pistol is then held stationary, and fired at the moment the moving target physically intersects the point of aim as described in the Trapping Technique section.

Each of these techniques are easily learned and mastered with a bit of practice.

Engaging Moving Targets: Additional Considerations

Engaging laterally moving targets is the most common type of moving target training provided to police officers. Most "running man" target systems are set up to provide a laterally moving target. In the real world, however, threat subjects are not limited to movement on this lateral plane.

To engage a threat subject moving **directly away from you**, simply engage as you would a stationary target that is slowly being reduced in size.

If the threat subject is moving **directly toward you**, you may feel overwhelmed or disoriented. While your eye will most likely be drawn to the subject's weapon, you should try to focus on a specific sighting location on the subject's body (a button on the shirt, for example) and engage as you would a stationary target. When practicing this technique in training, remember that the goal is *not* to hit the button, but the shirt and torso behind it! The button (or whatever aiming point is available) just serves to sharpen and narrow the focus.

Becoming the Moving Target: The Basics

Because the vast majority of police firearms training has traditionally been focused upon static (stationary) shooting skill development, the idea of moving before, during, or after shooting is relatively new to many officers.

This focus on stationary training is not right. It is, in fact, quite wrong.

Violent attacks and fights in general are typically dynamic affairs, with a lot of movement, confusion, and (very often) direct physical contact between combatants.

Conditioning officers to stand rigidly in one place before, during, and after shooting their pistols while training will most likely ensure that they will do one of three things when faced with an actual threat:

1) they will stand rigidly in one place before, during, and after exchanging rounds with an assailant. This often results in the officer standing stationary, exposed to incoming fire, even if cover is close by.

2) they will respond by moving, perhaps while firing their pistol. If they have never practiced this before, chances are great they will panic and fire ineffectively, or worse, injure themselves or others while leaving the assailant unscathed. Chances are also great that they may move in an inefficient and possibly inappropriate manner, placing themselves in greater danger as a result. (E.g., by running away from the threat while staying

exposed, or by running into traffic or other dangerous area, etc.)

3) they may enter a dissociative state, freezing in place. This obviously places the officer (and those around him) in great jeopardy.

There are ways to minimize the possibility of these undesirable responses being exhibited. A few are provided here for consideration.

Add Movement to Static Shooting Drills: Simply taking a step to the right or left before or after firing on static targets is the first step to breaking the static conditioning trap. Be advised, however, that if you have been shooting pretty much exclusively from a stationary position for any length of time, adding this simple step will actually be a BIG step! So don't be surprised (or disappointed in yourself) should you have a little difficulty doing this smoothly right from the start. Take your time, allow yourself the chance to "rewire" your conditioned responses, and stick with it! It won't actually take as long as it may seem to.

Learn to Move Safely in ANY Direction with Pistol in Hand: As a police officer, you will have many occasions to move through a variety of environments with a loaded pistol in your hand.

You *must* be confident in your ability to do this safely. Of even greater importance, your confidence must be based on having done this in training first, so the chances of your doing it unsafely are reduced. Too often I have seen officers pointing their pistols at other officers, innocent persons, and even themselves with no conscious realization while operating in the world. This can be directly attributed (in most cases) to the fact that they were never required to be concerned with keeping the pistol pointed in any other direction than **downrange** while in training. And as we all know, **THERE IS NO DOWNRANGE IN THE REAL WORLD!**

One technique that can be used to assist us in keeping our muzzles pointed in a safe direction when moving with pistol in hand is known as **Position "Sul."** (This technique is shown and described on page 224.)

Learn to Shoot Effectively While Moving: Learning to shoot effectively while you are moving is another critical skill that must be developed. You should learn to deliver rounds accurately to a static target while you're on the move during the initial stages of your training. Exercises that have you firing while moving directly toward, or while backing directly away from the target are an excellent first step.

Changing direction: Maintain your point shooting "ready" position when engaging threat targets by pivoting to face any threats you encounter. This includes when you are stationary as well as when on the move. (Illustration adapted from *Kill or Get Killed.*)

Once you have mastered these exercises, you should be exposed to more complicated drills such as the "Serpentine Drill." This drill is fully detailed in the *Police Pistolcraft* instructor's manual (Appendix O).

Condition Yourself to Move: The use of a conditioned threat response can be integrated into the training drills. Many departments already train their officers to sound off with a response such as "GUN!" when a threat firearm is observed. Simply by modifying this to "GUN! MOVE!" you can ingrain a verbalized threat response that will initiate a conditioned physical response in yourself.

In other words, you see the gun and automatically shout "GUN—

MOVE!" Your subconscious then responds to this command and compels you to move. How effectively this works, and how appropriately you respond will be directly influenced by the quality and amount of training you've previously participated in.

Courses such as the "Officer as the Moving Target Drill" are designed around this principle. (Reference *Police Pistolcraft,* Appendix O.)

Train Yourself to Look For and Move to Cover: Cover is defined as something that will stop bullets. If your body parts are behind cover, bullets will not penetrate them. This is known as "a good thing." The next section explains how and why you should become a true "lover of cover."

> **! REMEMBER: There is NO DOWNRANGE in the real world! Always control your pistol's muzzle!**

Vastly different than the sterile, controlled environment of the training range, the real world presents a dynamic and constantly changing environment populated primarily by innocent, law abiding people. It is up to us to control our pistols as well as any threat subjects we may need to deal with.

Position Sul

Position Sul is a ready position that allows for safer movement with pistol in hand while moving through environments where no immediate threat is perceived, but having the pistol in your hand is justified (e.g., stacking on a door prior to taking part in a warrant service entry; performing in an overwatch security capacity, etc.).

The technique was reportedly first developed in 1997 by Max Joseph of TFTT and Alan Brosnan of TEES while they were training Portuguese-speaking clients. (See www.tftt.com and www.tees-training.com for more information.) "Sul" means "south" in Portuguese, and was used as a short command for "muzzle down."

According to the developers, when performed correctly the muzzle is directed at the ground about 12-18 inches in front of you. **The muzzle must not be allowed to cover your body parts nor anyone else's.** The presentation (using a one- or two-hand grip) is fast and smooth from this position. The support palm is held flat against the solar plexus. The middle finger knuckle of the primary hand should be in contact with the index finger knuckle of the support hand as shown. Elbows are held against the torso.

This position is considered somewhat controversial in some circles. However, when taught correctly and employed properly, it provides an excellent, reality-based, alternative ready position for the armed professional. (See page 328 for more information.)

SECTION 7
Cover & Concealment

Assailant's View: These officers, approaching the darkened interior of a building, have failed to use either cover or concealment. This has placed them in great danger from any assailants who may be lying in wait!

As police officers, it is in our best interest to develop a strong sense of awareness of our surroundings. One of the things we want to be most aware of is the location and type of cover around us.

For our purposes, "cover" is defined as something that will stop bullets. While this definition is accurate, it's not as clear cut as it may seem simply because there are so many varieties of guns and ammunition in the world. As a result, some cover may stop some bullets but not others.

The important thing here is to take the time to train yourself to 1) be aware of cover and potential cover, and 2) make it a habit to use your environment to your advantage. To do this, you must also understand the concept of "concealment."

Concealment refers to the hiding or disguising of your body so your adversary cannot see and/or visually acquire you as a target.

PLEASE NOTE: *Being properly concealed does not equate to being in a position of cover!*

You can become completely concealed in a thick stand of hedges, yet be completely exposed to incoming rounds should an assailant decide to shoot wildly into the hedge on a hunch that you are there.

The same applies to using the improperly named "cover of darkness." Again, darkness may provide concealment, but won't stop rounds. This is especially true in today's technologically advanced world, as night vision devices are readily available (and affordable) in most sporting good stores or through the Internet.

Cover vs. Concealment Awareness Exercise

In regard to developing a good sense of "cover & concealment awareness," start by asking yourself these questions now:

- Where in the typical house can you find true cover?
- What part of an automobile provides the best cover?
- What is the best way to move from one position of cover to another?

Answers to these questions are provided on the following pages. The exercise, however, is for you to think about them first, then read the answers, and then think about them some more. For the answers will change as the questions change, and the questions will vary depending upon the environment you are operating in.

Movement to Cover

When moving to cover, or from one position of cover to another, get there as quickly as possible. Moving laterally from one point to another may allow you to utilize the next piece of cover with less exposure time than if you moved directly forward to it. Use the angles to your advantage! Check and clear any cover you may be approaching, especially if there is a potential for hidden hazards such as assailants, hazardous devices, etc.

Remember not to crowd your cover! Rather, stay back at least an arm's length plus the length of your weapon from it so long as you are still protected from incoming fire by it. This will help you avoid ricochet, spalling, or penetration damage, as well as give you a better field of view.

Angles of Attack

It is also critical that you understand the "angles" relating to the use of cover.

Since bullets travel in a (fairly) straight line, you can pretty much estimate their path of travel *if you are sure* of their origin point (the adversary's firearm). If that is the case, your primary concern will be to maneuver yourself so that something solid (that will stop that particular bullet) is between the point of origin and your body.

The tricky thing here is that the angles can be changed very quickly simply by you or the adversary moving just a few degrees. The further the distance between you, the less movement required to totally change the angles of view and therefore, the angles of attack.

Too Close for Comfort!

INCORRECT USE OF COVER! This is what your adversary would see if you were to snuggle up nice and close to your cover like people tend to . . .

(Above) BETTER USE OF COVER! . . . while this is what he would see if you maintained some distance as shown below. Make sure to choose your cover as wisely as you can. The empty plastic barrel shown is used only to demonstrate the technique. It would be much better if it was filled with cement!

Another aspect of these angles of attack that are often overlooked is this: even if you are in an excellent position of cover, unless you take care to ensure that *all* of your body parts are behind the cover, you can still get hit! This is another one of those things that seems to be so obvious that it doesn't need to be commented upon. However (and it *is* a big however), it is very common for people to be hunkered down behind cover and be totally unaware that their legs, feet, arms, elbows, or derrieres are sticking up, out, over, or around their cover. So take care to mentally inventory *all* your issued body parts when getting into a position of cover!

Additional Cover Considerations

Make it a studied habit to be aware of available cover anytime you are operational. If you suspect that a problem or danger is imminent, start picking out potential sites of cover, **as well as escape routes**.

Available cover should always be utilized to the best of your ability! As a general rule of thumb, it's best to look or **shoot from around the side of cover**, or even from beneath your cover, as opposed to shooting over the top of it.

Dwellings: In most modern houses or apartments, you may find there is actually not a lot of solid cover available. Bullets may pass easily through frame-built walls unless they hit one of the narrow studs. Appliances like refrigerators are actually of little use as cover; though they are large they have few solid metal components other than the compressor which is usually small and mounted on the very bottom. **Chimneys or foundations** may provide the best cover in these types of structures.

Vehicles: Vehicles also provide very little true cover. Most bullets pass easily through standard safety glass. Bullets also may penetrate through the sheet metal exterior panels of most vehicles unless the bullet hits something solid within the panel. As for the motor... the next time you open the hood of your car take a good look and see just how much open space is inder there, especially from a head-on perspective. If the bullet doesn't hit motor but strikes the firewall in front of the passenger compartment, chances are good it will penetrate into the interior.

On top of all this, should you come under attack, vehicles tend to be "bullet magnets," so unless you can drive immediately out of the line of fire your best bet may be to quickly exit the vehicle and get to any available cover. As for using the vehicle itself as cover, the strongest position is generally on the side, behind the wheel closest to the engine. You must also remember (so *much* to remember!) that bullets may "skip" or ricochet off a hard surface, which may change their angle of trajectory enough to allow them to strike someone otherwise in a good position of cover.

Last word on using a vehicle for cover: standing behind your cruiser, taking aim over the roof while your body is nicely framed by the windows, is a Hollywood technique that gets real people killed! Don't do it.

Miscellaneous items: In a pinch, a fireplug can provide outstanding cover. By getting low enough you can effectively employ a curbstone if the angles are right! Telephone poles or trees may provide some degree of cover, but, depending upon their diameter, can't actually be counted upon to stop high velocity projectiles. Hollow cement cinder blocks commonly used in construction are designed to support weight from above, not to stop high velocity rounds coming in from the side.

Body Armor: Your personal, portable cover. While most personal body armor will not stop high-velocity rifle rounds, it will stop or at the least slow down projectiles that would otherwise have easy access to your chest cavity. Body armor should be worn whenever you are in uniform or engaged in any potentially dangerous activity.

Bullet magnet! Unless you are in an armored vehicle, you must remember that a vehicle's primary purpose is transportation, not ballistic protection. Also remember that bullets can penetrate from the inside out as well from the outside in.

CHAPTER 6

Pistol Retention

SECTION 1
Pistol Retention Considerations

During a midnight shift many moons ago I tried to stop a car travelling at a high rate of speed on the Interstate and ended up in a full-blown lights and siren pursuit. From the highway into a tightly congested city I followed the two suspects in the large pickup truck, not knowing at that point why they were running.

Once we entered the city, a local police officer attempted to assist me in stopping the vehicle by blocking the suspect's path with his cruiser. The operator of the truck, however, brazenly maneuvered his speeding vehicle around the officer's cruiser and continued travelling deeper into the city.

I stayed with the truck, and attempted to radio in our position, which became difficult as I wasn't too familiar with that particular area, there weren't many street signs, we were moving fast, and it was pretty dark. This was also years before GPS so when the driver turned his truck down a dark, unmarked alley and bailed out while the passenger stayed in the now slowly rolling vehicle, I was momentarily alone and unsure of my location.

Holding the cruiser-mounted radio's microphone (no portables then, either), I advised "I'm out with two!" tossed the mike aside, slammed the gearshift lever into park and jumped out of my cruiser. The driver ran across the alley and up a short flight of stairs and tried to open a door at the top of the landing. I guessed the door was locked by the way he pulled at the knob with both hands with no result. I drew my pistol and tried to cover both suspects, still completely unsure of what I had. As I watched, the truck, driver's side door still open, rolled to a stop against a building.

The city police officer suddenly appeared in my peripheral vision and yelled to me that he would cover the suspect in the truck. As I made a bee-line for the driver I ordered, "Police! Show me your hands!" From his elevated position he suddenly turned toward me, dropped his right shoulder and something glinted in his right hand. I dropped to one knee and realized I was looking at him over the slide of my pistol. What saved his life right then was that I had my trusty old 3-cell Maglite in my left hand and had lit him up enough to see he was holding a set of keys.

"Leave me alone! I've got to go!" he screamed wildly, and turned toward the door again, keys extended toward the knob this time.

Glancing across the alley toward the truck I saw the passenger climb out. He was wearing a long trench coat and had a dazed look on his face. I trusted that the other officer had him under control and again ordered the driver to show me his hands.

He screamed something again, this time completely unintelligible and began to struggle harder with the door, trying to open it. I advanced two steps up the staircase and gave the order again, still holding both my pistol and flashlight. This time in response, the crazed driver, who looked to be about 30 years old, suddenly spun from the door and advanced two steps down and made a grab for me.

I swept his feet with the Maglite and dropped him hard onto the stairs, face up. Our legs tangled. I pinned him with my left hand, Maglite clenched tight, held horizontally across his chest. He grabbed at my light with his right hand as I reholstered my pistol and secured the retaining snap.

As I tried to wrestle him into a control position I felt a tug on my holstered pistol as his left hand found the grip.

From the corner of my eye I saw the other officer focused on dealing with the second suspect across the alley. Close as he was, he was as good as miles away as those critical few seconds passed.

Instantly, I clamped my right hand down hard over the driver's left hand, pinning it to my still holstered pistol. He grunted and began to struggle harder, pulling at both light and gun. The staircase was narrow and didn't leave much room to maneuver...

The story above is true. I relate it here because this is what we are talking about in this chapter: a down and dirty struggle between individuals for control of a pistol. *YOUR* pistol!

My thoughts on this subject have been formed by my training and experiences. My goal is not to try to convince you that one defensive tactics system is better than another, for there are a lot of approaches to defensive tactics and this includes pistol retention. There are many methods and techniques that can be learned. There are also quite a few options in regard to security holsters.

For many police officers, the choices of which retention skills to learn and the specific type of holster to be worn will be made by their department or agency. Other officers may have more leeway in this area. Still others will be given very little or no training and guidance at all.

I will not be attempting to cover all the options available here because this subject alone is worthy of an entire volume! Rather, in this chapter we will be exploring some common truths that apply equally across the spectrum of tactics and equipment.

I strongly suggest that you pursue additional knowledge and training about this specific aspect of police pistolcraft, for the time to consider what your options are, or how you will react to an assault on you and a fight for your pistol, is not at the moment it is happening!

A Three-Pronged Approach to Pistol Retention

Kevin Davis, police officer and the director of Advanced Tactical Concepts, describes his approach to pistol retention as "The Handgun Retention Triad: Mind, Holster, Skills." Kevin and I share a similar training philosophy in regard to many things, and this is one of them. Ensuring that your pistol remains under your control is not simply accomplished by practicing defensive tactics, or buying the best triple-retention holster available. It is accomplished by blending these two components, and by developing the proper mindset well before you encounter that person who is determined to take your pistol from you and use it against you and/or others.

As always, we lead off with the foundation of all survival skills: mental preparation.

1 **MINDSET:** Whenever we arrive at a scene, the first thing we must do is assess the situation. At the top of our immediate list is the threat assessment we make regarding any people present, either individuals or groups. The smaller the group, the narrower our focus becomes. Usually the focus will gravitate to people's hands and then their clothing and belt lines, looking for a telling bulge that would indicate a weapon.

Often, a police officer will become so involved in looking for an outside threat or weapon that he almost forgets that there is definitely at least one firearm on the scene for sure—his own service weapon.

There is an old joke that says you can always tell a rookie police officer because it appears that his weapon is wearing *him*—that is, because he is so conscious of the firearm on his hip, he unconsciously tends to highlight it. After a while, this awareness usually wears off. The weapon is put on and taken off day in and day out, usually only being fired at qualifications and all too often cleaned and lubricated only at these times as well.

It is soon regarded as simply another piece of gear on the belt.

Yet we must constantly remind ourselves that it is more than that. In reality we carry the potential instrument of our own destruction on our hips every day. And as any police officer can tell you, it is invariably this instrument that attracts the attention of just about anyone we come into contact with. Most people tend to glance at it, some stare, and then there are those few who give you pause to consider your stance and their proximity to your sidearm because of the way they seem to be "assessing" both you and your weapon.

Taking this into consideration, it becomes clear that one of the best ways to ensure pistol retention is through deterrence. And the primary deterrent to someone who may be thinking about making a grab for your pistol is your appearance and demeanor.

I believe it was Clint Smith of Thunder Ranch who once said, "If you look like food, you will be eaten!"

Not On the Menu

The best way to get it across to people that you are definitely *not* on the menu is by exhibiting the appearance of a squared-away, confident, and competent pistoleer. This relates to mindset because your outer appearance and demeanor are simply reflections of your inner preparedness, alertness, and resolve.

Another signal we send to potential predators that we are not food for the taking is by the way we position ourselves in relation to others. It is critical to maintain a safe distance or *reactionary gap* between yourself and others whenever working. We can not allow overconfidence, denial, or apathy to influence our behavior when working in close proximity to other people.

You needn't feel bad or rude about keeping people at a safe distance. The fact of the matter is that there is no need to let people you do not know and trust (and *trust* is not a word to be taken lightly) to get too close to you and your pistol. Should you find yourself closer than you would prefer for any reason, assume a tactically sound position and maintain your awareness of these people, your pistol, and their proximity to one another. (Standing in the "Interview Position" as discussed in Chapter 5 §2 is recommended for these times. More on that later in this chapter.)

Keeping your primary hand free whenever possible is also something you should consciously practice all the time.

The final thoughts on mindset in this section come from Kevin Davis:

> *If someone attacks and attempts to disarm you, more important than any other component is your* ***will to win****. Despite possible injuries, possibly being smaller, not as physically strong or even being outnumbered, you can and must win the fight for your life and retain your pistol. Other officers who have been hurt worse and in more dire situations have fought their way out, and you can too! Most times an intense will to win can overcome even the most vicious of attacks. You must not relinquish control of your pistol. Bite, claw, stab with your police knife, whatever and however long it takes, you can and must do it! Stoke your soul; there is not a suspect alive that can overcome the will and intent of a well-trained, hard-core street cop! There may be a day to die, but not here and not now, and not at the hands of this scum!*

I could not agree more, nor could I have said it better!

2 **HOLSTER:** I have been using holsters with thumb-break retaining devices for 23 years in a number of assignments, from patrol to SWAT to investigations. I have also worked with a number of security holsters over the years, but have never worn one on duty even though my department allows us the option. My reasons for doing this are simple: I prefer the basic thumb-break because it keeps my pistol secured in the holster and allows me to draw it out of the holster quickly and cleanly. I like it. I prefer it. But that doesn't mean it doesn't have its weaknesses.

One of the best experiences I had early in my career occurred during recruit training at the academy. We were required to participate in a drill during which one recruit would attempt to disarm another while grappling on the ground. During my turn as the disarmee I was shocked when I felt my S&W .357 Magnum revolver pulled from my holster during the struggle.

I was, however, able to gain control of my partner's gun hand (and my own damned gun!) before he could simulate using it on me and ending the drill.

The reason I consider this one of the best experiences I had is not because I was able to regain control of the pistol. That could have easily gone either way, and my success was probably attributable mostly to luck and adrenaline fueled by my acute embarrassment at being disarmed in front of the class.

No, the reason it was one of the best experiences I had is because it **completely woke me up** to the fact that my pistol could so easily be taken from my holster during a struggle. This knowledge, this "sense of danger" as the late Roger Ford used to call it, has influenced and guided me through more than two decades during which I have worked consciously and diligently to ensure no one would ever take my pistol again.

Now, having said all that, I would like to make it clear that using a Level 1, thumb-break retaining holster is *my* preference, based upon my training and experiences. But that hardly means it is the right choice for you or anyone else.

There are a number of holster types to choose from. If you are given a choice, you should make an informed decision.

Holster Security Retention Levels

Holster security retention "levels" are rated from Level 1 to 3.

Level 1 is the type of holster I prefer. These types of holsters only incorporate one retaining device.

Level 2 holsters incorporate two retaining devices and usually require the operator to perform an additional movement when drawing the weapon from the holster.

Level 3 adds one more device or component, and may require an additional movement or step as well.

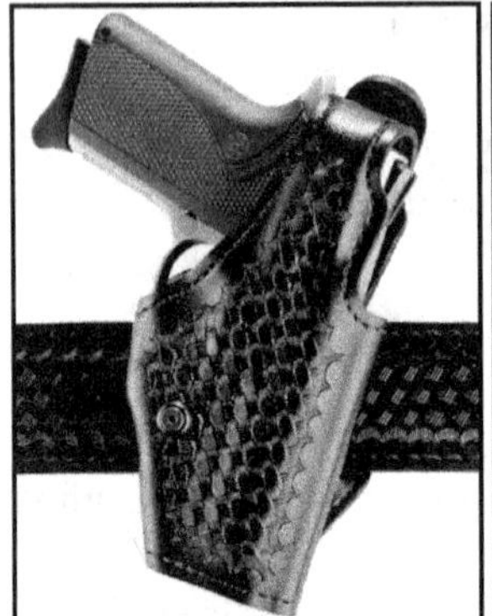
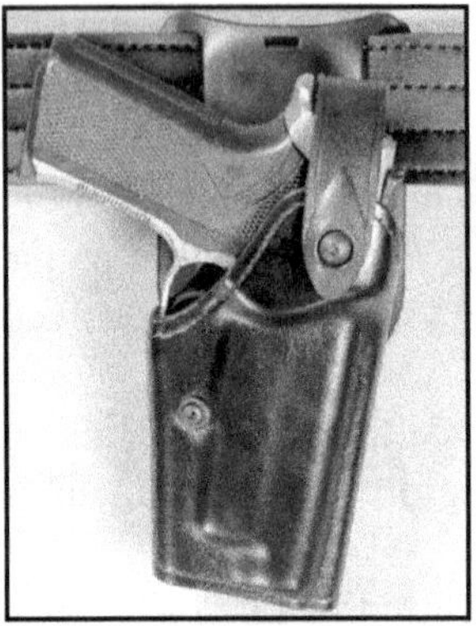
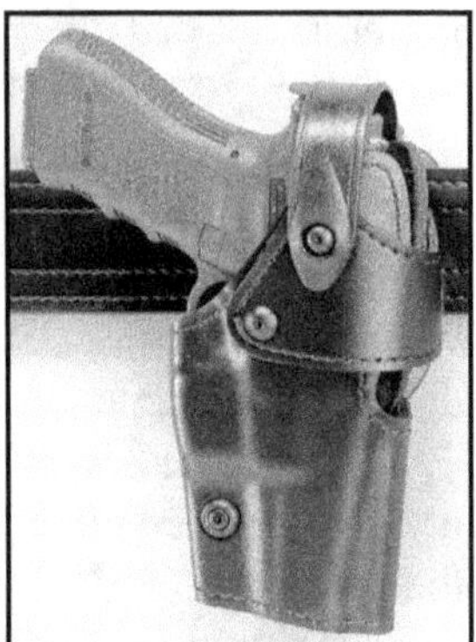

Safariland Retention Holsters, from left to right: Model 2 "Hi-Ride" (Level 1), Model 6285 Belt Drop (Level 2), Model 6295 Mid-Ride (Level 3). (Images courtesy of Safariland®.)

The key to using the higher security retention level holsters and ensuring they do not cause you a major problem when you need your pistol in your hand is practice. Pure, *proper* practice. That means no cheating when at the range by unsnapping or not fully engaging all the safety devices during training. And it means practicing the presentation and recovery until you manipulate the safety devices without conscious thought—and then practicing some more!

Security holsters can absolutely prevent or at least impede someone from getting your pistol from you during a struggle (or even after the struggle, should you be incapacitated and unable to defend your pistol). Without the proper practice, however, they can also prevent *you* from getting to your pistol when you need it most.

It's a definite series of trade-offs. So consider it well, make a choice, and practice diligently. Your life may very well depend upon it.

3 TACTICAL SKILLS: Allowing other people to get in a tactically superior position is a potentially fatal error, one which many of us have been guilty of at one time or another. If you want a clear picture of what I'm referring to, view the tape of the tragedy that befell Daryl Lunsford, a Texas constable who was killed in the line of duty in 1991. His death at the hands of three cold-blooded murderers was videotaped by a camera he had set up in his cruiser.

If you are not familiar with this tape, I strongly recommend that you track down a copy and view it. Much can be learned from it. It is probably one of the most graphic examples of what can happen when sound tactical doctrine is not employed.

While statistics compiled by the FBI indicate that the number of police officers killed with their own weapons has dropped dramatically over the past ten years (from approximately 14 percent to approximately 8 percent), the threat of an assailant getting to your pistol and using it against you is always present.

It is believed that the **two primary reasons officers are disarmed** are 1) because their **holsters are not properly secured**, and 2) because they **do not wait for backup** when it is appropriate.

As for not having your holster properly secured, consider this: you walk up to a vehicle. Something doesn't seem right. You place your hand on your holstered pistol and unsnap the retaining device. Situation seems all right after all. You interact with the occupants. One thing leads to another and you're suddenly in a physical struggle and your holster is still unsecured, whether you are now consciously aware of it or not...

Unsnap or Draw?

Some officers unsecure their holsters (without drawing the pistol) as described in the preceding paragraph. This is strongly discouraged! If the situation has you in fear for your safety to that degree, either draw the pistol or simply place your hand on the grip and be ready to immediately disengage the retaining device(s) should you need to draw it.

You also must condition yourself to resecure the retaining device(s) using only one hand when you reholster, every time! (See Chapter 4 §4.)

Two-to-One Rule

As for waiting for backup, a good concept to remember is the two-to-one rule:

It is always tactically desirable to have two police officers present for every suspect on scene.

Now, I realize it's not always possible to stick to this rule. In fact, it's often impossible, especially when working out on the highway or in rural areas. But this rule's primary purpose is to help us to change our way of *thinking* while we are working.

Many of us still harbor a resistance to calling for or accepting back-up, and we've got to get over this. There is nothing to prove out there to *anyone*.

Regardless of how much you may love being a police officer, the job we do is still just that, a job, and it's not worth taking foolish chances for, especially when we often don't have to.

Wait the extra few minutes for backup to arrive. Stack the odds in your favor. Run the risk of having a backup show up only to not be needed. You will never know how different the outcome may have been had he not been there.

Interview Position

The Interview Position, also known as the "on guard" position, allows you to interact with people while keeping your pistol not only physically away from them, but also out of their sight.

Both factors contribute to our goal of pistol retention. (This is the same stance illustrated and described in Chapter 5 §1.)

Position your feet wide for balance and stability. Your body is slightly bladed away from the threat area, and your back and neck are straight. Your hands are up and ready in a "nonthreatening" position. Some officers feel silly standing like this. You can modify it, as long as the basic position is preserved.

The most important elements of a proper Interview Position are found in the bladed-away, stable body position and in having the hands up to at least waist level.

This allows for quick movement and reduced reaction time should you need to take defensive or offensive action, such as employing a weapon-retention technique, administering a strike, or accessing your pistol.

One interesting thing I've observed when using this position while working is that this nonthreatening interview position takes on an almost ominous appearance when assumed correctly and seriously.

From experience, I can tell you, if three or more officers stand in this position while facing an unruly crowd, chances are they will observe a subtle uneasiness seep into the collective consciousness of the problem children. It also tends to bolster the confidence level of the attendant officers, for there is strength in unity, even in the mere *appearance* of unity.

Holster "Hand Lock"

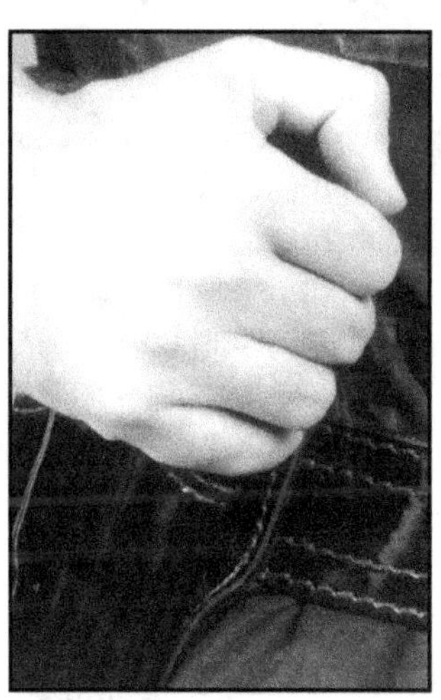

When working in crowds, a snug elbow or a hand around the snap closure (shown at right) may help prevent someone from beating you to the draw with your own weapon. But be advised, this commonly taught, one-hand weapon-retention grip can be easily defeated by people who know how—and they are out there.

What to do? Keep your distance, think tactically, and trust your instincts.

Stay Alert—Stay Alive!

Defensive Tactics

There are a number of defensive tactics that have been devised to aid in pistol retention. Like any tactic, the best will stand up to the following analysis.

Is the tactic:

- based upon gross motor movements?
- capable of being performed while operating under stress?
- designed to take into account probable responses?
- designed so that once executed, it controls the offender's movements?
- designed to allow for follow through?

If the tactic you are using does not allow you to answer "yes" for all of these questions, it is most likely a "dojo demo" technique. These techniques only tend to work well with a cooperative partner during training and often fall apart in the real world, much like old paradigm marksmanship-focused pistolcraft skills.

One of the best approaches I have seen in regard to reality-based tactics in this discipline has been developed by my colleague and friend, Joe Maffei.

Joe Maffei

Maffei, an accomplished martial artist, is the founder of the Integrated Martial Development Center.

In his system, Joe works a great deal from the ground, where, as we know, most grappling-type engagements eventually end up.

Joe's techniques are reality-based and designed to allow you to not only defend your pistol from an assaultive subject, but to prevail in the fight using a number of simple, strong, and effective tactics.

I highly recommend you research Joe's system as well as any other system made available to you. Once you have learned a system, it is also crucial that you practice the skills on a regular basis with a training partner.

As always, train hard and practice your skills as realistically as possible, for there are no "do overs" in the real world.

The Pin & Spin

The "pin & spin," one version of which is illustrated on the following page, is a commonly taught pistol retention technique. It is designed to provide the police officer with a sound method of retaining his pistol when an individual launches a direct assault on the officer with the specific intention of taking control of the officer's sidearm.

The technique is based upon leverage and body mechanics and is effective within a limited set of circumstances. Techniques such as these do not take into account the assailant (or assailants) who would launch an

The Pin & Spin Technique

The assailant, using his left hand, makes a direct frontal grab for the officer's holstered pistol. The officer immediately executes a weapon retention grip with his right hand, securing the pistol in the holster. The officer's left hand is then used to "trap" or "pin" the assailant's attack-hand to the weapon.

(Note that once established, the officer's grip on his pistol is never relinquished.)

The officer then rotates or "spins" into the elbow of the attacking arm delivering a strike using the forearm and elbow area of his right arm. Once the assailant's grip on the weapon is broken, the officer has the option of closing with the suspect and applying a physical control technique or creating distance.

attack directly against the officer's person with the intent of disabling him *before* retrieving his weapon. It is under these circumstances that tactical thinking skills are our most valuable of assets.

Unholstered Pistol Retention Considerations

Over the years I have participated in a number of defensive tactics (DT) training programs, including the excellent 80 hour FBI Police Defensive Tactics Instructor Course.

Every DT program (including the FBI's) intended for use by members of law enforcement invariably included a pistol retention component.

Just as invariably, the entire subject of pistol retention was dedicated to retaining only the *holstered* pistol.

While the FBI program and several others I have taken did include a handgun disarming technique element, this was directed toward teaching the officer how to disarm a pistol-wielding suspect—*not* how to keep the suspect from taking the officer's pistol from his or her hand.

Since there is not enough space in this book to do this subject justice, I offer the following few suggestions for consideration.

A future volume in the *Police Pistolcraft* series is planned to address this subject in greater detail.

Above: Bert DuVernay (on right) teaching a pistol disarming technique during a training course.

Protect Your Pistol

Whenever your pistol is in your hand, you must ensure that it is controlled at all times. This includes ensuring that it is under only your control! The best way to keep control (and possession) of your handgun is to keep it away from known or unknown dangers.

A **known danger** would be a suspect or suspects you are dealing with directly in order to achieve control of them and the situation. In these instances **keep your distance** and do not let a suspect close the space between you. Prison-trained convicts practice their own tactics and techniques, and one of the most common is to approach a potential "target" by holding the hands raised as if in submission and talking a steady stream of non-threatening, confusing words. The idea is to get close enough to the target to launch an attack. Prisoners have also been observed practicing disarming techniques on one another, with the armed "trainee" obviously playing the role of police officer.

An **unknown danger** is present anytime your pistol is in your hand and you are moving through any environment that doesn't permit a 360 degree field of view.

Most searches fall into this category.

While you should always try to stay behind your pistol, keeping the muzzle first to danger, you also do not want your pistol to enter a room or area ahead of you. It is very easy to strip a pistol out of someone's hand when this is done! Always try to visually clear a room or area prior to you or your pistol entering it.

The tighter the environment, the closer to your body you should be holding your pistol.

Fight for Your Pistol

Should someone grab hold of your unholstered pistol, you must do whatever is necessary to retain control of your weapon while simultaneously bringing the suspect's out-of-control behavior under control.

This is a deadly force situation *all day long* and cannot be interpreted as anything but!

Your response must be **immediate**, **violent**, and **decisive**. A loud war cry accompanied by a full-on attack is your best option. Keep your grip on the pistol with your primary hand and grab the slide with your support hand

Keep your pistol close to your body and be prepared to defend it and yourself when dealing with suspects at close ranges, or when approaching doorways or other environments where unknown dangers may be lurking.

(keeping clear of the muzzle). Attempt to rip the pistol out of the attacker's hands while stepping back, if possible. If not possible, ***EXPLODE*** into the attacker, striking him or her with your pistol as well as all your personal weapons. Drive your forehead into the bridge of the attacker's nose; deliver kicks or punches to the attacker's groin; kick his knees and shins, stomp his feet; deliver elbow strikes to the face and side of the neck; drive the fingers of your support hand into his eyes.

Remember, you must assume that he is trying to get your pistol for one reason alone—to murder you with it! For this reason, if all your attempts to get the attacker to release his grip on your pistol have failed, or, if you feel you are losing control of your pistol and the situation, you may be justified in shooting the attacker to stop the assault.

Just be advised, you cannot count on this option because it is very likely that the pistol may not fire if the struggling hands wrapped around it have taken it out of battery or otherwise impeded the mechanical functioning of the weapon.

If this is the case, and again, if you believe deadly force is required, you may try dropping to one knee while pulling your pistol out of the attacker's grasp and firing into the attacker's torso as soon as the pistol clears his hands.

This technique can be effective, but naturally, there are too many variables to guarantee anything except for this: ***YOU CANNOT LOSE THIS FIGHT!***

Train to Win

I strongly recommend you seek out or participate in a professionally-formatted and administered defensive tactics course of instruction, regardless of whether you have received such training previously.

If the topic of unholstered pistol retention isn't addressed, I strongly suggest you request training and guidance regarding it, for the threat of being disarmed while the pistol is in your hand is as great or greater than when it is secured in the holster.

We must always remember that training is a skill, and all skills are perishable. In regard to handgun retention, it is up to each of us to work on our own skills, and prepare for that moment when we are forced to fight off another's attempts to disarm us of our pistols.

It happens more often than one would imagine, oftentimes under strange or unexpected circumstances. When it does, as I stated unequivocally above, make no mistake about it—you will be dealing with a deadly force situation.

And you must be prepared mentally, physically, and emotionally to take proper legal, moral, and ethical action.

As is always the case, just what constitutes legal, moral, and ethical action will be dictated by the totality of the circumstances at hand, including the number of suspects, individual suspect's actions, number of officers present, your past training and experience, the specific events occurring at that moment in time, and your *perceptions* of those events as they unfold, moment by moment.

Epilogue

I started this chapter by recounting an experience I had while trying to subdue a suspect who had led me on a wild motor vehicle pursuit that ended with him and me wrestling on a staircase in a dark alley. Like most real-world police encounters, this entire event was neither pretty nor predictable. It unfolded as it did. Taking into consideration everything I have touched on in the rest of this chapter, I offer the conclusion of the story...

Based on the totality of the circumstances as I've described them, I feared for my life at this point in the struggle. Being all too aware of how quickly a violent engagement can change in an instant, especially while involved in a struggle for a holstered pistol, I acted swiftly and decisively.

While using my right hand to keep the suspect's left hand pinned to my still-holstered pistol, I used my personal weapons and my flashlight to bring his out-of-control, life-threatening behavior under control.

The fight ended quickly. By the time additonal backup officers arrived at the scene minutes later it was all but over.

Later that evening at the hospital, after reading the suspect the Miranda warning, I found out the rest of *his* story as he was being attended to in the emergency room...

While drinking late at night at home with his friend (the passenger wearing the trench coat), he received an automated telephone call indicating an alarm had gone off at his small office in the building by the alley.

Instead of calling the police to check the place, he and his buddy jumped in his truck and sped off to the office so he could check it himself.

In his alcohol-impaired state of mind his need to get to his office superseded everything else including speed limits, public safety, and the lives of anyone who got in his way.

He didn't have an answer when I asked him why he had tried to take my pistol. He simply stared blankly and said, "I don't know..."

He was later found guilty of a number of charges at trial.

The bottom line is, if he had gotten my pistol that night, or, if I had shot him when he turned on me with his keys in his hand, thinking them to be a gun, then someone would have ended up seriously injured or killed for no good reason at all.

Too often in our line of work, this is the sad reality.

Our job is to ensure that we are not the victim of this reality. 

CHAPTER 7

The Personal Survival Toolbox

SECTION 1

All Else is Supplemental

In this chapter we will look at some topics not commonly included in books about firearms training. The reason these topics are included is because this is *not* simply a book about firearms training. It is a book about *police* firearms training, and as such, this chapter is one of the most important in this volume.

This is because making the gun go "bang" and hitting your target are the *easy parts,* once the basic mechanical skills are learned.

Knowing *when* to make the gun go bang, *being able* to make the gun go bang when the target is human, and living with your actions after the smoke has cleared is where the true difficulties lie.

The construction of a "**personal survival toolbox**" starts with an individual, conscious decision. Only you can force yourself to actively consider and come to terms with the more unpleasant aspects of the profession. In order to do this, you must look at them directly and devote enough time and thought so you can achieve a true level of understanding of the threats, dangers, and difficulties they present.

Only after you have achieved this level of true understanding will you be able to learn to deal with these unpleasant aspects maturely, professionally, and effectively.

"The final weapon is the brain. All else is supplemental."

The above quote, attributed to John Steinbeck, captures the essence of the matter of building and stocking a personal survival toolbox.

Regardless of the strategic and tactical tools you may choose or develop, the "box" itself must be strong enough to hold them ready for use. And that box is the properly prepared human mind.

The fact is that if we are not mentally prepared to perform our jobs when the stress is high and the safety margins are low, all of the best strategies, tactics, and even mechanical equipment in the world will be useless to us.

While those who employ us, train us, and send us out into the world to perform our duty bear a significant responsibility to ensure we are prepared as well as possible, we too, share a great part of this burden.

Take your job seriously.

Learn as much as you can about doing it as safely and professionally as possible. In reality, it all starts and ends with you.

The Question of Judgment

For the law enforcement officer, the moment when he is faced with a situation during which he must decide whether to shoot or not may be the most important moment of his life.

Obviously, it may also be the most important moment of many other peoples' lives as well, including the officer's family, friends, and co-workers; any injured innocent bystander's, their families, friends, etc.; injured suspect's, their families, friends etc.; and the list goes on.

Reality demands that we recognize that the bullets fired from the officer's weapon may simultaneously take *and* save lives.

Reality also demands we acknowledge that hesitation on the part of the officer at this critical moment may cost *or* save lives.

> **"Reality demands that we recognize that the rounds fired from the officer's weapon may simultaneously take *and* save lives."**

There is nothing simple about this.

This is, in fact, the most difficult aspect of our profession, for we will often be required to make this life or death decision in a fraction of a moment, based on what we know, see, hear, feel, and believe *at that precise moment in time.*

The ultimate truth is that there are no easy answers. There are no hard and fast rules that apply to each and every officer, or to each and every situation. With rare exception, each human being—including those who may create situations that require police officers to employ deadly force against them—is responsible for his own actions.

That is why we, as law enforcement professionals, must prepare ourselves as best we can to meet this enormous responsibility, and, once prepared, we must *trust ourselves, our training, and each other* to do the absolute best we can in whatever situation we may find ourselves.

We must also be able to clearly articulate our reasons for employing deadly force, and be prepared to live with the consequences of our actions.

The Question of Reasonableness

Whenever a police officer uses any level of force while in the performance of duty, his actions will be judged according to a standard known as "objective reasonableness."

According to the Federal Law Enforcement Training Center (FLETC): "Objective reasonableness is not capable of being precisely defined or mechanically applied. It's based on the facts and comes down to this question: *Could a reasonable law enforcement officer believe that the force used was reasonable in light of the facts and circumstances and preexisting law?*"

It is also important to remember that while we always *want* to take the best possible course of action, we are not held to the "best possible

The determination of "objective reasonableness" is based on the facts known about the incident and this question: **"Could a reasonable law enforcement officer believe that the force used was reasonable in light of the facts and circumstances and preexisting law?"**

course of action" standard.

As long as the actions taken and force applied are deemed "objectively *reasonable*" under the circumstances, we have met the reasonableness standard.

Verbalization

Verbalization is a key component of officer survival and situational control.

Officers often tend to either say nothing during high-stress engagements, or, if more than one officer is present, they tend to all give commands and/or directions at the same time, creating confusion. This is especially true during dynamic situations when officers and/or suspects are on the move, constantly shifting position and realigning their angles of view, and as a result, influencing their perceptions.

The key to verbalization is simplicity.

If feasible, **give simple commands while speaking clearly and professionally.**

> **"Avoid using profanity no matter how heated the situation. Repeat the commands slowly until compliance is achieved or other means of control are required."**

Avoid using profanity no matter how heated the situation. Repeat the commands slowly and clearly until compliance is achieved or other means of control are required. If there is more than one officer present, the contact (initiating) officer should be the only one to issue commands.

Verbalization is also highly recommended during any type of entry or search process, as long as the officers are not conducting a stealth entry or stealth search and their presence is obvious to anyone in the area.

Issuing a Verbal Challenge

It is considered reasonable to issue a verbal challenge to a suspect before using force in most situations. However, if your issuing of a verbal challenge or command would most likely place you or others in greater danger based on the circumstances, then no verbal challenge should be made prior to taking reasonable action.

SECTION 2
Understanding Reaction Lag

Action Beats Reaction

Most people are aware on at least a basic level that action generally beats reaction. A simple example could be having two healthy adults facing one another at close distance, arms by their sides, and having one of them suddenly slap the other's face. Given no unusual circumstances and having both parties being relatively unexceptional in regard to training and experience, the chances of the recipient being able to effectively block, stop, or otherwise intercept that slap would be slim to none.

In regard to police firearms training, while the weapons, circumstances and other contributing factors are more complex than the example used above, the basic underlying principle remains the same.

Consider a dangerous suspect with a pistol hidden in his waistband.

The assailant, having made the decision to draw and fire at you, suddenly initiates the action — ATTACK!

You, meanwhile, must first observe the assailant's actions, comprehend what he is doing, and *then* respond by whatever means you have available to you, as in, 1) HE'S ATTACKING! and then 2) RESPOND!

Even when aware that we are facing a potential threat, we are still generally behind the proverbial eight ball because we tend to respond to a suspect's threatening actions rather than initiating our own physical action prematurely.

Just how much of a disadvantage this creates for us in most situations can be illustrated by the results of a recent study.

How Fast is Fast?

Dr. Bill Lewinski, a professor in the Law Enforcement Program at Minnesota State University, conducted a series of eleven experiments in order to determine just how quickly a number of typically criminal aggressive movements could be made. The results may surprise you. Two are synopsized below.

1. Operator of Motor Vehicle: Handgun hidden by right thigh, assailant shoots as officer approaches driver side door post.

Average time: **25/100ths of a second**

Fastest time: **15/100ths of a second**

According to Dr. Lewinski: "The movement is so fast that is unlikely that a street officer caught in this position would even be able to identify that the subject actually had a weapon in their hand until weapon was at the point of discharge."

2. Standing Suspect: Handgun hidden in waistband, assailant draws and fires from "combat tuck" position.

Average time: **23/100ths of a second**
Fastest time: **09/100ths of a second**

Again according to Dr. Lewinski: "An officer caught in the open in a 'Dodge City showdown' with even the average subject in this study literally would not stand a chance if the subject has their hand at their waistband, an actual weapon in that waistband, the intent to shoot and any accuracy at all with their weapon."

In regard to the average officer's speed, Dr. Lewinski advises the following: "To fully understand the implications of the research results… it is important to remember that the average officer, with their finger on the trigger and being psychologically set, is able to 'react' to a shot timer and pull the trigger of their weapon in about a quarter to a third of a second. I am currently working on research on this topic with a whole police department and the preliminary data indicates it is closer to a third of a second or even longer for most officers to react, at least with that department.

Some officers of course are quicker and others are slower. The reader needs to keep this 'average' reaction time in mind as they read about the different motions studied and learn just how really fast the suspect's action can be."

What it Means to Us

Understanding reaction lag is important to us for it will help us to better gauge the actual degree of danger we may be in. It can also assist us to better explain our actions should we be involved in a shooting.

If we are unaware of the principle of reaction lag, our perception of danger may be based upon a mistaken assumption of just how fast a suspect can act, and how fast we may be able to react in response.

SECTION 3

Mental Preparation for the Lethal Force Encounter

The term "mindset" is referenced throughout this book. In this chapter we are going to define and explore it.

Mindset describes a preset state of mind that is produced by mental conditioning and preparation. The goal is to prepare ourselves to deal with the realities of a lethal encounter.

All the firearms training that we do, all the practice we ideally perform on our own, and all the time we invest in physically exercising our bodies contribute to the tactical advantage we must possess while working in the field. But of all these contributing factors, achieving the proper mindset is considered the most essential to ensuring our survival.

And after all is said and done, the ultimate reality for us as police officers will always be found in those few terrifying moments when our life or someone else's hangs in the balance.

That is when it will all come together, as our training and conditioning take over and we act with purpose, determination, and valor. And it will all happen in those few terrifying moments we hope will never come. But when they do, if properly prepared, we will survive. We will win.

Often neglected in relation to other aspects of officer survival training, mental conditioning is the base upon which all other training and tactical skills must be built. It has been suggested that proper mental conditioning can play as much as 75 percent of the role involved in surviving violent, life-threatening encounters. In the absence of proper mental conditioning, luck becomes the major factor in determining our chances for survival.

The American Heritage Dictionary defines luck as "the chance happening of fortunate or adverse events." Since these chance happenings cannot be controlled by us, we must then strive to control those elements involved in lethal-force encounters that we can. By preparing ourselves mentally, we reduce luck's impact dramatically and put ourselves in greater control of our own destinies.

Too many officers working in today's environment still rely on what psychologists call a "**personal fable**." This occurs when an officer convinces himself that he is "special" and will never get hurt, will never run into that one individual who'll be truly intent—for whatever reason—on hurting, maiming, or killing him. The fable often becomes more believable to these officers than the events that occur around them. As years go by and nothing "really bad" ever happens to them personally, they begin to believe that their lack of training and practice doesn't matter or that poor or dangerous tactics they employ repetitively are good enough for them and anyone else who cares to listen.

Many of these officers may indeed complete their careers without having to face a lethal-force encounter, even though some statistics indicate that there is a definite possibility that all officers will experience at least one in their tenure. Too often, however, the results of one of these officers confronting his 1/10 of 1 percent chance encounter are added to the statistical database under the heading, "Summary of Law Enforcement Officers Killed In Line of Duty."

Understanding Proper Mindset

Contrary to common belief, proper mindset is much more than being alert and maintaining a fierce determination to survive and win a violent confrontation. These attributes, while important, do not address or compensate for the myriad physical and psychological factors we must be prepared to deal with during a life-threatening encounter. (Refer to Chapter 1 §3 and Chapter 1 §4 for a description of these factors.)

It's also important to note that many officers have survived extended life-threatening situations by turning normal, debilitating feelings, such as fear, into constructive, energizing feelings of controlled anger. This is especially important if you are injured during the incident. When the gloves come off, you must take any advantage you can to survive.

The following scenario combines a possible patrol situation with a description of some of the physical and psychological effects we might experience throughout its short duration.

A Possible Scenario

Getting out of the cruiser, you observe the operator of the vehicle you have just stopped as he appears to be yelling and thrashing about in the vehicle. Several times he pounds his hands on the steering wheel, while glaring at you in the rearview mirror.

His response is extremely irrational as far as you are concerned, because you have only pulled him over for a minor motor vehicle infraction. At this point, you are now alert and focused on this lone subject in the vehicle. If you have not experienced a situation of this sort before or been trained to deal with it through active scenario-based training or by using imaging techniques, you may find yourself hindered or even unable to plan a course of action.

As the large subject in the vehicle continues to carry on, you continue to approach slowly and cautiously. You think about the radio on your belt, press your elbow against your weapon. Psychologically, at this point, you are in a "what if" situation. Your breathing may get shallow and your heart rate may elevate slightly. You may find that your hands are cold and clammy, your mouth dry.

In response to the potential threat, your conscious mind may begin to create doubt; you may find yourself questioning your preparedness or ability. Any lack of training, real or imagined, may become magnified. You must counter these doubts with positive thoughts. Confidence in your training and abilities is critical at this point and must be real.

"Any lack of training, real or imagined, may become magnified. You must counter these doubts with positive thoughts. Confidence in your training and abilities is critical at this point and must be real."

Suddenly, the subject explodes out of the car. His face is red and angry. He turns his back on you, takes a few steps, and then spins around, all the while cursing and threatening. You order the subject to stop and show you his hands. He does neither.

Now he's coming straight at you. In one hand he is holding a large screwdriver. His other hand is clenched in a fist. Spittle spews out of his mouth as he screams incoherently. The next few seconds may seem like an eternity or may pass so quickly that you will have no conscious recollection of them or any actions taken during that time.

You may experience an uncontrollable upper body quiver. Your hands may shake and your knees may get weak as your heart pounds in your chest and your breathing becomes erratic. The doubts or negative thoughts may increase. You must now employ simplistic ideas and have true confidence in yourself and your training.

As the subject continues to move toward you, your perceptions may be altered. Visual distortions such as "tunnel vision" are among the most common. At this point, logic no longer functions. You may see things as being larger or smaller than they actually are, or as if they are happening in fast or slow motion. You may hallucinate, instantly relive a similar experience in your mind, or see a mental flash of your family. You may experience auditory blocking, hearing sounds only faintly or not at all. Or you may consciously "black out" altogether, reverting completely to your training.

It's important to remember here that your actions (or lack of actions) during this blackout will be totally dependent upon the amount and quality of training you have done. As you experience the fight-or-flight syndrome, your blood gets diverted to the larger muscle groups in your body and your arms and legs. It is inversely shifted from smaller muscle groups, affecting things like finger dexterity and hand-eye coordination. Again, at this point, you will only do the things you have trained to do.

As the subconscious mind takes over, you draw your weapon and order the subject to stop. He charges. You fire, or think you did, but you don't hear the gunshot. He stops for a moment, screams, and then keeps coming, slashing the screwdriver through the air.

You move backwards, strangely aware that your pistol is being fired again, almost as if by someone else.

As you watch, the subject appears to stumble in slow motion and fall soundlessly to the ground. Your head automatically scans left to right, opening up your field of view and allowing you to search for any secondary threats. You are suddenly aware that you don't know how many shots you have fired; yet as you look at the weapon in your hand, you see that you have decocked it and lowered it to the "ready position."

Your training has been effective, you have performed professionally, and, as unfortunate as it is that you have had to take a human life, you must accept that he gave you no other choice. This acceptance of our actions as well as our role in society is crucial to our surviving not only the lethal-force situation itself, but also its aftermath.

It is unique to the police and military professions that we go to work each day knowing that the possibility exists that one of us may have to kill another human being in the performance of our duty. Unlike the soldier, however, the police officer's duty will more than likely involve employing deadly force against a person who exists within his own society and shares equal protection under the laws of the same nation.

This most intense and complicated subject will be addressed more fully in the next section and will be (as its subject matter dictates) presented in a more introspective fashion, rather than in a mechanical or training format. This section, however, concerns mental and physical exercises we can use to ensure our survival, and these *are* mechanically performed and ingrained through training.

Repetition of the Basics

Ingraining the basic physical actions required to efficiently manipulate the pistol is best accomplished through practice. As we will discuss in Chapter 12, the more perfect the practice, the better the results will be when these actions are performed on the street for real.

Should our conscious mind suddenly shut off because of a violent sensory overload, it is the subconscious mind and the ingrained actions we have imprinted on it through training that will take over and see us through.

Imaging

Imaging has been successfully used by professional athletes for many years. It basically involves the user visualizing himself performing a physical task correctly and successfully in his mind. The more often it is done, the better the results are when the user actually performs the task.

The really interesting thing here is that studies have shown that the subconscious mind cannot distinguish between imagined memory and real memory. Adapting this unique quality to our occupation, the benefits become quickly apparent. Instead of actually having to experience a life threatening encounter to see what we would do, we can create them in our minds, examine options, decide on tactics, and engage and prevail in numerous scenarios. This advanced form of daydreaming is best when used in everyday situations, both on and off duty.

Simply by playing a controlled game of "what if," we actually provide our subconscious minds with an incredible variety of options, choices, and tactics. Then, when a real situation presents itself, we will experience an overwhelming sensation of having been here before, and we will not be engulfed by panic. We will act as we have rehearsed in our minds.

By using situations we individually encounter every day, we can tailor-make a training program for ourselves not unlike that experienced on Firearms Training Simulation (FATS) devices, where the officer interacts and may fire a laser-equipped weapon at moving images on a large screen.

For uniformed officers, imagine that while you are conducting a motor vehicle stop, the vehicle's operator suddenly starts acting irrationally or hostile. What would you do? Where would you move?

While speaking with two subjects you've stopped to help with a disabled motor vehicle, imagine what you would do if one suddenly ran at you or away from you or pulled out a weapon.

For narcotic and investigative personnel, scenarios should be geared toward your working environment and situations: while making an undercover purchase of narcotics in a bar, the suspects, believing that you're a small-time dealer, decide to rip you off and put a major hurt on you so you won't be back. What would you do? If a knife or gun was suddenly produced, where in the bar could you move to for cover? If you're acting as a cover person for the officer in the bar, what would you do if your partner was suddenly attacked?

The possible scenarios are endless and should also be used by officers while on off-duty status as well. Far from becoming obsessed with the job, this is a necessary part of being on the job. While in a pharmacy with your spouse, consider what you would do if the guy next to you pulled a gun to rob the pharmacist. What would be your best course of action? What options are open to you?

Of critical importance while using imaging is the incorporation of two points: 1) every scenario should end with you being successful, and 2) the scenarios and your actions in them must be realistic. Training ourselves to act foolishly brave or to ignore the realities of a threat or our own limitations will only serve to place us in jeopardy—when where we want to be is in the safest, most tactically advantageous position we can.

Mental Trigger

Another preparation that must be made well before becoming involved in an actual lethal-force situation is the setting of what is sometimes referred to as the "mental trigger." This means you must make a conscious decision before the moment is at hand as to what type of threatening actions will cause you to press your weapon's trigger.

Depending on your training, experiences, and perceptions, as well as the specifics of the individual situation itself, this moment could be when an assailant raises a firearm, or points or fires it at you or another person. Or it could be when an assailant, armed with a knife or some other potentially lethal instrument, rushes at you or is obviously about to injure someone else.

Unique situations such as dealing with a person you have probable cause to believe is carrying out a suicide/homicide bombing should also be prepared for. (Additional information on this can be found in Chapter 7 §6.)

This setting of the mental trigger can also be recalibrated several times during any given incident, as the situation changes and you reassess the danger to yourself or others.

This critical aspect of mindset can be aided by using the imaging technique described previously.

Resistance to Killing

In his book *On Killing*, Colonel Dave Grossman provides a window into the soul (and genetic programming) of the normal human being while simultaneously shattering the Hollywood-promoted myth of the police officer as "natural born killer."

I strongly recommend that every police officer read Grossman's book, for the information provided is critical to helping each of us better understand how and why we react as we do when dealing with deadly force situations before, during, and afterwards.

It is also important to remember that a civilian law enforcement-involved shooting is usually quite different from a military-involved shooting for a number of reasons. First of all, the civilian police officer is usually operating in his own, familiar society, as opposed to a foreign land where he may be dealing with people he does not identify with on many levels.

Second, most police-involved shootings occur while the officer is operating alone, as opposed to most military operations where soldiers act as part of an organized group, drawing support and direction from one another in regard to the employment of deadly force.

Third and perhaps most important is the differences in mindset. For while the soldier's basic and accepted operational objective is to seek out, close with, and destroy the enemy, the civilian police officer's duty (which is constantly drilled into him) is to use the least amount of force necessary to bring any given situation under control. This expectation, combined with generally-accepted societal "norms" regarding the taking of life and the fact that any incident involving deadly force administered by a police officer will be exhaustively scrutinized, analyzed, dissected, and second guessed, creates a much more restrictive mindset for most civilian police officers in

While responding to a hostage-barricade situation during a SWAT team call out, the author (in foreground) found himself unexpectedly facing the armed suspect at a distance of approximately 20 yards when the suspect suddenly walked out of a residence with his hostage.

Undetected by the suspect and afforded a degree of both cover and concealment by the terrain, Conti proned out, cocked the hammer on his pistol and took up the trigger slack to allow more precise shot placement if needed (it was at this moment that the above photograph was taken). The suspect, holding his pistol pointed at the ground, then released his hostage but had not indicated his intent to surrender. Conti's **"mental trigger"** was set to employ deadly force should the suspect make any threatening movements toward him or other personnel present.

Conti kept the suspect covered for several minutes from this position. While being fully prepared to shoot if necessary, Conti experienced the deep-seated and strong feeling of not *wanting* to shoot the suspect as described in the text. Being aware that this feeling is a normal reaction will limit the possibility of your being distracted or unsettled by it.

The suspect was eventually taken into custody with no serious injuries to him nor anyone else. (Photo courtesy Massachusetts State Police archives) regard to the use of deadly force.

On top of all this is the natural reluctance found in most people to seriously injuring or killing another human being. In regard to the specific matter of shooting a person in the line of duty, Grossman puts forth the argument that while a police officer must be *able* to shoot and take a life if necessary, no normally functioning and adjusted human being should *want* to do it. And in my experience, this *is* generally the norm.

This is one of the primary reasons that police officers often place themselves at greater risk than is necessary or prudent by not employing deadly force when it is clearly justified and necessary—not because they are *afraid* to do it, but because it goes against our *basic nature* to do it.

And when you think about it, this is a good thing, for we have enough psychopathic personalities amongst us to deal with as it is, and would be in serious trouble as a society if our police officers shared the psychopath's apparent absence of restraint in this regard.

While this reluctance to seriously injure or kill another person is a needed and desirable safeguard under most circumstances, it is another matter entirely when it comes to the police officer facing a person who is placing him or another in immediate, mortal danger. That is why our training is so critical, for when properly administered, it enables us to overcome this natural reluctance which can cause us to hesitate when deadly force is clearly called for.

Too many officers and innocent persons have been, and will continue to be, seriously injured or killed when the officers are not properly prepared to deal with this built-in human aversion. This occurs because the intense feeling of aversion causes officers to allow others to unlawfully injure or kill when the officers are in a position to stop the attack by a lawful application of deadly force against the assailant.

The first step to minimizing the possibility of this aversion causing you to hesitate is to realize that it does exist and that you will probably be affected by it. This will allow it to have less of an emotional impact on you should you experience it, so you can perform as needed in a timely fashion and stop the suspect's dangerous and immediately threatening actions.

Breathing

The "combat breathing" technique is described in Chapter 1 §5.

This technique, which can be used to calm the body and mind, is extremely beneficial for reducing stress caused by any activity or circumstances. Please refer to the noted text for more information.

Tactical Education

The final mental exercise presented for consideration is one you are currently participating in simply by reading this book: *exploring options*.

There is an abundance of solid, worthwhile police tactics and training manuals, books, magazines, videotapes, and web sites available on the market. While some of these materials are expensive, they are well worth the cost if you can learn even just one new, useful technique. You should also develop the habit of passing on any worthwhile ideas or tactics you learn to your fellow officers. You never know how your efforts will be rewarded.

Training ourselves and our people to the best of our abilities is something that must be done continually, because over time words are forgotten, techniques fade from memory, and we become lethargic and complacent.

It's human nature.

That is why learning new techniques as well as reinforcing old ones through personal, departmental, or specialized training sessions is so critical. The very nature of our jobs demands that we not allow ourselves to be caught off guard or unprepared.

Our investment in this facet of our profession is not only tax deductible, but it is our responsibility to ourselves, our families, and each other. We've got to be better than the ones who decide they just don't care anymore or the ones who just don't care, period. And we've got to be able to take care of ourselves and each other, because out there, for all intents and purposes, we're all we've got.

Recommended Online Training & Information Resources In Addition to www.sabergroup.com

alexisartwohl.com	**khybertraining.com**	**policeone.com**
calibrepress.com	**killology.com**	**posai.org**
cuttingedgetraining.org	**mlefiaa.org**	**taloninternational.org**
ialefi.com	**ntoa.org**	**theiacp.org**
ileeta.org	**jmjkd.com**	**forcescienceresearch.com**

SECTION 4

Aftermath of the Lethal-Force Encounter

In the previous section we took a look at some methods we can use to train and prepare ourselves mentally to confront and win a lethal force encounter. Practically all of our firearms and tactical training is geared to helping us achieve this end, and rightly so.

There is, however, one aspect of the lethal force encounter that, while often overlooked, is as serious a potential threat to us as the individual we may face who is holding a weapon or otherwise placing our life or someone else's life in jeopardy. It is sometimes called "afterburn," and unless we prepare ourselves for it, we leave ourselves prey to an attack from an enemy we may never escape—ourselves.

Practically everyone who wears the badge has at one time or another envisioned themselves in that "once in a career situation." The most common theme to these violent-encounter fantasies is that the officer runs up against a real bad guy, a violent career criminal who is well-armed and menacingly dangerous. After a spectacular gun battle, the bad guy is blown away—knocked off his feet and propelled backwards by a few well-placed shots from the officer's duty pistol.

This mental home movie may even finish with the police officer walking over to the dead scumbag, rolling him over with a well-placed foot, and looking into his cold, lifeless eyes. Add in a Dirty Harry voice, "Have a nice day," and you've got all the elements for a heart-warming scenario.

The problem, however, is that if this is how we envision a lethal-force situation, then we may be setting ourselves up for a severe crash when we do run into that individual who presents a threat to us or someone else. The sad truth of the matter is that if we do have to employ deadly force, it will more than likely be against someone who is mentally unwell, chemically impaired, or simply at the end of his rope.

In the "home movies" the bad guy is almost always a man, but in real life it could be a female, an elderly citizen, a young adult, or worse—a child on a killing spree in his or her own school.

The subject may be armed with something like a knife or a pipe or, in some cases, with nothing at all. That our actions as police officers depend not only upon the situation as it exists, but also upon our perceptions of the situation as it unfolds moment by moment is something often overlooked or ignored by the media and public.

And if it is a well-armed, well-trained criminal you encounter, and you do fire those two rounds and then stop and watch the subject, waiting for him to be knocked immediately to the ground or thrown 10 feet backwards, then you may be infinitely (possibly terminally) surprised when the subject not only continues to march in your general direction, but also gets more pissed off in the process—Hollywood doesn't direct real-life encounters. That's why real police officers shoot and keep on shooting until the threat is stopped.

No matter what the situation, we are now at that moment just after we have had to employ lethal force. Our ears may be ringing, we may or may not be injured, and there is a human being lying before us with blood spilling out of his body.

The person is dead, and nothing will bring him back. Our training has worked and allowed us to function during the incredible stress of a life threatening situation, and we have done what we had to do. But now that the threat has been stopped, we are faced with the enormity of what has happened, of *what we have done*.

As the reality of this suddenly sinks in, the mental and physical stress generated by the entire episode may cause various physical reactions to occur. We may suddenly burst into tears, vomit, or lose control of our bladder or bowels. We may experience uncontrollable shaking or feel suddenly drained. Or the effects may not be so severe or immediately evident, but fester for days, weeks, sometimes even years.

This psychological reaction is the "afterburn," and if not dealt with beforehand by mental and spiritual preparation, and afterward by counseling and therapy, it can, in some cases, destroy our careers, marriages, and lives.

Having now identified this subtle threat, we can take a look at some methods that have been developed to deal with it, counteract it, and minimize the potential damage it can cause.

Preparation—Mental and Spiritual

The reality-based thought of taking a human life is not a pleasant one. Our society struggles with it constantly in the form of the death penalty, and many people have strong religious beliefs that may conflict with a conscious application of deadly force.

No matter what your personal point of view on the matter may be, it is a core dilemma that we, as police officers, must face and come to terms with individually. The question, **"Can I take a human life if I have to?"**

must be answered honestly well before the moment is at hand. If the answer is a definite no, then you are endangering not only yourself, but your fellow officers and the public, and you must consider another line of work.

Once this question has been settled in your mind, you should then take it to the next step: "If I do have to kill someone, how will it affect me and my family?" Discussing this subject with your family is unique to our profession, but actually no stranger than ensuring that our spouses, parents, or children know what to expect or where the important papers are kept should something happen to us. Our families will likely be greatly affected should we be involved in a lethal-force situation and should be forewarned of the possible media coverage and social repercussions, both of which can prove greatly distressing.

At the Scene

At the scene of a shooting the officer involved will more than likely be extremely shaken or stressed, regardless of how he may appear outwardly.

We all have our rules and regulations and policies and procedures to guide us through the mechanics, but we must also be aware of other considerations.

An officer who is shaken or stressed may make a simple statement such as, "I didn't mean to shoot him," when his actual intent was to convey that he didn't *want* to shoot him. This statement could come back to haunt him in the form of an attorney saying, "Well, Officer, if you didn't *mean* to shoot my client's brother, what *did* you mean to do?"

That is why the first thing we must do (after securing the area) when we respond to a scene where one of our people has been involved in a shooting is to separate the involved officer from reporters, suspects, and crowds, and allow him to speak to no one.

A support officer (preferably a trusted friend) should be immediately assigned to stay with and take care of the involved officer. Someone from psychological services, an attorney, and a union representative (for union members) should be advised immediately, and the officer should be removed from the scene to the station as soon as possible.

At the station, the involved officer's family should be contacted and advised. Another officer should be assigned to the officer's home as needed to screen the media, provide departmental support to the family, and act as a communications link. (If possible, the involved officer or support officer should make a phone call and advise the family personally that he is all right before the support officer gets to the home. A cruiser pulling up to the house while the officer is at work can cause alarm.)

The involved officer should be kept isolated at the station and allowed to answer **no questions** regarding the incident until he has spoken with counsel. When the appropriate investigatory personnel are assembled, the officer should make a detailed statement once only. This does not necessarily need to be done immediately after the incident.

An evaluation should be done to determine the most appropriate time for the involved officer's written report, if he will indeed be required to write one. (Many departments leave the production of all written reports regarding the incident to the officer assigned to investigate the shooting.) The officer should then be secured from duty and taken home.

A high-ranking departmental officer should make contact with the involved officer during this time period to offer support. (This is very important.)

The support officer and psychological services should maintain contact with the officer, and immediate professional counseling is not only recommended but should, in my opinion, be mandatory. Many officers feel there is a stigma attached to the act of requesting any kind of assistance—never mind psychological assistance. This may cause them to decline to participate in any form of noncompulsory counseling session, even if they do feel a need to talk about their experience.

Simply by requiring any officer who has been involved in a lethal-force situation to attend at least one counseling session with a reputable therapist, the stigma would be removed. This would then allow the officer a chance to find out if the incident bothered him more than he thought and, if so, help him deal with it. And if not, then nothing is lost.

Direct to the Hospital?

Some departments mandate that any officer involved in a deadly force incident be taken to the hospital directly from the scene and examined by a doctor. This is done for two reasons: first, due to the excitement, confusion, and adrenaline, it is possible for the officer to have sustained an injury without being immediately aware of it.

Second, and just as important, the psychological shock combined with the powerful chemical cocktail coursing through the officer's system places a great deal of stress on the body. It is very common for a doctor to administer a mild sedative to someone in this state to reduce the pressure and reduce the time required to allow the system to return to a more normal state.

Of course, once the officer is sedated, he will not be able to answer any questions about the incident until he has had time to recover from both the effects of the trauma and the affects of the medication.

The Media

After a shooting situation, someone must deal with the media. Nothing generates quite the same interest as a police-involved shooting, and some sort of departmental guidelines must be put in place and followed so that no erroneous or inaccurate information is disseminated.

One of the best ways to prevent this from occurring is to designate a specific person (or persons) to be the departmental spokesperson. This person can be the chief, a public relations officer, or a designee. Regardless of who it may be, the spokesperson must make certain that any information he releases is accurate. He must also refrain from releasing any information prematurely or "off the cuff."

A brief initial statement should be issued, saying only that an officer (or officers) was involved in a shooting and that the matter is under investigation. Later, after the facts of the situation have been determined, the spokesperson should confer with investigating officers as well as a competent departmental firearms instructor to assist him in preparing a more definitive statement.

No one other than the designated spokesperson should make any statements or comment on the situation other than to read from these prepared statements.

It is not that we have anything to hide. The reality is that ours is an extremely litigious society. If the media report several versions of events, quoting members of the involved department, and these versions of events are incorrect or conflict with the actual events, a serious problem exists. More specifically, we have needlessly created a potential problem for the involved officer if there is later civil action.

So if you are not the designated spokesperson, and someone from the media questions you about the incident, the best thing you can do is to refer the reporter making the inquiry to the spokesperson or public relations unit.

Attitudes

A very important element of helping an officer deal with having employed lethal force is the attitude of his fellow officers. The Hollywood image of the stone-cold cop dispensing death while chewing on a hot dog is best left in the video stores—not projected on ourselves or one of our people.

Many officers who have had to take a life in the performance of their duty find it extremely disconcerting, even offensive, to have their fellow officers regard them with a sense of hero worship or awe. Far from celebrating, most officers feel bad to varying degrees about the experience, no matter how well justified their actions may have been.

Extreme guilt and anxiety are also common. Most police officers have a very black and white perception of the world and what is right and wrong, and, for the most part, our society still deems the act of killing as wrong. Considering that the involved officer may also be experiencing flashbacks, vivid dreams, or nightmares about the event, and a host of other psychological, trauma-induced reactions, it's easy to see why someone who will just lend a sympathetic ear or a supportive word would be so much more welcome than someone slapping the officer on the back and saying, "Good shot! Wish I'd run into that situation!"

Remember, it could happen to anyone of us. To quote the Roman statesman and philosopher Lucius Annaeus Seneca: "Do not ask for what you will wish you had not got."

What to Say?

The best advice I have ever heard regarding what to say to an officer who has come through a deadly force (or other equally traumatic situation) is simply this: "I'm glad you are all right, Brother/Sister."

A sincere offer to listen (*just* listen, no critiques, advice, or opinions unless specifically asked for by the officer) should the officer ever feel like talking about the experience or how he is doing is also recommended.

Returning to the Scene

As with any traumatic incident, it may be extremely beneficial for the involved officer to return to the scene at a later point (if possible) to visualize what took place. Distances may be greater or closer than imagined, lighting may be different—any of a variety of circumstances or environmental conditions may have been perceived differently because of the effects of stress on the conscious and subconscious mind.

Very often by returning to the scene, the misperceptions can be cleared up—as well as a great deal of residual stress and its effects.

Aftermath

No matter how well justified a shooting may be, the involved officer must eventually accept that he has had to injure or kill someone and then learn to go on with his own life.

If you've never had to take a life in the line of duty (I have not) and you think, "No problem, as long as it's justified," you must still take into consideration the fact that some officers involved in such situations have suffered negative, long term effects as a direct result.

That is why it is so important that we are prepared not only for the possibility of having to employ lethal force against anyone who presents an immediate threat of death or serious bodily injury to us or someone else, but also to live with our actions after the smoke has cleared and we return home to our families.

The Other Side of the Coin

While we must be cognizant of the potential negative effects we may experience as a result of being involved in a deadly force situation, it's also vitally important to acknowledge that this will not necessarily be the case for every individual and every situation.

There may be situations where the person we encounter *does* fit into our preconceived idea of a "professional bad guy," or after which we feel completely justified with no reservations about having taken the actions we did based upon the totality of the circumstances surrounding the incident.

Contrary to the views and opinions of some in our society, most police officers are well aware that there *are* predatory human beings out there who have made conscious choices and decisions in their lives and are decidedly criminal. We may very well face one of these people or, indeed, someone who just wants, for whatever reason, to hurt or kill someone.

If a police officer runs into one of these walking nightmares and prevails, then it is absolutely possible that the involved officer may feel downright good about defeating such a dangerous assailant.

And if that is the case, there is absolutely nothing wrong with that! Naturally, none of us *desires* to injure anyone, much less take a life. If you do, then you are obviously on the wrong side of the badge. But we are all human, and each of us is an individual. Therefore, each situation we are involved in will be unique, simply because the perceptions of these situations will be shaped by many factors unique to our individual training, experiences, and beliefs.

I think that common sense would indicate the bottom line to be to allow yourself to accept and then deal with whatever it is you truly feel, should you be involved in a lethal-force situation. The waters get muddy enough without people trying to dictate to us what it is we should or shouldn't feel about any experience. Just be aware that you are not alone in your experiences or the resulting emotional impact, be it positive, negative, or, as is most common, a bit of both.

The Dirty Little Secret

One of the more interesting aspects of a human being's response to employing deadly force is discussed in Grossman's book, *On Killing*. Grossman's research led him to believe that a human being faced with another person presenting an immediate deadly threat to him will most likely experience an intense feeling of euphoria immediately after defeating that threatening subject.

Now while this seems like a blatantly obvious response to having defeated an assailant and saved your own life, what Grossman discovered through numerous interviews with soldiers and police officers was that this intense feeling of joy is often misinterpreted by the victor as an indication that he enjoyed the *act* of killing. This glimpse into the apparent darkness of their own souls shocked and rocked many of these people! For while they were in actuality decent, normal human beings who were faced with an abnormal situation and did what was necessary, their self-image was forever altered and they perceived themselves to be some type of monster, even though this was far from the truth. Many of these people carried this perception of their "true self" hidden deep within, never discussing it with anyone else. It became, for many of them, their "dirty little secret."

Like most secrets we carry regarding our own flaws and feelings of guilt, this particular secret loses its power when exposed to the light of truth and understanding. The feeling of euphoria *is* a natural, human response to surviving a life threatening situation, and if you experience it, it is more than all right. It is *great*, because it means you not only survived but prevailed over a mortal threat! That is what the warrior culture strives for, and as members of law enforcement or the military, we are both living symbols and active members of that culture.

Warrior Culture

The members of any society who take up arms in defense of that society have been known for thousands of years as the "warrior class."

True members of the warrior class exist to serve and protect, and they live by a strict code, often referred to as a "Code of Honor." Codes of honor such as the Samurai's Code of Bushido and the Medieval Knights' Code of Chivalry are, in essence, as relevant today as they were then. Understanding the basic tenets of these codes and applying them to our daily lives can help us better prepare to deal with both the more difficult aspects of our professions as well as the aftermath of any violent encounters we may experience.

Warrior Code of Honor

The essence of these codes can be broken down into three parts.

1. Obligation: Understanding our obligations to those whom we serve is a key component of the Warrior Culture. We owe a debt to those who raise us, employ us, and do us any significant service during our lifetime. It is our solemn obligation to repay this debt honorably.

2. Justice: This simply refers to doing the legally, ethically, and morally right thing in order to repay the debt of service we owe.

3. Courage: A warrior must have (or find) the courage to do the right thing in order to repay the debt of service. This is, for many people, the most difficult aspect of the Code of Honor. Having the courage to do the right thing in order to repay the debt of service is not always easy. As one of my teachers has repeatedly instructed me over the years, however, while the "right thing" is rarely the *easy* thing to do, that does not make it any less the *right thing* to do.

This is true regardless of whether "doing the right thing" means speaking an unpopular truth; standing up for your principles or beliefs when doing otherwise would bring you into favor with powerful people; or using deadly force against a person who presents an immediate threat of death or serious injury to you or others even though you would prefer not to have to do so.

Regardless of whether you realized it at the time you raised your hand and swore an oath to protect and defend, and pinned on the shield and strapped on the pistol, you have joined the *Warrior Class*, Pistoleer.

How you live and serve as a member of that class will define not only your life, but will also reflect greatly upon the lives and reputations of the other members of that class, *especially* those who wear the same uniform or serve the same organization as you.

Joining that organization was a choice you made. Following the Warrior's Code of Honor is another choice you *can* make. A choice that can help you through difficult times and onerous decisions. For even if you are not able to live by the code in every instance, simply by understanding how to apply it will allow you to be able to determine what the honorable course of action is in any given situation.

Then you can work on developing the courage required to do the honorable thing. It is a process that requires a lifelong commitment, but one that is well worth doing. Like most other things, it also becomes easier to do the more you do it. (An excellent book on this subject I highly recommend is *Living the Martial Way*, by Forrest E. Morgan.)

Summary

As I was taught by my trooper coach years ago, we must take care of ourselves and watch out for each other—*all* ways. This includes not only while we're "out there," but also when the "out there" follows us home to our doorstep.

Remember, too, our chances of dealing successfully with the most difficult aspects of our profession are significantly increased when we have faith in our training, continually develop true faith in ourselves, and keep faith with each other.

This, too, is our solemn responsibility to ourselves, our families, and one another.

SECTION 5
Dangers of the Blade

These are some examples of the types of knives the author has encountered while working. Razors, machetes, axes, and swords are other edged weapons you may face on the street.

In this section we'll be taking a look at fighting knives and the threat they present to us in the hands of a skilled, unfriendly user. For even though an edged weapon in *anyone's* hands may constitute a deadly threat, in the hands of a determined, focused individual who has taken the time to develop proficiency with this type of weapon, the blade presents a particularly subtle and extremely dangerous threat.

Perceptions

Very often, the threat presented by an individual armed with some type of edged weapon is under-rated. Police officers in particular frequently justify this attitude by repeating the oft-spoken phrase, "Only an idiot would bring a knife to a gunfight."

Perhaps in some instances this is true. But in many, it is not.

In many cases the person who brings the knife to the gunfight has a distinct advantage, for he knows that if he can get close enough to initiate an attack on a police officer whose weapon is holstered, there will be no gunfight.

In our society, the chances of encountering an individual who is skilled with a knife are increasing. The blade has seen an increase in popularity over the past several years, and classes relating to its use as a defensive/offensive weapon are flourishing. Many people are also turning to the knife as gun laws become stricter.

And what these people are learning is that the knife is a very efficient and deadly weapon.

In order to prepare ourselves to deal with a skilled individual armed with an edged weapon, we must begin to understand not only the mindset of the person who would attack a police officer with a knife, but also the methods that he might employ against us.

Knife-Fighter Vs. Police Officer: Mindset

Think about it. You are armed with a knife. A weapon that requires you to get extremely close to your opponent in order to inflict damage.

Your opponent, in this case a police officer, is armed with a handgun. His weapon is holstered. If you are serious and determined, you must think about how to close the gap between you. Obviously, you will not telegraph your intent. Nor will you show your weapon to your opponent until it is too late for him to react effectively if at all.

In order for your attack to be successful, it will have to be fast, furious, and aggressive. Surprise also plays a crucial role in the successful knife attack, perhaps as much as 50%. After the attack is launched, all that is then required is to place the weapon into the primary target areas presented by the human body. If you are trained, skilled, and/or experienced, you will realize that it will be possible to terminate the fight before the victim officer is even aware that he has been engaged. If you have practiced your attacking techniques and perhaps studied your potential adversaries by watching shows like "COPS," your confidence level may be HIGH.

This is the mindset of the trained knife fighter. It must be understood.

Methods of Attack

There are several methods of attack that may be used against the armed police officer. As noted above, the first thing that the serious knife fighter

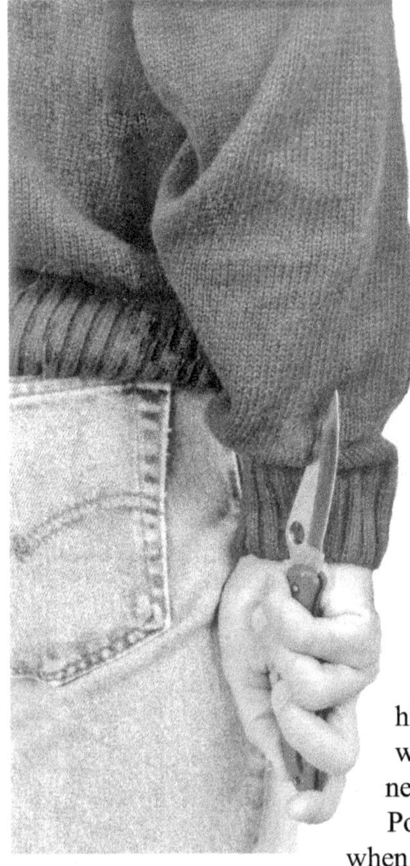

will want to do is to **close the gap** between you and him. In order to do this, the knife will often be held ready, but hidden from view.

One common knife fighting posture is to stand at a slight angle toward the potential victim, much as we do in the interview position. The knife is then held in the primary hand, arm extended down the side in a non-threatening manner, blade hidden behind the rearward leg.

The blade may also be palmed, held up behind the opened hand as shown in the photo at left.

Other fighting postures have the attacker hold the weapon close in at waist level, or up at shoulder height, blade forward, centered on the chest. In both of these cases, the knife may be hidden behind the other (support) hand, which is used to block or trap the opponent's hands during the assault. Positions such as these, usually assumed when the attack has been initiated, effectively hide the weapon from view. It is not uncommon for someone on the receiving-end of this type of attack to believe that they are involved in a fistfight, only to discover the presence of the blade *after* they have been cut.

The knife may be held in a straight grip with the edge down, or a reverse grip with the edge up with any of these techniques.

Most knife fighting systems teach a series of movements which may include slashes, thrusts, parries, and distraction techniques.

Of these, **straight thrusts** are considered the most deadly.

Target Areas

Target areas chosen for attack may vary depending upon the knife fighting system being used. A serious attacker armed with a knife, however, will generally be directing his efforts toward the most vulnerable target areas that the human body presents. From the front, this means the blade will be directed to the temple, eyes, throat, torso, and groin area. If the assailant's first objective is to disable the officer's response capability, he may target the inner wrist and upper arm before launching his mortal attack.

From the rear, the attacker may target areas such as the small of the back and the side of the neck, seeking to pierce the kidney and the carotid artery (or jugular vein), respectively. An assailant launching an attack from the rear may also target the femoral artery located inside the front upper thigh at testicle level, though when moving on an armed and trained police officer the faster, more efficient kidney/throat attack would probably be employed.

It is imperative that you understand that a penetration of mere inches can be enough to cause almost instantaneous unconsciousness and death, for the knife fighter knows this and will be directing his efforts to that end.

The Weapons

Many types and varieties of instruments fall under the heading of "edged weapons," to include knives, razors, machetes, swords, and axes. As our focus here is on knives, the discussion will be limited to them. It is important to note, however, that while a trained knife fighter may have only one or two specific weapons that he trains and feels comfortable with, the basic skills and techniques that are developed can be used with practically any other type of edged weapon.

While knives are produced in a myriad of sizes, shapes, and materials, they can generally be categorized as either fixed-blade knives or folding knives.

Some knife fighters prefer sheath or "fixed-blade" weapons. These knives, which may have a single or double-edged blade, can be carried on the belt, in the boot, or, in some cases, in specially designed, "speed-break" shoulder holsters. Rigs may also be encountered that allow the fixed-blade

Spyderco folding knives are easily opened with one hand.

knife to be secured to an arm or leg, or that permit it to be carried behind, or hanging from, the neck.

Other skilled knife fighters prefer single-edged folding knives, especially those similar in design to the one-hand opening Spyderco "clip-it" knives many police officers carry daily.

Besides attracting less attention than a concealed double-edged sheath knife, a single-edged, lock-back folder is generally legal to own, easy to conceal, strong of design, and best of all, easily explained: "I use it for work..."

Many people currently carry these types of knives inside the front of their pants, with the clip out over the pants but behind the belt, much like the appendix carry used for carrying a handgun. They may also be carried in the front pants pocket, clip exposed on the outside.

Other versions of fixed and folding knives include the double-edged boot knife, the push-dirk, (designed to be held in a closed fist with the blade protruding forward), the switchblade, (most of which are of mechanically weak design), and the Balisong or "butterfly" knife.

Regardless of the particular weapon chosen for carry and use, the serious knife fighter who decides to take on an armed police officer will probably possess, at the minimum, a level of confidence in his weapon and abilities that is at least equal to that of his intended victim.

Small knives like this TDI "Last Ditch" model can be hung around the neck inside a shirt or otherwise easily hidden. It is not uncommon for officers to miss such weapons during a cursory pat frisk search.

Police Officer Vs. Knife-Fighter: Mindset

The first thing that must be achieved by the officer is a true understanding of the danger that an assailant armed with a weapon, edged or otherwise, presents.

In order to do this, you must come face-to-face with the reality of the danger, and realize that you are susceptible to it. Many officers never allow themselves to admit this, preferring to live in a "personal fable" wherein nothing bad will ever happen to them. (See Chapter 7 §3.)

The dangers of this type of mindset become apparent in two ways: first, officers who believe that nothing bad will ever happen to them tend to miss or ignore danger signs, or take stupid chances that put themselves (or others) at risk needlessly; second, when something bad *does* happen to them, they tend to be totally surprised, shocked, and unprepared to respond appropriately.

One of the best ways to shock yourself or one of your people *out* of this dangerous mindset is to make yourself (or them) look at the results of the damage wrought by violent acts on others. In our profession, we will have many opportunities to do this, and do it we must, for this is how we develop the life-saving "**sense of danger**." (See Chapter 6 §1.)

Make no mistake—we *need* to do this. Whether it is a gunshot wound, knife wound, bludgeoning wound, etc., we need to *see it*, need to understand the damage that can be inflicted upon us by another human being. Only then can we begin to really appreciate how easily we can be seriously injured, and how crucial it is that we not allow it to happen to us or other innocent people.

(Right) This single fatal knife wound was inflicted using a small folding pocket knife.

The wound was 1/2 inch wide and penetrated approximately 2 to 3 inches deep.

The small blade severed the carotid artery.

Unconsciousness and death quickly followed.

Don't make the mistake of underestimating the danger presented by a knife-armed assailant, regardless of the size of the knife *or* the assailant!

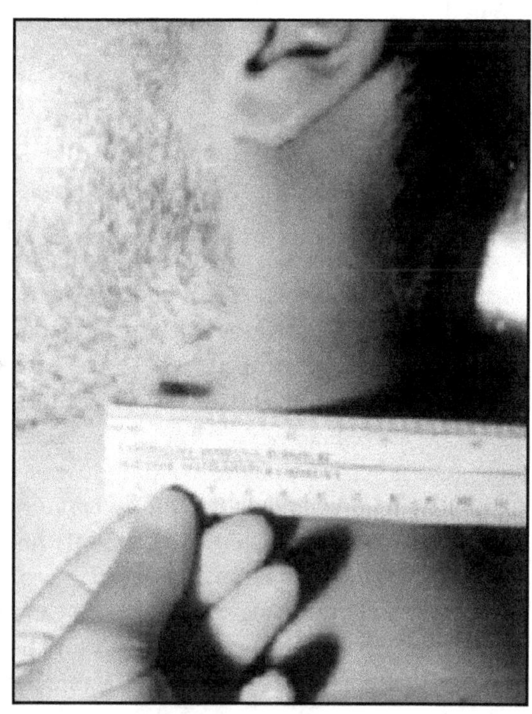

Know the Enemy

After developing a sense of danger, an understanding of how the trained knife fighter thinks, trains, and attacks must be achieved. These aspects were touched on above, though a more thorough study is recommended. In fact, I highly recommend that police officers take one of the many knife fighting courses that are offered throughout the country, both in order to achieve a greater understanding of this potential threat, as well as to enrich your own offensive capabilities. Let's look at that for a moment.

While I realize that the idea of a police officer using a knife as a weapon may seem incongruous to our profession, it is actually as reasonable as using any other means of deadly force, should the situation require it. The knife, commonly carried by police officers anyway, also makes for a dependable back-up weapon under extreme circumstances.

Warning Signs

The officer who has developed a sense of danger knows what a knife can do to the human body. The officer who has studied how knives can be used against him will be alert to the warning signs that indicate he is dealing with someone who a) has an edged weapon in their possession, or b) may be preparing to launch an assault against him while using one.

The first thing to look for is a knife itself. **Examine the hands:** Can they be clearly seen? Is one of them hidden or covered by the other? Is one being held in an unnatural position? **Look for clip-type knives:** is one attached to the belt, waistband of the pants, or pocket? **Examine the belt:** are there any pouches, cases, sheaths, or bulges visible? Also check the belt-buckle: some knives are disguised as buckles, with the belt itself serving as the scabbard. **Scan the chest area:** look for telltale shoulder holster straps or bulges, which could indicate a firearm or a knife. **Scan the immediate area:** vehicle, apartment, work area, or house interior. Especially beware of kitchens when responding to a residence or restaurant.

Remember to look both for weapons as well as empty knife cases, sheaths, or pouches; even frayed pants pocket edges can indicate that a clip-type knife is normally carried there.

Once the presence of an edged weapon is detected, it is prudent to assume that the person in possession of it knows how to use it. You should then act accordingly, taking all reasonable precautions.

The Defense

The best defense against a knife attack is not allowing it to occur!

Knowing what warning signs to look for helps you detect the threat. Should you detect such a threat and believe that an attack is imminent, you should then take action to prevent it. Since you understand that knife attacks are generally fast and furious and require the attacker to get close to you, you should immediately **cover the offender** with your firearm and **create distance** between you. At least 10 feet of distance (plus the length of the weapon) is recommended.

Clear verbalized commands should then be used to control the assailant's behavior.

If the assailant complies with your verbal commands, have him drop the weapon to the ground, back away from it, and assume some type of control position. You may choose to have him kneel down or prone-out away from the weapon.

Never allow a subject to approach you to hand you the weapon! Keeping the suspect covered, **call for back up**. Once the suspect is properly secured, check him thoroughly for additional weapons.

If, after challenging the suspect with your weapon drawn, he ignores your commands and decides to close with you, you should then employ whatever level of force you believe is necessary to stop the threat, up to and including the use of deadly force.

Remember, the edged weapon is considered second only to the handgun on the hierarchy of short-weapon deadliness.

Surprise Assault: Defense

Should you miss or ignore the warning signs of an impending knife assault, your options will be limited once the attack is under way. Depending upon your training and the circumstances, you may not even realize initially that you are being cut. If you even suspect that an assailant armed with an edged weapon is attacking you, you must either close with the subject and attempt some type of practiced physical control technique, or immediately disengage to increase space between you.

If you do disengage, try to get something solid between you and the assailant's weapon. Your sidearm should then be introduced into the equation. You must do whatever is necessary to prevent you from freezing up once you realize you are being attacked and/or cut. Standing in place and attempting to draw your weapon while under attack is not generally recommended, for the trained knife fighter will anticipate this and plan for it.

Does this mean you will die when attacked by a knife-wielding assailant? Absolutely NOT! However, it is probable that a determined assailant armed with a blade will more than likely cut you once he has penetrated the gap and closed with you. Far from being a defeatist attitude, this probability of sustaining some type of knife wound during a surprise attack must be accepted in order to mentally prepare for it as well as survive it.

So what gets cut? If you must "give something up" to block the attack, it is recommended that you use the outside or back of the support-arm forearm while creating distance and accessing your firearm.

Surprise Assault: Offense

In addition to defending, you can also **counter-attack**. Low kicks directed at the assailant's instep, knee and shin area, or groin may be effective. If you have been trained extensively in the martial arts and have true confidence in your techniques, you may close with and engage the subject and attempt some type of physical control technique. All of these options, however, should only be used if the firearm is immediately unavailable, or, if in attempting to access it you would leave your own vulnerable target areas open to attack.

Summary

Fighting knives and individuals trained in their use are becoming more common. The threat they present is real. Far from being "only a knife," the blade is a deadly, efficient weapon, and the chances that someone may launch an attack against you with one are increasing.

Is that an unsettling thought, brothers and sisters? You bet it is. But it is the truth, and since we have placed ourselves squarely in the arena by raising our right hands and accepting the weight of the gun and the badge, we must face it head on, prepare for the possibility of encountering a skilled knife fighter as best we can, and decide well before the moment is at hand that should we be the recipient of a skilled knife fighter's attack, not only will we survive the encounter, we will *win* the encounter.

And win it we must, for failure is not an option!

SECTION 6
Police vs. Terrorist

NOTE: The following information, while hardly definitive, is respectfully offered for consideration. As this specific threat continues to develop and evolve, so must our mindsets, training, and abilities. This challenge has had, and will undoubtedly continue to have, an enormous influence on the role of the individual U.S. law enforcement and security professional.

The threat of terrorist attacks within the United States has not abated since September 11, 2001.

Members of U.S. law enforcement have been kept busy actively working to detect, deter, and capture both individuals and groups intent on killing Americans and carrying out vicious acts to further their violent extremist political and religious goals.

While most people are aware that terrorist attacks occur on an all-too frequent basis throughout the world, we tend to forget or overlook the fact that there have been a number of terrorist incidents in America both before and since 9/11. With the exception of a major incident such as the Oklahoma City bombing (April 1995), many have not been given extensive press coverage. Even those that have been are seemingly quickly forgotten by the general public.

Just a few cases in point:

- **December 14, 1999:** Ahmed Ressam, an Algerian living in Canada, was arrested by U.S. Customs officials at Port Angeles, Washington, after they found nitroglycerin and timing devices concealed in his car. It was later revealed that Ressam and at least three other Algerians had conspired to bomb the Los Angeles International Airport (LAX). Ressam was tried, found guilty, and sentenced to 22 years in prison.
- **September-October 2001:** Letters containing anthrax spores were mailed to two U.S. Senators and several news media offices. Five people died and more than a dozen others were infected. Bruce Edwards Ivins, a senior biodefense researcher at the United States Army Medical Research Institute of Infectious Diseases (USAMRIID) in Fort Detrick, Maryland

was eventually identified as the primary suspect. Ivins committed suicide on August 1, 2008, after learning that formal charges were to be brought against him.

• **December 2001:** Richard Reid, the "shoe bomber," tried to detonate explosives aboard a flight from Paris to Miami. He was subdued by flight attendants and passengers and taken into custody by the Massachusetts State Police and FBI at Logan International Airport. Reid was found guilty of charges of terrorism in 2003 and sentenced to life imprisonment.

• **July 4, 2002:** An Egyptian immigrant, Heshem Mohamed Hadayet, launched an unprovoked attack inside the Los Angeles International Airport. Armed with two handguns and a knife, Hadayet opened fire on a group of people lined up at the El Al ticket counter, killing two and wounding seven others. Hadayet was shot and killed by a pistol-armed El Al security officer moments after he began his attack.

• **May 2003:** Iyman Faris, a naturalized U.S. citizen originally from Kashmir and living in Columbus, Ohio, was arrested for planning to collapse the Brooklyn Bridge. The New York City Police Department developed information about the conspiracy and deterred the attack. Faris was sentenced to 20 years.

These are just a few examples of the types of terrorist activities that have been attempted or committed on U.S. soil. Other acts such as the Beltway Sniper Attacks, the Jose Padilla "dirty bomb" case, the arrests and convictions of members of the "Buffalo Six" (also known as "Lackawanna Six"), a group with ties to al-Qaeda, and numerous other cases that have been made public indicate that we will be seeing terrorist attacks here in the future.

In addition, based upon terrorist attacks that have occurred in other parts of the world and Intelligence that has been developed, we can also reasonably anticipate further attacks of a more brutal nature to take place in the U.S.

The specter of multiple, coordinated small-unit ground attacks such as carried out during the London bombings on July 7, 2005 is one such likely scenario. Another is the horror of a school attack, siege, and ultimately a massacre as experienced at Beslan's School Number One in North Ossetia, Russia, on September 1, 2004. During this horrific terrorist incident, 186 school children and 158 adults were murdered.

The likelihood of members of U.S. law enforcement having to deal

The author (center) with two members of the Israeli Border Police (Magav) outside the Old City of Jerusalem. All Magav officers, male and female, receive combat and counter-terrorism training. These officers are on the front line in the war on terrorism in an extremely active environment. Yet they carry out their duties day after day professionally, demonstrating both courage and restraint.

with such a determined individual or group grows each day. Yet, for the most part, training to prepare for these types of incidents has largely been focused on responding to the aftermath of such an attack, rather than on how to act when faced with the threat itself.

We must do more.

I have had the opportunity through the years to observe and work with police officers in different parts of the world who have had to deal with these types of attacks on a fairly regular basis. In my experience, police officers from our allied nations for the most part tend to be of similar mind, temperament, and approach to their duties, regardless of country of origin.

That is why I believe, having also been privileged to have worked with officers from all across the United States, that we will rise to the occasion as our brother and sister officers in Europe and Asia have done when this menace again strikes here.

How the Terrorists Operate

Terrorists employ premeditated, politically or socially motivated violence against persons or property in order to intimidate or coerce a government or the civilian population.

The terrorist's basic goal is to induce fear by intimidation.

Their violent acts are neither spontaneous nor random. A determined terrorist attack will generally be well-planned and conducted very deliberately.

While most terrorist groups are organized into "cells"—small, relatively isolated groups—individuals acting alone may also carry out terrorist acts.

Because most terrorists employ the small-unit tactical concept, they are generally able to move about, plan, and attack with limited exposure. The nature of these types of activities generally dictates the use of hit & run type operations, the suicide/homicide attack, and the use of weapons of mass destruction (WMD). Elements from each of these tactical options may be combined in the initial plan (Plan "A"), or may be transitioned to (Plan "B") should Plan "A" not work out as intended.

Hit & Run Attack

This is a small unit attack utilizing small arms, vehicles, explosive devices, etc. In this type of operation the attackers generally have an exfiltration plan. If cornered, they may surrender or transition to a suicide attack mode.

Suicide/Homicide Attack

This tactic is often referred to as either a "suicide attack" or a "suicide/homicide attack" by those who suffer the attack.

July 12, 2005: The author (center) with two members of the British Metropolitan Police Service, outside New Scotland Yard in London. Conti was sent to London to participate in a coordinated anti-terrorist, intelligence-sharing operation with members of the British law enforcement and emergency services establishments days after the 7/7 London bombings. The attack was the first suicide/homicide incident in Western Europe. Fifty-two people were killed and more than 700 were wounded. All four bombers died during the attacks.

A second, similar attack was attempted two weeks later. Fortunately, the devices failed to detonate. On July 22, while searching for the suspects involved in the second bombing attempt, police shot and killed a Brazilian man at the Stockwell tube station. The officers had pursued the man believing him to be one of the second wave bombing suspects. Police later confirmed he was not related to the bombing incidents and issued an apology, accepting full responsibility. Mistakes such as these are an unfortunate by-product of the stress, confusion, and sense of extreme urgency that the suicide bombing threat produces. Even experience dealing with these types of threats and training designed specifically to address them will not eliminate the chances for this type of unfortunate mistake. We must, however, make the effort to reduce them.

Six men were eventually arrested and charged with conspiracy to commit murder as a result of their involvement in the July 22, 2005 bombing attempt. Four of the men were convicted in 2007 and sentenced to 40 year prison terms. The other two suspects may be retried.

Those who employ it however, refer to it as a "Martyr Operation."

Think about that clear distinction in mindsets. Unlike most criminals we may encounter while working, the suicide attacker has no exfiltration plans or desires. The objective of the attack is to kill as many people as possible while dying yourself. This was the mindset of the 9/11 and the July 7th London subway attackers.

There are a few common tactics used by suicide attackers. The first is to have an individual (or individuals) carrying a high-explosive device on his or her person detonate the device in a crowded area.

The second is to have an individual (or individuals) deliver a vehicle that has been equipped with a high-explosive device by driving or flying it into the target area and detonating the device.

Obviously, unless the suicide bomber is exposed by others or detected during the early stages of preparation by trained personnel, these types of attacks are very difficult to defend against. Since a suicide bombing operation can be planned and carried out by persons without professional training or assistance, and for very low monetary costs (such as the London bombers are believed to have done), this threat is made all the more terrifyingly real and probable.

In addition, the psychological impact of multiple suicide bombings on the population can be devastating.

It must be remembered that a suicide attack is a proven tactic with a strategic objective. Chances are great we will see this type of attack in the U.S. again.

WMD Attack

This describes a small unit attack utilizing a chemical, biological, radiological, nuclear, or high explosive (CBRNE) device, or combinations thereof.

The series of coordinated Madrid train bombings executed on March 11, 2004, provide an example of this type of attack. Carried out just three days before Spain's general election, this attack resulted in 191 people murdered and more than 1,700 wounded.

The explosive devices were concealed in backpacks. While the London bombers also used backpacks to deliver the devices, the Madrid bombers left their backpacks on the trains using cell phones as timers to detonate the devices at the height of the morning rush hour.

Less than a month later, four Arab terrorists believed to be involved in the Madrid bombings died in an apparent suicide explosion, killing one police officer and wounding eleven others.

Our Response Options

As police officers, we will most likely respond to these types of incidents after the attack has been launched and completed. In these cases, we need to be aware of the possibility of secondary attacks or devices and act accordingly.

Should you be present while an attack is being initiated, however, while on duty or off, you need to keep in mind that we know from captured documents, past operations, and other Intelligence that the terrorist's standard operating procedures include 1) immediately detonating their suicide/homicide device should they be confronted or challenged by a member of law enforcement, and 2) immediately and systematically murdering anyone identified or believed to be a threat to them—*especially* a member of the military or law enforcement—during the first stages of a hostage-taking or siege operation. This is not hard to believe, considering that these types of operations are intended to result in the deaths of both the terrorists and all the hostages anyway.

So if you find yourself in this type of situation, and you are sure you are dealing with homicidal attackers as described above, your best response option will be to 1) take out your pistol (remember, the serious Pistoleer is *always* armed) and 2) launch your own counterattack as quickly, violently,

The Boston Globe

FRIDAY, JUNE 13, 2003

NEW WEAPONRY AT LOGAN

State Police Lieutenant Thomas Coffey (left) and trooper Edward F. Powers patrolled with MP5SD submachine guns yesterday as Logan Airport added to its security measures. Massport acquired 30 of the guns at a cost of $2,500 each, making Logan the first airport in the nation to employ such high-tech weaponry. B4.

Israelis kill 9 in strike on Hamas

Palestinians slay one; war of words grows

By Dan Ephron

June 2003: Members of the Massachusetts State Police assigned to Logan International Airport in Boston, MA become the first airport police in the nation to patrol with submachine guns on a regular basis. Logan was the site from which half of the hijacked aircraft used in the 9/11 attacks originated.

and effectively as possible, showing no mercy to the attackers. Your ability to do this will depend almost exclusively on the confidence you have in your abilities to wield your pistol professionally and skillfully.

And this confidence will only come through practice and experience.

Train hard. Train well. Much is at stake. For the response of the first U.S. law enforcement officer to an actual suicide bomber or siege operation will resonate throughout the world, and let our enemies know what they can expect from us in the future.

Perceived Suicide Bomber Incidents in U.S. since 9/11

While there have been a number of threats and bomb scares over the years, the specter of a suicide bomber since 9/11 has put many people on edge and in a heightened state of awareness regarding this specific threat. Two incidents in particular stand out as indicators of how the members of U.S. Law Enforcement will respond should the threat be realized, and there is enough time to react.

December 7, 2005: Two federal Air Marshals shot and killed a 44 year old man, Rigoberto Alpizar, at Miami International Airport after he bolted from his seat on an American Airlines flight, saying he had a bomb. When confronted by the Air Marshals and ordered to the ground, Alpizar instead reached into his backpack at which point the Marshals fired their pistols. The Air Marshals were found to be legally justified in their actions.

September 21, 2007: A 19 year old female MIT student wearing a black hooded sweatshirt and an electronic circuit board device on her chest that included lights and wires set off a suicide bomber scare when she approached an information booth in the terminal at Logan International Airport in Boston. Star Simpson, who was also holding a large lump of Play-Doh, walked away from the booth, saying simply, "It's a piece of art" when the employee at the booth asked her what she had on her chest. She refused to answer any more questions and began to roam the terminal, causing several employees to flee while others called the Massachusetts State Police. Simpson was then challenged by state police officers armed with MP5 submachine guns. She immediately complied with their orders. After EOD experts determined the device was not a bomb, Simpson was arrested and charged with disturbing the peace and possession of a hoax device.

SECTION 7

Respirators: The *Other* Body Armor

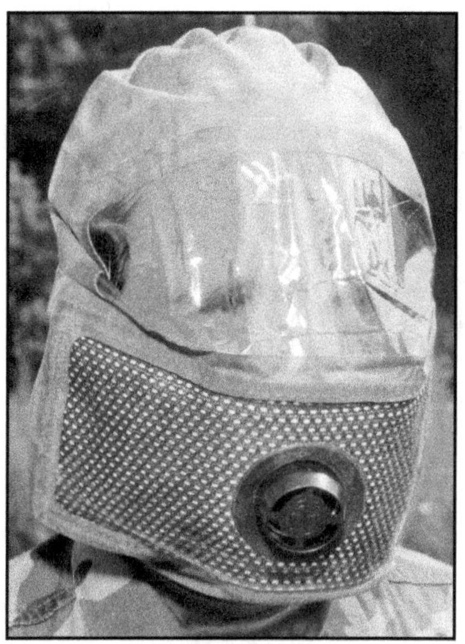

The QuickMask Respirator can be carried in a small pouch attached to the duty belt. Unlike more conventional respirators, the Quick Mask is an emergency escape mask designed for single-use applications.

The final section in this chapter will be brief, but do not gauge the importance of the subject matter based upon the brevity.

The reason I am including this section is to make and stress one critical point: *Every police officer should have, and know how to maintain and use, an air-purifying respirator!*

What is an Air-Purifying Respirator?

Commonly referred to as a "gas mask," an air-purifying respirator is a critical piece of protective equipment that can keep you safe from a number of dangerous materials.

In addition to riot agents like CS and CN, a quality respirator equipped with the appropriate filter can provide protection against chemical and biological warfare agents; blistering and blood agents; radioactive and highly toxic nuclear particles; aerosols and micro-organisms; and bacteria and viruses, as well as numerous other hazardous contaminants used in industrial applications.

Why Should You Have One for Other than Riot Control Incidents?

If you find yourself in an area that has been contaminated as a result of a nuclear, biological, or chemical (NBC) attack by an individual or group, or should you need to respond into a contaminated area to stop a threat and/or rescue innocents, you will want to have the best respirator available—and you will want it NOW!

The time to consider whether or not to acquire a respirator, or to try and remember where you stashed your issued mask or how to use it, is *not* when you are watching the cloud of unidentified material coming your way! It is also definitely not while standing outside a building listening to the screams of the innocent because a madman has deployed a couple of canisters of CS and is creating havoc while wearing the $20.00 surplus respirator he bought on the Internet.

The specter of an individual walking into a crowded environment and throwing around a powder or liquid, or releasing a gaseous substance while proclaiming it to be anthrax, ricin, sarin, or some other terror-inducing material is another consideration the modern law enforcement officer needs to think about. For while it may be a hoax in the vast majority of cases, what if in the particular instance to which you are responding it's for real? Do you really want to just wade into the area without any type of protection for your eyes, face, and lungs—especially when the protection is so readily available?

If You Really Needed One, Wouldn't It Be Issued To You?

This is the same question some officers asked for years regarding personal body armor. I, like many other officers, purchased my own body armor when I first got on the job because my department didn't issue it at the time.

I still wear body armor every time I wear the uniform, and have for more than 22 years. Thankfully, I have never needed it to stop a bullet from entering my body, but just having it has always provided me with a greater sense of safety.

The same can be said for a respirator (which I also keep accessible when working), for with either piece of equipment, should you need it, you will need it very badly, and its presence could mean the difference between living and dying for you and others.

You because both pieces of equipment can protect you and save your life.

Others because if you are incapacitated or killed, then you will be unable to do your job and protect them.

There Are Many Like It, But This One is Mine

Like any piece of equipment, respirators will only work as designed when assembled and used correctly. Most modern respirators are composed of a

The M95 Full Facepiece Respirator is an ergonomically designed, comfortable and effective respirator. The author has worked extensively with this and many other respirators over the past 26+ years in the military, police, and private industries, and believes the M95 to be one of the best negative-pressure respirators available for tactical applications. It is shown here with the M95 filter cartridge attached.

number of modular components which must be installed properly prior to use. While the filter cartridge (shown attached to the mask in the photo above) is the most obvious, other components such as inhalation and exhalation valves, eyelets, head harnesses, and straps, etc. must be checked and maintained on a regular basis as well. If any components are apparently missing, distorted, or damaged, do not use the respirator until it has been professionally inspected and repaired.

Prior to employing any respirator, you must be familiar with the design, operational capabilities, and limitations of the specific device you have. Take nothing for granted. Read all the information provided by the manufacturer. Listen to your trainers and follow their advice and instructions. If you have purchased your own respirator, you should seek out additional information as well as professional instruction in its maintenance and use.

As always, professional instruction in the operation and employment of this type of equipment is mandatory to ensure the highest margin of safety for you and those around you.

Certified, knowledgeable, and competent instructors should be sought prior to purchasing, training with, or employing any critical equipment. Considering what the respirators are intended to be used for, there are few more critical pieces of equipment we may possess.

Additional information about the selection, care, and use of respirators is available in the book, *BEYOND PEPPER SPRAY*, by Michael E. Conti. Available from Saber Press.
www.sabergroup.com

CHAPTER 8

Low Light Considerations

SECTION 1
How Our Eyes Work

The human eye is a complex organ that can be likened to a camera.

The **cornea**, a protective layer of transparent tissue at the front of the eye, focuses light as it is passed into the eye.

As light enters the eye, it passes through the **iris**, which is the colored part of the eye. Depending on how much light there is, the iris may contract or dilate like the aperture of a camera, allowing more or less light to enter the **pupil** (the black "dot" in the center of the eye). This constriction and dilation in response to the amount of light present is what makes the pupil appear either smaller or larger.

The light then enters the **lens**, which changes its shape to better focus on light reflecting from near or distant objects. This changing focus is called **accommodation**. As we get older, the lens hardens and accommodation becomes more difficult, causing a loss in visual acuity. This is most obvious in people over 40 years of age, who often develop **presbyopia**. Presbyopia is a condition that makes it difficult to focus on objects near to the eye.

Both the cornea and the lens at the front of the eye focus light through the center of the eye onto the **retina**, which lines the back of the

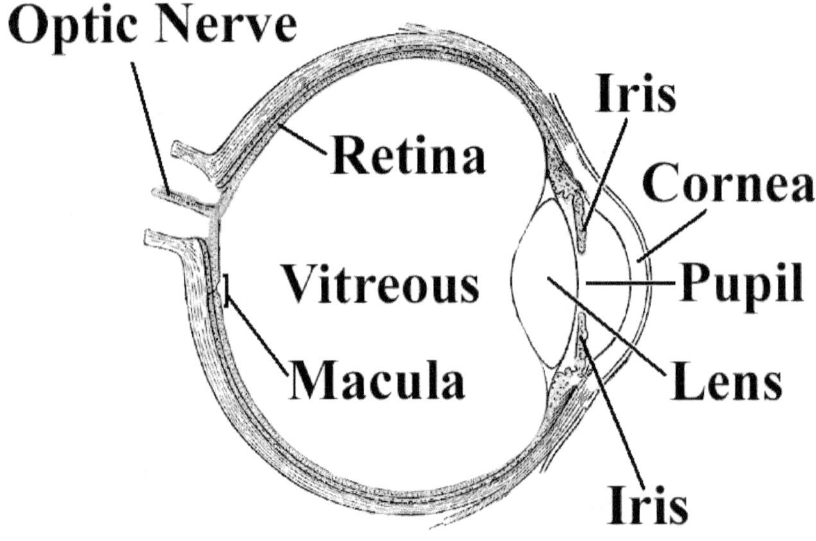

Diagram of the human eye.

eye. On its way through the eye to the retina, the light passes through a clear jelly-like substance called the **vitreous**.

Once the light reaches the retina, light-sensitive nerve endings known as **photoreceptors** (or **rods** and **cones)** in the retina act like film, in that they record light images and then instantly convert them into nerve signals. At the center of the retina is the **macula**, which contains more specialized photoreceptors than any other part of the retina. The center of the macula is called the **fovea**.

Groups of photoreceptors within the retina then convert all the light images into meaningful **neural patterns** (or electrical impulses) and transmit this information to the brain through the **optic nerve**.

The brain then receives and interprets this information and vision occurs.

How We See In Low Light Conditions

Humans have evolved so that we see best under daylight conditions. Because of this, we are considered to be "**diurnal**" as opposed to "**nocturnal**." The reason we are diurnal is because our eyes contain many more cones (130 million) than rods (7 million).

The rods are the more sensitive of the two types of photoreceptors in our eyes. Compared to the cones, the rods are actually about 1,000 times more sensitive to light. The rods are used to detect shades of light, shape, and movement. They work by producing a chemical called **rhodopsin** or "**visual purple**." Under low-light conditions, it usually takes the eyes about 30 minutes to produce enough rhodopsin to allow images to be detected.

After approximately 1 hour, our eyes will be completely adapted to the low light conditions. This is as good as our personal night vision gets.

It is important to remember that our vision is drastically impaired when we transition from a brightly-lit environment to a lowly-lit environment. In fact, for at least the first 30 minutes our vision will be approximately 20/180, which is considered legally blind!

It is also important to remember that once we have achieved our highest level of night vision or **adaptation**, we can lose it in an instant if our eyes are exposed to a bright light, even for a moment, because the rhodopsin will be "bleached out" as a result. This means it will take another 30-60 minutes before your night vision is at its peak again. This can be a long time when seconds count during a search or other tactical activity.

Maintaining Night Vision

There are a lot of beliefs about how best to maintain night vision when operating in low light environments. One technique I was taught in the U.S. Army was to close one eye when exposed to any white light, so as to maintain the night vision in "at least that one eye..."

This technique actually does seem to work to a degree, even though it doesn't make sense when you consider that the pupils of the eyes are dilated or contracted in a *sympathetic fashion*. In other words, if one eye is exposed to bright light and the pupil constricts, so should the other, regardless of whether the eyelid is closed or not.

As I said though, it does seem to help, as does the practice of immediately looking away or shielding the eyes when white light is observed. Of course some types of intense white light (even momentary light) can completely blind you, in low light or not. (Think of a camera's flash and the resultant visual impairment it can induce even during daylight conditions.)

Tips for Seeing Better in Low Light

Another technique I was taught in the Army for working in low light was to never look directly at the object you are trying to observe. Rather, look off to either side of it, or rotate your eyeballs in quick jerky movements around the periphery of it. The object can then often be "seen," even if not in the normal manner.

This works because it allows the rods, which are located around the edges of the fovea, to take in information about the object and translate it into a pattern that can be decoded by the brain.

This technique takes a little time to get used to, and even more time to learn to trust the images produced by the brain.

While your ability to see well during either the day or night is primarily dependent upon your age, other factors such as proper nutrition, health, and even cigarette smoking can have a significant impact.

While the first two are positive factors, the last, smoking, is definitely in the negative category.

As for nutrition, believe it or not, Mom was right about eating carrots to help you see better. Carrots contain beta-carotene, which the body converts into vitamin A or "retinol." Vitamin A is also found in fish oil, liver, eggs, and fortified dairy products.

SECTION 2

Challenges & Benefits of Low Light Environments

Why We Need Low Light Skills

Most police-involved shootings take place during the hours of darkness or under low light conditions. While some people might, at first blush, believe this to indicate that only officers working the evening or midnight shifts need be concerned about low light skills, the fact is that even officers working primarily during the day may find themselves in a dimly lit environment should they enter a house, office building, barroom, etc.

Accordingly, all of us need to be familiar with the challenges and benefits presented by the low light environment

Challenges of Low Light Environments

One of the core aspects involved in the justifiable use of force by a police officer concerns **identification of the threat**. This is often difficult enough in a well-lighted environment, let alone a dimly lit one. While the ability to positively identify an immediate threat may be more difficult under low light conditions, the responsibility for employing deadly force appropriately remains.

Fortunately, there are tactics, techniques, and equipment options available to assist us to do this to the best of our ability.

Reading the Light

When operating in a brightly lit environment under normal conditions, we should be able to distinguish a high degree of detail, possess excellent depth perception, and be able to identify threats reasonably well.

As the available light is changed or diminished, however, the number and types of challenges we will be presented with will increase.

When outdoors, the "gray" times of the day, dawn and dusk, may prove to be more problematic than one would think. This is because our eyes tend to have a tough time distinguishing colors, shapes, and textures in this lighting. Vision under these lighting conditions actually becomes, for most people, a bit monochromatic, almost as if the world had changed to varying shades of black and white.

Under these conditions, our ability to visually identify things, including threats, becomes diminished. The less available light present, the more our difficulties increase.

Artificial light sources can be a help or hindrance to us under darker lighting conditions, as they change our ability to accurately determine shapes and colors as well as negatively affect depth perception.

Should we find ourselves in a completely lightless environment (such as in a sealed room or cave), we will be, for all intents and purposes, unable to operate effectively unless we possess or can improvise some type of light source.

Benefits of Low Light Environments

The darkness can be your friend, if you are comfortably familiar with it.

Many people are not. Many are actually afraid of the dark, a fear that often carries over from childhood.

One interesting theory about this innate human fear of the dark is that it is a holdover from the time in our history when we lived in small groups and sought protection from the elements and predators by holing up in caves. Supposedly, children (and sometimes adults) see "monsters" in the dark as a result of this "genetic memory," because there once *were* monsters out there in the dark, and this fear developed to keep the children close to the adults and protected while the nocturnal beasts prowled.

One way to make this common human phobia work for you is to come to the conscious realization that 1) there *are* still predators out there in the dark, and 2) you can turn this to your advantage if you decide to develop yourself into a *superior* predator, so you are the hunter and not the hunted.

It is important to remember that we humans are, by design, predatory animals; highly evolved hunter/gatherers who still seek protection from the elements and other predators by holing up in our homes, the modern version of the cave—enhanced with central heating and wide-screen televisions, of course!

Learn to use the darkness. It can provide concealment, a tactical edge, and a psychological advantage if you adapt to it better than your adversaries.

Low Light Rules

A few good rules to remember when operating in low light environments:

- If you can see yourself in a low light environment (look down at your arms and legs), then so can someone who may be in the shadows. In that case, get yourself into the shadows as quickly and safely as possible. Doing this may require you to briefly illuminate the area into which you are moving so you can ensure no threats currently reside there. (More on this in the next section.)

- If you *can* see yourself but cannot get to the shadows for any reason, then LIGHT UP THE AREA as much as possible to take away the tactical advantage of anyone hiding there.

- If possible, always try to avoid backlighting yourself. When entering a dark area or room through a doorway or other opening, do so quickly so you are not "framed" in the opening.

- You can use the light from your flashlight, vehicle, or another source to create a wall of light to dazzle or blind your adversary. Called "masking," this may allow you to maneuver unseen behind the wall of light. You can also use light to deny an area to your adversary, for he/they will have difficulty seeing who or what is behind it in most cases, and may choose avoidance rather than risk facing the unknown.

- Always carry a backup flashlight.

SECTION 3
Flashlights & Pistols

The Flashlight: Another Basic Tool of the Trade

Along with a good quality handgun, the professional pistoleer must possess at least two good, high-quality flashlights. Owning both a larger, rechargeable model and a smaller belt or pocket-carried model powered by lithium or alkaline batteries is recommended.

Possessing *at least* two high quality lights is a necessity, not a luxury!

The difference between having a flashlight when you need it or not can be the difference between life and death—for you or someone else.

And the difference between having a high-quality, dependable flashlight as opposed to a low-quality, undependable one can be just as significant. So do not skimp when it comes to your flashlights any more than you would when it comes to your pistol—get the best quality light you can possibly afford.

You also need to understand that there is a major difference between a household or utility type flashlight and a flashlight specifically designed and intended for hard tactical use. The difference is significant.

Basic Desirable Characteristics of the Tactical Flashlight

The following criteria are provided to assist you in assessing the tactical qualities of a flashlight.

- The tactical flashlight should be made of **superior materials**. While anodized aircraft aluminum is preferred, steel or high-impact phenolic (polymer) materials are also acceptable as long as they are manufactured to high standards. Aluminum is generally preferred over steel because it offers less electrical resistance than steel (meaning more power is delivered to the light), and is more corrosion resistant. Naturally, aluminum also tends to be stronger and more durable than most polymers.
- The tactical flashlight must be **waterproof** and **shockproof**.
- Regardless of the length of the flashlight, **you should be able to grasp it comfortably and control it using only one hand**. You should also be able to find the activation switch quickly, easily, and consistently. Smaller flashlights equipped with end or tail-cap activation switches best satisfy this requirement. Since it is recommended that you own both a large,

Common Characteristics of the Tactical Flashlight

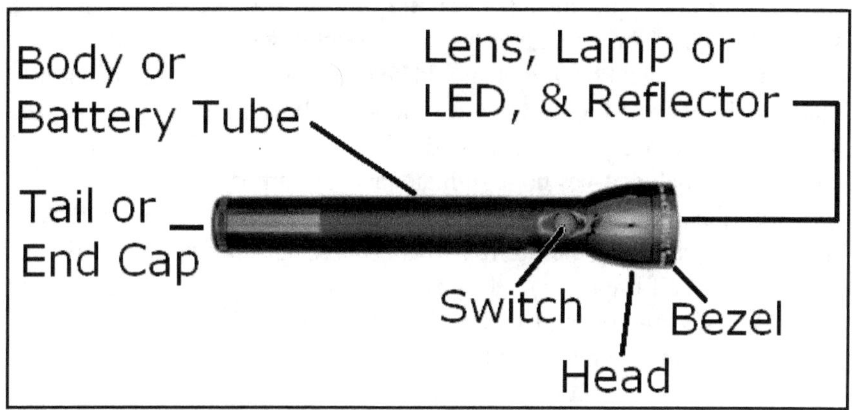

Common characteristics of hand-held tactical flashlights. Top: Full-size 3-cell Maglite® flashlight. Below: Pocket-size 1-cell Brite-Strike® Tactical Blue-Dot™ flashlight. Advances in technology allow the 3.5" Brite-Strike model shown below to produce more than 2 times the lumens of the foot-long D-Cell model pictured above!

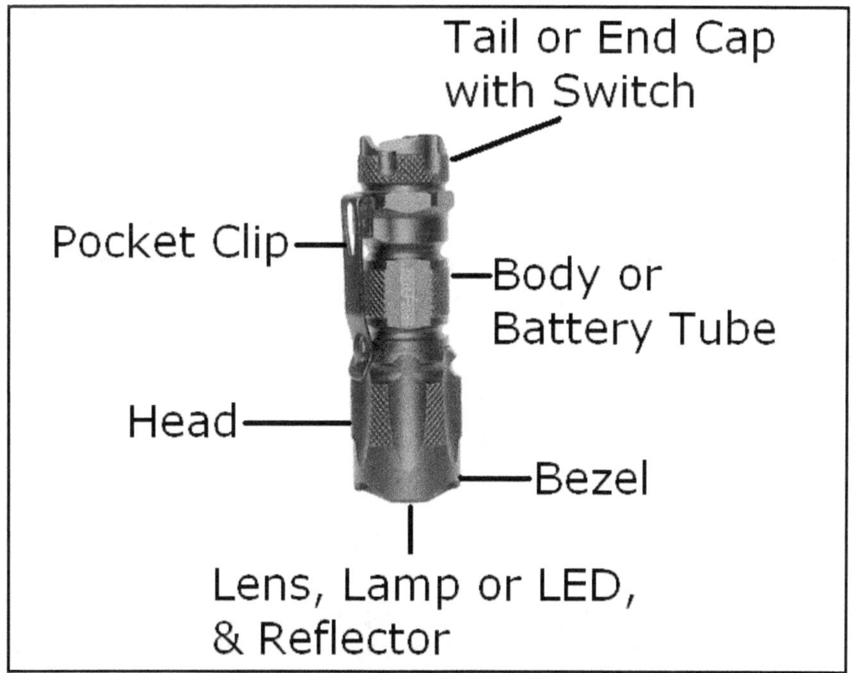

rechargeable flashlight as well as a smaller model, you should know that most longer models are produced with the activation switch on the side of the body, or tube. This means you will need to work and become familiar with both lights well enough to minimize fumbling during operation.

- The tactical flashlight should be equipped with a **non-adjustable**, clear and bright **pre-focused beam**. Adjustable beams tend to produce dark spots and shadows within the field of the beam and this "adjustment" capability actually serves no legitimate tactical purpose.
- For flashlights using batteries other than the rechargeable type, lithium batteries are the preferred power source because they are powerful, have a long shelf life (usually 10 years), and perform well in cold weather.
- The brighter and whiter the light output, the better. Be careful when evaluating lights based on reported **candela** or **candlepower**, because different flashlight manufacturers measure it differently. **Lumens** on the other hand, is a measurement of the actual light output that doesn't take into account the focus of the beam. **Lights that produce 80 lumens and better are available and recommended**.
- There are a variety of switching mechanisms available that range from simple ON/OFF to MOMENTARY ON/OFF, LOW/HIGH/OFF, and STROBE capability. At the very least your light should be **capable of being positively turned on as well as having momentary or "pressure flash on" capability.**

Types of Flashlights

Flashlights are available in a variety of sizes, shapes, and configurations. Some are designed to be **hand-held** while others are intended to be used as **weapon-mounted** lights. Your choices will be influenced by the environment you will be working in, the mission you are tasked with, and the resources available to you.

Your department or agency may also determine the specific types of lights you will be using, and how they are to be used. A few examples of high quality, tactical flashlights are shown on the following pages.

A Cautionary Word Regarding Weapon-Mounted Lights

Weapon-mounted flashlights are becoming more popular. One indication of this popularity is the current trend toward the production of pistols with

Hand-held Flashlights

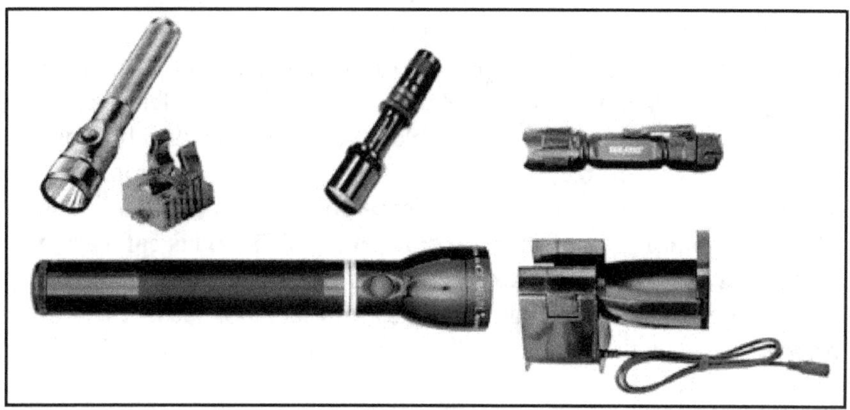

Examples of high-quality, hand-held tactical flashlights (Shown Clockwise from top left): Rechargeable LED Surefire® Stinger with charging cradle, Surefire® Model 6Z CombatLight™, one of the Tactical Blue-Dot™ Series LED lights from Brite-Strike®; the large flashlight at the bottom of the photo with its charging cradle is from the Mag Charger® rechargeable flashlight line produced by Maglite®.

Weapon-mounted Flashlights

Examples of high-quality, weapon-mounted tactical flashlights. At left, the SSL-1™ Rail-mounted LED Tactical Light from Insight Technologies®. This light allows ambidextrous operation when mounted. On right, the Safariland RLS™ or "Rapid Light System." This versatile LED light can be locked on the rails after mounting simply by rotating it to either the left of right side of the pistol. The RLS system allows for safer mounting and dismounting of the light on a loaded pistol under field conditions than do the more common spring-loaded lever designs.

integral rails. While these rails can accommodate other accessories, they are predominantly intended and used for the attachment of lights.

While options are always good, they must be thoroughly thought out and examined. In regard to the practice of mounting an illumination device to the pistol so that the beam and the muzzle are aligned (referred to as co-axial alignment), one significant problem becomes immediately apparent: obviously, **if you utilize the pistol-mounted flashlight for illumination anytime other than under deadly force circumstances, you will most likely be violating one of the cardinal rules of firearms safety as you point your muzzle in unsafe directions as you search with the light.**

This serious operational and tactical consideration must be addressed prior to the adoption and use of any type of weapon-mounted lighting system.

Employing the Tactical Flashlight

When operating with a flashlight while trying to locate, identify, and control or engage a threat subject, some general principles apply.

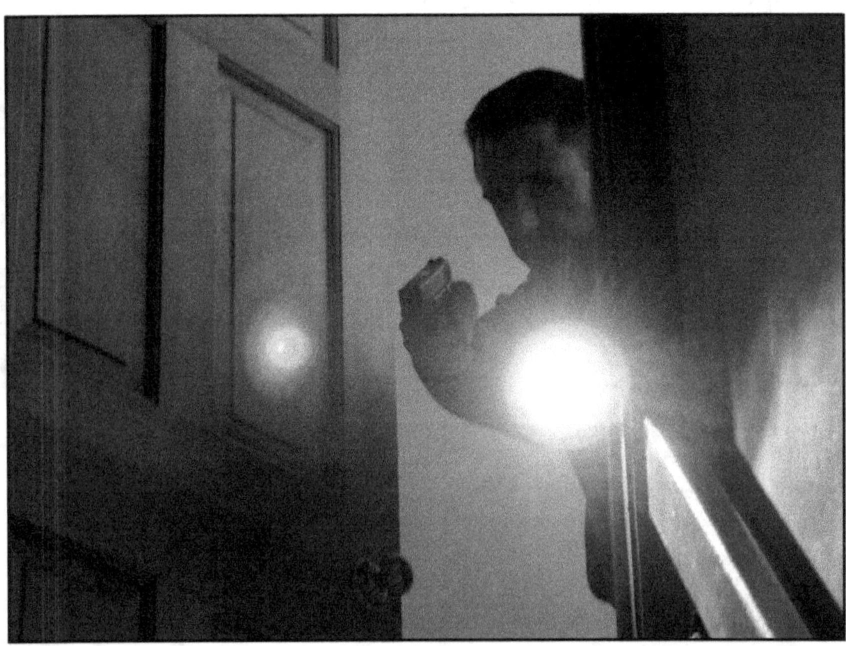

Tactical Flashlight Basics

When operating tactically, we use flashlights to assist us to do four basic things:

1) NAVIGATE from place to place

2) LOCATE obstacles, friendlies, and threats

3) IDENTIFY obstacles, friendlies, and threats

4) CONTROL and/or ENGAGE threats

We can also use flashlights for:

5) "MASKING" or concealing yourself, others, or an area by directing the light into another's eyes

6) DISTRACTING someone

7) DISORIENTING someone

8) SIGNALLING

First, you need to remember that while you are using your flashlight to locate and illuminate the threat, he or she may use *your* light to do the same, for *you* may be illuminated to a certain degree by your own flashlight while it is on.

This is why the technique of "**light and move**" is so often taught. In its basic form, light and move simply means that you should flash the light on momentarily to illuminate your way or to identify something, and, if no immediate threat is detected, immediately shut the light off and move to another spot.

Should you locate and identify a threat, some trainers advocate you should engage and then shut off the light and move, while others suggest that once located, the threat should be kept illuminated until fully controlled; otherwise, you run the risk of losing track of the suspect and having to start the entire process over.

Because this entire matter is so subjective (based upon the situation, environment, training, etc.), I am not inclined to try and deliver any hard and fast rules or recommendations other than those already noted.

You will need to apply your own training, experience, and common sense when operating in the real world with your flashlight and pistol in hand.

Handgun-Flashlight Combination Holds

A few basic techniques for simultaneously controlling both your weapon and your flashlight are illustrated in the following photos.

It is imperative that while assuming a combination hold you **extend the weapon toward the target or threat area *first***. Only when the pistol is extended is the flashlight-holding support hand brought into position. This is done to prevent your support hand from being passed in front of your pistol's muzzle.

The techniques shown all have strengths and weaknesses. I believe each of them merits consideration, however. The situations and circumstances the average police officer will encounter during the course of his career will vary, as will his responses to them. Being familiar with multiple techniques provides officers with options and, it is hoped, a tactical edge.

Because the length of the flashlight is no longer a determining factor as to how bright it is, some officers may choose to use one of the smaller models that can be carried unobtrusively on the belt or in a pocket as their primary flashlight. The choice is yours to make.

Personally, while I always have a 1-cell Brite-Strike HLS LED model clipped in my support-side pocket, I still like to carry a full-size Mag-Lite while working in the field.

Flashlight-Assisted Shooting Positions

Side / FBI Technique

The light is held to the side and forward of the body. Keeping the light away from the body allows you to direct the beam into darkened areas without placing your torso directly into potential lines of fire. It also may prove beneficial should an assailant shoot at the light, as your body is not directly behind it. Can be used with any size flashlight, the brighter the better.

While this technique is considered obsolete by some, it is extremely versatile and comes in handy when searching multi-angled, complex environments. It is highly recommended for inclusion in your personal survival toolbox.

Flashlight-Assisted Shooting Positions (Continued)

Harries Technique

The primary hand extends the pistol while the support hand grasps the flashlight in an overhand hold (bezel down). The flashlight is brought up and under the primary hand. The backs of the hands are pressed and "locked" together, creating a fairly stable shooting platform.

Technique is shown using a large rechargeable light. Works equally well with smaller, tail-cap activated flashlights.

Flashlight-Assisted Shooting Positions (Continued)

Chapman Technique

Used with lights equipped with tube- or side-mounted activation switches. Grasp the light, palm up, in the support hand. Hold the light with your thumb and index fingers wrapped around the tube in the "OK" position with the thumb on switch. Grasp pistol securely in primary hand as you press against the extended middle, ring, and pinky fingers of support hand. Once you get used to it, this technique is very comfortable and effective to shoot with. May take some time getting used to.

Flashlight-Assisted Shooting Positions (Continued)

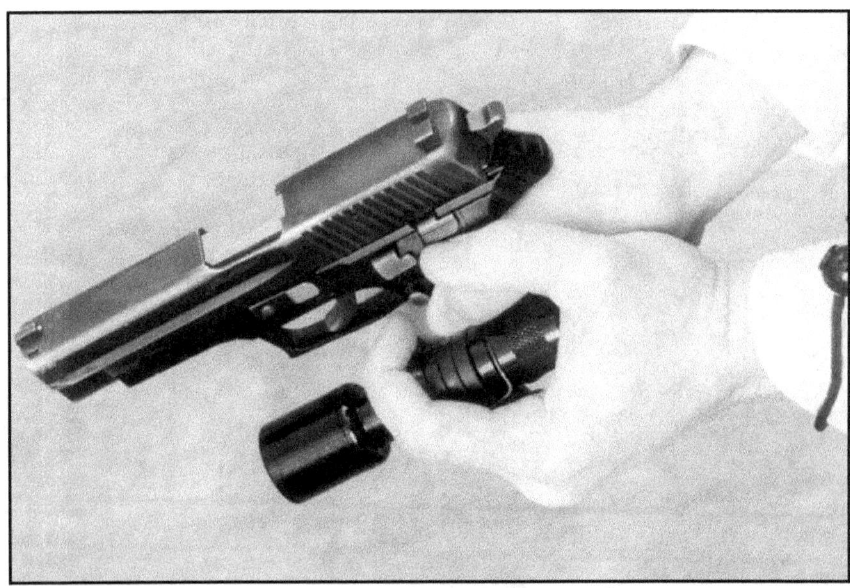

Rogers / SureFire Technique

This technique was developed specifically for use with the Surefire® CombatLight™ series of flashlights. The light is activated by palm pressure on the tail cap-mounted switch. This hold allows for thumb-over-thumb grip position. Middle, ring, and little finger of support hand also wrap around front of the primary hand's grip, stabilizing both the light and weapon.

Below: Surefire's Z2 LED CombatLight® features a light emitting diode that generates 80 lumens.

Flashlight-Assisted Shooting Positions (Continued)

U.S. Marine Corps Technique

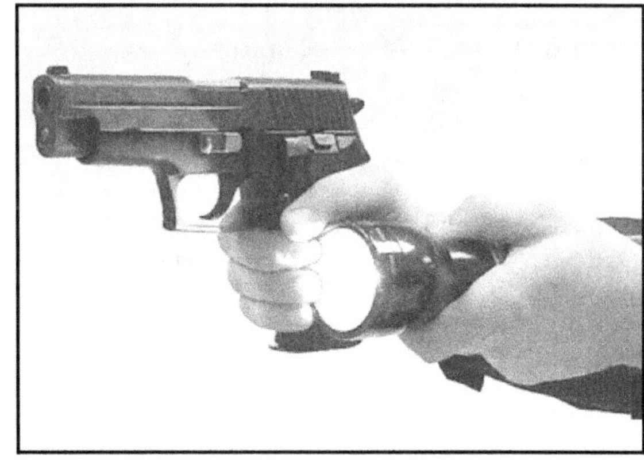

Grasp the pistol securely in the primary hand. The support hand grasps the flashlight securely as shown, with thumb on switch.

Press the tips of the primary hand's middle and ring fingers against the bezel of the flashlight, exerting enough pressure against the bezel to stabilize the shooting platform.

Paul Wosny (above) served as an M-1 Tank Commander in the United States Marine Corps during Gulf War I. Not surprisingly, he claims *this* is the best flashlight-assisted shooting technique... *Semper Fidelis!*

Flashlight-Assisted Shooting Positions (Continued)

Chin or Cheek Weld Technique

While this technique can be used with flashlights equipped with either side-mounted or tail cap-mounted activation switches, it works best with the latter.

The primary hand grasps the pistol securely. The support hand grasps the flashlight securely as shown, thumb on switch.

The flashlight is held pressed against the side of the chin or cheek as shown.

Note: When the light is activated, the target area will be illuminated as will your hand, arm, and pistol. This assists in accessing the sights if they can be employed, but also increases the ability of an adversary to get a good fix on your position and body posture.

Technique demonstrated by Donna Losardo.

When *NOT* to Use a Flashlight

1) When you have located trouble, but "trouble" doesn't yet know you are there.

2) When your light is overwhelmed by the size of the darkened area you are moving through. In other words, if the darkness may be full of predators but your light can't help you see them, don't let it help *them* to see *you*!

3) When you are badly outnumbered. Remember, the darkness can be your friend if you are the superior predator.

4) When gunfire has already erupted. Better to find cover and concealment and use *their* muzzle flash to help you locate *them*.

(Adapted from Tom Aveni's Reduced Light Instructor Course.)

CAUTION: HOT BULBS!

Some high-intensity incandescent flashlight bulbs burn bright and hot. So hot, in fact, that there may be an "after-glow" from the bulb once the power is shut off.

In the dark it is possible for someone to track your movements by following this glow. To minimize this possibility, simply point the light either straight up or down after switching off the power.

This problem will eventually be eliminated as more tactical flashlight manufacturers move toward the cooler burning, long lasting, and practically shockproof light emitting diode (LED) technology instead of incandescent bulbs.

Flashlight-Assisted Shooting Positions (Continued)

Flashlight Supported Pistol Stabilization Technique

The author (above) was first shown this technique by Bob Taubert years ago while attending Taubert's excellent *Close Quarters Pistol* course at the Smith & Wesson Academy in Springfield, Massachusetts.

The position is assumed by bracing the top of the pistol's backstrap against the flashlight's end cap, and then bracing the flashlight's head against your shoulder.

A surprising degree of stability can be achieved using this technique. The addition of the improvised stock for the pistol allows for more consistent and effective delivery of precision-aimed shots. Since the pistol is only braced against the flashlight and not attached in any manner, there is no violation of federal law governing the affixing of a stock to a pistol.

(Pistol in the photo is a Glock 22 equipped with a set of HexSites and a Storm Lake precision barrel.)

CHAPTER 9

Plainclothes Pistol Techniques

SECTION 1
Concealed Carry Considerations

Concealed carry, whether on or off duty, means exactly that—*concealed.*

Sometimes new officers will *accidentally* let their weapons be seen while carrying off duty, this usually being simply a case of immaturity and television training. Forget the "coolness" factor and resist these impulses if you experience them! Unless the situation requires it, the last thing you should desire when operating in the real world in plainclothes is to be "made" or identified as a police officer. This applies equally to when you are roaming the world while off duty as well as when operating on duty in an undercover capacity. Unless you are in uniform, Pistoleer, you are wearing "urban camouflage" and should act accordingly.

Predators All

While the term "predator" often has a negative connotation when used to describe a human being, it is actually an accurate description of our species.

Like most predators, our **eyes face forward**. This provides us with good depth perception which enables us to see how close or far away a prey animal is. This binocular vision is especially helpful when chasing and catching prey, as it allows us to focus on a single forward point. In contrast, the eyes of prey animals are located along the side of the head. This allows them to see to the side and rear without moving the head while they are grazing. In this way they can better detect predators who may be stalking them.

Our teeth provide another indication of our predatory nature; like the coyote and bear, we are **omnivores**, possessing both sharp and flat teeth for holding, cutting, tearing, and grinding meat and plants.

The fact that we are **bipedal plantigrades** (we walk on two legs on the soles of our feet) gives us a distinct advantage, for we are the only mammal to do so exclusively. While this makes us a little slower than if we walked on four legs, it also allows us better elevation from which to survey the surrounding terrain and locate other predators and/or prey. This aids us in the **stalk**.

As for the stalk, while some humans prefer to **hunt in packs**, others prefer to **hunt alone**. Some of our species use their predatory natures and instincts in positive ways, while others use them in decidedly negative or harmful ways. And then, of course, there are many who suppress and deny this aspect of our nature all together, unless and until something happens that triggers it.

As police officers, we use our predatory natures for the good of our society primarily by seeking out and capturing the criminal predators in our midst.

The Art of Blending & The Element of Surprise

It is always better to go unnoticed in a world full of two-legged predators. This allows you to possess and control the element of surprise should you and one of the criminal predators happen upon one another.

Be advised: *it is going to happen.* And when it does, it is always best if you recognize the criminal predator before he recognizes you. Just be warned that this may be more difficult than it sounds. For even if you do the smart thing and avoid wearing hats, shirts, jackets, or other articles of clothing emblazoned with your department's name or logo (or that scream "cop" and "gun" like the popular 5.11 Tactical Vest), the truth is that after working as a police officer for a number of years, you will most likely start to *look* like one even when you don't think you do.

This happens because people tend to become what they do. If you truly live the profession, soon enough you will start to walk, talk, think, and move like a cop *all the time.*

This is especially so in regard to the way we look at the world—not philosophically, but actually, physically *observe* the world around us—because we develop true "hunter's eyes."

And the criminal predators among us will pick that up right away, recognizing us as a threat and being on guard as a result.

This recognition can have fatal results.

Oftentimes, a criminal predator actively engaged in illegal activities will sense the danger from the police predator and act quickly and decisively to eliminate the threat if he has the advantage. (This is especially true should the predator you encounter be engaged in terrorist activities, for they actively train to immediately dispatch anyone who even *appears* to be a police officer in the early stages of any type of "take over" operation.)

That is why it is so important that the professional pistoleer is *always armed*, especially if you carry any type of police identification with you.

Learn well how to access and employ your pistol smoothly, efficiently, and effectively when dressed in plainclothes. And remember that the fact that you are armed should be evident to *no one*, unless and until the pistol is in your hand and being used to control someone else's out of control, threatening behavior. (For more information, refer to Chapter 3 §3.)

The following sections are provided as a general overview of basic equipment and techniques that can be employed while operating in plainclothes. A more complete study will be provided in a future volume.

SECTION 2

The Investigator

One of the biggest adjustments that must be made when transitioning from uniform patrol work to plainclothes investigations is in regard to the carrying and employment of the pistol and other tactical equipment.

Very often, no specialized training is offered to assist the newly-assigned investigator with this transition. The selection of carry gear and attendant equipment specifically suited for plainclothes use is another aspect that is often left up to the individual officer to figure out.

Basic Tactical Equipment

Some officers make do with whatever equipment may be given to them, or improvise based on what they see other officers do. Some officers make it a point to equip themselves with the best gear they can afford. And some officers give little thought to the matter at all, using their newfound plainclothes investigator status as an excuse to not carry even the basic tactical equipment, sometimes even including the pistol.

While I do not believe that the plainclothes investigator needs to routinely carry as much tactical equipment as the uniformed officer, I do know for a fact that he needs to have a basic complement of gear on his person every day if he is to do the job safely. The **basic required gear** is shown at left and listed in order of importance below the photograph:

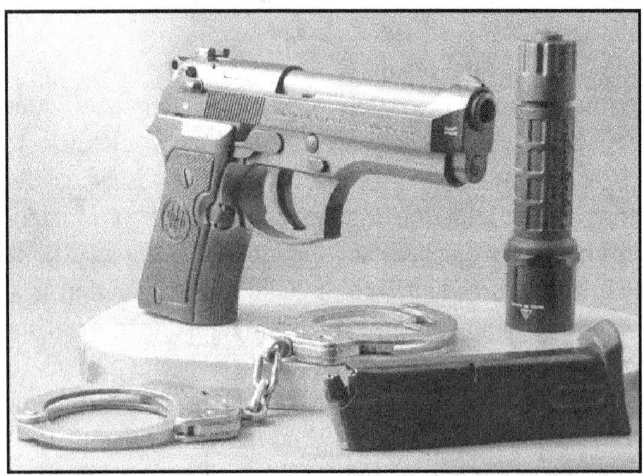

- **Pistol:** *Should be fully loaded with a round in the chamber*
- **Flashlight:** *Smaller, easily concealed LCD lights are recommended*
- **Extra Magazine:** *Should be carried in the same place all the time*
- **Handcuffs:** *Should be carried in a case as opposed to hung over the belt*

(See Chapter 2 §3 for more information on equipment and accessories.)

Recommended Accessories

As for carry gear, the following is recommended (*Quality is key*!):

• A *high quality* **belt** is the foundation of your plainclothes carry gear. This is a critical piece of equipment that will either serve you well or cause you grief. Spend the money necessary to buy a belt specifically designed to carry the weight of the pistol and other basic equipment without deforming or breaking down. I have been wearing the same Uncle Mike's Reinforced Holster Belt for years. It looks like a dress belt but wears like iron.

• A *high quality* **holster** for the pistol. Leather or Kydex are preferred over nylon. A belt holster that employs the same type of security level/device as the uniform duty holster and is worn on the dominant side is strongly recommended. This will help avoid confusion and minimize training conflicts.

• A *high quality* carrier for the extra magazine and set of handcuffs. **Combination carriers** are available that allow the convenient carrying of both magazine and handcuffs. Combination carriers designed to carry a magazine and a flashlight or handcuffs and a flashlight are also available.

I prefer to carry the magazine and handcuffs together in a clip-on combination carrier such as the Galco model pictured at right. I've been using the one shown for more than 8 years. Invest in good gear and it will serve you long and well.

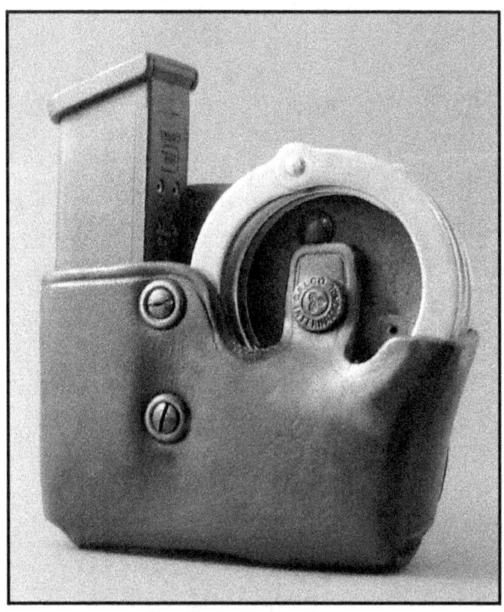

As for the flashlight, I currently carry a small but powerful Brite-Strike LCD model that clips in my pocket but have also carried models that require a holder (such as the SureFire CombatLight) with great confidence.

Again, *quality* is the defining factor when selecting your personal equipment.

PLAINCLOTHES PRESENTATION

Presentation From Concealment, Hip Holster

NOTE: The pistol (Glock 22) is being worn concealed in an OWB hip holster on the right side.

Bring the primary hand to the centerline of the body and curl the fingers inside the edge of the outer garment as shown.

The support hand is also brought to the centerline; from this position it is ready to either establish a two hand grip on the pistol, or it can be used to defend the officer and/or the pistol at close quarters.

Simultaneously slide the primary hand down and back, vigorously sweeping the jacket back. (A set of keys or a magazine in that pocket will aid with the rearward sweep.)

As the jacket clears the pistol, the primary hand immediately establishes a grip on the holstered pistol high on the backstrap. Note how the elbow points back instead of out to the side.

The retaining snap is released at the same moment the grip is established.

Presentation From Concealment, Hip Holster (Continued)

Draw the pistol up and out of the holster and present as described in Chapter 5 §2.

In the photo above the pistol has been cleanly presented to the full extension low ready position. It is pointed at an approximate 45 degree angle to the ground. Note placement of trigger finger along the side of the slide.

The support arm has been extended to the side for balance and the aggressive, forward-leaning crouch has been assumed.

When you decide to fire, raise the primary arm like the handle of a pump. The arm pivots from the shoulder. Keep the **wrist and elbow locked**.

When point shooting, the pistol is raised until it interrupts your line of sight to the target.

As you raise the pistol, place your finger on the trigger. At the moment the pistol is locked on target, convulse the primary hand and fire the weapon. EYES ARE ON THE TARGET!

Presentation From Concealment, Shoulder Holster

NOTE: The pistol is being carried concealed in a shoulder holster on the left side of the torso in the vertical, muzzle-down position.

You must be able to access your concealed pistol using only one hand!

Each of the presentation techniques illustrated in this section should be practiced using both one and two hands to access the pistol.

The primary hand moves directly to the pistol. The grip is established as any retaining devices are unsecured or manipulated as required.

NOTE: The support hand may be used to clear the outer garment to the side; however, you need to ensure you can present the pistol with only one hand if necessary.

The outer garment(s) should be worn in a way that allows easy access to the pistol.

Presentation From Concealment, Shoulder Holster (Cont.)

Safety Circle Concept

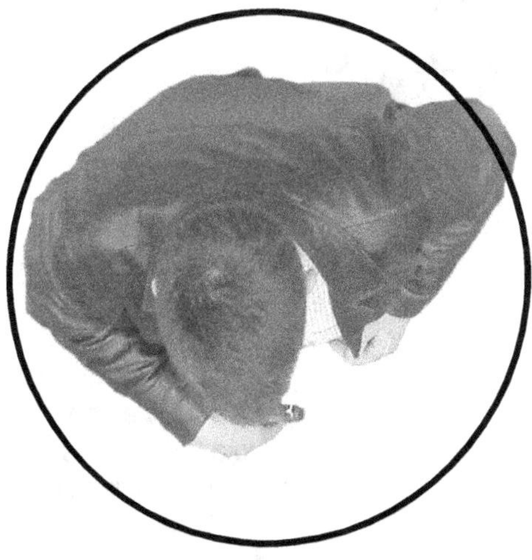

Left & Right Above: Draw the pistol out of the holster cleanly and then rotate it vertically 180 degrees. It is imperative that you control the muzzle at all times throughout the presentation. You do not want to cover your own body parts or anyone else with the muzzle while it is being brought into alignment with the threat. Pistol being drawn is a Colt Officer's ACP.

The controlled track of the muzzle is sometimes visualized as occurring within a "safety circle" around your body as illustrated in the image at left.

Presentation From Concealment, Shoulder Holster (Cont.)

Once the pistol has been brought into alignment with the threat, the muzzle tracks up through the center of the threat and the pistol is fired if necessary.

The muzzle-control "safety circle" concept should be employed anytime the pistol is drawn in a cross-draw fashion. This includes when drawing from a shoulder, hip, or inside-the-pants holster worn on the support side of the body. The safety circle concept should also be used when employing Position Sul as illustrated in Chapter 5 §6.

Presentation From Concealment, Ankle Holster

(Left) Ankle holster draw from the high position.

(Right) Ankle holster draw from the low position. Pistol being drawn is a .380 SIG-Sauer P230. The holster is made by Uncle Mike's. As ankle holsters go , it's very comfortable and holds the pistol securely. This combination of comfort and security is crucial when selecting both the ankle holster and the pistol you will carry in it.

NOT SHOWN: Drawing from the ankle holster while laying on the ground should also be in your personal survival tactical toolbox. In addition, as with all of the presentation techniques, you need to be able to access the pistol with one hand as well as with two when presenting from the ankle holster. The primary hand should be used to clear the pants, then access and draw the pistol when the support hand cannot be used. (Space limitation prevents all of the presentation techniques and their variations being shown.)

SECTION 3
The Undercover Operator

Working undercover is well-known to be one of the most dangerous assignments in law enforcement, if not the most dangerous. That's why one of the things that truly surprised me when I was assigned to a narcotics task force in the late 1980s was the attitude some of the officers in the unit had about gear. Some chose not to carry any type of tactical gear, including pistols, while working in an undercover capacity.

To Carry or Not to Carry...

The decision to carry a firearm or other type of weapon while involved in undercover operations must ultimately be made by the officer performing in an undercover (UC) capacity.

However, the UC officer's supervisors and co-workers must also be aware that their words, actions, and examples may influence the decision of the UC officer in this matter—*especially* the newly-assigned officer who has little or no experience working in that capacity.

While many officers have successfully performed numerous undercover operations while unarmed, some have also found themselves at a distinct disadvantage when faced with an armed criminal adversary. This disadvantage is compounded when, in the criminal's mind, the UC has either been identified as a police officer or worse, is believed to be simply another criminal "player" possessing drugs and/or money ripe for the taking.

One of the common arguments made for not carrying a firearm is that should the weapon be discovered, the UC will be identified as a police officer and the operation will be blown. Some officers counter this argument by stating the fact that persons involved in criminal activities routinely carry firearms; therefore this should not factor into the decision.

The argument can be made further that anyone—criminal or law enforcement officer—involved in dangerous activities such as the illicit sale and purchase of narcotics or other felony acts would naturally desire to possess some means of self-protection.

Finally, it is highly recommended that this entire matter be kept in its proper perspective, as the focus of any police operation must be first and foremost on **officer safety**, second on the **safety of innocents**, third on the **apprehension of suspects**, and LAST on the **recovery of evidence**.

Concealed Pistol Indicators

Keeping your pistol concealed is desirable for any officer wearing plainclothes, but keeping it truly invisible is especially important to the UC officer. There are a number of indicators that can telegraph the presence of a concealed pistol. You need to be aware of them so you can watch for them in others and eliminate them in yourself.

- **Printing** occurs when the outline of a pistol or accessories shows through clothing.
- **Exposing** occurs when the pistol is exposed to view while reaching, leaning, bending, or kneeling.
- **Touching** occurs when you habitually touch or reposition your pistol. If it is necessary to adjust your pistol on your person, you should only do it from a position of concealment so no one can observe your actions.
- **Looking** occurs when you habitually glance at your concealed pistol whether to verify it is still there or is visible.
- **Telegraphing** that you are carrying a concealed pistol can be done in a number of ways in addition to those noted above. Letting the concealed pistol hit or bump something will produce a distinct sound. If you pass too close to a person, or allow someone to get too physically close to you, the pistol may be felt through the clothing. And the big one, dropping your pistol onto the ground when getting out of a vehicle or up from a chair because it has shifted and come loose from the place you had it secured. It happens!

What is needed is a method of carrying your pistol concealed so it is secure and invisible and yet can be quickly and efficiently presented when the situation requires it.

One solution to this problem is the appendix carry.

The Appendix Carry

The appendix carry, also known as "Mexican carry," is a simple, effective, and reasonably safe way to carry the pistol concealed when in plainclothes.

The pistol is slipped into the top of the pants behind the belt to the left or right of the front centerline of the body. While the pistol can be carried this way without any additional equipment to keep it in place, a special holster or clip as shown in the photo on page 334 is highly recommended to assist in keeping the pistol secure. These options are far superior to using nothing, and will help eliminate the possibility of the pistol slipping into your pants, only to fall out onto the street through one of the legs of your trousers.

PLAINCLOTHES PRESENTATION

Presentation From Concealment, Appendix Carry

NOTE: The pistol (SIG-Sauer P226) is being carried concealed in an inside-the-pants holster.

The support hand grabs the bottom of the garment and pulls it vigorously upward, clearing the pistol. This movement should be exaggerated in training to prepare for the actual execution of the technique while wearing heavy or layered clothing and operating under stress.

The primary hand then establishes a secure grip on the pistol.

Presentation From Concealment, Appendix Carry (Cont.)

The pistol is drawn straight up and out, clearing the belt line. Use the "safety circle" concept to assist you to control the muzzle while it is being brought into alignment with the threat.

No bystanders should be covered by the muzzle during the presentation.

Once the pistol has been brought into alignment with the threat, the muzzle tracks up through the center of the threat and the pistol is fired if necessary.

Should you decide to use an inside-the-pants holster as shown in these photos, make sure you work with the holster enough so you can be sure the holster will not impede the presentation in any way—including by coming out with the pistol.

Presentation From Concealment, Appendix Carry (Cont.)

Equipment Options

Shown here are two excellent options that can be used should you decide to carry your pistol using the Appendix Carry as described in this section.

(Left) One of the easily-mounted "**Clipdraw**" clips shown installed on a Colt Officer's .45 ACP pistol. These simple, robust clips are available in a variety of styles to fit just about every handgun. Once mounted, the clip allows you to secure your pistol inside your pants, with the clip over the pants and belt, or over the pants and under the belt. These clips hold your handgun tight to the body, while allowing a fast, smooth presentation of the pistol. They don't impede the operation of the weapon in any way. Cost: around $25.00. (www.clipdraw.com)

(Right) One of **Uncle Mike's Inside-the-Pant Holsters**. Made of ultra-thin synthetic material, these holsters have an internal moisture barrier that keeps perspiration off the pistol, and a smooth nylon lining that allows for a fast, smooth presentation. The suede-like exterior helps anchor the holster inside the pants or skirt. Cost: around $13.00 at the time of this writing. (www.uncle-mikes.com)

SECTION 4
The Off-Duty Officer

The first consideration regarding carrying a pistol off duty is to ensure you are in compliance with all applicable laws as well as your department's policies and procedures.

This may be a more complicated issue than you would first imagine. Firearms carry laws are different in many parts of the country. Departments in the same jurisdiction may have different policies and procedures regarding the carrying of the issued duty pistol while off duty. It is your responsibility to find out what these laws and policies are, and to ascertain if and how they apply to you before you start carrying off duty.

If your department does authorize you to carry your issued duty pistol while off duty, and, if you are a qualified current or retired law enforcement officer who meets certain requirements, you may carry the pistol concealed anywhere in the United States (as of this writing) under the auspices of **H.R.218: The Law Enforcement Officers Safety Act of 2004**.

H.R.218 exempts "qualified law enforcement officers from state laws prohibiting the carrying of concealed firearms."

The required qualifications cited in this Act include (but are not limited to) the following:

You must be a current or former "qualified" law enforcement officer, which is defined as an employee of a governmental agency who:

- is authorized by the agency to carry a firearm
- is authorized by law to engage in or supervise the prevention, detection, investigation, or prosecution of, or the incarceration of any person for, any violation of law, and has statutory powers of arrest
- is not the subject of any disciplinary action by the agency
- meets standards, if any, established by the agency which require the employee to regularly qualify in the use of a firearm
- is not under the influence of alcohol or another intoxicating or hallucinatory drug or substance
- is not prohibited by federal law from receiving a firearm

You must also be in possession of the "photographic identification issued by the governmental agency for which the individual is employed as a law enforcement officer."

H.R.218 does not exempt you from federal laws or regulations. There are also additional restrictions and requirements that must be met.

For additional information, the **Fraternal Order of Police** website provides an excellent overview of the Act. (**www.fop.net**)

After you have checked to ensure you can lawfully carry your pistol while off duty, you must then make the decision to do so or not. While I touch on this subject throughout this book and frequently offer my own opinion on the matter, the final decision is yours to make.

Should you decide to carry off duty, and should your department or agency not dictate how you do this, you will need to choose the pistol and carry gear that best suits your lifestyle.

The Off-Duty Pistol

Some people are adamant that only certain calibers and/or types of pistols are worthy of carrying. Frankly, while I always prefer to carry a larger caliber weapon myself, I also believe that a .22 caliber pocket pistol absolutely beats no pistol at all. Make no mistake: the diminutive .22 or even the much maligned .25 caliber round will produce a fatal injury when fired into the vulnerable target areas of the human body, *especially* at the close quarter distances they will most likely be used at. Multiple rounds fired quickly in a **vertical track** up the centerline of the body, throat, or head tend to produce the most effective result when using smaller caliber ammunition while attempting to achieve incapacitation.

Regardless of make, model, or caliber, as always let quality guide you should you need to choose a handgun for off-duty use.

Techniques, Equipment, & Other Considerations

Any of the techniques demonstrated in this chapter can be used when wearing plainclothes, off duty or on duty. Same goes for any of the equipment shown in this chapter. The big difference is going to be found in mindset. Just having the pistol in your possession, though, generally tends to motivate you to be a little more aware than you may normally be, as well as a little more careful about becoming involved in any type of petty argument or disagreement. Indeed, carrying the pistol should influence you to be *more* reserved and cautious than you might be without it.

Remember when carrying off duty to ensure the pistol is both well concealed and secured on your person. And you will want to ensure that you are in complete control of it at all times. This requires that you first and foremost be in control of *yourself* at all times. Keep your head and keep it clear.

This means no alcohol or other judgment-impairing substances should ever be used when you are carrying your handgun. *Ever.*

CHAPTER 10

The Left-Handed Pistoleer

SECTION 1

Not Just for the Ten-Percenters!

The modern day, competent pistoleer is equally adept at operating his pistol with his non-dominant hand as he is with his dominant hand.

Since the vast majority of people in the world tend to be right-hand dominant (approximately 90 percent), that means more people need to learn and develop left-hand pistol skills than right-hand skills!

I am by nature right-hand dominant but have also trained myself to be proficient shooting left-handed with a variety of weapons. Initially, I did this because of the very real possibility of injury to my primary hand during an encounter. There are also certain tactical situations where it is beneficial to be able to employ a weapon with either hand—such as when moving around cover from your support side.

This ability again proved useful when I became involved as a trainer. I was able to help lefties with their unique weapons-handling problems because I was familiar with them. Again, this sounds like common sense, because it is—yet I cannot tell you how many times I've heard instructors admonish left-handed shooters to simply, "Do the best you can," or "Do what you have to," when asked about left-handed operation. After speaking with numerous left-handed police officers, I've come to believe that this attitude is, unfortunately, fairly common.

Following are a few simple techniques that may make life a little easier for you oppressed lefties out there, as well as a little longer for any of the rest of us who may find ourselves having to get our pistol up and running with our left hand during a real world engagement.

SAFETY NOTICE

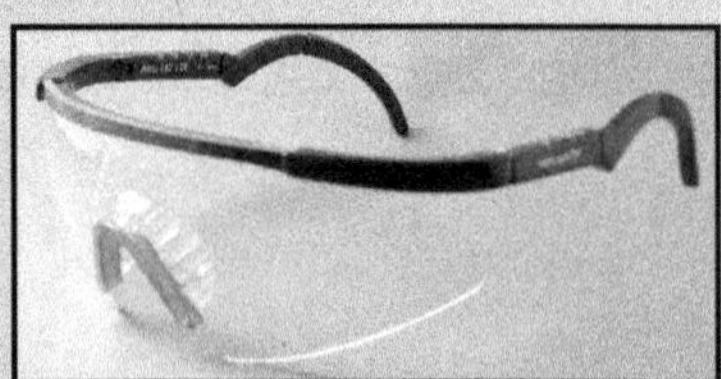

Proper wrap-around eye protection is especially important when firing semiautomatic pistols with the left hand during training, for the vast majority of pistols eject hot, spent shell casings to the right. Wrap-around eye protection such as shown above decreases the possibility of a hot casing striking the eye directly, or finding its way behind the lens of your safety glasses.

SECTION 2

Problems & Solutions

Common Problems & Solutions

The major problems left-handed shooters experience with departmental-issued handguns are related to the "gears and levers," the manipulation and use of which are generally taught by right-handed shooters. Everything else, such as the stance, presentation, grip, aiming, and firing of the weapon, and recovery to the holster are simply mirror-image duplicates of those used by the right-handed shooter.

One of the interesting things I discovered while working left-handed with the semiautomatic pistol is that in many cases, if the proper techniques are used, the left-handed shooter actually has an advantage over the right-handed shooter. Magazine-release buttons are a good case in point. Once accustomed to depressing the magazine-release button with the firing hand's index finger, you may begin to wonder why the weapons are not configured that way by design. It is especially advantageous for the shooter with small hands or shorter fingers, as less manipulation of the weapon in the firing hand is required when performing a magazine change.

Locking the slide to the rear in the manner illustrated in the accompanying photographs is also much "cleaner" and simpler than when performing this same task with a right-handed posture.

This and several other suggestions for dealing with left-hand pistol operation "problems" are provided in the rest of this section.

I strongly suggest you take the time to learn them well.

Locking the Slide to the Rear

Watching a left-handed person lock the slide to the rear is similar to watching the typical right-handed American eat a steak. I know this because while living in Europe, I had my unconscious American steak-eating ritual pointed out to me on several occasions. It works like this: holding the fork in the left hand, the right-handed steak eater sticks the fork into the steak, pinning it in place. While keeping it pinned to the plate, the right hand works the knife, cutting off a piece of steak. Nothing unusual so far. What happens next though, is pretty much unique to citizens of the U.S.

The American steak eater then *puts down his knife*, switches the fork to his right hand, and only then does he insert the piece of steak into his mouth. Why does he do this? Beats me. I never even realized I did it until quizzed by my puzzled hosts. Once I had it pointed out to me, however, I adopted the European steak eating technique, which is much more efficient for it eliminates an unnecessary step. You simply keep the utensils in the same hands before, during, and after the cut, and pop the steak into your mouth with the fork in your left hand. This makes eating a simpler and more efficient affair, as well as eliminating a habit that makes it easier for people to identify you as an American while travelling abroad, if this is of concern to you.

As for locking the slide to the rear, left-handed people also tend to add a step that not only isn't needed, but could cause you to fumble the gun while trying to run it when operating under stress during a real world engagement. What usually happens is this: the pistol, held in the left hand, is passed to the right hand before the slide is locked to the rear "righty style." Once the slide is locked to the rear, the pistol is then passed back to the left hand to continue whatever operation is desired next.

Here's how we clean it up:

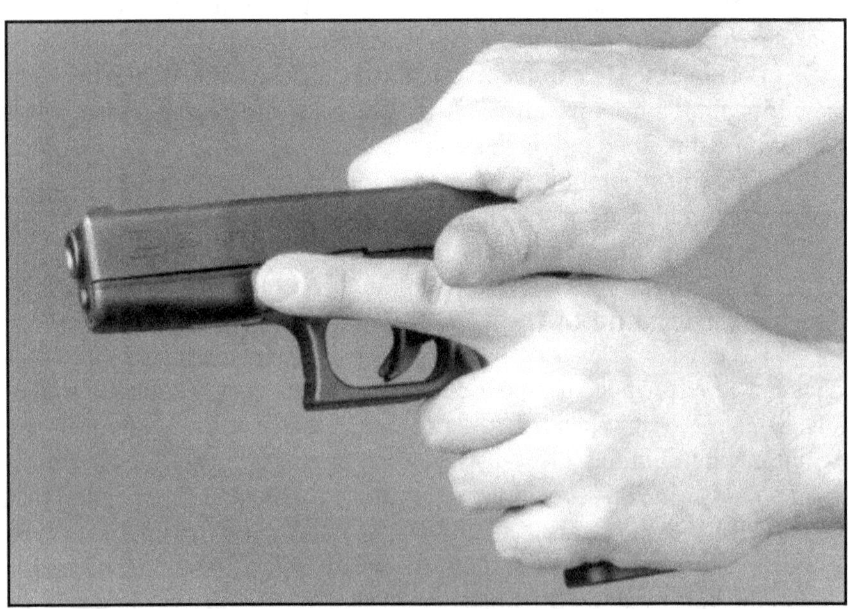

1. Hold the pistol securely in the left hand. It may be canted to the right as needed to allow a proper grasp of the slide by the right hand (as illustrated). Ensure that the ejection port is NOT COVERED by the right hand and that the right-hand thumb can move freely.

Locking the Slide to the Rear (Continued)

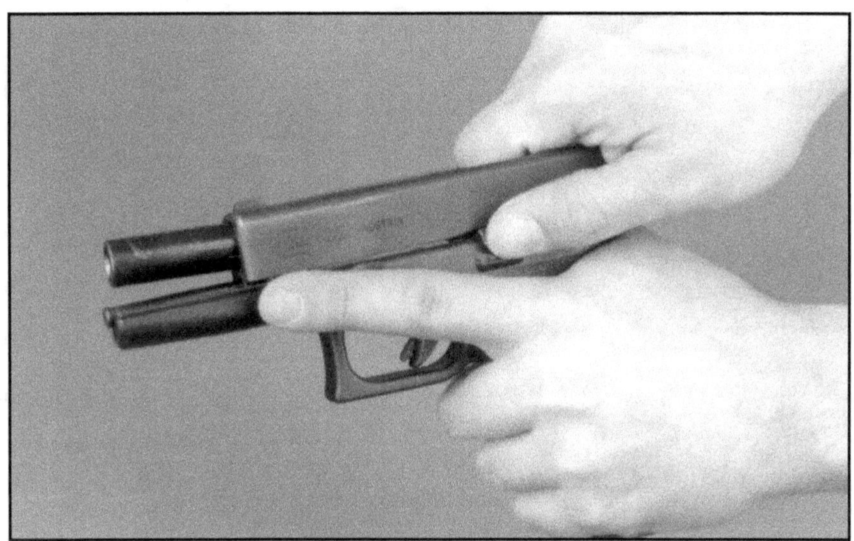

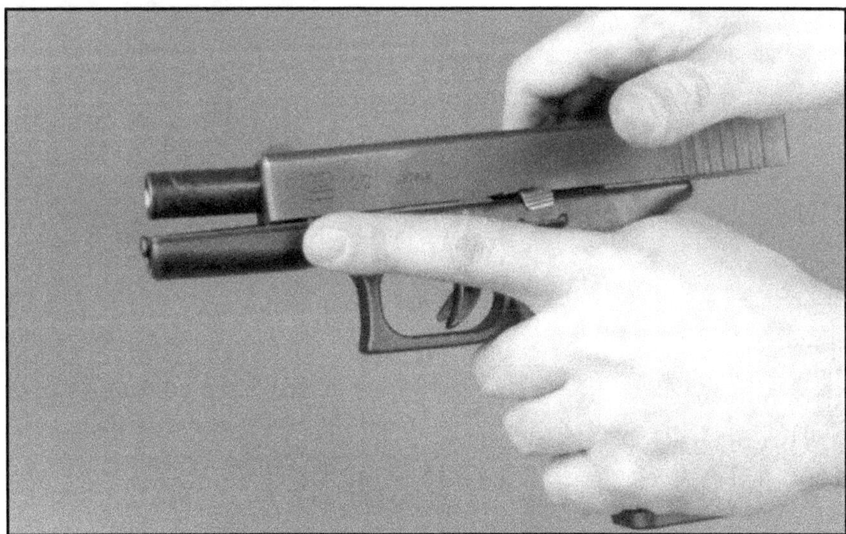

2-3. Draw the slide rearward. At full retraction, the right thumb presses the slide stop lever upward. Allow the slide to move forward just enough to engage the slide stop lever solidly and you are done! Locking the slide to the rear in this manner eliminates the need for changing the hands or the possibility of having the muzzle inadvertently pointing in an unsafe direction.

Releasing the Slide Stop

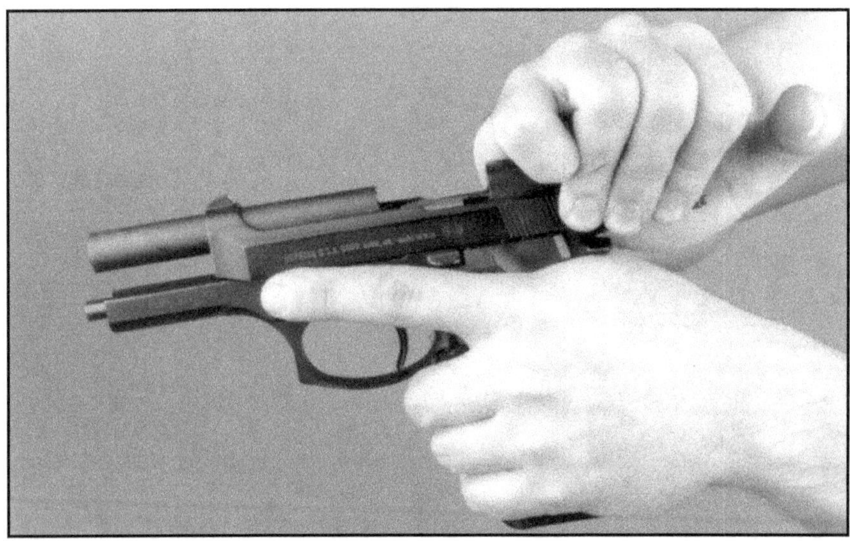

The overhand (shown above) and sling-shot methods are preferred for their simplicity and reliability. Refer to Chapter 4 §3 for additional information.

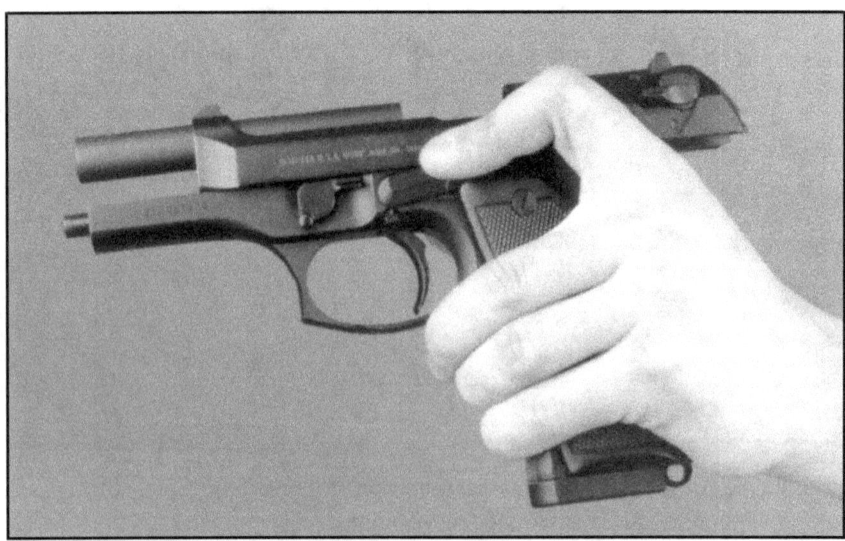

For one-handed operation, the index finger can be used to press the slide stop lever down, allowing the slide to go forward.

Decocking

The index finger should be used to operate the decocking lever on pistols that do not possess ambidextrous decocking levers.

Magazine Release

Again, the index finger should be used to depress the magazine release button. Many semiautomatics, such as the SIG-Sauer P226 pictured here, have reversible magazine release buttons. If you wish, an armorer can make the change for you in a matter of minutes.

Simple Hand-Switch

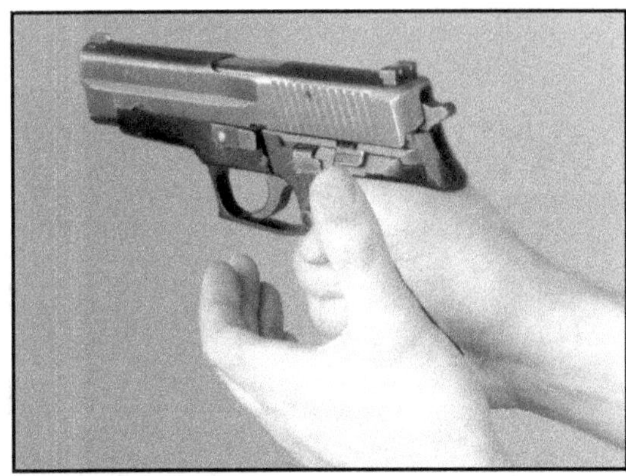

Passing the pistol from one hand to the other is one of those "simple things" that often becomes unnecessarily complicated. Illustrated here is one technique to put the simple back into it.

1. First, bring the receiving hand up to the holding hand.

2. Then move the thumb of the holding hand to the opposite side of its normal gripping position.

The pistol is now being controlled by the fingers of the holding hand.

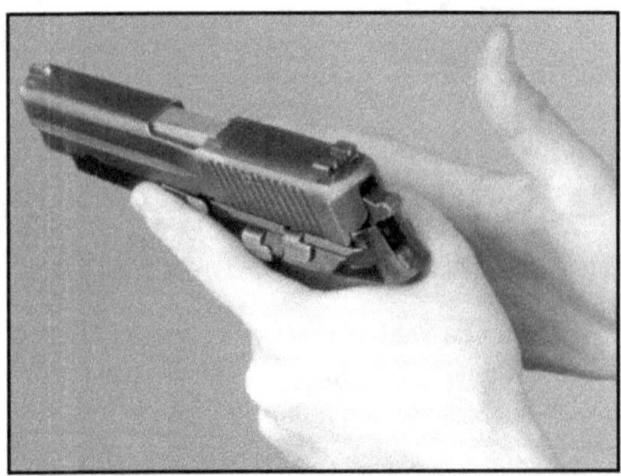

3. Place the pistol securely into the receiving hand, web of the receiving hand high up on the backstrap. A firm grip is immediately established.

When performed correctly, the need for grip readjustment is minimized, as is the time required to engage if necessary.

CHAPTER 11

The Female Pistoleer

By Donna Losardo

CHAPTER INTRODUCTION

Donna M. Losardo

This chapter was written by Donna Losardo, who is, in my professional opinion, one of the finest instructors my department has ever produced.

Donna was instrumental in the creation of both the MSP Firearms Training Unit (FTU) and the New Paradigm Police Firearms Training Program. She succeeded me as the Director of the FTU where she served with distinction, providing cutting-edge training to literally thousands of recruit and veteran police officers.

Donna also blazed another trail when she was selected to serve as the first female Senior Drill Instructor in the history of the Massachusetts State Police Academy. Appointment as the "Senior Drill" is a high honor reserved only for the most capable and qualified members of the department.

In addition to her years of hard work dedicated to training others to survive and win violent encounters, Donna has also "walked the walk," successfully performing in a number of capacities to include uniformed patrol, undercover narcotics investigations, and VIP security operations. She was also recruited to serve as a trainer and operational member of the MSP Logan International Airport Anti-Terrorist Unit (ATU), where she further distinguished herself both as an MP5 Submachine Gun Instructor and while performing in highly-specialized security enhancement operations.

She is a uniquely qualified individual and I am honored to have her contribution included in this volume. I am also honored to be able to call her my friend, for her character and integrity are as admirable and dependable as her shooting skills and teaching ability.

— Mike Conti

SECTION 1
Mindset

In my world, the mindset of the female pistoleer must be similar to that of an American Pit Bull: a combination of intelligence and, when needed, a level-headed, focused, and *fierce* fighting spirit.

Achieving this mindset for some female officers is more difficult than one might first think. For while it is equally true that both male and female officers need to have a "don't ever quit, keep fighting" mentality, the fact is that female officers are often at a bit of a disadvantage in this regard for two primary reasons.

The first is physical, as most females are smaller statured than their male counterparts. The second is actually cultural, for the traditional socialization of females in our culture has generally been as peacemakers and nurturers, not as warriors or aggressors, though this has been changing somewhat over the past few decades.

This combination can prove especially challenging when facing a larger male adversary who may make the mistake of underestimating our ability to control him and the situation, and decide to act on his perceived advantage.

This is why developing an alert, appropriately aggressive mindset is so very important for all officers, but especially so for the female officer.

We must use all of the tools at our disposal. We must constantly strive to practice and refine all of our physical, mental, and persuasive survival skills. We must practice with the gear that we use and carry each and every day and in doing so we will develop true competence and confidence in our gear and our abilities.

This is a *must*, not a luxury! I live by this way of thinking.

Being a smaller statured female type myself, I have learned that I must work harder and smarter than those blessed with superior size and strength, and I have dedicated myself to this goal. Why?

There is an expression that says, "We are the makers of our own destiny." Well, if you are someone who carries a gun to work every day, your destiny—and your reality—may be much different than most other people's. If you want to truly take charge of your destiny, it requires work.

And in order to work efficiently, you first need a *plan*.

Planning for Survival

The first steps involve gaining as much knowledge as possible from a variety of different sources. This is where basic formalized training programs, books, specialized training courses, videos, and Internet sources prove their value.

Of even greater value, however, are the things learned by actually doing. In this realm it is important to realize that our experiences will not always be positive. However, if we make it our goal to study and analyze our experiences and those of others honestly, then we will be able to truly learn from them, taking the good and using it, and learning from the bad how to do better next time.

It is necessary to take control of this aspect of your profession and to decide for yourself that learning will be an intensely personal and ongoing matter for you, for I have found that training offered by most police departments is fairly scarce after the initial basic training has been completed.

I know when I was fresh out of the MSP Academy my head was filled with new techniques and proper procedures on the way things should be done. After just a short time working the road, I realized that nothing can take the place of learning by experience, by using in real world situations all the things you've learned in a controlled training environment.

I also learned that in the "real world," techniques don't always look so "pretty and perfect" as they did in that safe, controlled training world!

Time was beginning to go by in my career when I also realized that if I didn't go out and find additional training on my own, I probably wouldn't get much. That's when I became aware that there were instructor courses being offered through the Academy, because there was always a need for qualified people to provide training on both the recruit and in-service levels. Since becoming "qualified" meant that you would receive additional training well beyond the basic courses, I saw this as a way to improve my own skills as well as helping others improve theirs.

Getting involved in instructor level courses was the best thing that could have ever happened to me early on in my law enforcement career. I started to understand that I could not teach someone else if I wasn't competent and *especially* confident with the material I was trying to teach.

I knew if I were to succeed as an instructor in whatever discipline I was working in, I would need to train hard, practice, and train some more. Becoming an instructor and being an instructor is a constant evolution. For me, being an instructor has undoubtedly made me both a better student and a better officer.

When we initially rolled out the New Paradigm Program for the

Donna Losardo (right) instructing members of an MSP Recruit Training Troop.
(Photo courtesy Massachusetts State Police Archives)

Massachusetts State Police, Mike Conti took the lead and ran with it. He taught each and every day for the first iteration of training. I watched, took notes, and practiced each day with the hope and anticipation that I would someday be able to run a class of officers through the program. When that day finally came, Mike knew I was ready, but I still wasn't sure if I could carry the day and have the group learn and absorb not only a new way of training, but also a new way of *thinking* about training.

Apparently, Mike could see something I couldn't because my first day of teaching the program was one of the best days I have ever had as an instructor! I began speaking at 0800 hours that morning and didn't stop until sometime after 1530. I had several adrenaline dumps throughout the day and when we finally sat down in the office after all of the students had left, I could not believe how truly drained I was from a single day of training. I was also amazed that I knew as much as I did and was able to convey what I knew to my students. It was truly an enlightening experience.

The point I'm trying to make with this little story is that if we are thinking about and practicing the skills that we may need to save our lives or someone else's, we will become competent and confident in those skills and they will be there if and when we need them.

As an instructor I need to believe in what I am teaching and I need to be able to "practice what I preach."

I have been very fortunate to have worked for and with incredible human beings that have made me a better instructor, better operator, and better person, and I have tried to do that in turn for those I work with and teach. This philosophy of "giving back" to your people and your organization is perhaps the true driving force behind the mindset for survival.

For in our profession, when we truly apply ourselves, we work hard to ensure not only our own survival, but each others' as well.

It's really something to think about.

Donna Losardo (right) and Paul Wosny were instrumental in ensuring that the members of the MSP Logan Airport Anti-Terrorist Unit (ATU) were well-trained and properly prepared to employ the highly-accurate, MP5 Submachine Guns chosen for use in the terminals of the busy Category "X" airport post 9-11. The MSP MP5 program established Logan as the first airport in the U.S. to employ such weapons on a regular basis. Here they are pictured in 2008 while conducting an MP5 Instructor Course for the members of the department's FTU. Losardo, who served as the second Director of the FTU, was succeeded by Wosny. Both were subsequently recruited to assist in the formation and training of the ATU.

SECTION 2
Pistol Considerations

The Duty Pistol

As we train for survival, we need to keep in mind that the members of the law enforcement profession are made up of all different sizes and shapes of people.

I would be curious to look at the different make up of police departments throughout the United States. I know just from looking at my own department that we have officers that range in height from 4'11" to many well over 6 feet tall. With the difference in height obviously comes a difference in weight, foot size, hand size, and so forth. You get the idea. When trainees are in the Academy they get measured for field boots, shirts, jackets, and all of their other issued uniform parts. One item that tends to get overlooked in the size department, however, is the handgun.

Realistically, I know that we can't take a hand measurement of each officer and have a gun custom-made for a perfect fit. That's not what I am driving at. However, I do believe that reasonable accommodations as to handgun size for officers with both smaller and larger hands should be considered and explored.

There are a lot of reasonable options available out there that bolster the already strong argument for why the GUN SHOULD FIT THE HAND and not the other way around!

I am not plugging for a specific brand of gun when I say that in my department we do now have several different options when we encounter an officer with smaller hands.

The pistols we use are all made by the same manufacturer and employ the same operating system. The difference comes in the size of the grips, slides, frames, and triggers. In many cases simply changing the trigger makes a huge difference for the officer with smaller hands!

When we initially began to introduce the concept of fitting the gun to the hand by offering a smaller version of the duty pistol to those who needed it, we were met with much skepticism, for our department had never done this previously. This pushback was not just from cautious administrators, it was also from many of our own officers within the department.

It was not uncommon to hear some vocal members of the department stating the sentiment, "If he/she can't shoot with the big gun than we don't want them!"

My response to this, based upon my experiences as both a police

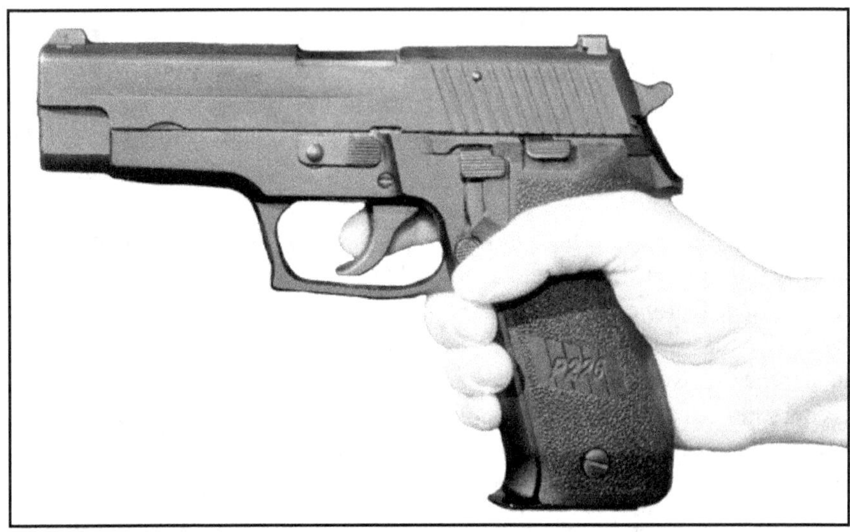

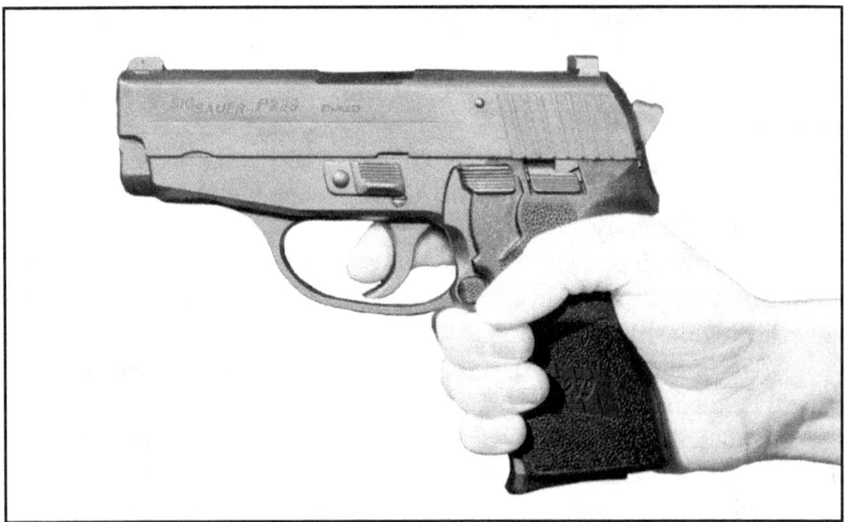

Fitting the Pistol to the Hand

The .40 S&W Caliber SIG P226 pistol in the top photo is obviously too large for this person's hand to adequately grip and reliably control. The .40 S&W Caliber SIG P239 in the bottom photo is a much better fit.

If this were your hand, and you knew you may be required to use your handgun to save your own life, which pistol would you prefer?

officer and a firearms instructor, is that it's time to let go of this juvenile mentality!

Saying that a person is unqualified to be a police officer because his or her hand is too small to adequately control a larger framed pistol is as nonsensical as saying that a person with long legs is unqualified to be an officer if he or she needs to adjust the seat position in a cruiser.

Seats *are* adjustable. Pistols *do* come in different sizes. Some pistols now come with adjustable grip inserts for just this reason! That's because equipment is meant to serve our needs—not the other way around.

Other comments we heard about this subject included concerns such as, "Can my magazine fit in their gun or visa versa, so if we are in a gun fight we can share ammo if we need to?"

This concern was addressed by noting that the need for sharing magazines is a fairly rare occurrence in civilian law enforcement, while the need for effective pistol control and first-round hitting ability is crucial! We also pointed out that officers from different departments routinely carry different weapon systems, meaning that the ability to share magazines and/or ammunition was already fairly limited on a large scale anyway. The common sense approach indicated it was more logical to make decisions based upon the more probable and immediate need than the statistically much less-likely event.

Once these concerns were addressed, then other, less reasonable questions were lobbed such as, "So why can't I get the smaller gun if I want one so I don't have to carry the heavier gun?" Comments such as these from a few disgruntled individuals deteriorated from there, so we knew where they were going—nowhere. So we left them to their self-manufactured misery and turned to helping others escape their institutional-inflicted misery.

We acquired alternate pistols, and documented the accommodation experiment with photos and facts, including hand measurement (which was the only criteria used for the issuance of the smaller framed weapons).

Our thinking was that if we could help even just one of our people who will be out there on their own become more efficient and effective with their pistol simply by providing them with this reasonable accommodation, then we would do whatever it took. So we did.

This all happened back in 2000. In the years since, what we have documented is a dramatic decrease in "problem shooters" because most of the problems disappeared once the shooters had a pistol in their hands that they could control effectively. We have also had zero negative issues relating to this practice. Rather, all the feedback has been positive, and this "radical approach" has now become an accepted and normal practice.

Now when we see newer officers wearing the alternate pistol with no undue attention given to it, we just smile.

The final point I'd like to make about this issue is this: hand size and stature are not an *excuse* to try (or to request to try) some of these accommodations; they are *reasons*. If you fall into this category, whether you are male or female, younger or older, or larger or smaller than average, and your issued pistol is unwieldy in your hand due to its size, then you must be willing to act as your own advocate. Be prepared to explain and defend why you are requesting the accommodations you are. There are plenty of articles and information out there for you to arm yourself with to get the point across on just how important reasonable accommodation for duty guns is.

For those of you who don't have this problem, consider this: if you're involved in a situation where weapons are drawn, wouldn't you rather have an officer next to you with a pistol they were confident with than one that just felt like a big piece of steel in their hand that they could not control? Just a thought.

As far as off-duty guns are concerned, if you are authorized to carry your own personally-owned pistol when not working, make sure you buy one that properly fits your hand. I also strongly recommend you try to stay with the same type of operating system that your duty weapon has.

Why, you ask? When we as human beings have to operate under stress, with adrenaline running through our bodies, we revert to our training. If we train with a pistol that uses one type of operating system for working hours, and then carry a pistol that employs a different system when we are off duty, we are doing ourselves a disservice.

For example: if your duty pistol doesn't have a mechanical safety that disengages the trigger but your off-duty weapon does have one, odds are that under stress you will be pressing the trigger on your off-duty pistol without ever disengaging that safety. This could prove fatal should you be trying to stop an immediate threat to you or others.

The saying "Train like you fight because you will fight like you train" is so true. That pertains to all that we do.

Just keep in mind that when operating under stress, you will automatically go to what you know.

And what you know will be what you have practiced.

SECTION 3
Carry Considerations

In the previous sections we addressed the necessity of adopting a "Pit Bull" survival mentality, regardless of whether you are a male or female officer.

We have also looked at the matter of fitting the gun to the hand of the individual shooter. This too is another subject that affects both men and women, and so it has been treated as such.

The last subjects we'll discuss in this chapter concern carry and clothing considerations. However, as Mike has covered this subject from a primarily male perspective elsewhere in this book, in the final two sections of this chapter I am going to focus specifically on carry and clothing considerations for the female officer. This seems appropriate, especially since the title of this chapter *is* "*The Female Pistoleer!*"

So you males can either stop reading and step out of the room, or keep reading and maybe learn a thing or two about what your sister officers must deal with on a daily basis.

Uniformed Duty Carry Considerations

Most of us in the police and security fields are issued our uniforms and other basic gear. If not, we are usually told what specific types of uniforms and gear we need to purchase. Either way, the fact remains that while the desire for uniformity of appearance is understandable, one size does *not* always fit all. This is especially so when it comes to the female officer.

Obviously, women are built different than men. Women's hips, waists, and torso lengths are not the same as a man's, therefore wearing the same uniform pants, duty belts, and holsters may not always be the optimum choice. There are *some* options out there, but not many.

One available option I have experimented with is a **low-rise holster**. It is believed that this type of holster may work better for women with larger hips. I once tested and evaluated this type of holster, as well as a duty belt that was made specifically for the female law enforcement officer. I personally did not like the rig because I thought it was not sturdy enough, but I gave it to another female officer who used it while participating in drug raids and she thought that it was great!

Once again, it comes down to personal preference. You must find the equipment options that work for *you*. Finding out exactly what does work for you, however, requires research and testing. You must be willing to do this, and to encourage those who dictate the types of uniforms and gear you use to allow you to do this. This brings us back to the idea of taking control of our own destinies again.

Of course, just how much say we have in deciding exactly what types of uniforms we wear, or how we will carry our gear (to include the pistol) may be fairly limited.

Surprisingly, as restrictive and unyielding as many departments and agencies are regarding uniformed carry considerations, when it comes to plainclothes carry, the complete opposite is often found to be the case.

Plainclothes Carry Considerations

Let's once again go back to my early days on the job... to the day I graduated from the State Police Academy.

The graduation itself had ended, with all of its military precision and ceremony; pictures had all been taken, and then it was time for my classmates and me to change into our civilian business attire, grab our gear and head out with all of our proud family members in tow.

Well, things were going great; there were plenty of hands to help with the gear, except for one very important piece -- the issued handgun and magazines that were now filled with "real bullets."

While we had been issued both a shoulder holster rig and a nylon off duty hip holster, we hadn't been given any instruction on their use; nor had we thought we required any at the time. "After all," the rationale must have been, "how hard can it be!?"

The first problem came when we took the shoulder holster out of the pristine packaging that it came in and tried to figure out how to put the holster on properly. Well, with the many straps and Velcro attachment points on the shoulder holster, most of us could not even venture into the realm of trying to assemble the item, never mind trying to put it on and then put a gun in it! After just a short time we all realized that the shoulder holster option was out.

We then looked at the nylon hip holster in *its* pristine packaging. We went through the same process of opening the package and taking the holster out. Thankfully there was nothing complicated about this one. Then all at once we realized that some of us had a little bit of a different issue. While it was obvious where the holster went and how you would put it on, for most of us female officers there was one thing missing: our business attire didn't include pants with belt loops on them. Hence: no belt loops, no using the holster that needed to be attached to a belt.

At this point, all any of us wanted to do was get out of there so we could go celebrate our great accomplishment with our families. So what to do? I thought about it for a long minute and then made my decision. I loaded my gun, tucked it into the front of my pants, concealed it with my jacket, put my extra magazines in my jacket pocket and "hit the road," so to speak! Out I went, just like that to the restaurant for well-deserved chow, suddenly realizing that I wasn't as prepared to be out in the world on my own with a pistol as I had imagined myself to be. The reality was that I still had much to learn about the most basic aspects of pistolcraft, starting with how to carry my gun in plainclothes.

This experience stays with me to this day and influenced me greatly during my time at the FTU. It especially influenced my approach to training recruit officers in regard to plainclothes and off-duty carry considerations, for it inspired me to put together a course that allowed the trainees to come to the range in their business attire and practice with their newly issued, off-duty holsters.

I must admit that it was quite a sight to see all of the trainees on line

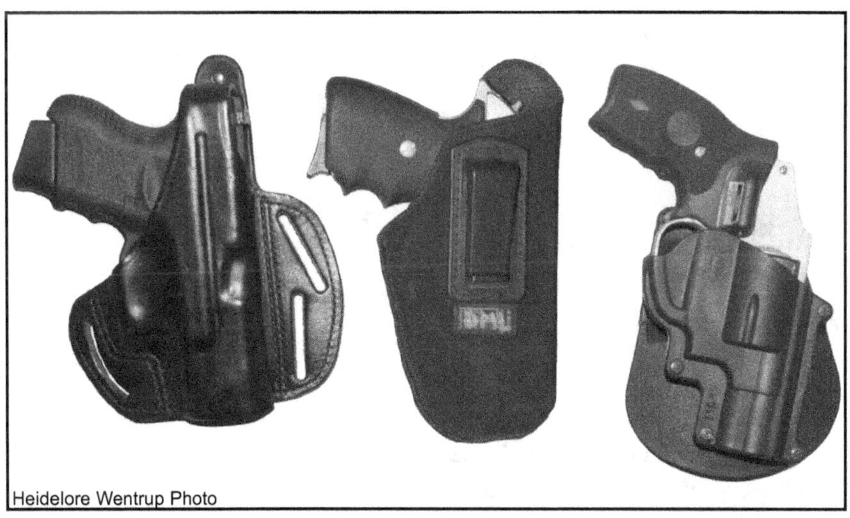

Heidelore Wentrup Photo

A few plainclothes holster options: (Left) Pancake holster for outside the waistband (OWB) hip carry. (Center) Inside the Waistband (IWB) holster used for Appendix carry. (Right) Paddle holster for OWB carry. Smaller framed pistols such as the ones shown are easier to conceal, but there are trade-offs. A smaller pistol means fewer rounds in the weapon, a smaller caliber bullet, or both.

in business attire being taught proper accessing and drawing techniques with suit jackets on, but I was sure by the end of the training that they were truly ready to go out on their own with all of the equipment and skills they needed.

While this may seem like a common-sense approach (and it is), the fact is that this type of training is not always offered in many law enforcement training programs.

I think part of the problem may be that as instructors we sometimes forget who our audience is. Sometimes we do not think that we need to tell people how to load their guns when they're not at the range or how to carry their firearm when they are not in their uniform with their issued duty belt and holster. Because these issues are so familiar to us, we assume it is so for those around us.

After my experience with the holster issues at graduation, I made it a point to ensure that the recruit officers I trained would not have to repeat that experience.

Our hope with this book is that it helps you avoid other problems that many officers have had to deal with, us included. We are all novices at one time. It is nothing to be embarrassed about!

What *can* be embarrassing, though, is making novice-like mistakes after being on the "Job" for years, because a) no one ever taught you better ways of doing even the simplest things, or b) you never thought to ask.

While the former is usually not in your control, the latter absolutely is. So *ask*!

Options & Accessories

When we talk about plainclothes carry options and accessories we think of holsters, concealment purses, fanny packs, and all of the other available gear that actually houses the gun and extra magazines while we are operating in "urban camouflage."

While options are good, many may also prove problematic. This is another case where you will need to experiment with these different types of carry options to determine what works and what doesn't work for you or your specific operational needs.

If you choose to carry your pistol in a briefcase, concealment purse (a specially-designed purse with a compartment intended to secure the pistol), or fanny pack-type carrier, for example, I strongly recommend you first

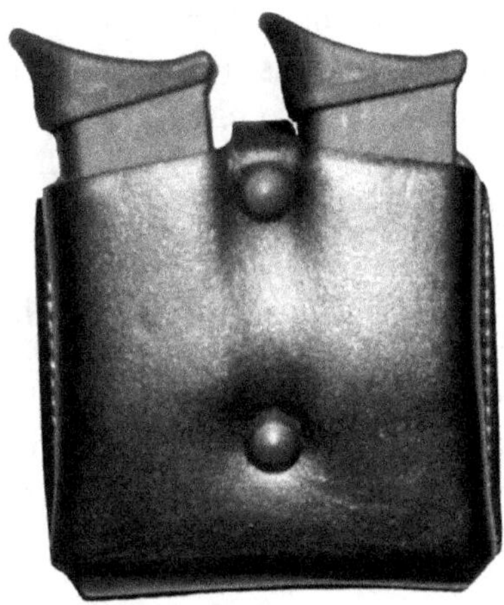

Double Magazine Pouch with paddle attachment for plainclothes carry use. (H. Wentrup photo)

try it out on the range—*thoroughly*.

For while the item you've chosen may initially seem like a great idea because it provides a more convenient means of carrying the pistol when involved in activities that don't necessarily bring you into contact with suspects (such as processing crime scenes), should you need to access your pistol in a hurry under stress you may find that there was a steep price to pay for that convenience.

During my time as Director of the FTU, I once again had the opportunity to work with Mike Conti on a special project. Mike had developed a specialized training course specifically for officers performing in an undercover capacity, and I was lucky enough to be able to assist him while he implemented the 3-day course.

I remember one of the first times we ran the course: we had a class full of hard-charging narcotics officers from the State Police. Mike told them to wear the same type of clothing and use the same type of equipment as they would while actually working on the streets. This meant that if they wore a t-shirt or sweatshirt or some type of jacket untucked that covered their pistol, then that's how they would operate during the course.

Sounds like a simple and straight-forward request, but most of our undercover officers had never trained with the clothing and the gear they worked in. Why? Because historically during "qualification" training all officers had been required to wear the uniform duty belt, regardless of their actual assignments.

This obviously left our officers performing in an undercover capacity at a disadvantage, for they hadn't been given the opportunity to train realistically with their gear. That changed with this course.

We first showed them methods that could be used to carry their pistols concealed, and then taught them how to access the concealed pistols in a smooth and efficient manner.

Carry positions on the hip area or the belly area were recommended. We did not recommend carrying in the small of the back, but we did review the process for accessing the weapon from that position and explained why we discouraged it (see the box on following page). The use of a fanny pack (or "man purse" as it was jokingly referred to) was also discussed, especially as we had two officers in the class who were wearing them and had been using them while working.

Mike also went over methods to retrieve the gun from inside the pack and present it, discussing the need for smoothness and a plan to identify yourself as a police officer once the pack was open and the pistol out. After a little more work, the basics were covered on accessing and presenting the weapon from various positions, holsters, and packs. We then began the drills with safe, clear, and empty weapons so the students could get used to and develop their new skills as safely as possible.

Just as we had expected, the officers with the fanny packs had some issues accessing the gun. We reiterated that if they were to continue carrying the gun in the pack that they needed to be able to get to it quickly, smoothly, and safely in order for that to be a viable carry option for them. They continued to practice and did smooth out quite a bit, but the reality of accessing the pistol from the compartment started to become clearer to them, especially as they saw their fellow students quickly developing a smooth and fast presentation from concealment positions on the hip and from the appendix carry position.

Fanny Pack

Not ready to give up their fanny packs and convert by the time we were ready to introduce live fire drills, these two officers participated in the first drills using the black pouches strapped around their waists.

I believe it took about three repetitions on the first live fire course

"Small of the Back" Carry is Discouraged Because:

1) **The spine may be injured as the result of an impact to the weapon from a blow or fall.**
2) **The pistol is easily felt by others, especially in crowded environments such as a bar.**
3) **Accessing and/or protecting the pistol may be difficult in crowded or close environments.**
4) **Accessing the pistol from the SOB carry position is more obvious and entails more "telegraphing" movements than from the Appendix carry position.**

before we observed the two fanny packs on the ground behind the firing line, and observed the two officers to be carrying their pistols "appendix" or "Mexican" style (in the front of the pants carry).

Just that one exercise made the course worth doing; for even if we had gotten nothing else accomplished during the course, at least we may have saved these two officers from not being able to get to their pistols if and when they needed them to save their own lives or someone else's in the course of their duties.

Based upon the results of the training and the feedback from the students, the course was a success and we all learned a great deal about training like we fight.

Training *Matters*

The little story related above sums up the message that I am trying to convey regarding carry considerations. Train with the gear and the clothing that you wear while you're working and never settle for gear that doesn't work for you.

Your life or someone else's life may depend on you being able to access your pistol and other equipment. You may be efficient and effective with your pistol in your hand, but if you can't access it to use it, then it will be of no use to you when the time comes.

Take the time to research and experiment because there is an awful lot of gear out there, some good, some not so good. One motto that we lived by in the FTU was, "We never want any of our people to have to do something for the first time for real; we want them to do it in training first."

We tried to replicate in training challenges and situations that we could reasonably anticipate happening in the real world, and that included the gear that we used and the manner in which we used it.

We should also try to make sure we train in the attire that we will be wearing while on duty. This includes jackets, shoes and any other gear or accessories we may wear when engaged in our various duties as law enforcement or security professionals.

Heidelore Wentrup Photo

Drawing from concealment must be practiced until the presentation is smooth, efficient, and consistent.

You must train in the attire you will be wearing on duty!

In this photo Donna is using an OWB hip carry holster.

SECTION 4
Pistolera Attire

Each of us is built differently and has different needs when it comes to preparing our wardrobe. The one common thread we all share, however, is the need to be able to carry our pistol and attendant gear in a manner that allows us to be efficient and effective when the time comes and we need to access it.

Locating the type of clothing and equipment that allows this is not always easy, though, especially for the female officer.

I do know that if you surf the Internet you will be able to find at least one company that does cater to women in law enforcement and their wardrobe.

As for clothing, in my experience, online or off, I find it very difficult to get a **professional woman's business suit** with adequate (if any at all) belt loops. It may also be a challenge to find a suit type jacket that is long enough to cover the various gear, such as your handgun, extra magazines, handcuffs, and whatever else you may be carrying.

So shop around until you do locate an appropriate business suit with pants that have belt loops and a suit jacket that is a little longer than standard. Then buy at least two and pass along the store location to your sister officers! We *are* all in this together.

After finding an adequate business suit with belt loops, your next issue may be finding a **belt** wide enough and sturdy enough to support your pistol and other equipment.

Most belts that are made for women tend to be thin and quite flimsy, as they are often used just to make a fashion statement, not for what a belt was intended for: actually holding up your pants! A thicker-style, heavier leather type belt may work best to actually hold the holster and pistol closer to your body so it is not "flopping around" on your hip.

Another suggestion would be to shop online or at your local police supply store and ask about a tactical style "dress belt." This type of belt looks like a fashionable leather belt on the outside, but on the inside there is a strip of hard plastic that gives it strength. These belts are much sturdier and will not stretch or deform from the weight of the gear as a typical leather dress belt will.

One more belt option you may consider is a nylon type tactical belt with a buckle and Velcro to hold the belt in place. I find that this type of belt works best if you have a black suit and the tactical belt is also black.

I would be remiss if I did not talk about what type of **shoes** I recommend with your business attire. We need to remember that although we want to remain stylish in our business attire we must also remain tactical.

If a situation presents itself and we need to act, we need to be able to move, possibly access our pistol, and very possibly run after a suspect. If this is the case then a good sturdy pair of rubber soled shoes is your best option.

Once again, we are all different and some may be able to maneuver better than others in shoes with heels, but remember that we are working and we need to be ready for what we may actually need to do.

"Urban Camouflage" Considerations

Jacket should be long enough to cover the pistol and accessories and loose-fitting enough to avoid having the pistol "print" through the material. Jackets must not restrict your arm movements or otherwise impede the presentation of the pistol or self-defense tactics.

Belt should be strong enough to bear the weight of the pistol, accessories, and carry gear, as well as hold your pants or skirt up.

Pants or skirt should allow free range of motion to allow for running or self-defense tactics.

Shoes should be both stylish and sensible. Rubber soles that you can maneuver and run in are preferable to heels. Remember when shopping that you are buying work clothes.

Heidelore Wentrup Photo

CHAPTER 12

Perfect Practice

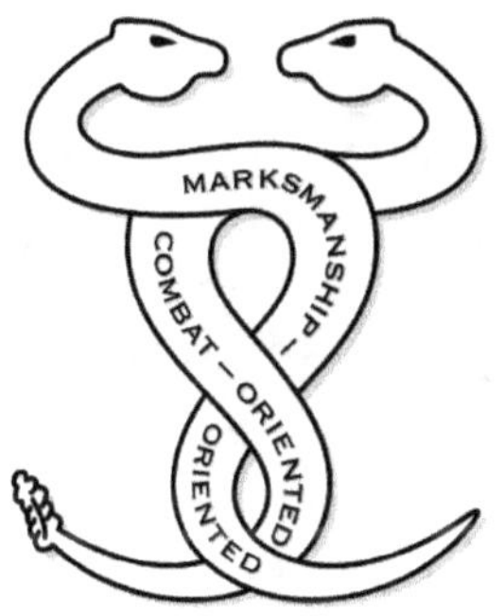

SECTION 1

Perfect Practice Makes Perfect

The final chapter in this book is provided as a reference to assist you in developing good, basic pistolcraft practice habits and techniques. *Habits* is listed first for a reason. The best way to develop and polish your pistolcraft techniques is to practice with your pistol on a regular, frequent basis, making it part of your normal routine.

If your first response to this advice is that it is impractical because your department doesn't provide you frequent opportunities to train with your pistol, or because you only have limited access to ammunition and/or range time, please keep reading! For some of the best practice you can do with your pistol and equipment can be done without firing a shot, and in small increments of time.

> **"Some of the best practice you can do with your pistol and equipment can be done without firing a shot..."**

Practicing the presentation is one example. During most active law enforcement officers' careers, the pistol will be drawn numerous times in the real world but fired only a few, if that. Often, the ability to get the pistol into your hand quickly and smoothly will preclude the likelihood of your having to fire it, for if your pistol is presented *first* you will most likely be able to achieve control of the situation.

The opposite also tends to be true as well. Officers sometimes feel they have no choice *but* to fire if they initially have trouble getting their pistol into their hand when facing what they perceive to be an immediate deadly threat. The feeling that they are "running out of time" can become overwhelming, especially if they experience significant difficulty unsnapping or drawing the pistol from the duty holster or concealment position.

The best way to prevent this possibility is to develop a smooth, lightning-fast draw.

Information and illustrations to help you achieve this are provided in Chapter 4 §5 and Chapter 5 §2. Additional information and a suggested practice regimen for developing a smooth presentation and other critically needed police pistolcraft skills is provided in the next section.

Keep in mind that when practicing, only *perfectly executed* repetitions count! It is infinitely more beneficial to perform 5 perfect repetitions than 100 sloppy or technically incorrect repetitions. So take your time, pay attention to detail, and make every moment you dedicate to training count.

SECTION 2

Practicing Techniques: Dry and Live Fire

DRY EXERCISES

SAFETY ALERT! It is strongly recommended that only a DRY (*SAFE, CLEAR and EMPTY*) pistol be used during the initial stages of training.

All of the movements and/or techniques shown or described in this book should only be used with live ammunition after they have been mastered, and after your competency has been evaluated and validated by a professional police firearms instructor.

1 Developing a Smooth Presentation & a Consistent Tactical Recovery

When practicing the **presentation**, begin with slow, deliberate movements.

Your initial goal is to develop smoothness, *not* speed! Speed will increase naturally the more you practice. So do your best to avoid the common mistake of pushing yourself too hard and fast in the early stages of training. The presentation is covered in Chapter 4 §5 and Chapter 5 §2.

Because a smooth, fast presentation is such an important skill to have, daily practice is recommended, at least at first. If you follow the basic practice session recommendations on the following page, this means you will only need to devote less than 5 minutes a day to practicing both the presentation and recovery. Positive results should be quickly realized.

Keep in mind when practicing that while the presentation will eventually be performed fast, the **recovery** is always performed SLOWLY.

Never rush the recovery during practice, and *especially* not when operating in the real world. The Tactical Recovery is fully described and illustrated in Chapter 4 §11.

BASIC PRESENTATION & RECOVERY PRACTICE SESSION (DRY) Time: 3:00 Minutes

(NOTE: All basic and advanced drills are performed while standing unless otherwise indicated.)

	Exercise Description	Repetitions	Practice Time
1)	**Holster to Body Point Position & Recover;** One-Hand Hold **Reference Chapter 5 §2**	5	1:00 minute (total)
2)	**Holster to Full Extension Position & Recover;** One-Hand Hold **Reference Chapter 5 §2**	5	1:00 minute (total)
3)	**Holster to Full Extension Position & Recover;** Two-Hand Hold **Reference Chapter 5 §2**	5	1:00 minute (total)

ADVANCED PRESENTATION & RECOVERY PRACTICE SESSION (DRY) Time: 5:00 Minutes

	Exercise Description	Repetitions	Practice Time
1)	**Simple Hand Changeover** (Present pistol with Primary Hand, and then switch to Support Hand. Then switch back to Primary Hand and Recover to holster.) **Reference Chapter 10 §2**	5	1:30 minute (total)
2)	**Holster to Position Sul & Recover;** (Standing) One-Hand Hold **Reference Chapter 5 §6**	5	1:30 minute (total)
3)	**Holster to Position Sul & Recover;** (Seated) One-Hand Hold **Reference Chapter 5 §6**	5	2:00 minute (total)

Additional Presentation and Recovery Hints & Tips

Although the majority of your presentation and recovery practice will be dedicated to performing them while standing, other positions should also be used. It is very possible that you will need to access or secure the pistol while seated, moving, kneeling, or prone; uniform and/or equipment limitations imposed by these various positions may interfere with the actions involved in drawing or securing the weapon and must be prepared for.

Practice in drawing the weapon with only the support hand is also necessary, should the primary hand be disabled or otherwise engaged.

The selection and **placement of the holster** on the duty belt is critical to the speed and efficiency of your presentation. While a discussion of the common types of holsters available for use is provided in Chapter 2 §3 and Chapter 6 §1, a closer look at the placement or positioning of the holster on the duty belt is warranted.

Regardless of which type of handgun you carry, the uniform duty holster should be worn high on the primary side hip, never slung low in a "gunslinger" manner. (Drop down or "thigh carry" holsters that are popular with some tactical unit personnel are discouraged for general duty use.)

The holster should be mounted in a vertical position, in line with your primary arm. To check its placement, stand with your arm hung naturally by your side, your weapon holstered. Then slide your hand straight up the side of your pants, following the seam. If the holster is positioned correctly, your hand will be brought directly and easily to it and fall naturally upon the grip of the weapon. You should not have to reach back to secure a grip high on the weapon's backstrap.

The bottom (muzzle end) of the holster may be slightly canted to the rear, bringing the top (grip end) slightly forward. This makes carry comfortable while you are seated in a vehicle.

As Donna Losardo noted in the preceding chapter, female officers may experience difficulty in drawing from a standard-issue holster, as women's torsos tend to be shorter than men's. In effect, this means their hips are often "higher," which can cause the holster and pistol to ride extremely high, inhibiting a clean presentation of the weapon. Specialized gear as noted in Chapter 11 §3 is available to help address this issue.

Final note: Presentation of the pistol from the holster using the support hand should also be practiced to prepare for the possibility of the primary hand/arm being disabled prior to drawing the weapon.

2 Developing a Smooth Reload

The goal is to achieve a smooth, consistent reload. As with the presentation, speed will increase naturally as you progress. Both the combat and tactical reloads are fully described and illustrated in Chapter 4 §7.

RELOADING PRACTICE SESSION (DRY)

(NOTE: Dummy Rounds as shown in Chapter 5 §3 should be used when initially practicing these drills both for safety and to prevent the slide from locking to the rear.)

Exercise Description	Repetitions	Practice Time
1) **Combat Reload**, Standing	5	3:00 minutes (total)
2) **Combat Reload**, Kneeling	5	3:00 minutes (total)
3) **Combat Reload**, Prone	5	3:00 minutes (total)
4) **Tactical Reload**, Standing	5	2:00 minutes (total)
5) **Tactical Reload**, Kneeling	5	2:00 minutes (total)
6) **Tactical Reload**, Prone	5	2:00 minutes (total)

Additional Reloading Hints & Tips

When practicing the reload, the object, as with the presentation, is to perfect the form before you attempt to increase the speed of the actions. The exercises described above should be performed paying as much attention as possible to proper sequencing of the actions.

It is a must, especially when practicing the combat reload, to have the fully-loaded magazine out and up to the weapon before you eject the empty or half-empty magazine from the weapon.

Total practice time estimates are based upon both the execution of the drill and the re-staging of magazines.

3 Practicing the Pistol Refunction Technique

The Pistol Refunction technique is fully illustrated in Chapter 4 § 9. It should be practiced using the dominant and support hands alternately.

Make sure to perform enough repetitions so you can execute the technique effectively.

SEMIAUTOMATIC PISTOL REFUNCTION PRACTICE SESSION (DRY)

(NOTE: Dummy Rounds as shown in Chapter 5 §3 should be used when initially practicing these drills both for safety and to prevent the slide from locking to the rear.)

Exercise Description	Repetitions	Practice Time
1) **Refunction Drill**, Standing, Dominant Hand	As Needed	N/A
2) **Refunction Drill**, Standing, Support Hand	As Needed	N/A
3) **Refunction Drill**, Kneeling, Dominant Hand	As Needed	N/A
4) **Refunction Drill**, Kneeling, Support Hand	As Needed	N/A
5) **Refunction Drill**, Prone, Dominant Hand	As Needed	N/A
6) **Refunction Drill**, Prone, Support Hand	As Needed	N/A
7) **Refunction Drill**, Supine, Dominant Hand	As Needed	N/A
8) **Refunction Drill**, Supine, Support Hand	As Needed	N/A

 Practicing Stoppage Clearing Drills

Stoppage clearing is explained and illustrated in Chapter 4 §10. It is important that you understand the various types of stoppages as well as their causes and cures.

SEMIAUTOMATIC PISTOL STOPPAGE CLEARING PRACTICE SESSION (DRY)

(NOTE: Dummy Rounds as shown in Chapter 5 §3 should be used when initially practicing these drills both for safety and to prevent the slide from locking to the rear.)

Exercise Description	Repetitions	Practice Time
1) **T.I.R.R. Clear Drill**, Standing	10	1:00 minute (total)
2) **Double-Feed Clearing Drill**, Standing	5	1:45 minute (total)

Additional Stoppage Clearing Hints & Tips

Stoppage clearing using both the TIRR Clear Drill and the Double-Feed Clearing Drill should also be practiced from other positions such as kneeling, prone, and supine. This is necessary because there are no guarantees that you will be in a standing position when you experience a stoppage during an actual engagement.

Another important consideration regarding stoppage clearing concerns time; it must be remembered that while the actual clearing of the stoppage can usually be completed in seconds, *realizing* that the pistol has experienced a stoppage often takes much longer! For this reason it is suggested that officers be conditioned to reflexively observe their pistol after firing to ensure it is fully in battery, either when moving to a new position of cover or during the recovery.

LIVE FIRE EXERCISES

ALWAYS WEAR YOUR SAFETY GEAR!

WARNING: The following LIVE FIRE drills are intended for use by qualified personnel who have already completed, at a minimum, a basic firearms training and certification course.

Firearms training is a dangerous activity that can lead to serious injury or death if not properly and safely performed.

All training should be conducted at approved ranges and under competent supervision.

Practicing Stoppage Clearing Drills (Continued)

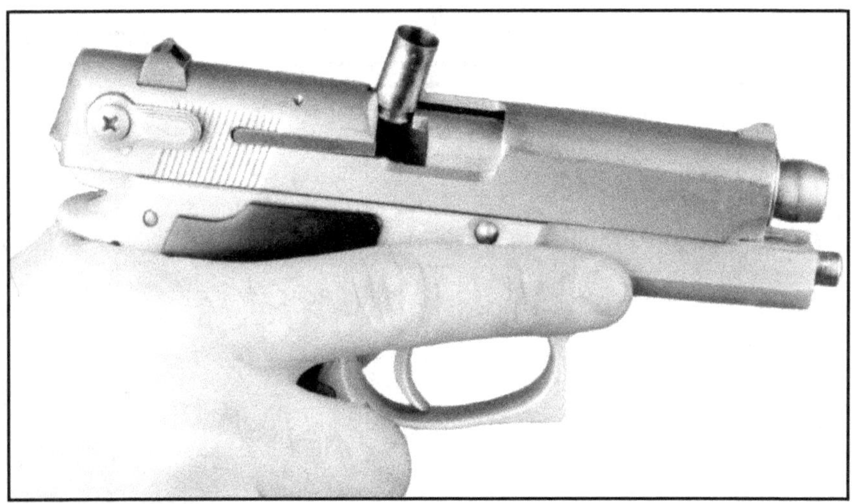

SEMIAUTOMATIC PISTOL STOPPAGE CLEARING PRACTICE SESSION (LIVE FIRE)

(NOTE: Dummy rounds as shown in Chapter 5 §3 should be mixed in with the live ammunition when practicing these drills so you can experience the stoppage while firing. As double-feed type stoppages are difficult to reliably generate, you should substitute the predictable "failure to fire" stoppage caused by the dummy rounds to practice the Double-Feed Clearing Drill.)

Exercise Description	Repetitions	Practice Time
1) **T.I.R.R. Clear Drill, Standing**	At least 4	1:00 minute (total)
2) **Double-Feed Clearing Drill,** Standing **Reference Chapter 4 §10**	At least 4	1:45 minute (total)

Live fire stoppage clearing should also be practiced from other positions such as kneeling, prone, and supine.

5 Developing Your Basic Point Shooting Skill Set

Before attempting to perform any of the techniques shown in this book using live ammunition, you should dry practice thoroughly until the movements can be performed safely, fluidly, and correctly.

Make sure to perform the drills very slowly in the initial stages of dry practice. Check yourself in a mirror to ensure your body positioning is correct. Then continue to practice until the movements begin to feel natural to you. Smoothness will lead to speed. After you have achieved both and can consistently perform the drills safely, it is time to begin live fire practice.

When live ammunition is introduced, you must begin the entire process again, starting with slow, deliberate movements. Never rush yourself or your training, especially when live firing! Remember, some mistakes can only be made once. We are working with deadly weapons and involved in a serious business. There is no margin for error.

The Full Extension (left) & Body Point (right) Positions are fully explained and illustrated in Chapter 5 §2.

POINT SHOOTING SKILLS DEVELOPMENT PRACTICE SESSION 1 (LIVE FIRE)

(NOTE: Refer to Chapter 5 §2 for illustrations and additional descriptions of the techniques referenced below.)

	Exercise Description	Repetitions	Distance
	FULL EXTENSION POSITION		
1)	One-Hand Hold, from **LOW READY** Position: Raise pistol to **LINE OF SIGHT** while staring at a specific point on target; **CONVULSE HAND** and **FIRE 1 ROUND**. Continue to hold pistol at line of sight for 2 seconds, then **SLOWLY LOWER** to **LOW READY**. (Remove finger from trigger and DECOCK or ENGAGE SAFETY if required.) After completing initial 10 repetitions, rest, reload, and then repeat. **Reference Chapter 5 §2**	10	3 Yards
2)	One-Hand Hold, from **HOLSTER** to Full Extension Position, **FIRE 1 ROUND** & Recover. Remember to allow pistol to interrupt the **LINE OF SIGHT** before firing with **CONVULSIVE GRIP**. Keep your **EYES ON THE TARGET**! After completing initial 10 repetitions, rest, reload, and then repeat. **Reference Chapter 5 §2**	10	3 Yards

Remember: the initial goal is **ACCURATE,** and **CONSISTENT SHOT PLACEMENT**, not speed. Speed will increase naturally with practice.

POINT SHOOTING SKILLS DEVELOPMENT PRACTICE SESSION 2 (LIVE FIRE)

(NOTE: Refer to Chapter 5 §2 for illustrations and additional descriptions of the techniques referenced below.)

Exercise Description	Repetitions	Distance
FULL EXTENSION POSITION		
1) One-Hand Hold, from **LOW READY** Position: Raise pistol to **LINE OF SIGHT** while staring at a specific point on target; **CONVULSE HAND TWICE** and **FIRE 2 ROUNDS**. Continue to hold pistol at line of sight for 2 seconds, then **SLOWLY LOWER** to **LOW READY**. (Remove finger from trigger and DECOCK or ENGAGE SAFETY if required.) After completing initial 5 repetitions, rest, reload, and then repeat. **Reference Chapter 5 §2**	5	3 Yards
2) One-Hand Hold, from **HOLSTER** to Full Extension Position, **FIRE 2 ROUNDS** & Recover. Remember to allow pistol to interrupt the **LINE OF SIGHT** before firing with **CONVULSIVE GRIP**. Keep your **EYES ON THE TARGET**! After completing initial 5 repetitions, rest, reload, and then repeat. **Reference Chapter 5 §2**	5	3 Yards

Remember: the initial goal is **ACCURATE, CONSISTENT SHOT PLACEMENT**, not speed. Speed will increase naturally with practice.

POINT SHOOTING SKILLS DEVELOPMENT PRACTICE SESSION 3 (LIVE FIRE)

(NOTE: Refer to Chapter 5 §2 for illustrations and additional descriptions of the techniques referenced below.)

	Exercise Description	Repetitions	Distance
	BODY POINT POSITION		
1)	One-Hand Hold, from **HOLSTER** to **BODY POINT** Position: Keep **EYES ON TARGET;** staring at a specific point, **CONVULSE HAND** and **FIRE 1 ROUND**. Continue to hold pistol locked in position for 2 seconds, then **SLOWLY LOWER** to **LOW READY,** (Remove finger from trigger and DECOCK or ENGAGE SAFETY if required.) **& RECOVER TO HOLSTER.** After completing initial 10 repetitions, rest, reload, and then repeat. **Reference Chapter 5 §2**	10	5 Feet
2)	One-Hand Hold, from **HOLSTER** to **BODY POINT** Position, **FIRE 2 ROUNDS** & Recover as described above. Remember to **LOCK** primary arm elbow tight against your ribcage, keeping pistol **CENTERED ON YOUR MIDLINE**. Fire with **CONVULSIVE GRIP** while keeping your **EYES ON THE TARGET**! After completing 5 repetitions, rest, reload, and then repeat. **Reference Chapter 5 §2**	5	5 Feet

Remember: the initial goal is **ACCURATE, CONSISTENT SHOT PLACEMENT**, not speed. Speed will increase naturally with practice.

6 Developing Your Basic Precision Shooting Skill Set

When initially training a combat pistol shooter, it is highly recommended that the point shooting skills be established *prior* to the precision shooting skills for the reasons cited in the text in Chapter 1 §6.

This in no way diminishes the importance of precision shooting skills development, however! The ability to deliver a precision-aimed shot, should the circumstances allow you to access and employ the sights of your pistol, is a critical skill that must be mastered by the competent police pistoleer.

The suggested training module outlined below is offered for consideration. These exercises, or exercises of a similar nature, should be included in your regular training regimen along with the point shooting and other physical skills development exercises described in this section.

In addition to the Live Fire drills noted below, it is also strongly suggested that **dry drills** such as the **Wall Drill** and the **Coin Drill** described in Chapter 5 §3 be utilized as well, both before and after live firing.

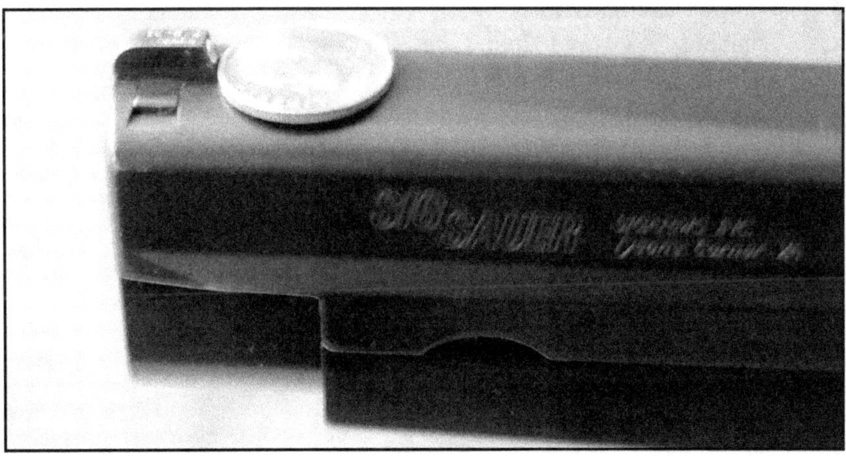

The dry fire **"Coin Drill"** should be performed with a **SAFE, CLEAR, and EMPTY** pistol. The objective is to repeatedly manipulate the trigger while keeping the sights aligned without causing the coin to fall. You should be able to complete at least 10 repetitions with just a little practice. Reps will increase as smooth trigger manipulation develops. (**Note:** When performing this drill with most Beretta pistols, you will have to place the coin against the rear sight; Glock and similar "Safe-Action" type pistols require a manual cycling of the slide between reps.)

PRECISION SHOOTING SKILL DEVELOPMENT PRACTICE SESSION 1 (LIVE FIRE)

(NOTE: Refer to Chapter 5 §3 for illustrations and additional descriptions of the techniques referenced below.)

Exercise Description	Repetitions	Distance
1) **Ford's Rawhide Drill**, Standing, **Two Hand Hold**, (Alternate Dominant Hand & Support Hand)	As Needed	3 Yards
2) **Ford's Rawhide Drill**, Standing, **One Hand Hold**, (Alternate Dominant Hand & Support Hand)	As Needed	3 Yards
3) **Dummy Round Drill**, Standing, **Two Hand Hold**, (Alternate Dominant Hand & Support Hand)	As Needed	3 Yards
4) **Dummy Round Drill**, Standing, **One Hand Hold**, (Alternate Dominant Hand & Support Hand)	As Needed	3 Yards
5) **Reset Drill**, Standing, **Two Hand Hold**, Dominant Hand	As Needed	3 Yards
6) **Reset Drill**, Standing, **One Hand Hold**, Dominant Hand	As Needed	3 Yards
7) **Reset Drill**, Standing, **Two Hand Hold**, Support Hand	As Needed	3 Yards
8) **Reset Drill**, Standing, **One Hand Hold**, Dominant Hand	As Needed	3 Yards

PRECISION SHOOTING SKILL DEVELOPMENT PRACTICE SESSION 2 (LIVE FIRE)

(NOTE: The drills listed below are to be fired one after another in the order shown. Reload as needed to complete all the drills. Take your time and make each shot count. Refer to Chapter 5 §3 for additional information about the techniques referenced below.)

Exercise Description	Repetitions	Distance
1) **Reset Drill**, Standing, **Two Hand Hold**, Dominant Hand (Decock if pistol so equipped)	3 Rounds	7 Yards
2) **Reset Drill,** Kneeling, **Two Hand Hold**, Dominant Hand (Decock if pistol so equipped)	3 Rounds	7 Yards
3) **Reset Drill**, Prone, **Two Hand Hold**, Dominant Hand (Decock if pistol so equipped)	3 Rounds	7 Yards
EXECUTE SIMPLE HAND SWITCH		
4) **Reset Drill**, Prone, **Two Hand Hold,** Support Hand (Decock if pistol so equipped)	3 Rounds	7 Yards
5) **Reset Drill,** Kneeling, **Two Hand Hold**, Support Hand (Decock if pistol so equipped)	3 Rounds	7 Yards
6) **Reset Drill,** Standing, **Two Hand Hold**, Support Hand (Decock if pistol so equipped)	3 Rounds	7 Yards

PRECISION SHOOTING SKILL DEVELOPMENT PRACTICE SESSION 3 (LIVE FIRE)

(NOTE: The drills listed below are to be fired one after another in the order shown. Reload as needed to complete all the drills. Take your time and make each shot count. Refer to Chapter 5 §3 for additional information about the techniques referenced below.)

Exercise Description	Repetitions	Distance
1) **Reset Drill**, Standing, **Two Hand Hold**, Dominant Hand (Decock if pistol so equipped)	3 Rounds	15 Yards
2) **Reset Drill,** Kneeling, **Two Hand Hold**, Dominant Hand (Decock if pistol so equipped)	3 Rounds	15 Yards
3) **Reset Drill**, Prone, **Two Hand Hold**, Dominant Hand (Decock if pistol so equipped)	3 Rounds	15 Yards
EXECUTE SIMPLE HAND SWITCH		
4) **Reset Drill**, Prone, **Two Hand Hold**, Support Hand (Decock if pistol so equipped)	3 Rounds	15 Yards
5) **Reset Drill,** Kneeling, **Two Hand Hold**, Support Hand (Decock if pistol so equipped)	3 Rounds	15 Yards
6) **Reset Drill,** Standing, **Two Hand Hold**, Support Hand (Decock if pistol so equipped)	3 Rounds	15 Yards

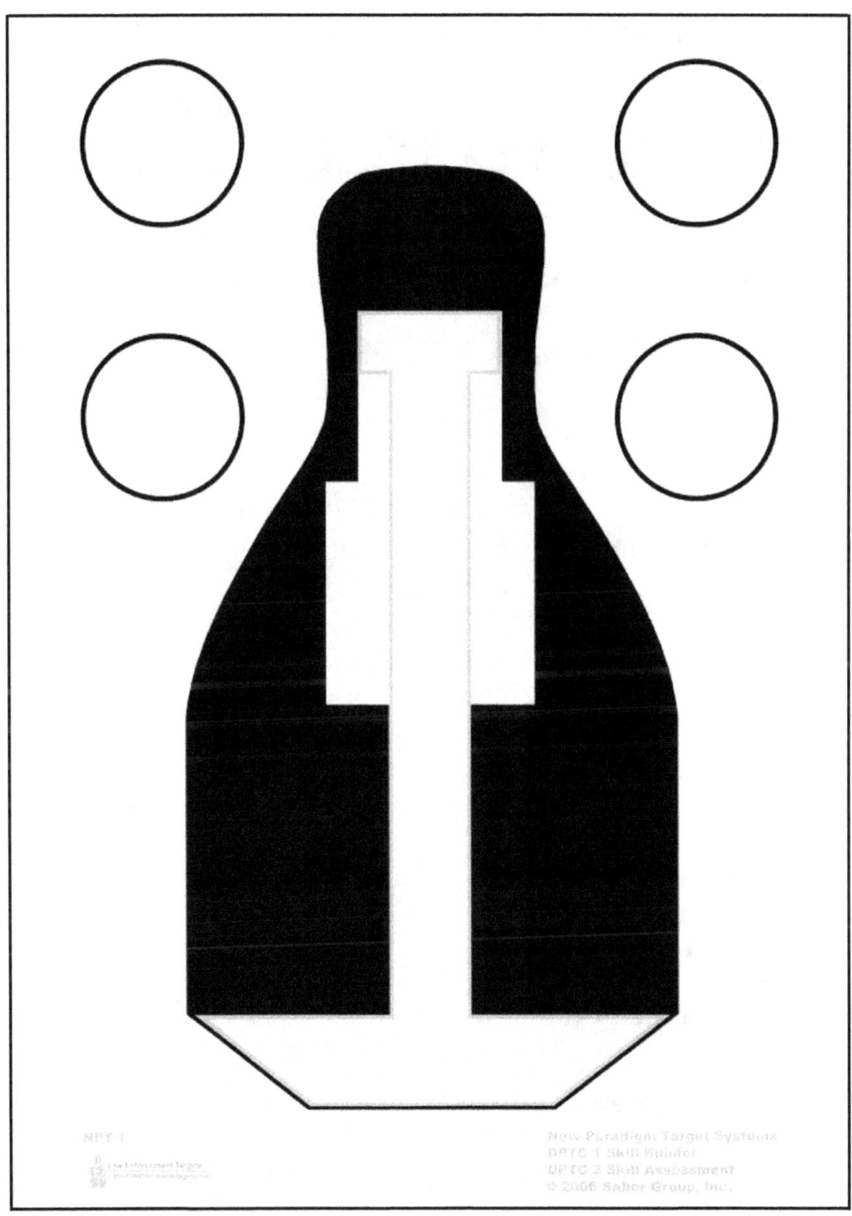

The NPT-1 Target produced by Law Enforcement Targets, Inc., is specifically designed for use with the drills described in this section.

Visit www.letargets.com for more information.

7 Additional Skills Development

In addition to the practice sessions suggested in the previous sections, you should seek out additional training and devote time to developing your pistolcraft skills in the following areas as well:

- **Continued Speed and Accuracy Development**
- **Reduced Light Shooting**
- **Transitioning Drills**
- **Moving Target Drills** (Including drills during which the target moves, the officer moves, and both move simultaneously.)
- **Close Quarter Pistol Combat Skills**

It is also important to note that while pistolcraft combat skills are critical, very few civilian law enforcement use of force situations will actually require or call for the use of the pistol. For this reason, the competent police or security officer must develop other use of force related skill sets.

These skill sets include, but are not limited to:

- **Empty Hand Combat Skills**
- **Chemical Agent Weapon Skills**
- **Impact Weapon Combat Skills**
- **Edged Weapon Combat Skills**

More information pertaining to training materials, programs, and recommended training entities relating to these disciplines is available on our website (www.sabergroup.com).

SECTION 3

Living as a Professional Pistoleer

Pis-tol-eer ***n.*** **1. a professional-at-arms, trained and equipped with a handgun as the primary weapon; 2. a person noted for speed and skill in handling a pistol; may also be referred to as a pistolero (*m*) or a pistolera (*f*)**

There are many people in the civilian realm whose profession requires them to carry a pistol. Police officers, security officers, and professional body guards are routinely issued pistols and trained in their use.

Despite the formality of the processes used to select, train, and verify the competency of these people with their handguns, the truth of the matter is that most people who carry a handgun professionally do not think of themselves as professional pistoleers. Surprisingly, this is especially true in the civilian police industry.

There are many reasons for this. Many police officers are not thrilled with the idea of carrying a handgun, much less the possibility that they may need to use it to shoot another human being.

A lot of police officers are also unsure of their abilities with the handgun; this lack of confidence often translates into a general feeling of discomfort or even disdain for the pistol they are required to strap on daily.

Other officers who do develop substantial skills with the pistol are loath to acknowledge or display any type of pride in this. In my experience, I have found this to be largely based on the fear of being branded as a gun nut, cowboy, or "feeler"—a brand, incidentally, that is often applied by people from the first two groups described above.

There is also, unfortunately, another, much smaller group within the police subculture that embraces the notion of police officer as pistoleer to the extreme. Sometimes referred to as a "Tackleberry" after the gun-crazed character in the *Police Academy* movies, these officers often serve as a detriment to the widespread development of much needed police pistolcraft skills, as well as a danger to themselves and others with their immature and sometimes foolish actions.

That brings us to the last group, the professional police pistoleers. The officers in this group, like many officers in the other groups noted above, take their profession as a whole very seriously, and work hard to develop proficiency in the myriad disciplines they employ throughout their careers. The members of this group, however, differ from the other groups in that they realize that while all their professional law enforcement skills are important, it is their skill with the pistol that is most likely to determine the outcome of a deadly force encounter, when lives are at stake and the threat is presented by another human being.

In recognition of this reality, these officers dedicate themselves to mastering their abilities to employ the pistol, *especially* for close combat use, as they know that the majority of violent and deadly encounters take place up close and personal.

The professional police pistoleer not only acknowledges and accepts the enormous responsibility that comes with the taking up of the badge and gun, but embraces it proudly as both an honorable duty and an obligation.

I have been privileged to have been taught by, and to have served with, such people for more than two decades now. We have entrusted our lives to one another on many occasions, and would do so willingly again, without hesitation. We have an understanding based upon mutual trust, honor, and respect.

Outside of our group, we are sometimes misunderstood. Over the years we have even occasionally been branded with barely hidden derision as the "gun guys" by a few others in our department. We pay it no mind. We are, actually, usually amused by this, because as some of these people look at us and see zealots, we look at them and see fellow officers who are either living in glass bubbles of denial, or who have not yet developed the critical and life-saving "sense of danger" discussed in Chapter 7.

For our part, we try and help them break their glass bubbles and develop a sense of danger by providing reality-based training that drives home the critical need for the development of relevant police pistolcraft skills. We have them use the pistol in training the same way they will use it on the street: the time frames short, the distances close, the threats immediate and as real as we can manage.

We do this because we have seen—firsthand—the aftermath of too many violent, police-involved, real world encounters. We have seen the blood on the ground. We have shaken the hands of grieving family members at funeral homes and in cemeteries. And we have listened to the mournful call of the bagpipes and bugles and sworn we would do all we could to prevent it from happening again.

We have also seen the effect on officers whose bubble of denial was shattered though they survived the incident. I have listened on several occasions as these officers (who had previously looked upon the pistol and training as simply job-required nuisances) explained to me with great emotion just how important training and preparation are, because when it happens "it happens so fast" and there's "no time to think, you just react like you've been trained to" and how "God-awful scary it is when you realize that this other person is intent on *actually killing you*" and there is no one there to save you but—*you.*

You and your pistol.

The Professional Police Pistoleer is Always Armed

Always armed. By now you have seen this admonition several times in this book. I stress it because I believe it so strongly.

I have been carrying a pistol every day for more than 20 years both on duty and off. I will not leave the house without one. I freely admit that I do so out of fear.

Not the fear of being unable to defend just myself should I encounter a deadly threat situation, but primarily the fear of being unable to defend others—especially my loved ones.

Think about it: we are trained to defend life. We are issued equipment that enables us to do so in extreme situations. We have taken an oath to do so. We go about our days carrying the pistol, ready to put ourselves in the line of fire to defend ourselves or others while working—and then, when off duty, many of us relinquish this responsibility to others by choosing to go about unarmed.

This is something I have never been able to understand: how police officers, being aware of the potential dangers that lurk all around us, could choose to go out into the same society they police while leaving the means to defend themselves or their family members at home.

We, more than anyone, must understand that when seconds count, on-duty police officers are most likely *at least* minutes away!

How can you justify not being prepared to do what you are trained and obligated to do, just because you are "off the clock?"

The common arguments for going about unarmed usually include the following: **1.** ***When I'm off duty, I don't get involved no how, no way. I leave the job—and the gun—at work.***

This argument usually self-destructs the first time the officer saying it actually runs into a bad situation while off duty. The feeling of nakedness and vulnerability (so I am told) is something one never forgets, especially if you are drafted into participation as opposed to volunteering. A good example of this is the unarmed, off-duty police officer who was standing in a pharmacy several years back when a drug-addled, knife wielding desperado demanded cash and pills from the person behind the counter. The terrorized clerk, meaning no harm but grasping for a lifeline, turned to the officer and blurted out, "You're a cop! Do something!" Though he survived this situation, it did not end well for the officer as he received several lacerations as the crazed subject decided to slash his way out of the store.

2. *The duty pistol is uncomfortable to carry.* First off, to paraphrase Clint Smith, guns aren't meant to be comfortable so much as comforting. Just the same, if you can, buy a pistol that comfortably fits both your hand and your lifestyle and carry it when off duty. If this is not an option, then invest in a good concealment holster and carry your duty pistol every day. You will get used to it. It's like buckling up your seatbelt. After a while you don't even realize it's there, but if you crash, you'll thank God that you went to the trouble and put up with the slight discomfort.

3. *The gun makes my family members uncomfortable.* More than likely this is because you are also uncomfortable with it, consciously or not. This can be overcome on your part with the development of a proper mindset and training as described throughout this book. If this is not the case, then perhaps it is because you have never explained to your family members why you feel the need to carry off duty. They should be told this, as well as what to do should you become unavoidably involved in something while with them. (See Chapter 3 §3 for more information on this.)

My own wife and children know that I always carry. They also understand that they must do exactly as told should a situation develop that requires my response. They have come to accept the presence of the pistol as both normal and necessary, based upon my duties and obligations as a law enforcement professional.

In fact, on more than one occasion, my beautiful daughter, sensing potential danger in an urban setting or wooded terrain, has turned to me and asked, "Have you got your pistol with you, Daddy?" Upon hearing my response of "Yes, I do," she has invariably replied, "Good."

Why? Because it makes her feel safe.

And why shouldn't she? She has her own highly trained, well armed police escort near at hand, something many people willingly pay for.

Why deny your family members the same?

Be safe. Be smart. Be strong. And most of all, *be ready.* 

APPENDIX A

The Revolver: Rolling with the "Wheelgun"

The Revolver: A Primer

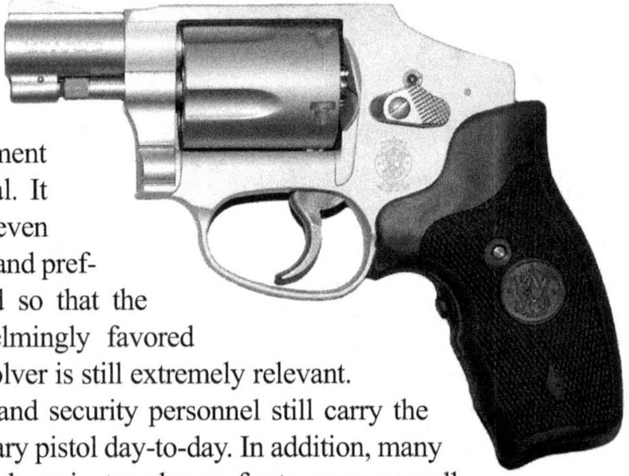

This appendix is included to provide a basic overview of the revolver for the modern law enforcement or security professional. It is included because even though pistol designs and preferences have evolved so that the semiauto is overwhelmingly favored for use today, the revolver is still extremely relevant.

Many officers and security personnel still carry the revolver as their primary pistol day-to-day. In addition, many officers who are issued semiautos also prefer to carry a small revolver as a back-up or off-duty weapon. This is hardly unusual, as the revolver has been serving the members of law enforcement, security, and the military for more than 150 years with great distinction. In addition to the continued presence of the "wheelgun" in the hands of professional pistoleers, revolvers of all types can also be found in great numbers throughout our society, in the hands of law-abiding persons as well as criminals.

Regardless of this continuing presence and availability, there are many officers who have come into the law enforcement, security, and military industries during the past decade or so who have never handled a revolver.

In fact, when training new recruits and showing how a late model revolver is operated for familiarization purposes, I have actually been asked if it used black powder! This lack of knowledge is, unfortunately, becoming more common in our high speed, low drag, "guns of the future" oriented society. This appendix, therefore, is provided to help fill that gap a bit, as well as to provide a rudimentary review for those of us who may still prefer, or be required, to "roll with a wheelgun" daily or even just now and then.

Please understand that we will not be going into great depth regarding the handling and use of the revolver in this appendix. A future volume in the *Police Pistolcraft* series dedicated to the combat revolver is in production and will focus on this reliable alternative to the semiautomatic pistol.

Pistols shown in photo on preceding page, from top: Colt 1851 Navy Model, Colt 1849 Pocket Model, Colt Police Positive, S&W Military & Police, Colt Lawman MK III, S&W Model 19, S&W Model 65, S&W Model 36. Pistol shown on this page is a S&W Model 642 Airweight Revolver.

SAFETY NOTICE

All safe firearms handling rules should be reviewed prior to handling any type of firearm. (Reference Chapter 3)

If you are not familiar with revolvers, you should seek out training from a professional and competent firearms instructor prior to handling them.

Common Characteristics of the Revolver

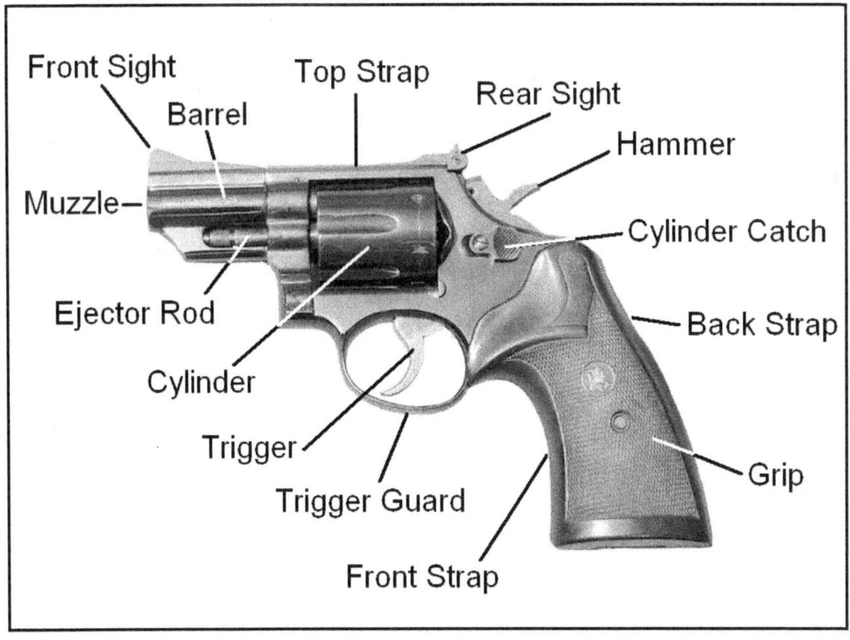

How Revolvers Function

Modern revolvers are relatively simple to load, fire, and unload. The basic functioning of a double action revolver is described and illustrated below.

Loading the Revolver

Always keep the muzzle pointed in a SAFE DIRECTION!

1 First, depress the cylinder catch to release the cylinder and push the cylinder into the open position with the middle and ring fingers as shown.

With the cylinder opened, the revolver cannot fire. Nevertheless, ensure you keep the muzzle pointed in a safe direction.

Holding the revolver as illustrated allows you to maintain control of it while loading and unloading the cylinder.

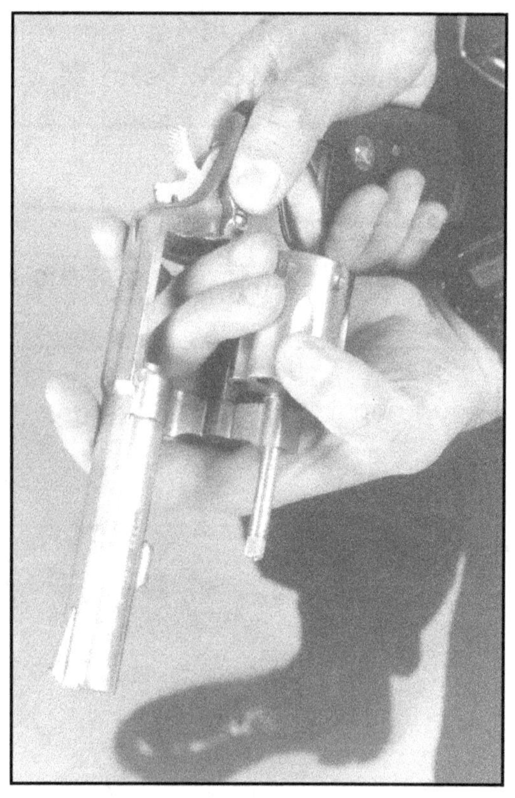

Loading the Revolver (Continued)

2 Insert one round of ammunition into each of the chambers.

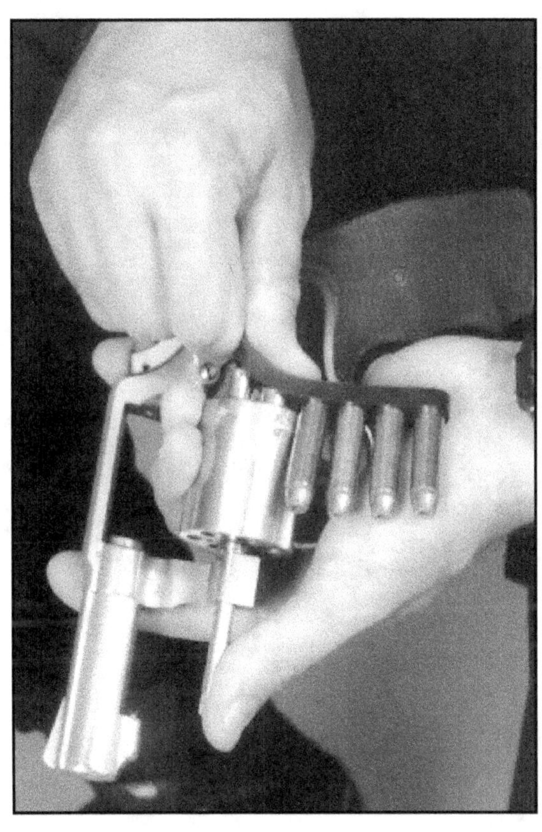

Rounds can be drawn and loaded individually, loaded two at a time using a speed strip as shown in this photo, or all chambers can be loaded simultaneously using a speed loader.

Below: Speed strips (left) and speed loaders (right) provide for efficient and fast reloading. Older model double "dump pouch" shown in center. Six loose rounds are carried in each pouch.

Loading the Revolver (Continued)

3 Close the cylinder by pressing it into position and rotating it slightly. You should feel it lock into place.

The revolver is now ready to fire.

Note: Avoid forcefully swinging or snapping the cylinder closed as this can damage the revolver and adversely affect its performance.

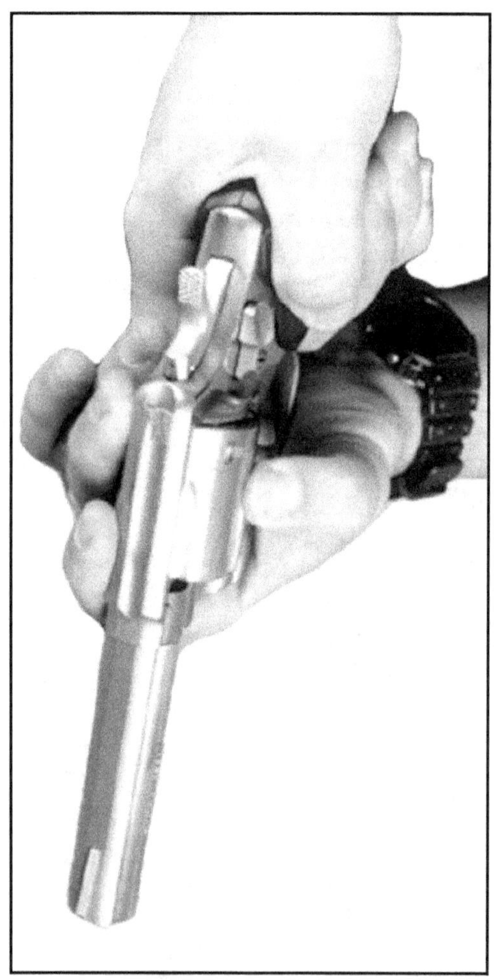

Always keep your fingers off the trigger until ready to fire!

Firing the Revolver

Press the trigger to fire. The vast majority of modern combat revolvers can be fired in both double and single action modes. (Refer to Chapter 2 §1 for a more detailed explanation of trigger actions and terminology.)

Trigger Actions

Double action — a single press of the trigger raises the hammer from the forward position fully rearward, and then releases the hammer to fire the weapon.

Single action — the pistol is fired by pressing the trigger with the hammer at the full-cock position. The hammer must be brought to the full-cock position manually. This is usually accomplished with the thumb of the firing hand.

When firing **double action,** each time you press the trigger while the hammer is forward, the cylinder will rotate one position as the hammer moves rearward. The cylinder will then automatically lock into place immediately before the hammer falls, with a loaded chamber aligned with the bore of the barrel and the hammer.

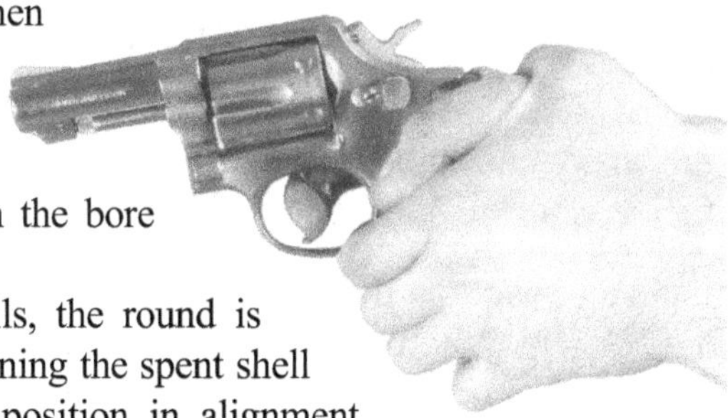

When the hammer falls, the round is fired, and the chamber containing the spent shell casing remains locked into position in alignment with the bore. The revolver will fire one round each time the trigger is pressed in this manner until all of the rounds have been expended.

If so designed, the revolver may also be fired **single action**. To do so, first manually cock the hammer to the rear. As the hammer is cocked, the cylinder will rotate one position and lock into place, bringing a different chamber into alignment with the bore and the hammer.

Pressing the trigger releases the hammer and the round is fired.

Unloading the Revolver

To unload the revolver, first open the cylinder as previously described. You may then either:

1) Keep the **muzzle pointed down** and depress the ejector rod with your thumb. This will cause the star extractor to lift the shell casings from the cylinder wells, at which point you may remove the live rounds (or the empty casings) manually.

or:

2) Maintain control of the revolver with the cylinder open and point the **muzzle up**. (Be conscious of where it points.) The live rounds (or empty casings) may fall out when you do this.

If the weapon has been fired or is dirty, however, you may need to depress the ejector rod. Striking the rod with the heel of the hand as shown at right is recommended, especially if you are clearing the cylinder in order to perform a reload.

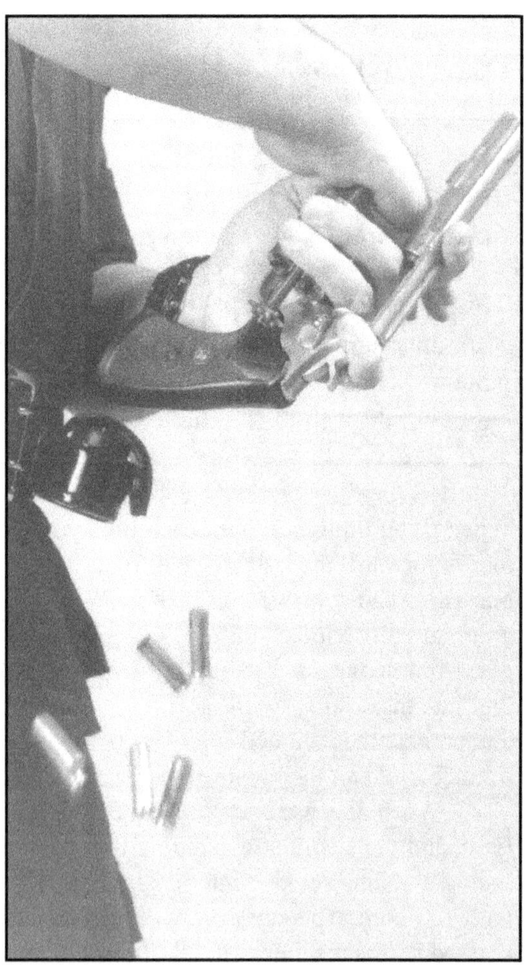

Remember: *Smooth is Fast!*

Maintaining the Revolver

Cleaning and maintaining the revolver is as necessary as cleaning and maintaining the semiautomatic. Some people seem to believe that the revolver is not only easier to use than a semiauto, but that it is also maintenance free to boot! Nothing can be further from the truth.

The revolver, like any complex mechanical device that has multiple moving parts, should not be needlessly abused. It must also be kept clean and lubricated, *especially* if your life may depend upon it!

As for handling, you need to ensure that you employ all safe firearms handling rules as described in this book when working with *any* handgun, regardless of design or action.

I would offer a warning regarding a particular "Hollywood stylization" unique to the revolver that you should avoid if possible; when closing the cylinder, some people mimic the movie star gunslingers by snapping the open cylinder shut by flicking the revolver to the side. While this does work, if you do it repeatedly it can also damage the gun and adversely affect its operation. You are better served by closing the cylinder with your support hand as shown on page 394, and not forcefully slamming or snapping the cylinder into the frame.

Of course, the snap-closing method may be used in an emergency should one of your hands be injured or otherwise unavailable, and you need to close the cylinder after reloading. Other than for emergency use, though, you should steer clear of this damaging practice.

Cleaning Basics

Since the general aspects of handgun cleaning covered in Chapter 2 §1 apply to both the semiauto and the revolver, I will refer you to that chapter and not cover the same ground again in this section.

Instead, in this section, we will examine a few specific details as they relate to the general issues of cleaning and maintaining the wheelgun.

With the revolver, it is especially important to remove any dirt, carbon fouling, corrosion, or lead buildup from around critical areas such as the forcing cone, star extractor, and ratchet, as well as around the firing pin hole, pawl, and hammer groove. The cylinder face and chambers must also be thoroughly cleaned.

More information on these components follows.

Cleaning the Revolver (Continued)

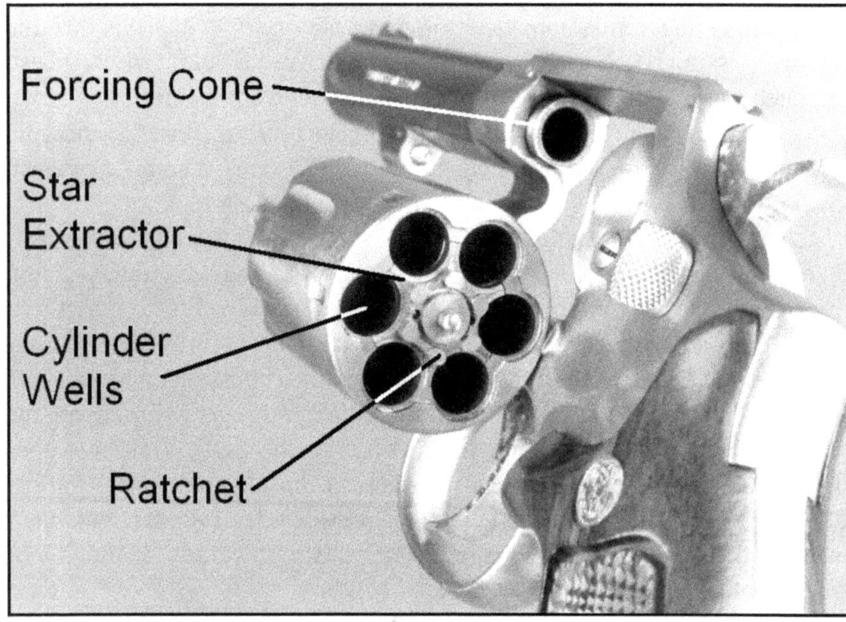

With the cylinder opened, the forcing cone, star extractor, and cylinder wells are visible. All must be kept clean and clear of fouling and debris.

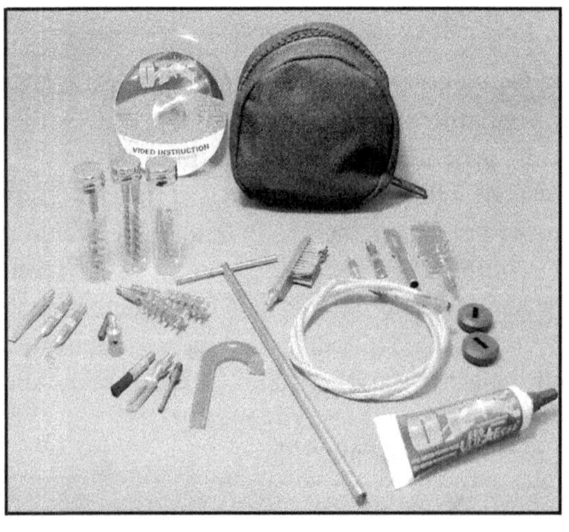

The **OTIS Premium Gun Cleaning Kit** shown at left is extremely versatile. This one small kit can be used to clean pistols, rifles, and shotguns! All the contents fit into the small belt pouch shown rear right. While you can make do with a basic pistol cleaning kit as noted in Chapter 2, it is always a good idea to have a complete firearms cleaning kit in your range bag.

Cleaning the Revolver (Continued)

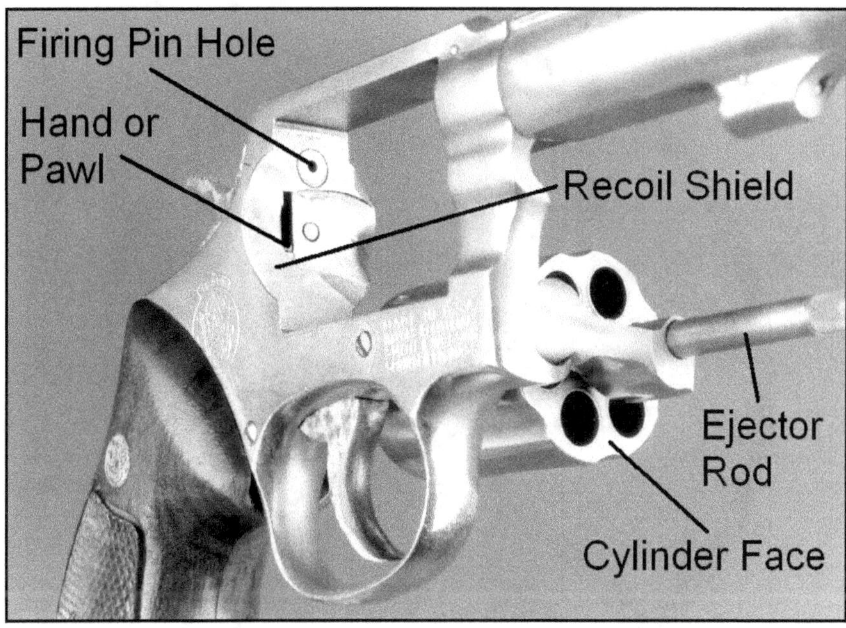

In this photograph, you can see the firing pin hole, recoil shield, and pawl, as well as the ejector rod and the face of the cylinder. Screws such as those visible on the frame above the trigger as well as grip screws should be checked periodically for tightness. Make sure you use the right size screwdriver when doing this so you do not damage or score the screw slot or frame, and be careful not to over-tighten.

Other areas to clean include the bore, frame, sights, grips, etc. More information on cleaning the handgun is included in Chapter 2 §1.

Lubrication: Remember to lubricate all metal surfaces after cleaning. Pay particular attention to all moving parts, as well as any areas that show wear due to friction. Avoid over-lubricating parts, especially in the area of the recoil shield. Too much oil will not only attract and hold dust, dirt, and lint, but may adversely affect the ammunition if the revolver is kept loaded for extended periods of time.

Storing / Securing the Revolver

Any of the options described in Chapter 3 §3 for storing and/or securing the handgun can be used with the revolver.

One method that is **not recommended**, however, is illustrated in the above photograph. As noted in Chapter 3, this less than desirable option utilizes the handcuffs as a firearms disabling device. With the revolver, this is done by securing one of the cuffs around the top strap with the cylinder open as shown. With the semiautomatic, the slide is removed and one of the cuffs is secured through the ejection port, the other through the trigger guard.

Even though this practice is effective at rendering the weapon inoperable, I strongly recommend against it because the metal on metal contact can easily damage the weapon's frame or slide, possibly causing problems in operation.

SAFETY NOTICE

The two-handed grip shown below is generally safe to use when firing a revolver, but is extremely dangerous to use when firing a semi-automatic pistol! It is best to keep your support hand thumb clear of the rear of the slide in order to avoid severe injury as the slide cycles. (See below -- *Ouch!*)

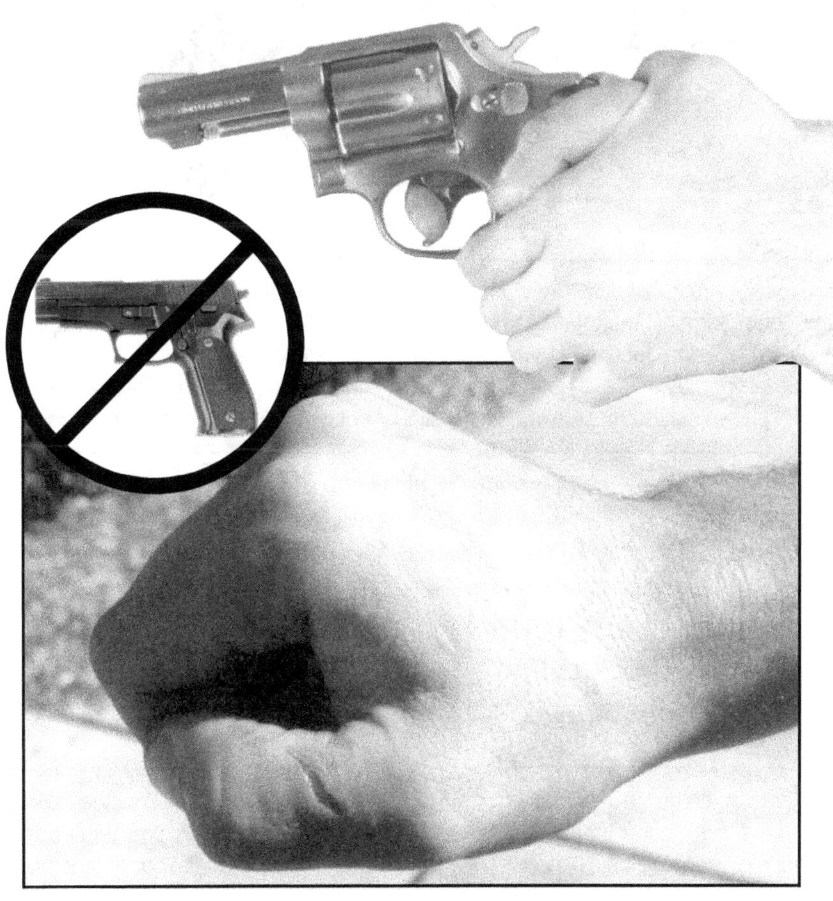

APPENDIX B

How to Load a Pistol Magazine

Understanding how to properly load the semiautomatic pistol magazine is one of those things that is often taken for granted by experienced shooters.

One method is illustrated here for those new to the business and the gear. Regardless of how you load it, try to remember that this vital pistol component is properly referred to as a *magazine*, not a "clip."

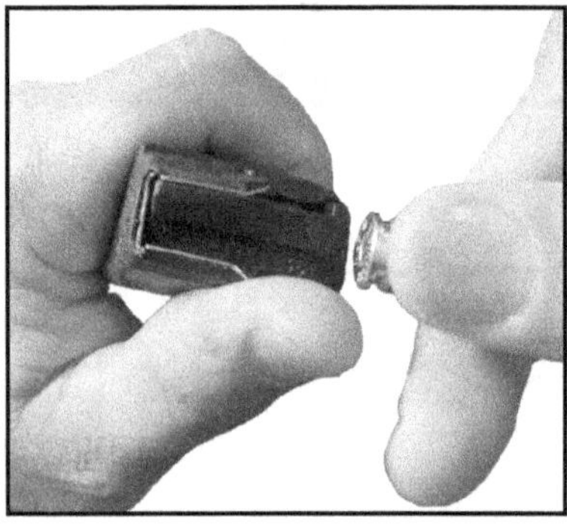

1. Grasp the magazine securely, with your thumb against the top-front side of the magazine feed lips. Hold a round in your other hand, with your thumb placed on top as shown.

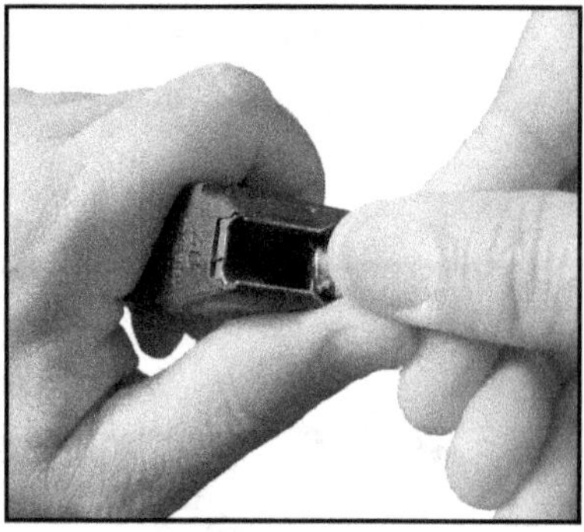

2. Using the thumb placed against the side of the magazine feed lips as a guide, press the base of the round against the follower while slipping it between and under the feed lips.

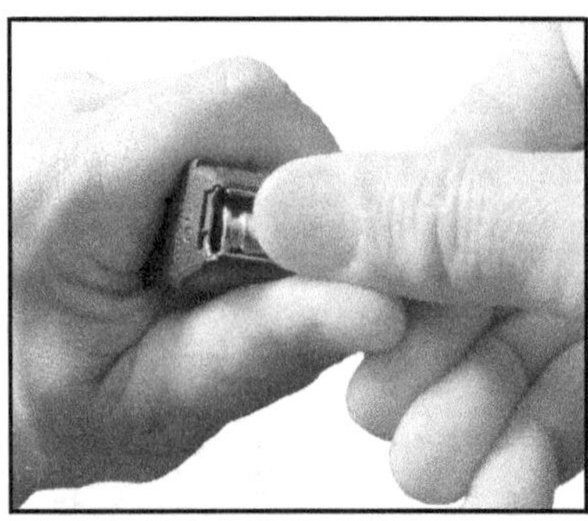

3. Keeping downward pressure on the round with your thumb, slide the round fully rearward until it stops.

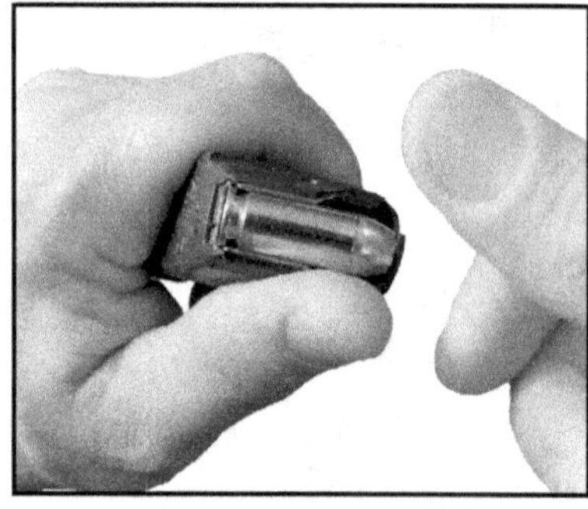

4. Release pressure on the round. Repeat as needed, pressing subsequent rounds against one another.

INDEX

B

C

E

G

H

I

Q

R

S

PHOTO CREDIT INDEX

The author wishes to acknowledge and thank the following individuals for contributing their time, talent, and photographs to this book.

Photograph Contributions

The late *Rex Applegate*......Page 26

Lou Chiodo......Page 24

The late *Jim Cirillo*......Page 105

Kathryn T. Conti......Pages 136, 137, 138, 139, 246, 308

Katie Conti......Pages 205, 326, 327, 328, 332, 333

Margie Conti......Page 99

Joe Maffei......Page 242

Al Pereira......Pages 66, 67, 78, 110, 114, 115, 118, 119 (bottom), 120, 121, 141, 152, 153, 155, 209, 213 (center and bottom), 227, 228, 240, 241, 243, 252, 278, 293, 314, 329, 340, 341, 342, 343, 344, 374, 392, 393 (top), 394, 395, 396, 398 (top), 399, 400, 401 (top)

Heidelore Wentrup......Pages 79 (bottom), 316, 357, 359, 362, 364, 390

Archival photographs, various sources......Pages 16, 17, 20, 23, 28, 35, 55, 57, 75, 113, 172, 173, 263, 287, 289, 291, 346, 349, 350

***About the Author* photograph**, Page 423, courtesy of MLEFIAA

All of the other photographs and illustrations in this book were produced by the author. Many of these photographs would not have been possible without the generous contributions of time and patience by the following people who allowed themselves to be talked into serving as models:

Paul Wosny, Donna Losardo, Paul Damery, Joe Thibodeau, Jim Cirillo, Bob Taubert, Kathy Conti, & Nick Conti

Police, at all times,
should maintain
a relationship with the public
that gives reality to the historic tradition
that the police are the public
and the public are the police;
the police being
only members of the public
who are paid to give full-time attention
to duties which are incumbent
on every citizen
in the interests of
community welfare and existence.

— **Sir Robert Peel**
(1788-1850)

Sir Robert Peel, considered to be the
father of modern policing, established the Metropolitan
Police Force for London based at Scotland Yard.

The above quote is taken from Peel's
Nine Principles of Law Enforcement.

About the Author

Photograph courtesy MLEFIAA

Mike Conti has been a proud member of the Massachusetts State Police (MSP) since 1986.

During his career he has worked in uniformed patrol, SWAT, undercover narcotics, and death investigations. He has been involved as a professional trainer since 1991 and holds numerous instructor certifications in various use of force disciplines.

In January 2000, Conti was assigned to the MSP Academy and tasked to organize, staff, and train the first fulltime Firearms Training Unit (FTU) for the department. During the creation of the FTU he developed the reality-based *New Paradigm* police firearms training program, which has since been adopted by departments both nationally and internationally. In 2001 Conti was awarded the *Massachusetts State Police Medal of Merit* for his work on this project.

After September 11, 2001, Conti was assigned to Logan International Airport in Boston to assist in the formation and training of the first-in-the-nation, commercial airport Anti-Terrorist Unit (ATU). This project entailed the development of a comprehensive, highly-specialized training matrix, which included the adoption and deployment of submachine guns for regular patrol use in the airport, another first in the U.S. In 2003 Conti was awarded the *Commonwealth of Massachusetts Citation for Outstanding Performance* in recognition of his work in the development and administration of specialized training programs for both the FTU and the ATU.

In addition to his work for the MSP, Conti has served as the law enforcement contributing editor for *Guns & Ammo* magazine, and as a consultant for the Law Enforcement Training Network (LETN), Calibre Press, and the History Channel. He has also authored three other books and more than 100 articles.

Conti continues to serve as a member of the MSP and currently holds the rank of lieutenant. He also continues to serve as the Director of Saber Group, Inc., a private training and consulting services company he founded in 1997.

Saber Press Quick Order Form

Postal Orders: **Saber Press**
268 Main Street
PMB 138
North Reading, MA 01864

Website Orders: www.sabergroup.com

Contact us: Telephone/Fax: 978-749-3731
Email: Booksales@sabergroup.com

Please send me the following SABER PRESS Titles:

☐ ***THE OFFICER'S GUIDE TO POLICE PISTOLCRAFT***
Price: **$40.00 (Includes S&H)**

Ship-to **Massachusetts** addresses **ONLY** add 5.00%
Sales Tax ($1.75 per book) for a total of **$41.75**

☐ ***POLICE PISTOLCRAFT*** (Instructor's Textbook)
Price: **$40.00 (Includes S&H)**

*(**NOTE:** Please check website or call to check on availability of this title before ordering.)*

Ship-to **Massachusetts** addresses **ONLY** add 5.00%
Sales Tax ($1.50 per book) for a total of **$41.50**

International Shipping Costs (Canada & Overseas):
ADD $18.00 for first book, **$8.00** for each additional book.

I have enclosed a cheque or money order for $ ____________

Ship to: Name: ________________________________

Mailing Address: ________________________________

____

____

Postal Orders: Cheque or money order made out to Saber Press.

Special Orders: Contact us about discount rates for larger orders.

www.ingramcontent.com/pod-product-compliance
Lightning Source LLC
LaVergne TN
LVHW020040110826
845155LV00029B/561

* 9 7 8 0 9 7 7 2 6 5 9 0 9 *